Palgrave Studies in the History of Economic Thought

Series Editors

Palgrave Studies in the History of Economic Thought publishes contributions by leading scholars, illuminating key events, theories and individuals that have had a lasting impact on the development of modern-day economics. The topics covered include the development of economies, institutions and theories.

More information about this series at
http://www.palgrave.com/gp/series/14585

Maria Cristina Marcuzzo · Ghislain Deleplace ·
Paolo Paesani
Editors

New Perspectives on Political Economy and Its History

palgrave
macmillan

Editors
Maria Cristina Marcuzzo
Department of Statistical Sciences
University of Rome La Sapienza
Rome, Italy

Ghislain Deleplace
Laboratoire d'Economie Dionysien
(LED)
Université Paris 8
Saint-Denis, France

Paolo Paesani
Department of Economics and
Finance
University of Rome Tor
Vergata
Rome, Italy

ISSN 2662-6578 ISSN 2662-6586 (electronic)
Palgrave Studies in the History of Economic Thought
ISBN 978-3-030-42924-9 ISBN 978-3-030-42925-6 (eBook)
https://doi.org/10.1007/978-3-030-42925-6

Cover illustration: Heritage Image Partnership Ltd/Alamy Stock Photo

This Palgrave Macmillan imprint is published by the registered company Springer Nature Switzerland AG
The registered company address is: Gewerbestrasse 11, 6330 Cham, Switzerland

Contents

Notes on Contributors

Richard Arena is Full Professor at the University Côte d'Azur of Nice, France. He has been Visiting Professor at the Universities of Cambridge (UK); Catane; Hitosubashi/Tokyo; Hohenheim/Stuttgart; Milan/Bicocca; Oxford; Paris-I La Sorbonne; Pise and Sfax. His main research fields concern behavioural economics, industrial economics, business cycle theory, structural economic dynamics, economic methodology and history of economic analysis.

Alberto Baccini is Full Professor of Economics at the University of Siena, Italy. He started his research activities by working on various aspects of applied economics and history of the theory of choice under uncertainty. His current research interests are focused on scientometrics and bibliometrics with a special emphasis on the application of network analysis techniques to the study of scientific communities.

Carlo Benetti is Emeritus Professor at the University of Paris Nanterre, France. He has worked on monetary theory and on classical and Marx's theories of reproduction and prices.

José Luís Cardoso is Research Professor at the Instituto de Ciências Sociais, University of Lisbon, Portugal. He is author and editor of several books on the Portuguese history of economic thought from a comparative perspective, with special emphasis on the study of the processes of diffusion and assimilation of economic ideas. He was co-founder of the *European Journal of the History of Economic Thought* and President of the European Society for the History of Economic Thought (ESHET) in 2014–2016.

Jean Cartelier is Emeritus Professor of Economics at the University of Paris Nanterre, France. His fields of interest are monetary theory and history of economic thought.

Ghislain Deleplace is Emeritus Professor at the University Paris 8, France. He has published *Private Money and Public Currencies* (with M.T. Boyer-Xambeu and L. Gillard; Sharpe, 1994), *Money in Motion. The Post Keynesian and Circulation Approaches* (co-edited with E. J. Nell; Macmillan, 1996), *Ricardo on Money: A Reappraisal* (Routledge, 2017), *Histoire de la pensée économique* (Dunod, 3rd edition 2018).

Christophe Depoortère is Full Professor of Economics at the University of the Reunion Island, France. His research deals with classical political economy. He works on the method of political economy, monetary economics and the theories of value and distribution. He is also engaged in the search for unpublished manuscripts of classical political economists, especially David Ricardo.

Sheila Dow is Emeritus Professor of Economics at the University of Stirling, Scotland, UK, and Adjunct Professor of Economics at the University of Victoria, Canada. Her main academic focus is on raising methodological awareness in the fields of macroeconomics, money and banking, and the history of economic thought (especially Hume, Smith and Keynes).

Luca Fantacci teaches Economic History and History of Economic Thought at Bocconi University in Milan, Italy, where he is co-director of the research unit on Monetary Innovation, New Technologies and Society (MINTS). His research focuses on the works of John Maynard Keynes, on the history of monetary and financial systems and, more recently, on complementary and cryptocurrencies.

Christian Gehrke is an Associate Professor in the Department of Economics at the University of Graz, Austria, and a co-director of the Graz Schumpeter Centre. His main research fields are theories of growth and distribution, and the analysis of technical change.

Masashi Izumo is Professor at Kanagawa University, Yokohama, Japan, and President of the Japanese Society for the History of Economic

Thought (JSHET). He has worked on classical political economy, the reception and diffusion of Western economic thought in Japan, and recently on John Ruskin and William Morris.

Elisabeth Klatzer is a free-lance researcher and university lecturer. She researches on feminist economics, gender budgeting and economic policies. She has been involved in gender budgeting also as an activist and consultant in Europe and beyond. She is co-editor with Angela O'Hagan of *Gender Budgeting in Europe: Developments and Challenges* (2018).

Jan Kregel is Director of Research at the Levy Economics Institute of Bard College, USA, and director of the Levy Institute master's programs in economic theory and policy. Elected in 2011 to the Accademia Nazionale dei Lincei, he is a Life Fellow of the Royal Economic Society (UK) and elected member of the Società Italiana degli Economisti. In 2010, he was awarded the prestigious Veblen–Commons Award by the Association for Evolutionary Economics.

Heinz D. Kurz is Emeritus Professor at the University of Graz, Austria, and Fellow of the Graz Schumpeter Centre. His main fields of research are economic theory, especially value and distribution, economic growth and development, innovation and technical change, and the history of economic analysis.

André Lapidus is Emeritus Professor of Economics at PHARE, University Paris 1 Panthéon-Sorbonne, France. He has recently worked on the Scottish Enlightenment (especially David Hume and Adam Smith), on classical economics, on medieval economics and on the methodology of the history of economic thought.

Maria Cristina Marcuzzo is Professor at the University of Rome La Sapienza, Italy, and Fellow of the Italian Academy of Lincei. She has published about 100 articles in journals and books, plus authoring or editing 20 volumes, among which *Fighting Market Failure* (Routledge, 2012), in Japanese by Nihon Keizai Hyoronsha (2015) and *Essays in Keynesian Persuasion* (Cambridge Scholars Publishing, 2019).

Nerio Naldi is Associate Professor at the University of Rome La Sapienza, Italy, where he teaches economics and economic history. He has worked on classical and pre-classical political economy, Keynesian economics, Keynes investments in commodity markets and Piero Sraffa's intellectual biography. The latter interest has led him to devote part of his research to study Sraffa's relationship with Antonio Gramsci and some aspects of Gramsci's biography.

Angela O'Hagan is a Reader in Equalities and Public Policy at Glasgow Caledonian University, Scotland, UK, where she teaches on gender, equality and human rights from a critical public policy perspective. She has been an activist for gender budgeting as well as an academic researcher publishing on gender budgeting in Scotland, Wales and comparatively in Europe. She is co-editor with Elisabeth Klatzer of *Gender Budgeting in Europe: Developments and Challenges* (2018).

Paolo Paesani is Associate Professor at the University of Rome Tor Vergata, Italy. He has published articles in books and academic journals including *History of Political Economy*, *Cambridge Journal of Economics*, *Journal of Post-Keynesian Economics*. His research focuses on post-war monetary controversies, history of the Phillips curve, theory of speculation.

Jean-Pierre Potier is Emeritus Professor of Economics at the University Lumière-Lyon 2, France, and a member of the CNRS research staff *Triangle*. Author of numerous essays concerning the French and the Italian economic thought in the nineteenth and twentieth centuries, he is preparing the edition of J.-B. Say's correspondence. His last publication is *Léon Walras, économiste et socialiste libéral* (Garnier, 2019).

Alessandro Roncaglia Emeritus Professor at the University of Rome La Sapienza, Italy, member of the Accademia Nazionale dei Lincei and of its presidency council, has been editor of *Moneta e Credito* and *PSL Quarterly Review* and President (2010–2013) of the Società Italiana degli Economisti. He authored more than 200 publications—among these, *The Wealth of Ideas* (CUP, 2005) and *The Age of Fragmentation* (CUP, 2019).

Eleonora Sanfilippo is Associate Professor of Economics at the University of Cassino and Southern Lazio, Italy, where she teaches macroeconomics and history of economic thought. Her research interests concern Keynes's theory and practice as an investor and speculator, the Cambridge School of Economics, Keynesian macroeconomics and consumption theory.

Yuji Sato formerly Professor at Shonan Institute of Technology is now Professor of Economics at Rikkyo University, Tokyo, Japan, where he teaches history of economic thought. He has worked on Adam

Smith, David Ricardo and Thomas Robert Malthus. His current research projects focus on classical monetary theory and the history of monetary economics.

Mario Sebastiani formerly Full Professor of Political Economy at the University of Rome Tor Vergata, Italy, until retirement, is currently teaching antitrust and markets regulation at the same university. After dealing with history of economic thought and development economics, his present research interests are in law and economics with special reference to competition law and regulation of public utilities markets.

Nathalie Sigot is Full Professor of Economics at the University Paris 1 Panthéon-Sorbonne, France, and member of the research centre PHARE. She authors articles on Bentham, Jevons, John Stuart Mill and French Liberals, all of these works dealing with the way utilitarianism, or its critics, may have influenced the theoretical positions of economists about justice, money, gender or the role of the State.

Antonella Stirati is Professor of Economics at Roma Tre University, Italy. Her research interests are in the history of economic thought, particularly the classical theory of wages, and in the modern development of the Classical-Keynesian approach in the fields of output and employment determination and income distribution. Currently, she is president of STOREP (the Italian association for the history of economic thought), a member of the Institute for New Economic Thinking academic council and associate editor of *Review of Political Economy.*

Richard Sturn is Joseph A. Schumpeter Professor of Economics and Chair of the Graz Schumpeter Centre and of the Institute of Public Economics at Graz University, Austria. He works on the economics of the public sector and institutional change, normative theory, economic liberalism and the history of economics in the context of a more general interest in the history of ideas.

Susumu Takenaga is Emeritus Professor at Daito Bunka University in Tokyo, Japan. His research interests include the economic theories and thoughts of Marx and Ricardo. His recent publications in English include *Ricardo on Money and Finance* (co-edited with Yuji Sato, Routledge, 2013) and *Ricardo and the Japanese Economic Thought: Selection of Ricardo Studies in Japan During the Interwar Period* (Routledge, 2016).

Paolo Trabucchi is Assistant Professor at Roma Tre University, Italy, where he teaches history of economic thought and foundations of political economy. His research interests are in the theory of value and distribution and in the history of economic analysis. He has worked on Hicks and the theory of capital and on Sraffa's unpublished papers. His current research project focuses on the origins and development of the Neowalrasian theory.

Richard van den Berg is an Associate Professor at Kingston University Business School, UK. He has published on a variety of topics relating to French and British economic thought of the eighteenth century. He has also edited the economic writings of Richard Cantillon and of Achille Nicolas Isnard.

Paola Villa is Full Professor at the University of Trento, Italy, Department of Economics and Management. She is the author of numerous studies on labour economics with particular reference to internal labour markets; labour market regulations; gender equality; women in the labour market; fertility and female participation; care work; youth labour market performance. She is an expert of gender studies and equal opportunities policies in a comparative perspective.

List of Figures

List of Tables

CHAPTER 1

Introduction

Maria Cristina Marcuzzo, Ghislain Deleplace, and Paolo Paesani

In contrast to the reorientation of political economy implemented by Keynes with his *General Theory* less than seven years after the 1929 Wall Street crash, no substantial change in the mainstream approach to economics can be detected twelve years after the collapse of Lehman Brothers. The same Dynamic Stochastic General Equilibrium (DSGE) model which had been unable to anticipate the crisis still rules research, teaching and economic policy, only marginally modified to take account of

M. C. Marcuzzo (✉)
Department of Statistical Sciences, University of Rome La Sapienza, Rome, Italy
e-mail: cristina.marcuzzo@uniroma1.it

G. Deleplace
Laboratoire d'Economie Dionysien (LED), Université Paris 8, Saint-Denis, France
e-mail: ghislain.deleplace@univ-paris8.fr

P. Paesani
Department of Economics and Finance, University of Rome Tor Vergata, Rome, Italy
e-mail: paolo.paesani@uniroma2.it

M. C. Marcuzzo et al. (eds.), *New Perspectives on Political Economy and Its History*, Palgrave Studies in the History of Economic Thought,
https://doi.org/10.1007/978-3-030-42925-6_1

the most obvious flaws of the economic system. In this intellectual environment, going back to past authors may be of some help, not to fuel nostalgia for times gone by but to explore modern economic issues along new perspectives—in short to build theory and understand facts. This is the task of the history of economic thought, when it is not understood as a graveyard for respected albeit no longer read authors but as a living corpus of debates on the same old issues shrunk and distorted by the present mainstream.

This conception of political economy and its history has been applied byAnnalisa Rosselli during her long and prolific academic life. The present volume in her honour bears testimony to her commitment, bringing together contributions by scholars who share it to some extent. It is no surprise that specific sections of the book are devoted to 'big names' who incarnate unconventional ways of thinking in political economy today: Ricardo, Keynes and Sraffa. Another section deals with the Old Classical tradition from Quesnay to Marx which gave centre stage to the relationship between the distribution of income and the accumulation of capital—an issue neglected in modern mainstream economics. And the volume opens up with a section on history of economic thought method and scope; it includes new perspectives in gender studies and illustration of the fecundity of the link with economic history.

Drawing on previous research by Maria Cristina Marcuzzo, a recent study empirically identified three trends in the evolution of the history of economic thought during the past 20 years: '1) a sort of "stepping down from the shoulders of giants", namely a move towards studies of "minor" figures and/or economists from a more recent past; 2) the blossoming of archival research into unpublished work and correspondence; 3) less theory-laden investigations, connecting intellectual circles, linking characters and events' (Marcuzzo and Zacchia 2016, p. 39). With this quantitative investigation, it has been possible to 'demonstrate that there is some evidence to support these claims' (ibid., p. 29). How does the present volume fit into these trends?

First, it is unquestionably an act of resistance against 'stepping down from the shoulders of giants'. Of the ten 'giants' considered in the study by Marcuzzo and Zacchia (Smith, Ricardo, J.S. Mill, Marx, Walras, Marshall, Wicksell, Schumpeter, Keynes, Hayek), all except Wicksell and Hayek show up here. If we add to this list three other authors who can hardly be called 'minor' (Quesnay, Bentham, Sraffa), eleven of the eighteen chapters deal explicitly with their theories (with frequent overlapping). The winning trio is Ricardo–Keynes–Sraffa, each of them being considered in at least four chapters. Two reasons may account for this unconventional bias. As mentioned above, this volume brings together contributors who wished to express their respect for Annalisa Rosselli's scholarly achievements. Obviously some sort of accord appears between the way she has practised history of economic thought and the selection of authors she has studied most. However, a deeper reason also underlies this bias: the common belief that going back to these 'giants' is not a sectarian ratiocination about 'what they really said' but a defence against the conceptual impoverishment of modern economics and a useful tool to open new paths to a broader understanding of present issues.

If the volume aims to resist one of the trends detected in the above-mentioned quantitative study, it nevertheless also illustrates the third trend detected there: the growing interest in the appraisal of intellectual circles and historical networks, seen from an interdisciplinary standpoint. Seven of the eighteen chapters explicitly adopt this method, and in doing so, they trace out new perspectives in various fields and subjects: the state of the history of economic thought in the economics discipline, gender studies, and political and intellectual history. More generally, nearly all the chapters in the volume bear out the importance of history in their way of doing history of economic thought. This is a distinctive aspect which calls for further examination.

1.1 History of Economic Thought and Economic History

Many chapters in the volume draw on the relationship between history of economic thought (HET) and economic history (EH). Working two-way, this relationship is not to be understood (as it all too often is) as mere historical contextualization of theory or, symmetrically, as a departure from theory in favour of history. Things are more complex.

In her presidential address to the 2012 annual conference of the European Society for the History of Economic Thought, Annalisa Rosselli summarized the reconstruction of Ricardo's theory of money she had put forward with Maria Cristina Marcuzzo (Marcuzzo and Rosselli 1991) and asked: 'If this reconstruction of Ricardo's monetary theory is correct, what is the contribution of EH to it? Could it be arrived at on textual evidence alone, or does a knowledge of the working of the economic system in Ricardo's times constitute a significant contribution to it?' (Rosselli 2013, p. 872). Her answer was that EH had been 'the source of three major contributions to this reconstruction' (ibid.): (1) factual knowledge of the working of the foreign bills of exchange market avoided the risk 'to misinterpret the text' (ibid.); (2) it threw some light on 'the implicit assumptions of his [Ricardo's] theory which reflect the behaviour of some of the agents involved' (ibid., p. 873)—particularly the (inverse) causal relationship between the quantity of money and the exchange rate generated by the liquidity of the bullion traders; and (3) with a knowledge of the *ancien régime* monetary system—characterized by the duality of the unit of account and the means of exchange—we could appreciate the fact that 'at the theoretical level it was Ricardo with his Ingot Plan who decreed the end of th[is] system' (ibid., p. 877).

It will be observed that this type of approach to HET is both analytical, thanks to its careful attention to the texts (what did past authors say, was it original and consistent, and what link, if any, did it have with today's economics?), *and* historical, thanks to its detailed study of the facts (how did the theories reflect and incorporate social relations, institutions and practical issues?). To simplify, we will call it a historical-analytical way of doing HET. It is not an easy way, because its specificity may fail to be recognized among historians of economic thought and among economists at large. This is due to two possible confusions which reinforce each other. Since it is concerned with economic analysis and often refers to issues also debated in modern theories, it is confused by some historians of economic thought with what is usually called a 'Whig' approach—one which evaluates past authors through the lens of present-day economics, considered as the scientific achievement of a long historical process. This assimilation neglects the fact that most of the advocates of the historical-analytical way of doing HET share a profound dissatisfaction with modern economics, if not a critique of it. This aspect leads to further confusion, this time not only on the part of some historians of economic thought but also of many other economists. This second confusion is with what is usually called 'heterodox' economics and it is all the more likely to be made since, reconstructing past theories in their own right, it often focuses on some 'big names' neglected or misrepresented by standard economics (e.g. Smith, Ricardo, Marx, Keynes, Sraffa), and stresses the role of historically determined institutions in the working of the economy. Acknowledging the specificity of the historical-analytical way of doing HET thus requires dissipation of these two confusions.

1.2 Economic Analysis, but No 'Whig' History of Economic Thought

Addressing the History of Economics Society in 1987, Paul A. Samuelson declared: 'I propose that history of economics more purposefully reorient itself toward studying the past from the standpoint of the present state of economic science. To use a pejorative word unpejoratively, I am suggesting Whig Economic History of Economic Analysis' (Samuelson 1987, p. 52). He praised Schumpeter's *History of Economic Analysis* as 'an evident leading example' (ibid., p. 56) and borrowed from history of science in general: 'Remember that working scientists have some contempt for those historians and philosophers who regard efforts in the past that failed as being on a par with those that succeeded, success being measurable by latest-day scientific juries who want to utilize hindsight and ex post knowledge' (ibid., pp. 52–53). HET should thus be a story of success, equated with the present state of economics, as the Whig politician and historian Thomas Babington Macaulay viewed the history of civilization as a progressive march towards nineteenth-century England. Whig HET may nevertheless take past failures into consideration, provided study of them contributes to scientific progress by preventing their being repeated. The following observation by Takashi Negishi (1992, p. 228) illustrates this view:

> To develop our science in the right direction, I believe more theoretical resources should go into the study of the history of economics from the point of view of the current theory. This of course does not mean to cut or stretch a past theory into a Procrustean bed for the current theory. The history of our science should be used as a mirror in which the current theory reflects the knowledge of how it failed to succeed in the past. To learn from past theories does not impede the progress of our science. Progress often means, however, sacrificing something old. To make sure that we are going in the right direction, it is always necessary to see whether we have sacrificed something in error.

The presupposition that past theory 'failed to succeed' leads to using HET as a device to confirm that current theory is developing 'in the right direction', by making sure that it only 'sacrificed something in error'.

By contrast, the historical-analytical way of doing HET does not presuppose that the shortcomings that may be found in past theories are necessarily errors but considers them as symptoms of difficulties which may also plague modern theory since they arise in the treatment of issues which, in spite of different historical contexts, are common to past and modern political economy. One example is the difficulty faced by any distribution theory in accounting for an economy with heterogeneous capital goods—an issue much debated during the 'Capital Controversy' of the 1960s and which is still unavoidable in any theory going beyond the modern models based on one good and one representative agent. HET—in the case of Piero Sraffa's reinterpretation of Ricardo's economics in the introduction (Sraffa 1951) to his edition of the latter's *Works and Correspondence*—had a decisive part in resurrecting this issue by showing that Ricardo's value theory was not an error (mocked by Stigler 1958 as a '93% labour theory of value') but a device to overcome this difficulty and lay the foundations for a consistent way of solving it—a road further pursued by Sraffa in his own 1960 book *Production of Commodities by Means of Commodities*.

This example also illustrates a broader role played by historical-analytical HET, namely testifying to the consistency and relevance of ways of thinking in economics which were sacrificed not because they were erroneous or obsolete but because, for one reason or another (also to be investigated), they were submerged by different views. This role lies not only in keeping alive the memory of what was valuable in past theories and has been lost, but also in offering alternative approaches to modern standard economics. This means two things: it can only be played within the economic discipline—contrary to the proposal that HET should 'break away' from economics (Schabas 1992)—and it implies a critical eye on its present state. This latter aspect is often the source of a second type of confusion.

1.3 Critical History of Economic Thought, as Distinct from Heterodox Economics

Linking HET with EH raises the issue of how specific historical aspects may be introduced in the reconstruction of past theories without losing the generality required by comparison of authors situated in periods distant from one another, including modern times. Here, the historical-analytical way of doing HET may find itself in the company of heterodox economics. The matter is all the more complex since some of the advocates of this way of doing HET also envisage their work in the perspective of a critique of orthodox economics and construction (or reconstruction) of alternative approaches to it. There is nevertheless a difference in the way history is considered, and this may be viewed in contrast to the approach of one of the most prominent living heterodox economists—and also someone open to the historical-analytical way of doing HET: Luigi Pasinetti.

In his book *Keynes and the Cambridge Keynesians*, Luigi Pasinetti explains the method which, he holds, opens the way to '"a revolution in economics" to be accomplished' (the subtitle of the book). In particular, money is singled out as illustrating the major methodological distinction (a 'separation theorem') between the level of '*pure theory*', where 'natural' phenomena are studied, and '*the* institutional *stage, where social and institutional types of behaviour may be explored*' (Pasinetti 2007, p. xviii; LP's emphasis). In a section of the book entitled 'On Monetary Theory and Policy', he gives some clues about this necessary 'clarification' indicating 'three *degrees of freedom that in monetary production economies open up and need to be closed from outside the foundational basis of the natural economic system*' (ibid., p. 337; LP's emphasis): the *numéraire*, the rate of inflation and the money rate of interest.

This notion of 'degrees of freedom … to be closed from outside'—e.g. by history—suggests that the basic structure of a theory should be left open, in contrast to the orthodox attempt at subjecting all economic phenomena to the same methodological tools. However, this openness may be understood in two different ways. One, it seems, is Pasinetti's way: 'pure theory' may be completely determined abstracting from the 'outside' and as such applies to different historically defined economies. History does not affect fundamental economic relations; as applied to particular economies, theory is indeed incomplete but this incompleteness only concerns the possibility of moving from pure theory to applied economics. The other way is to consider that these relations cannot be completely determined unless the 'degrees of freedom' are 'closed', so that their meaning depends on how they are closed. The incompleteness then affects the 'pure theory'.

An illustration of this distinction in the Sraffa system is the treatment of the rate of profit as an independent variable. Many Sraffians rely on Sraffa's famous phrase 'It [the rate of profits] is accordingly susceptible of being determined from outside the system of production, in particular by the level of the money rates of interest' (Sraffa 1960, p. 33) to introduce money and finance as institutions—and the social relations they shape—into the Sraffa system, so that the same fundamental price and distribution relationships described by this system also apply to a monetary economy. It must be noted, however, that, if the existence of an inverse relationship between the rate of profit and the wage share in the aggregate income can be demonstrated for any level of the independently determined rate of profit, the meaning of this wage share and the associated price system remains unclear without a theory of the determination of the rate of profit. In terms of the three 'degrees of freedom' listed by Pasinetti in relation to money, there is a need for a theory to link them up, before the Sraffa system can be considered as applying to a monetary economy or, to put it in a few words, the observable world.

This issue of how exactly to open up theory on history is important for the historical-analytical reconstructions that HET performs. The openness of a theory may also derive from its being restricted to a particular field—in the case of Sraffa (1960) the theory of natural prices and distribution—to be complemented with other special economic theories (e.g. concerned with capital accumulation, or effective demand, or money and finance, etc.). In this case, history does not take its place outside 'pure theory' but in the combination of these special theories.

What can be said of the questions raised by the treatment of history in the Sraffian heterodoxy could also be said of other heterodoxies—whether post-Keynesian, Marxian, Hayekian, etc.—whenever the temptation arises to separate pure theory from history. Here lies the distinction between the historical-analytical way of doing HET and heterodox economics: the former is interested in testing the consistency of the historical combination of special theories rather than extracting a core of fundamental principles from them. The eighteen essays contained in this book, with their focus on different special theories and their historical and institutional dimension, reflect the historical-analytical approach to the history of economic thought as a source of new perspectives on political economy and its protagonists. The essays are divided into five parts respectively devoted to new methodological approaches (Part I), issues in Classical political economy (Part II) and new perspectives on Ricardo (Part III), Sraffa (Part IV) and Keynes (Part V).

1.4 New Approaches

Sheila Dow, whose contribution opens Part I of the volume, explores the methodological role of the history of thought in economic theorizing, tracing a connection between Adam Smith's use of the history of ideas for his own theorizing on the one hand and his espousal of the Newtonian experimental method on the other. On this basis, the argument is then developed that study of the history of economic thought contributes to the modern development of theory within a pluralist, open-system approach. Further, the significance of different approaches to history itself is highlighted both for an understanding of Smith and to consider modern-day debate on the history of thought.

While Sheila Dow's chapter offers arguments affirming the important role there is for the history of economic thought in economic teaching and practice, the following chapter in this Part I offers a quantitative assessment of how scholars do their work in the field of history of economic thought. The field is operationally defined by Alberto Baccini as limited to the research articles published in the six professional journals indexed in the Web of Science database, namely *History of Political Economy*, *The European Journal of the History of Economic Thought*, the *Journal of the History of Economic Thought*, *History of Economic Ideas*, *Research in the History of Economic Thought and Methodology*, and *History of Economic Thought and Policy*. History of economic thought occupies a small and stable niche in the economic literature, with a production relatively concentrated in a few countries. Books still represent a major part of the primary sources used by HET. Historians cite a relatively small number of journals, and references are relatively concentrated.

One of the findings by Alberto Baccini is that writing in HET is still an individual male enterprise. This is one sign among many of the significance of gender issues in academia as well as society, and of the need to carefully investigate them. In this spirit, we chose to address the issue of gender in two directions. The first—Gender Budgeting (henceforth GB)—is a topic to which Annalisa Rosselli has contributed significantly. GB emerged in the 1980s, building on feminist economic analysis of public resource allocation processes based on male bias in economic models and policy institutions. Elisabeth Klatzer and Angela O'Hagan take a historical perspective on GB, tracing its conceptual development and contestations, and offering a critical perspective on the transformational adoption or institutional co-option that is characterizing GB as it moves from the margins to the mainstream. Klatzer and O'Hagan propose a refined set of favourable conditions necessary to underpin the claim made by Annalisa Rosselli in her work on the topic that GB is a powerful instrument for feminist transformation.

GB aims to promote gender equality by engaging with public finance from a transformational perspective that results in integrating the provision of care in economic policy and deconstructing gender norms which perpetuate inequalities. The second path the book takes as it explores connections between gender issues and new perspectives on socio-economic analysis appears in the chapter by Paola Villa. Villa focuses on the family as a key socio-economic unit in society. The nature of its organization is shaped by cultural values and gender norms that change slowly over time. This implies that history matters in the sense that social institutions (e.g. the family, values, norms) tend to reproduce themselves over time, revealing a certain inability to make the necessary adjustments to new challenges. This chapter argues that in familistic societies—where family ties are strongly rooted in traditional values and gender norms—women bear the burden of unpaid work, with negative effects in terms of both gender equity and fertility decisions. Moreover, economic growth—entailing more job opportunities for women—tends to be constrained in societies where the family still plays a strong economic role (i.e. where there is a disproportionally large share of small family firms).

Part I ends with a chapter by José Luís Cardoso, which reinforces the idea that social constraints play a decisive role in the evolution of institutions and underlines the importance of history in understanding the transformation of socio-economic units, including firms and banks. Cardoso provides a case study—the creation of the Bank of Lisbon in December 1821—in the context of the particular period of political change, namely the Portuguese liberal revolution, which had begun in August 1820. As Cardoso reconstructs, public debt management and control of the paper money in circulation are central themes for an understanding of the origins of, and the reasons for, the modern organization of banking. These themes invaded public debate in Portugal at the turn of the nineteenth century, promoting confrontation and convergence of doctrinal and theoretical views on monetary and financial issues in which the overall credibility and trustworthiness of the state were at stake. Study of this example in Portuguese banking history, which shows parallels with other examples of European banks, also enables us to better understand the rhetorical use of political economy in the course of political action.

1.5 Classical Political Economy

The chapters in Part II deal with analysis of the two pillars of Classical political economy, namely distribution of income and accumulation of capital. Paolo Trabucchi goes over the main stages in the development of Quesnay's *Tableau Économique*, confirming the traditional interpretation of this development as a fundamentally continuous process of clarification and elaboration. On discussing the opposite view, however, i.e. the existence of a significant change in Quesnay's position, a clearer picture of the path he followed between the first drafting of the *Tableau* and its first public appearance is obtained. Retracing that path, Trabucchi ascribes the formulation that marks the last stage in the development of the *Tableau* to the difficulties Quesnay met in reaffirming the sterility of the manufacturing sector, as a temporary alternative to a price theory, and not as an essential component of any such theory.

Antonella Stirati takes up another well-known and amply discussed topic in the literature on Classical political economy, namely the analytical contents of the criticisms levelled at J.S. Mill's theory of the wage fund and accepted by him in his famous 'recantation' of 1869. One reason for the interest in the analytical issues that emerged in the criticisms of the wage fund theory, raised by Longe and Thornton, lies in the fact that they take up and revive many aspects of Smith's approach to wage determination. In so doing, those arguments show its inconsistency with the wage fund theory presented (and eventually recanted) by Mill; that is, they bring out the conflict between Smith's views, representative of the theory of wages proper to the Classical political economy (from Petty to Ricardo), and the subsequently established theory of the wage fund.

The final chapter in Part II explains why modern readers can benefit from studying Classical economists today. As Christian Gehrke, Heinz Kurz and Richard Sturn argue, the Classical approach to studying an economic system in motion under a cumulative process of division of labour offers a superior starting point for analysing the salient properties of capitalist market economies. While modern mainstream economics has adopted, but variously restricted, some of the ideas contained in particular in the works of Adam Smith and to a lesser extent in the works of David Ricardo and Karl Marx, its historical development involved a growing distance and even opposition to the concerns, methods and analytical approaches of the Classical economists. This implied a considerable loss of the huge analytical potentialities they offered.

1.6 New Perspectives on Ricardo

Among the towering figures of Classical political economy, David Ricardo stands out in this book also because Annalisa Rosselli has dedicated particular attention to him. Appropriately, therefore, Part III is devoted to various aspects of his life and works. Christophe Depoortère, André Lapidus and Nathalie Sigot discuss the possibility, often alleged and widely accepted, that Bentham had an influence on the development of Ricardo's economics. Three possible points of contact have been mooted: the first mediated by the key figure of James Mill and the other two being unmediated reactions to their respective works, Bentham's *Sur les prix* and Ricardo's *Essay on Profits*. Yet, they argue, none of these claims for influence has firm foundations. Regarding the first proposed *rendez-vous*, Depoortère, Lapidus and Sigot show that if Mill had an influence on Ricardo at the beginning of their friendship (say, around 1808), he was at this time Stewartian and not yet Benthamian. The second *rendez-vous manqué* turns on Ricardo's reading of Bentham's manuscript *Sur les prix*: they show that (i) this reading could not have exerted an influence on Ricardo's monetary thought at an early stage—that is, before his first monetary writings—and (ii) Ricardo expressed such disagreement with it that any influence from it on his views about money is inconceivable. The third *rendez-vous* was also *manqué*: commenting on Ricardo's *Essay*, Bentham accused him of confusing 'cost' and 'value'. Examining this criticism by turning the focus on the different aims of both authors, related to their explanations of, respectively, inflation and the evolution of distribution, and their different conceptions of price, Depoortère, Lapidus and Sigot conclude that the assumption of Bentham's influence on Ricardo's economics seems hardly defendable.

On a similar line of thought, i.e. how the literature has interpreted Ricardo, the following chapter in this Part looks at the long-standing tradition of Ricardian studies in Japan, which Annalisa Rosselli has visited on a number of occasions by invitation of Japanese scholars. Masashi Izumo, Yuji Sato and Susumu Takenaga recall that, due to the policy of isolationism pursued for more than two hundred years, from the seventeenth to the mid-nineteenth century, the Japanese knew practically nothing about the European economic thought of the time. It was only after the Meiji Restoration that various kinds of economic thought, including that of Ricardo, came to find dissemination in Japan. The state of Ricardo studies in Japan is different from that in Western countries in several respects.

To understand this evolution, the chapter deals with three distinct periods: from the 1860s to the 1910s, the interwar period and post-World War II. Dealing with the first period, the authors describe how Ricardo was introduced in Japan in the late nineteenth and early twentieth centuries. Subsequently, the chapter illustrates the development of Ricardo studies in Japan during the interwar period and, finally, the controversial interpretations of Ricardo's theories that have been advanced from 1945 to the present day. The chapter focuses on several topics such as the theories of value, rent, wage, money and finance that were passed on to later generations of scholars, paying particular attention to the Japanese studies that offer original approaches and thus afford interesting comparisons with similar debates in foreign countries.

The publication of *Production of Commodities by Means of Commodities* by Sraffa in 1960 was another landmark, after his *Introduction* to *Principles* in 1951, in Ricardo scholarship. Carlo Benetti and Jean Cartelier inquire into what could or should be a Classical theory of money and prices sixty years after Sraffa's *magnum opus.* They take as granted three basic propositions: (i) Sraffa's system of prices is relevant for determining Classical natural prices; (ii) a monetary standard (gold) is central to a Classical theory of money; and (iii) the Cantillon-Smith rule is pivotal to Classical market price determination. They contend that: (i) the coexistence of a natural price and a legal price of gold is a necessary condition for a Classical theory of money; (ii) the market price of gold cannot be different from its legal price (no arbitrage); and (iii) regulation of the quantity of money remains an open question.

1.7 New Perspectives on Sraffa

It is a logical step in the structure of the book to turn to Sraffa, who, subsequent to the opening of his Archives, has been receiving greater attention from scholars interested in forming a better idea of his life and work. In the first chapter of Part IV, Jean-Pierre Potier examines the relationship with Antonio Gramsci, in particular on Ricardo, Classical political economy and 'pure economics'.

For Gramsci, the importance of Ricardo in the formation of Marx's ideas must be reassessed from the point of view of the conception of the world and history. In 1932, he asked the opinion of Sraffa, who was highly sceptical about any Ricardian historicism, sending him bibliographical indications. Unfortunately, Gramsci received none of this bibliography and was unable to react to Sraffa's remarks. On the other hand, he commented on Pantaleoni's *Principii di economia pura* and advanced an opinion on *An Essay on the Nature and Significance of Economic Science* by Robbins, through an indirect source. On the questions raised in these books, Gramsci would have appreciated some dialogue with Sraffa, a critic of marginalism, but unfortunately it did not come about.

On the origin of the equations which became the building blocks of Sraffa's book, there has been some disagreement in the literature. Nerio Naldi tackles the issue from a new angle, namely how Sraffa came to introduce price variables into his equations. Building upon Garegnani's analysis (e.g. Garegnani 2005), Naldi shows that Sraffa's earliest equations included only things and no price variables, and he aims to explain why Sraffa still tried to maintain his earliest formulation for the case of a no surplus economy even after he had decided to introduce price variables into his positive surplus equations.

But what can still be learnt from Sraffa's study of prices in a surplus economy? From the 1960s to the 1990s, drastic changes occurred in our real economic system and in the meaning of what can still be called the global reproduction of this system. Today, it is therefore crucial to reconsider the ability of Sraffa's intellectual legacy to grasp the working of our present economic system, taking into account the opening of his unpublished papers in 1993. This is the issue addressed in Richard Arena's chapter, which closes Part IV. Arena reminds us that before the 1990s, two opposite interpretations of Sraffa's economic theory prevailed. The first consisted in defining what was called the 'Classical theory of general economic equilibrium'. It was intended to differ from the old version, described as 'neo-Walrasian'. The second rejected the view of Sraffa's contribution as a new version of the theory of general economic equilibrium (GEE) and tried to provide alternative constructions. However, today things have changed. Using both *Production of Commodities by Means of Commodities* (based on a scheme of general interdependence) and Sraffa's criticism of Marshall's partial equilibrium, Arena shows that price theory no longer offers sufficient scope. A broader view has to be considered, seeking to understand the right approach to analysing how the surplus of a production economy is distributed among economic agents and social groups, within various given historical systems of institutions, whether including markets or not.

1.8 New Perspectives on Keynes

Finally, the first two chapters in Part V, which proposes new perspectives on Keynes, take a long view of the issues connected to the notion of liquidity, at both the substantive and methodological levels. Richard van den Berg begins his investigation by looking into Joseph Schumpeter's inclination to read Keynesian precedents into 'mercantilist' monetary writings. He focusses on a single instance in which Schumpeter argued that a passage, which he attributed to the eighteenth-century author Malachy Postlethwayt, 'reads like' Keynes's theory that money interest depends on liquidity preference. The fact that Schumpeter did not fully understand the circumstances under which the much earlier passage was written, and did not even realize who originally wrote it, does not necessarily invalidate his interpretation of it. Rather, it illustrates the historicity of historiography, or how the emergence of new economic theories, like Keynes's theory of interest as a monetary phenomenon, prompts new readings of old texts. The main point which van den Berg makes is that what readers 'made of' a text is an object of historical study that is distinct from the 'original purposes' that its author may have had. Later, commentators will predictably bring concerns and perspectives of their own time to bear when interpreting earlier economic writings. Simply condemning such interpretations for being 'retrospective' is often all too simple.

In the same vein—searching for the original meaning of a concept by placing it in the context in which it originates—Luca Fantacci and Eleonora Sanfilippo examine the idea of 'the liquidity trap', starting from the observation that its definition is not univocal. Fantacci and Sanfilippo turn back to the original meaning of this expression in the works of the economists that first introduced it into economic analysis, namely Keynes and Robertson. Building on primary sources and unpublished material, this chapter provides a reconstruction and contextualization of the original use of this expression in economic analysis with the aim of contributing to a better understanding of its meaning. In particular, Fantacci and Sanfilippo point out that, in the early theoretical debate among the first economists who addressed this issue, the notion did not designate merely a specific circumstance, characterized by the ineffectiveness of monetary policy at the zero lower bound or at low interest rates, but referred to a more general problem concerning the nature of liquidity as a shelter from uncertainty and the related structural tendency of a monetary economy towards stagnation.

The last two chapters enlarge on the issue of the relevance of these methodological aspects to present-day issues, both in terms of reconstructing an alternative to neoclassical economics and for policy considerations.

As we know, Keynes formulated a 'monetary theory of production' that led to a liquidity-preference theory of financial asset prices, while Sraffa developed a theory of prices of production. Jan Kregel and Alessandro Roncaglia charter a less known territory and explore similarities between Keynes and Sraffa, suggesting a fruitful symbiosis of the two approaches. Both challenged neoclassical price theories. Keynes rejected the idea of a natural rate of interest determined by conditions of production, arguing, rather, that the rate of interest is endogenously determined by asset preferences subject to policy decisions of the central bank, while Sraffa rejected the productivity determination of the rate of profits, suggesting a monetary determination of the rate of interest influencing income distribution. As for the analytical method, both isolated a specific objective and identified the most important elements relevant to the problem under consideration. Kregel and Roncaglia outline the Classical 'circular-flow' notion, the 'photograph' interpretation of Sraffa's analysis and the structure of Keynes's theory.

The final chapter addresses the issue of the relevance of the Keynesian approach to policy. Mario Sebastiani reminds us of a passage in *The End of Laissez-Faire* in which Keynes ([1926] 1972, p. 295) asserted:

> For my part I think that capitalism, wisely managed, can probably be made more efficient for attaining economic ends than any alternative system yet in sight, but that in itself it is in many ways extremely objectionable. Our problem is to work out a social organisation which shall be as efficient as possible without offending our notions of a satisfactory way of life.

This observation encapsulates Keynes's 'manifesto', his economic and social—in a word, political—vision and programme; a far-reaching vision, to be implemented not on the macroeconomic level only, but by rethinking the *laissez-faire* creed as a whole. The clash between individual and social calculation is not a passing ailment, negligible as a transitory deviation from a steady state of good health, but a structural condition affecting every aspect of economic and social life and calling for structural remedies. Accordingly, Keynes's fundamental aim was to reform the relationships between the 'State' and the 'market'—not the State *vs.* the market—searching for a way to reconcile them, with a view to promoting a more efficient and just economic and social system.

In their attempt to provide new perspectives on political economy and its history, the eighteen essays collected in this book try to respond to the wish that economics might embark along a different route, whereby economists take into serious consideration past theories and concepts which have failed to survive in the evolutionary struggle of ideas for no good reason, but simply because they have been 'submerged and forgotten' with the shift of paradigms. This is a wish that we are certain Annalisa Rosselli fully shares.

Acknowledgements We are very grateful to Iolanda Sanfilippo for her excellent editorial assistance in preparing this volume and to Graham Sells for his first-rate language revision.

References

Garegnani, P. (2005). On a Turning Point in Sraffa's Theoretical and Interpretative Position in the Late 1920s. *The European Journal of the History of Economic Thought, 12*(3), 453–492.

Keynes, J. M. ([1926] 1972). *The End of Laissez-Faire*. London: Hogarth Press. As reprinted in: D. E. Moggridge & E. Johnson (Eds.), *The Collected Writings of John Maynard Keynes, Vol. 9: Essays in Persuasion* (pp. 272–295). London: Macmillan for the Royal Economic Society.

Marcuzzo, M. C., & Rosselli, A. (1991). *Ricardo and the Gold Standard: The Foundations of the International Monetary Order*. London: Macmillan.

Marcuzzo, M. C., & Zacchia, G. (2016). Is History of Economics What Historians of Economic Thought Do? A Quantitative Investigation. *History of Economic Ideas, 24*(3), 29–46.

Negishi, T. (1992). Comment on Schabas. *History of Political Economy, 24*(1), 227–229.

Pasinetti, L. L. (2007). *Keynes and the Cambridge Keynesians: 'A Revolution in Economics' to Be Accomplished*. Cambridge: Cambridge University Press.

Rosselli, A. (2013). Economic History and History of Economics: In Praise of an Old Relationship. *The European Journal of the History of Economic Thought, 20*(6), 865–881.

Samuelson, P. A. (1987). Out of the Closet: A Program for the Whig History of Economic Science. *History of Economics Society Bulletin, 9*(1), 51–60.

Schabas, M. (1992). Breaking Away: History of Economics as History of Science. *History of Political Economy, 24*(1), 187–203.
Sraffa, P. (1951). Introduction. In P. Sraffa (Ed., with the collaboration of M. H. Dobb), *The Works and Correspondence of David Ricardo, Vol. 1: On the Principles of Political Economy and Taxation* (pp. xiii–lxii). Cambridge: Cambridge University Press for the Royal Economic Society.
Sraffa, P. (1960). *Production of Commodities by Means of Commodities: Prelude to a Critique of Economic Theory*. Cambridge: Cambridge University Press.
Stigler, G. J. (1958). Ricardo and the 93% Labour Theory of Value. *American Economic Review, 48*(3), 357–367.

PART I

New Topics for the History of Economic Thought

CHAPTER 2

The Methodological Role of the History of Economic Thought

Sheila Dow

2.1 Introduction

The place of the history of economic thought (HET) within economics has reappeared on the agenda thanks to the global student movement for the reform of the economics curriculum. This movement forms an important part of the response to the financial crisis and the resulting re-examination of both the content and the teaching of economics.[1]

Current discussions about the role of HET in economics call to mind the last flurry of debate, in the 1990s and over the millennium, on how best to promote HET. A focal point was the HOPE conference organized by Roy Weintraub at Duke University in 2001[2] to reflect on the place of the history of economic thought in the academy. In particular, the conference addressed concerns that the future of HET was under particular threat. The HET community (as represented by journal activity

S. Dow (✉)
University of Stirling, Stirling, UK
e-mail: s.c.dow@stir.ac.uk

M. C. Marcuzzo et al. (eds.), *New Perspectives on Political Economy and Its History*, Palgrave Studies in the History of Economic Thought,
https://doi.org/10.1007/978-3-030-42925-6_2

and attendance at relevant annual conferences) seemed to be burgeoning. Yet the field was losing its traditional place in the economics curriculum and its journals were not looked upon favourably in the rankings increasingly being used for assessing research quality. A particular focus was provided for the conference by the (hotly-debated) strategic proposal put forward earlier by Weintraub on the History of Economics Society listserv to ensure a future for the field by separating it from economics itself and moving it into the history of science.

The paper presented by Annalisa Rosselli and Maria Cristina Marcuzzo challenged this strategy, arguing instead for a strategy addressed rather to maintaining the history of thought's place *within* economics, albeit as a separate subdiscipline. They approached the topic by tracing the way in which the role of HET in Italy had evolved since the 1960s, when history of thought was integral to economics, to a state of marginalization. This evolution was identified with the encroachment of a 'Whig' approach.

> The difference between the traditional American and British 'Whig' approach … and the Italian style of doing HET in the 1970s is that for the former the past is sifted for the predecessors of modern theory and present ideas ('quest for ascendancy'), while for the latter the past is searched for what has been lost and can no longer be found in modern theory ('quest for an alternative'). (Marcuzzo and Rosselli 2002, p. 102)

They saw this evolution towards a 'Whig' approach to the history of thought as reflecting the rising power in the profession of the mainstream approach to economics. Addressing the place of HET in economics therefore involved a critique of this mainstream approach.

> What we are advocating is a thorough questioning of the present practice of doing economics, fostering the critical thinking and openness of mind that are essential to the social sciences. This critical attitude is also a means to draw attention to principles and methodologies alternative to the present set, rooted in past theories. … We cannot do HET *as if* doing economics; we should make room for it as an autonomous subdiscipline with its own agenda, methods, and standards of achievement. As in the 1970s, however, we must reposition HET at the center of the battlefield of economic ideas. (Marcuzzo and Rosselli 2002, p. 108)

This was a general methodological argument for history of thought being integral to economics, one which directly challenged the mainstream methodological approach. Their argument was therefore that HET had a special role to play in making economics better.

The purpose of this contribution is to pursue further the argument for the history of economic thought as an integral element of the discipline of economics, building on the Marcuzzo–Rosselli argument. In this spirit, we approach the argument through the history of thought. The Italian approach of the 1970s reflected the classical approach which traces its origins to Adam Smith. In what follows, we will consider the role of history, and specifically of the history of ideas, in Smith's epistemology and methodology. The third section takes the Smithian approach forward to the present day in order to consider the continuing methodological role of the history of economic thought.

We will return to arguments already made for keeping HET 'at the center of the battlefield of economic ideas' and the related arguments for retaining HET in the economics curriculum—or returning it to the curriculum. Blaug (2001) surveyed these well at the time of the last debates; see also Weintraub (2002a). These arguments refer variously to the role of HET in promoting better conceptual understanding of modern theory and its subject matter by means of historical (rather than rational) reconstruction; in recovering old ideas; in explaining historically different approaches to economics rather than assuming the best from the past already to be subsumed in the present. In the process, we draw on Smith's particular historical approach in order to address the controversial issue of whether or not methodological or theoretical critique of the mainstream disqualifies research as HET.

2.2 Adam Smith's Epistemology and Methodology

Adam Smith's pioneering economics built on a long history of ideas, but it is generally up to editors and other scholars to make the connections to that history, illuminating the evolution of ideas behind Smith's thinking. The exception is when he seeks to relate his thinking to alternative traditions. But this was not 'Whig' history in the conventional sense; Smith was mindful of the different contexts in which other ideas were developed and expressed.

Thus, for example, while arguing against both the approach and content of physiocracy, Smith ([1776] 1976, IV.ix) nevertheless expressed appreciation for the physiocrats' achievements. In the multiple examples from a wide range of countries which had supported agriculture over manufacturing, he further demonstrates an appreciation of context. Indeed, Smith ([1776] 1976, II.v) had earlier discussed the merits of devoting capital to agriculture rather than manufacturing and trade at early stages of development, with capital scarcity.

Similarly, while arguing against mercantilism, Smith ([1776] 1976, IV) demonstrated appreciation for the context within which it had emerged, drawing further on his stage theory of socio-economic development. According to Coats (1975, p. 220), Smith 'treated the mercantile system on two distinct, but interrelated levels: in terms of his atemporal ideal system of natural liberty, and by reference to the actual past and current practices of various European nations'. Coats (1975, p. 221) goes on to criticize the conventional 'habit of viewing Smith's attack on the mercantile system simply and solely as an analysis of impediments to the smooth functioning of the competitive market economy, rather than an integral part of a larger system of moral, socio-philosophical, historical, and political ideas'.

In terms of presenting his own theories, Smith ([1762–63] 1983; [1795] 1980) distinguished between theory development and the rhetoric employed to persuade others to accept theoretical developments. While assiduous citation is more a matter of modern style, the absence of citation by Smith of precursors also served the forcefulness of his presentation. Indeed, Smith at times depended on actively downplaying the contributions of contemporaries (see, e.g., Dow 1984). Persuasion was required because of the inability to *demonstrate* the superiority of one theory over another. Here, Smith drew on Hume's ([1739–40] 1978) critique of French rationalism and its substitution by a non-rationalist approach to knowledge (which sat well within the Scottish moral philosophy tradition as it had emerged from the seventeenth century; see Broadie 2003).

Hume had concluded that rationalism was a dead end: reason alone was insufficient for knowledge as the basis for action, but rather required input also from real experience and moral sentiment. Yet, given the complexity of physical and social systems, the causal mechanisms underlying experience were too complex to be categorically identified. This was his problem of induction; there was no definitive basis for assuming that a hypothesized causal connection would be repeated in future. Rather, much of our knowledge must rely on conventional understandings which have built up over time, while drawing on the human faculties of sentiment and imagination as well as reason. Thus, even the physical sciences and mathematics required a foundation in a theory of human nature.

In the absence of a demonstrably superior body of knowledge, different theories could therefore legitimately be defended. In particular, different theories held sway, and indeed had legitimacy, in different periods and different contexts. The history of ideas was thus a major part of the current body of knowledge and was a central focus for Adam Smith. Although largely unfulfilled, he had aimed to produce a 'Philosophical History of all the different branches of Literature, Philosophy, Poetry and Eloquence' (Wightman 1975, p. 44). Indeed, the history of ideas was just part of a more general historical approach to knowledge typical of the Scottish Enlightenment.

The historical approach was already embedded in Scottish education, whereby all subjects, including mathematics, were taught historically. It followed from the epistemological position that no one theory could be demonstrated to be true, that a range of theories should be taught, explained in terms of their own context. Indeed, the curriculum was conditioned, not only by the historical approach, but also by the early classes in moral philosophy and logic by which the Scottish epistemological tradition was taught. However, various reform efforts throughout the nineteenth century eroded these practices to conform more with the English approach to higher education. This approach emphasized rather classical literature, greater specialization with a focus on the latest theories and deferment of any philosophical training until this specialization had been achieved (Davie 1961; Anderson 1983). Yet courses in philosophy and logic continued to be a compulsory element at the start of the arts degree programme in Scottish universities until the 1960s.

Smith pursued a particular approach to history itself, variously called philosophical, conjectural or analytical history (Skinner 1965, 1972). It involved identification of patterns in order to suggest to the imagination causal mechanisms behind historical events, including the emergence of ideas.

> The distinctive nature of [this] theory of history ... may be found in its scientific temper and emphasis on economic forces as fundamental to historical and sociological investigation. The particular feature of this contribution ... [may be] ... that of finding principles which reduce the apparent

chaos of history to order and thus enable us to understand our *present* condition. (Skinner 1965, p. 22, emphasis in original)

Indeed, this historical approach to ideas as well as society provided the route for applying Newton's experimental methodology to the social sciences (Dow 2009a). Newton had set out a process of abduction whereby provisional theoretical ideas emerged from study of experience in some experiments/contexts, to be reviewed in the light of experience in other experiments/contexts. Rather than the duality of deduction (French rationalism) and induction (English empiricism), Newton had applied the method of abduction whereby observation and analysis were complements rather than substitutes. Newton's experimental methodology was thus to combine analysis and synthesis: 'analysis consists in making Experiments and Observations, and in drawing general Conclusions from them by Induction . ... Synthesis consists in assuming the Causes discover'd, and establish'd as Principles, and by them explaining the Phaenomena proceeding from them' (Newton [1704] 1730, pp. 380–381). This methodology was readily absorbed into the Scottish tradition (Comim 2006; Montes 2006).

Unlike in the physical sciences, it was history which provided the experimental evidence in the social sciences. Thus, Smith drew on a wide range of historical (geographical and cultural) circumstances to illustrate and support his arguments. This was evident, for example, in his discussion of the way in which the extent of the market limited the division of labour (Smith [1776] 1976, I.iii), the history of money (Smith [1776] 1976, I.iv) and the role of public works and institutions in supporting the conduct of commerce (Smith [1776] 1976, V.iii).

In their introduction to the 1976 edition of the *Wealth of Nations*, the editors include a section on Smith's use of history, noting that he 'frequently wrote as a historian' (Campbell and Skinner 1976, p. 50, the former, Roy Campbell, being a historian by discipline). They identify aspects of Smith's historical work as 'orthodox history' (or Oxford history) and assess his marshalling of facts from different sources accordingly. But they also explain how these facts served as inputs to Smith's 'philosophical history' whereby 'he tried to distil an ideal interpretation of an historical process ostensibly from the facts he had accumulated' (Campbell and Skinner 1976, p. 51). Thus, having arrived at a hypothesis (the principle of the division of labour) as a result of applying the method of abduction to his wide reading, Smith ([1776] 1976, I.1.1) started his presentation with a statement of the principle in the very first sentence. Only later did he adduce the evidence to support the principle, reversing the order of presentation of 'orthodox history'.

Since the priority for Smith was to build a system and persuade that it was the best way of understanding the economy, this inevitably influenced Smith's understanding, selection and presentation of facts. But the editors point out that no incontrovertible presentation of facts is possible, even for the purely orthodox historian, and deny that there is any evidence in Smith of active distortion. Rather, they argue that Smith paid particular attention to evidence which was at odds with his system and endeavoured to understand why the circumstances deviated from the ideal. What might appear to the orthodox historian as inconsistencies (between the general principles of Smith's system and the historical exceptions to which he draws attention) were in fact what we would expect from the Newtonian methodology of seeking provisional principles which require adaptation to different contexts.

Smith used this Newtonian experimental method, not only to develop his economic system, but also within the history of scientific ideas themselves. In particular, he sought to review evidence in relation to his theory of human nature, whereby the aim of the philosopher is to provide a psychologically satisfactory account of the real subject matter: 'A system is an imaginary machine invented to connect together in the fancy those different movements and effects which are already in reality performed' (Smith [1795] 1980, IV.19). He took the history of astronomy as a set of case studies by which to provide supportive evidence for this theory of mind (Smith [1759] 1976, II.12)—not for appraisal or to identify a general theory of astronomy. Anticipating Kuhn's ([1962] 1970) account of the history of astronomy, Smith explained the successive coexistence of different systems of astronomy, all grounded to a greater or lesser degree in reason and evidence, in terms of their respective appeals to the imagination within their own contexts (see further Skinner 1972). In the process, Smith puts forward his own system for understanding science, not least in seeking to categorize different approaches (in a manner consistent with his more general analytical historical approach).

The history of ideas thus not only played an important role in *promoting understanding* of current theory, but also contributed directly to the *formulation* of current theory. But it also played a third role in *shaping the subject matter* of theory. Smith contributed directly to policy thinking with respect to trade and development, altering attitudes to mercantilism for example. Indeed, he contributed directly to efforts to promote development in the Scottish Highlands and Islands: along with Hume he belonged to the Edinburgh Society for Encouraging Arts, Sciences, Manufactures, and Agriculture in Scotland, which had grown out of the Select Society founded in 1754 (by the portraitist Allan Ramsey). Specifically, he argued that ideas (in the form of the 'arts') are critical to innovation and thus development, while development in turn prompted the emergence of new ideas (Dow and Dow 2015).

Smith sought to soothe the imagination by presenting the evolving character of the economy as a system, just as Newton had done for the heavens. But Smith also challenged conventional understandings, such as those of the mercantilists. While conventional knowledge makes up for some of the shortcomings of rationalism, it was the role of the philosopher to apply more powers of reason to examining these conventions, sometimes to flout them. It was in this context, of specialization in knowledge, that Smith first developed the idea of the division of labour. Here, we have a further application of the Newtonian method, this time in the case of non-philosophical knowledge. Society builds up conventional knowledge on the basis of long historical experience, but this knowledge is necessarily provisional when considering application to new contexts. It is the role of the philosopher to expose conventions to abductive reasoning.

In turning to consider what we might glean from Smith to help us consider HET in the modern context, we need to be very mindful of the fact that the context of Smith's epistemology and methodology was very different from our own. Nevertheless, there was a prior economics literature which included not only precursors to Smith but also alternative approaches. As we have seen, Smith explicitly engaged with alternative frameworks: physiocracy on the one hand and mercantilism on the other. He paid due respect to each, as befits a non-absolutist epistemology. History played an integral part in Smith's analysis, as was inevitable given the historical nature of Scottish epistemology, even though the focus was on practical policy questions. Indeed, arguably, it was this cast of mind which facilitated the inventive success in addressing practical problems which characterized Scotland in the eighteenth and nineteenth centuries. When it came to economic theorizing on socio-economic issues, the history of ideas and epistemology more generally were woven into the fabric of argument and the emphasis on economic history was considerable. In the meantime, Smith ([1795] 1980) provided an exemplar, with respect to astronomy, for considering HET in modern times.

2.3 Modern Application

In the last major debate over HET, some (such as Weintraub 2002b) expressed concern that HET was being (mis)used as a vehicle for inter-paradigm debate, at the expense of quality of scholarship. Weintraub's strategy of separating HET from economics was aimed at promoting the field and maintaining standards. There is an interesting echo here of the orthodox-history critique of Smith's alternative, philosophical or analytical, approach to history: that approaching history from a prior perspective involves bias and distortion. But this argument provoked a Smithian response that there are several approaches to history, none of which can be demonstrated categorically to be superior to any other. This response was most fully developed with respect to HET by Marcuzzo (2008) who detailed a range of such approaches.

In fact, the concerns of the pessimists were somewhat misplaced. The field has succeeded in maintaining a high standard of scholarship in what is now a multiplicity of HET journals, HET monographs and HET fora addressed to a growing community of specialists. And this has been achieved while retaining HET as a subfield of economics. But there is now far less evidence of the 'battlefield of ideas' within the HET specialism. The 'battlefield of ideas' has shifted to the outlets and venues of the community of non-mainstream economists, where relevant HET is both produced and incorporated in theoretical and methodological argument.

The success of HET as a specialist subdiscipline has thus coincided with the proliferation of journals, organizations and conferences developing economics outside the mainstream, which has provided an additional home for work in HET. While this work too is high quality and specialist, it differs in focusing on the history of ideas most relevant to the community being addressed, where HET is only one subdiscipline on which the discourse draws. Thus, for example, specialist HET work on Keynes appears in the outlets and venues of the post-Keynesian community. This development accords with Marcuzzo and Rosselli's (2002, p. 108) conclusion that the future of HET lay not in separating it from economics, but in promoting its role within an open, critical approach to economics whereby a 'critical attitude is also a means to draw attention to principles and methodologies alternative to the present set, rooted in past theories'.

But is the HET produced for non-mainstream audiences tainted by bias in favour of one focus and interpretation which supports a particular approach? Weintraub (2002a) reports this as a concern raised by several participants in the 2001 HOPE conference (see also Lodewijks 2003, p. 667). Any historian of thought of course should accept scrutiny over sources, logic of argument and basis for interpretation. But to imply that HET can be devoid of interpretive judgement is to take a very particular view of history. We have seen that several approaches to history are possible, and legitimate, including 'philosophical history' whereby textual evidence is referred to a conceptual system of thought. Non-mainstream discourse tends to apply the philosophical approach whereby both historians of thought and non-HET specialists approach the material from a particular systemic perspective. Particular inconsistencies between a piece of evidence and the system are bound to arise and require analysis in order to understand why they arose and what that might imply for the system.

So when Marcuzzo and Rosselli (2002) argue that the *production* of HET as a specialist subdiscipline is separable from its *use* by economists, the subdiscipline may still apply the philosophical approach to history, or any of the others. Of course this does not preclude any HET specialist from arguing in favour of one approach to history; indeed when none can be demonstrated to be superior, persuasion is an inevitable requirement of discourse. Thus, the case can be made that a strict separation of HET between 'objective/orthodox history' and 'subjective/philosophical history' is not sustainable. The issue comes back to the difference between a Whig history approach and one which identifies in history, not only different theories, but different approaches. The focus of Italian HET in the 1970s, just as in Smith, was as much on difference of approach as on theoretical difference.

Most modern HET (whether or not Whig) reflects Q. Skinner's (1969) approach of seeking to identify the intention of the author, in context, in a historical reconstruction. But such an approach tilts HET away from a Whig approach by tending to encourage the possibility that an author's conceptual framework, in her context (in space, culture or time), would be different from authors in a different context. This is why HET became associated particularly with non-mainstream approaches which draw on different historical traditions (Theocarakis 2014). But it is leading mainstream economists that Blaug (2001) identifies as taking a Whig approach to HET, rationally reconstructing older economic ideas in terms of modern intentions and context.

This implies that the many modern HET scholars, focusing on historical reconstruction, cannot avoid the possibility of identifying different approaches to economics in different contexts. They must therefore be open to the possibility that the modern context might have enough in common with an earlier context to justify applying an earlier approach (or theory) to modern economics. Or indeed it could provide the basis for an argument that economics had taken a 'wrong turning'. This was the Italian approach identified in the 1970s. HET thus provides a body of 'experimental' evidence for a Newtonian/Smithian analysis of economics.

Some specialist HET scholars choose (quite reasonably) not to draw any conclusions for modern economics, indeed (controversially) identifying that limitation with their definition of HET (Lodewijks 2003). But others who are more likely to address non-mainstream audiences make a different choice, engaging in the battlefield of ideas with respect to modern economics. Then, there are non-specialists who draw on the specialist HET work of others to inform their economics. For the economics curriculum, there is scope on the one hand for specialist HET courses, but also for embedding HET within all other courses (Roncaglia 1996; Dow 2009b). This too goes back to the Smithian tradition. In this context, the tradition was applied within Scottish higher education, where everything was taught historically in order to convey the range of possible approaches and theories, and also to promote understanding of conceptual evolution.

It has thus been argued (e.g. by Roncaglia 2014, pp. 5–7) that HET can provide a valuable contribution to all economists, mainstream as well as non-mainstream, and to economics education in particular. Our understanding of modern theory is enhanced by understanding how it evolved, particularly conceptually. Even accepting the Whig history argument that modern ideas reflect the highest achievement relative to history, the standard teaching approach is to present modern theories as being like rabbits out of a hat. But why is modern theory the way it is? As Blaug (2001, p. 156) put it: 'No idea or theory in economics, physics, chemistry, biology, philosophy and even mathematics is ever thoroughly understood except as the end-product of a slice of history, the result of some previous intellectual development'.

Blaug (2001) also points out that intellectual history is open to different interpretations, which are subject to periodic revision. He gives as an example the way in which the Whig history interpretation of Smith ([1776] 1976) as providing the basis (without the technical content) for the rational-economic-man interpretation invisible hand has been challenged. But he explains the problem of approaching HET as rational reconstruction (using the modern framework) rather than historical reconstruction (trying to tease out the relevant context-specific framework). In particular, given the difficulties of historical reconstruction, he argues that the history of ideas cannot be taken for granted as having been settled. Support for HET research is thus necessary for its *continuing* contribution to modern understanding in economics. Blaug also argues that assessment of modern theory can benefit from its history, giving as an example a critique based on HET of the whole approach of general equilibrium theory. HET thus itself can in fact be an important ingredient in justifying the Whig approach to HET. The overall conclusion is therefore that some knowledge of HET is necessary for developing a rounded (even if contestable) understanding of modern theory.

The history of economic ideas is important, not just for understanding theory itself, but also for understanding the subject matter of theory and how it has absorbed particular economic ideas. Karl Niebyl (1946) presented a stage analysis of Classical monetary theory and policy whereby the dominant economic ideas of each stage are both the product of real experience, but also shape real experience, all mediated by power structures (Chick 1999; Dow and Dow 2002). Prevailing academic ideas about monetary policy, the product of past experience, provide the basis for monetary arrangements and monetary policy, which then enable and constrain future possibilities for monetary policy. Given this temporal sequence and the tendency for past experience to be a poor guide to the future, these developments get out of phase, so that monetary arrangements and monetary policy get out of phase with reality and academic ideas take time to catch up, and so it goes on.

So understanding the evolution of ideas is necessary for understanding the evolution of policy and institutions and their real consequences. As Keynes (1936, p. 383) had already put it, 'the ideas of economists and political philosophers, both when they are right and when they are wrong, are more powerful than is commonly understood. Indeed, the world is ruled by little else. Practical men, who believe themselves to be quite exempt from any intellectual influences, are usually the slaves of some defunct economist'.

At the very least, we need to understand what these 'defunct economists' thought and how that fitted into the evolution of ideas. As Niebyl (1946, p. 2) put it, we need to study the historical development of monetary theory in relation to the contemporary real economic context within which it developed so that 'we shall be able to attain an invaluable insight into the necessary technique of coping with our own concrete problems'.

While a strong case for HET can be made even from a Whig perspective, it rules out the basis for HET in Italy in the 1970s which Marcuzzo and Rosselli (2002) outline: the scope for rescuing from the past good ideas which have subsequently been ignored. Thus, for example, even Blaug (2001) downplays the force of their argument by suggesting that successful rescues of old ideas are very rare. But this is to ignore the significance of difference of approach to economics; for modern economics, as important as theoretical ideas is the approach of key historical figures. Thus, for example, it is Keynes's approach to policy discourse which is arguably of even greater direct relevance to modern economics than specific theories (see, e.g., Carabelli and Cedrini 2014). It is important therefore for the 'thought' in HET to refer to the level of approach as well as theory.

2.4 Conclusion

We have considered here the arguments for HET to play an integral role in economics, even when the specialist research into HET is carried out within HET as a separate subdiscipline. These arguments follow from a non-positivist view of economics, which legitimizes the possibility of a range of approaches to economics, both now and in the past. At the very least, then, HET serves to enhance our understanding of modern economics. This applies even to a Whig HET perspective, which limits the scope for difference of approach to the past. If only for that reason, HET should be part of the economics curriculum.

But an acceptance of the incompleteness of economic knowledge means that HET plays a much broader and active methodological role in both the development of economic theory and debate between different approaches to developing theory. HET provides a range of ideas from the past, developed in relation to a range of contexts, from which we can draw ideas for the present. It also provides evidence from a range of contexts as inputs to a Newtonian experimental methodology, for developing and reviewing a system of economic ideas.

Adam Smith's work is a notable case in point, with a wealth of ideas on epistemology and methodology and their application to the social, as well as natural, sciences. A similar exercise could of course have been conducted with respect to Keynes, and indeed, there are many parallels with Smith. To seek such patterns is indeed to apply the philosophical approach to history.

In terms of the future for HET, it is perhaps Smith's approach to history which is most pertinent. His philosophical approach to history was addressed to distilling patterns from history in the full understanding that actual circumstances might well deviate from the patterns, thus requiring particular investigation and discussion. This corresponds to the approach to history employed by non-mainstream economists. But it is approaching HET from this perspective which has been classified by some as bias and subjectivity, in contrast to the 'objectivity' of an orthodox-history approach to HET.

But, just as a non-positivist epistemology allows for a range of approaches to economics, so also it allows for a range of approaches to history. Each approach of course requires justification through debate, but there is no basis for any one approach to be demonstrated as the best—in economics or in history. It is therefore clear that, for historians of economic thought within non-mainstream economics, the battlefield of ideas needs to include explicit discussion of history itself.

Notes

1. Annalisa Rosselli has played a key role in promoting HET, not least through her own research within the field, but also in encouraging the research of others, e.g. through ESHET, the European Society for the History of Economic Thought, and as a founding editor of *Economic Thought: History, Philosophy and Methodology*.
2. Annalisa and I both attended that conference.

References

Anderson, R. D. (1983). *Education and Opportunity in Victorian Scotland: Schools and Universities*. Oxford: Clarendon Press.

Blaug, M. (2001). No History of Ideas, Please, We're Economists. *Journal of Economic Perspectives, 15*(1), 145–164.

Broadie, A. (Ed.). (2003). *The Cambridge Companion to the Scottish Enlightenment*. Cambridge: Cambridge University Press.

Campbell, R. H., & Skinner, A. S. (1976). General Introduction. In R. H. Campbell & A. S. Skinner (Eds., textual editor W. B. Todd), The Glasgow Edition of *The Works and Correspondence of Adam Smith, Vol. 2a: An Inquiry into the Nature and Causes of the Wealth of Nations* (pp. 1–60). Oxford: Oxford University Press.

Carabelli, A. M., & Cedrini, M. A. (2014). Chapter 18 of *The General Theory* 'Further Analysed': Economics as a Way of Thinking. *Cambridge Journal of Economics, 38*(1), 23–47.

Chick, V. (1999). *Karl Niebyl's Methodology: Classical Monetary Theory in Historical Context.* Paper presented to the History of Economic Thought Conference, Glasgow Caledonian University.

Coats, A. W. (1975). Adam Smith and the Mercantile System. In A. S. Skinner & T. Wilson (Eds.), *Essays on Adam Smith* (pp. 218–236). Oxford: Clarendon Press.

Comim, F. (2006). Adam Smith: Common Sense and Aesthetics in the Age of Experiments. In A. C. Dow & S. C. Dow (Eds.), *A History of Scottish Economic Thought* (pp. 123–145). London: Routledge.

Davie, G. E. (1961). *The Democratic Intellect: Scotland and Her Universities in the Nineteenth Century.* Edinburgh: Edinburgh University Press.

Dow, A. C. (1984). The Hauteur of Adam Smith: An Unpublished Letter from James Anderson of Monkshill. *Scottish Journal of Political Economy, 31*(3), 284–285.

Dow, S. C. (2009a). Smith's Philosophy and Economic Methodology. In J. T. Young (Ed.), *Elgar Companion to Adam Smith* (pp. 100–111). Cheltenham, UK and Northampton, MA: Edward Elgar.

Dow, S. C. (2009b). History of Thought and Methodology in Pluralist Economics Education. *International Review of Economics Education, 8*(2), 41–57.

Dow, A. C., & Dow, S. C. (2002). The Relevance of Historical Experience for Economics. In P. Arestis, M. Desai, & S. C. Dow (Eds.), *Methodology, Microeconomics and Keynes* (pp. 39–50). London: Routledge.

Dow, A. C., & Dow, S. C. (2015). Economic Development in the Scottish Enlightenment: Ideas as Cause and Effect. In N. Perdikis & K. Ruziev (Eds.), *Development and Financial Reform in Emerging Economies* (pp. 7–22). London: Pickering and Chatto.

Hume, D. ([1739–40] 1978). *A Treatise of Human Nature* (2nd ed., K. A. Selby-Bigge & P. H. Nedditch Eds.). Oxford: Clarendon Press.

Keynes, J. M. (1936). *The General Theory of Employment, Interest and Money.* London: Macmillan.

Kuhn, T. S. ([1962] 1970). *The Structure of Scientific Revolutions.* Chicago: Chicago University Press.

Lodewijks, J. (2003). Research in the History of Economic Thought as a Vehicle for the Defense and Criticism of Orthodox Economics. In W. J. Samuels, J. E. Biddle, & J. B. Davis (Eds.), *A Companion to the History of Economic Thought* (pp. 654–668). Oxford: Basil Blackwell.

Marcuzzo, M. C. (2008). Is History of Economic Thought a 'Serious' Subject? *Erasmus Journal for Philosophy and Economics, 1*(1), 107–123.

Marcuzzo, M. C., & Rosselli, A. (2002). Economics As History of Economics: The Italian Case in Retrospect. In E. R. Weintraub (Ed.), *The Future of the History of Economics* (pp. 98–109). Durham, NC: Duke University Press.

Montes, L. (2006). Adam Smith: Real Newtonian. In A. C. Dow & S. C. Dow (Eds.), *A History of Scottish Economic Thought* (pp. 102–122). London: Routledge.

Newton, Sir I. ([1704] 1730). *Opticks: Or, a Treatise of the Reflections, Refractions, Inflections and Colours of Light* (4th ed.). London: William Innys.

Niebyl, K. H. (1946). *Studies in the Classical Theories of Money.* New York: Columbia University Press.

Roncaglia, A. (1996). Why Should Economists Study the History of Economic Thought? *European Journal of the History of Economic Thought, 3*(2), 296–309.

Roncaglia, A. (2014). Should the History of Economic Thought be Included in Undergraduate Curricula? *Economic Thought, 3*(1), 1–9.

Skinner, A. S. (1965). Economics and History: The Scottish Enlightenment. *Scottish Journal of Political Economy, 12*(1), 1–22.

Skinner, A. S. (1972). Adam Smith: Philosophy and Science. *Scottish Journal of Political Economy, 19*(3), 307–319.

Skinner, Q. (1969). Meaning and Understanding in the History of Ideas. *History and Theory, 8*(1), 3–53.

Smith, A. ([1759] 1976). *The Theory of Moral Sentiments.* In D. D. Raphael & A. Macfie (Eds.), The Glasgow Edition of *The Works and Correspondence of Adam Smith* (Vol. 1). Oxford: Oxford University Press.

Smith, A. ([1762–63] 1983). *Lectures on Rhetoric and Belles Lettres.* In J. C. Bryce (Ed.), The Glasgow Edition of *The Works and Correspondence of Adam Smith* (Vol. 4). Oxford: Oxford University Press.

Smith, A. ([1776] 1976). *An Inquiry into the Nature and Causes of the Wealth of Nations.* In R. H. Campbell & A. S. Skinner (Eds., textual editor W. B. Todd), The Glasgow Edition of *The Works and Correspondence of Adam Smith* (Vols. 2a and 2b). Oxford: Oxford University Press.

Smith, A. ([1795] 1980). The History of Astronomy. In W. P. D. Wightman & J. C. Bryce (Eds.), The Glasgow Edition of *The Works and Correspondence of Adam Smith, Vol. 3: Essays on Philosophical Subjects* (pp. 33–106). Oxford: Oxford University Press.

Theocarakis, N. (2014). A Commentary on Alessandro Roncaglia's Paper: 'Should the History of Economic Thought be Included in Undergraduate Curricula?'. *Economic Thought, 3*(1), 10–20.

Weintraub, E. R. (Ed.). (2002a). *The Future of the History of Economics*. Durham, NC: Duke University Press.

Weintraub, E. R. (2002b). Will Economics Ever Have a Past Again? In E. R. Weintraub (Ed.), *The Future of the History of Economics* (pp. 1–14). Durham, NC: Duke University Press.

Wightman, W. P. D. (1975). Adam Smith and the History of Ideas. In A. S. Skinner & T. Wilson (Eds.), *Essays on Adam Smith* (pp. 44–67). Oxford: Clarendon Press.

CHAPTER 3

A Bibliometric Portrait of Contemporary History of Economic Thought

Alberto Baccini

3.1 Introduction

Rankings are ubiquitous in the public debate about science, and research metrics are pervasive. Scientometrics and bibliometrics, i.e. the disciplines devoted to the quantitative studies of science, are usually considered as producing instruments and indicators for evaluative purposes. Economists are particularly and exclusively interested to this evaluative side. Backhouse and colleagues showed that the American Economic Association (AEA) started to publish institutional rankings since the 1930s (Backhouse et al. 1997, p. 2). League tables of individual economists' journal output, based on the AEA's *Index of economic journals*, started to appear at the beginning of the 1970s (Hansen and Weisbrod 1972). Since then economists have produced a watershed of rankings of journals, departments, articles or whatever. One example for all: the RePEc project (https://ideas.repec.org/top/) permits to rank documents, people, journals, regions, countries and universities by adopting a variety of

A. Baccini (✉)
Department of Economics and Statistics, University of Siena, Siena, Italy
e-mail: alberto.baccini@unisi.it

M. C. Marcuzzo et al. (eds.), *New Perspectives on Political Economy and Its History*, Palgrave Studies in the History of Economic Thought,
https://doi.org/10.1007/978-3-030-42925-6_3

bibliometric indicators of production or impact. RePEc distributes also 'IDEAS-Fantasy League' (https://ideas.repec.org/fantasy.html) where economists compete by imagining to be 'at the helm of an economics department. Your goal is to improve its ranking relative to other departments in the league. You can do this by trading economists and by choosing which ones to activate in your roster'.

Actually, bibliometric and scientometric tools may serve more useful and less narcissistic purposes than rankings. Bibliometric indicators were indeed originally developed for the quantitative study of science (De Bellis 2014) and *descriptive* bibliometrics is currently used for enriching our understanding of the structure and dynamics of science (Lucio-Arias and Leydesdorff 2009; Mingers and Leydesdorff 2015; Todeschini and Baccini 2016). From the 2010s only, historians of economics have started the so-called quantitative turn in the history of economic thought (Cherrier and Svorenčík 2018; Edwards et al. 2018). Bibliometrics and citation analysis have been embarked into the methodological toolbox of historians, along with other quantitative methods such as network analysis (Catherine and Doehne 2018) and topic modelling (Ambrosino et al. 2018). Claveau and Gingras (2016) for example advanced a 'bibliometric history' of economics from the late 1950s to present days. Jovanovic (2018) used citation analysis to reconstruct the history of the efficient market hypothesis. And Oliveira (2018) showed how bibliometric analysis can be useful for studying the formalization of economics. In 2018, the *Journal of Economic Methodology* devoted a special issue to quantitative HET in which pros and cons were debated.

In general, bibliometrics and quantitative methods permit to draw a landscape of scholarly fields, because they allow to consider an amount of documents that cannot simply be processed by humans. This paper attempts to use bibliometric techniques for investigating the field of the *history of economic thought* (HET) itself. The goal is to offer to the historians a *bibliometric portrait* of the contemporary state of their own field. Specifically, this paper contains some preliminary answers to descriptive questions about the field: What are the most productive countries, institutions and authors in HET? How frequent is the collaborative writing of papers in HET? What is the gender distribution of the authors? What are the main interests of HET scholars in terms of authors, journals and documents? Do they cite more books or articles? What are the main clusters of references?

3.2 HET as a Research Field: Quantitative Analyses

A couple of studies recently started the quantitative study of HET. Zacchia and Marcuzzo (2016) used the EconLit database, maintained by the AEA, for retrieving the papers belonging to the sub-field of HET. They selected any paper classified with a JEL code 'B', according to the EconLit subject descriptors (https://www.aeaweb.org/econlit/jelCodes.php), and having a subject description SU = 'History of Economic Thought'. They report that, from 1955 to 2013, 930 distinct journals in the database published at least one HET article. However, they note a steady decrease over time in both journals and articles dealing with HET. Between 1993 and 2013, the journals specialized in HET (*History of Political Economy*, *Journal of the History of Economic Thought*, *History of Economics Review*, *History of Economic Ideas*, and *European Journal for the History of Economic Thought*) have published more than 24% (2938 papers) of all the HET articles in *EconLit*. Based on the quantitative analyses of HET articles, the authors detect three trends in the evolution of HET in recent years: (1) an increasing interest for minor economists from a more recent past, (2) the flourishing of archival research into unpublished work and correspondence, and (3) the tendency to move out from the focus on individual authors towards the collective dimension of economic thought, namely groups and networks. They highlight also the concentration of HET articles in a small set of specialized journals.

Duarte and Giraud (2016) investigated, with a mix of quantitative and qualitative analysis, the weight of HET literature in eight leading economic journals. They are the so-called Top-Five (*American Economic Review*, *Econometrics*, *Journal of Political Economy*, *Quarterly Journal of Economics*, *Review of Economic Studies*) (Heckman and Moktan 2018), plus *Economic Journal*, *Journal of Economic Literature* and *Journal of Economic Perspectives* (Duarte and Giraud 2016). In order to identify the papers belonging to the sub-field of HET, they selected any paper classified with a JEL code 'B'. The quantitative analysis shows that the rate of HET articles published in top economic journals is decreasing over time. Between 1969 and 2011, around 3% of the articles published in the top journals were related to HET, with a notable decrease after mid-1990s. Adopting a close reading approach, Duarte and Giraud classified the 196 HET research articles appeared in the top journals according to the methods and narrative styles used by their authors. According to the authors, only few of these articles employ archival research, whereas most of them are surveys or overviews with a few of citations to historical sources. As for the narrative styles, one of the most common uses of HET is to trace the origins of current economic ideas in past developments, or to point out the great figures of the past.

3.3 The Production of Contemporary HET

In this work, the focus is on HET specialized journals, that is on journals publishing exclusively HET articles. This choice permits to define in a very simple way the domain of analysis, i.e. all the papers published by specialized journals. The rationale of this choice consists in restricting the HET field in such a way that only articles produced for a field-specific audience are considered. It is possible to conjecture that choosing HET specialized journals permits to select the stream of literature conceived and written by historians of economic thought for a professionalized audience, i.e. in view of having other historians of economic thought as readers.

This point of view is different from the one adopted by Zacchia and Marcuzzo (2016) who define the HET field by considering all kinds of HET papers according to their EconLit classification irrespective of the journal where they were published. It also differs from the one of Duarte and Giraud (2016) who considered only HET articles written for an audience of economists. It is worthwhile to note that the quantitative approach adopted by Duarte and Giraud (2016) and by Zacchia and Marcuzzo (2016) is limited to the metadata of the considered articles, i.e. title, abstract, type of contribution, names of the authors, journal, publication year, subject classification and so on. The aim of this paper is to enlarge the domain of the quantitative approach by considering also references and citations of HET articles. Consequently, the coverage of this work is necessarily limited to the set of HET journals indexed in the bibliometric database used for retrieving data. The Web of Science (WoS) database, maintained by Clarivate Analytics, indexes six HET journals:

1. *History of Political Economy* (HOPE), founded in 1969 and published by Duke University Press, is the most ancient professional journal of the HET field (coverage 2006–2018);

2. The *European Journal of the History of Economic Thought* (EJHET) started in 1993 and it is published by Taylor and Francis (coverage 2005–2018);
3. The *Journal of the History of Economic Thought* (JHET) started in 1979 as *History of Economics Society Bulletin* and adopted the current name in 1990; it is published by Cambridge University Press (coverage 2009–2019);
4. *History of Economic Ideas* (HEI) was funded in 1983 as *Quaderni di storia dell'economia politica*; the current name was adopted in 1997 together with a complete switch to English language; it is published by Fabrizio Serra editore, Pisa, Italy (coverage 2009–2018);
5. *Research in the History of Economic Thought and Methodology* (RHETM) is both a journal and a book series; it started publication in 1983; from 2009 it is published by Emerald (coverage 2009–2018);
6. *History of Economic Thought and Policy* (HETP) started its publication in 2012 by incorporating the experience of the Italian journal *Rivista di Storia del Pensiero economico* started in 2004; it is published in Italy by Franco Angeli publisher (coverage 2005–2018).

Some HET specialized journals, such as *Revue d'Histoire de la Pensée Economique* or *History of Economics Review*, are not included in this paper simply because WoS does not index them. Actually, WoS index policy induces an English language bias, i.e. only articles published in English are considered. Moreover, for HET, two journals out of six are published in Italy and this probably induces an over-exposition of the Italian HET community with respect to other national communities of scholars.

WoS coverage imposes also the choice of the period analysed. Articles considered are those published in 2005–2018, since, before 2005, WoS indexed HOPE only.

According to WoS, in the considered period, these journals published 2837 items; in view of focusing on original research only, the book reviews are removed from the analysis, by lasting a corpus of 1780 research articles (hereinafter HET corpus).[1] HOPE represents 31% of the corpus, EJHET 29% of the HET corpus, the JHET and HEI follow with 15 and 14%, respectively, whereas RHETM and HETP cover around 8 and 3% of research articles considered.

In order to have a rough measure of the representativeness of these articles over the entire production of HET, it is possible to consider the total number of scholarly peer-reviewed articles indexed in the EconLit database in the same period. EconLit has a coverage of economic literature much wider than WoS. The research articles published in the six HET journals represent about 20% of the total number (8940) of peer-reviewed articles indexed in EconLit and classified as 'history of economic thought' (JEL CODES: B00, B10–B31). The peer-reviewed journal articles represent about 64% of the total number of items (book reviews, chapters of book, books, etc.) indexed in EconLit and classified as HET (14,059). It is worthwhile to stress that HET articles represent about 1.5% of the total number of EconLit articles (627,480). Figure 3.1 draws yearly data about the relative dimensions of HET corpus with respect to the number of HET research articles, to the number of HET items and to the total number of items indexed in EconLit. It reports also the percentage of the

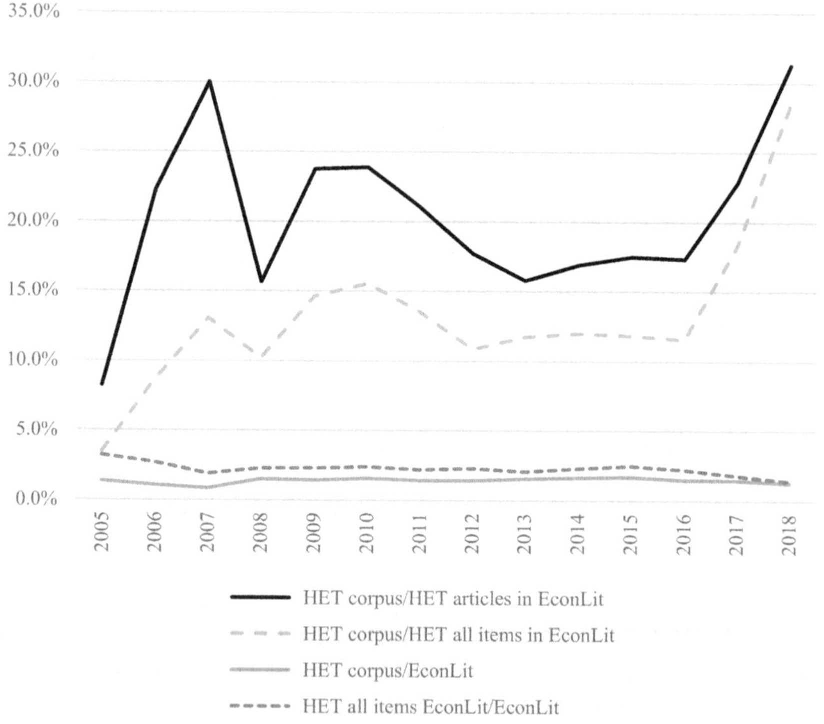

Fig. 3.1 The relative size of HET corpus. Yearly data (*Source* WoS and EconLit)

items classified as HET in EconLit on the total number of items indexed in EconLit.

From these data, it appears that HET represents a very small niche in the economic literature. The share of this niche is stable over the considered period, whether all the items classified by EconLit as HET or HET corpus are considered. These results are compatible with the finding of Duarte and Giraud (2016) that the share of HET articles in eight top economics journals has declined over time. If both trajectories are considered together, HET seems to evolve by locking itself up more and more in specialized journals, as suggested by Zacchia and Marcuzzo (2016).

All the results presented in what follows refer to HET corpus only. The question whether these results can be extended to the whole HET production is not at stake here. The generic expressions used hereafter referring to HET have to be considered, therefore, as indicating evidence limited to HET corpus. For instance, the expression 'HET most prolific authors' is a short label for 'the most prolific authors according to the data of HET corpus here considered'.

The analysis of the HET corpus metadata permits to investigate the contemporary scholarly production by following a macro- to micro-trajectory, i.e. from the country to the single authors.

What are the most productive countries in HET? Table 3.1 shows the ten most productive countries in the HET corpus. According to WoS,

Table 3.1 Top ten most productive countries in HET

Rank	*Country*	*Number of articles*	*%*	*Rank in EEF*	*%*	*Specialization in HET*
1	USA	426	24	1	28.2	0.9
2	France	310	17.5	4	4.6	3.8
3	Italy	297	16.8	9	3.6	4.7
4	England	149	8.4	2	9.8	0.9
5	Canada	85	4.8	8	3.8	1.3
6	Germany	64	3.6	3	6.1	0.6
7	Australia	61	3.4	7	4.2	0.8
8	Netherlands	49	2.8	10	2.8	1.0
9	Brazil	48	2.7	19	1.2	2.3
10	Switzerland	41	2.3	15	1.6	1.4

Source WoS

countries are attributed to articles based on the address of the institution to which the publication's author is affiliated. Thus, a publication authored by an Italian scholar working in the USA increments the USA score, not the Italian one. An international article co-authored by two scholars of two different countries increments both countries' scores. HET production is highly concentrated in the ten countries that represent about 85% of the total HET articles produced in the considered years. Unsurprisingly, the USA ranks first for number of authored articles, followed by France and Italy, two countries with a strong research tradition in HET studies.

It is possible to compare these data with Scopus data about the production of research articles in the field of economics, econometrics and finance (EEF) for the years 2005–2016 (data are available in Baccini et al. 2019). The top ten countries in HET represented only the 66% of the total production in EEF. The column 'Rank in EEF' of Table 3.1 reports the position of the countries in the ranking of EEF production. Eight countries in the HET top ten are also in the EEF top ten. Brazil and Switzerland are out from the EEF top ten, substituted by China (6th) and Spain (10th).

On the basis of these data, it is possible to build a very simple index of specialization of a country in the HET, by calculating the ratio between the percentage of world publication in the HET of a country, and the percentage of publication of the same country in EEF. A value of the index equal to 1 indicates that the share of HET articles produced by a country is equal to its share of EEF production. Values of the index less than 1 indicate a relative de-specialization of a country in the production of HET articles, i.e. the share of the HET production of the country is less than its share in EEF. Finally, values of the index greater than 1 indicate a relative specialization of a country in the HET production, i.e. the share of the HET production of the country is greater than its share of EEF production. The most HET specialized country is Italy: its share of HET production is 4.7 times greater than its share in EEF. France follows with share of HET production 3.8 greater than its production in EEF. The USA, UK and Germany, the top three countries for EEF production, are all relatively de-specialized in EEF production.

The USA produced in the considered period about a quarter of the total number of HET articles, but they are relatively de-specialized, i.e. their contribution to the HET literature is less than proportional to their production in EEF. Italy and France had lower share of total production but strong specialization in HET. This specialization is probably the result of national research traditions, more than of a European more historically way to do economics. Indeed, other European countries, mainly Germany, have strong HET de-specialization. In the case of Italy, as anticipated, the possibly unbalanced coverage of WoS may have contributed to the high level of the specialization indicator.

That intuition is reinforced when the ten most productive institutions in HET are considered. To this end, each article is counted as belonging to the primary affiliation of its first author as indexed in WoS. Table 3.2 lists the top ten most productive institutions. The French CNRS ranks first, by probably collecting articles of members of universities who work in labs sponsored by CNRS. It is followed by the University of Pisa, seat of HEI, and by the Duke University, seat of HOPE.

Writing HET. The articles in HET corpus are authored by 2235 non-unique scholars, for an average of 1.26 authorships per article. Only one scholar authors most of the articles (77.9%). Only two articles are authored by the maximum number of five co-authors (Table 3.3). Hence, writing HET continues to be mostly an individual enterprise. Collaboration in the form of multi-authored papers is rather uncommon.

In the considered corpus, there are a total of 1147 unique authors. Few authors produce a large fraction of the publications: the 20 most productive authors produced the 19% of the total number of articles. The big

Table 3.2 Top ten most productive institutions

Rank	*Institution*	*Country*	*Number of articles*
1	Centre National de la Recherche Scientifique (CNRS)	France	65
2	Università di Pisa	Italy	45
3	Duke University, Durham	USA	43
4	Université Panthéon Sorbonne, Paris	France	35
5	Université de Strasbourg	France	26
6	Université de Lausanne	Switzerland	26
7	HESAM Université, Paris	France	25
8	Université Paris VIII	France	25
9	Universidade de Brasilia	Brazil	24
10	Università di Palermo	Italy	24

Source WoS

Table 3.3 Proportion of multi-authored papers

Number of authors	*Number of articles*	%
1	1386	77.9
2	351	19.7
3	27	1.5
4	14	0.8
5	2	0.1
Total	1780	100.0

Source WoS

part or the authors (66.5%) produced only one article, 14.7% produced two articles and 6% produced three articles.

Since the WoS author field contains the full name of the authors, it is possible to investigate the gender distribution of HET authors. For genderizing authors, the R package *genderizeR* (Wais 2016) was used, which automatically recognizes gender by using a multi-language database of first names. The results were then checked manually and the recognized wrong attributions were corrected.

On the total of unique authors, 201 are women (17.5%), whereas 946 (82.5%) are men, a ratio of 4.7 men per woman. The ten most productive authors are shown in Table 3.4 and none is a woman. Their institutional affiliation and country varied: only Duke University-USA has two of the

Table 3.4 Most productive authors in HET journals (all male)

Institution	*Country*	*Number of articles*	*Number of co-authored articles*	*% of co-authored articles*
Universidade de Brasilia	Brazil	25	6	24.0
University of Birmingham	UK	21	11	52.3
Università di Palermo	Italy	18	9	50.0
Brock University	Canada	18	4	22.2
Duke University	USA	17	1	5.9
Université Paris II	France	14	6	42.9
Université de Lausanne	Switzerland	16	3	18.8
Universität Graz	Austria	12	1	8.3
Duke University	USA	11	1	9.1
Université of Montpellier	France	11	2	18.2

Source WoS

Table 3.5 Women authors with more than five publications in HET journals

Institution	*Country*	*Number of articles*	*Number of co-authored articles*	*% of co-authored articles*
Trinity University	USA	8	0	0
Institut National d'Etudes Démographiques	France	8	2	25.0
Université de Strasbourg	France	8	1	12.5
Università di Padova	Italy	7	3	42.9
Università di Cassino	Italy	7	0	0
Université de Cergy-Pontoise	France	7	1	14.3
Università di Pisa	Italy	7	1	14.3
Università del Salento	Italy	6	0	0
Università di Roma Tor Vergata	Italy	6	1	16.7
Université Lyon 2	France	6	2	33.3
Université Paris 1	France	6	2	33.3
Université Nice Sophia Antipolis	France	6	2	33.3
Università Roma La Sapienza	Italy	6	1	16.7

Source WoS

most productive scholars. Table 3.5 shows the list of the ten most productive women. Indeed, there are 13 women in the list since six scholars are *ex-aequo* with six papers. Their institutional affiliation is varied, but all but one (USA) are affiliated with French (6) and Italian institutions (6).

In the last column of both Tables 3.4 and 3.5 is reported the percentage of the articles written in collaboration by the most prolific authors. Some of them, especially male authors, collaborate significantly, while others prefer a more individual style of work.

At the level of the articles, 347 publications are authored by at least one woman (19.5%), whereas the articles authored entirely by men are 1434 (80.5%). Among the mono-authored articles, 13.4% are authored by a woman and 86.6% by a man.

In sum, the gender analysis of the corpus reveals a remarkable gender disparity in HET from a point of view of production of articles.

3.4 The Sources Used by Contemporary HET

In this section, the analysis is focused on articles and books cited as references in the articles of HET corpus. It contains 87,554 non-unique references and 63,790 unique references.

For historical disciplines, and then also for HET, references of papers are of two types (Nederhof 2006; Hellqvist 2010):

1. *Source references* pointing to primary sources, i.e. to historical published materials that are the *object* of study of historians; and
2. *Scholarship references* pointing to secondary literature, i.e. published materials produced by other scholars, that an historian uses for contextualizing her/his achievements or for discussing previous reconstruction or ideas about his/her object of study.

A first question is about the diffusion of different outlets such as books and journal articles in the reference lists. For calculating the proportion of references to books and to journals, it is necessary to classify the considered references as books or articles. The standard technique consists in considering as 'books' all the references that lack both the volume and the page number (Larivière et al. 2006). In the case of HET, this technique may generate wrong classifications for the collected works of economists, e.g. William Stanley Jevons or John Maynard Keynes, that may be classified as articles since a correct reference contains both a volume number and pages. Here the standard technique is adopted, but the resulting classification was checked manually.

As shown in Table 3.6, 46.6% of the unique references point to books and 36.3% to journals, whereas 17% of the references remain undetermined by this method since they contain either the page or the volume number. Possibly these remaining references consist mainly of book chapters or archival material. The high proportion of references to books is not unexpected: it is possibly originated by source references pointing to

Table 3.6 Estimation of the proportion of books and serials in the HET references

	Number	*Percentage*
Estimated unique book references	29,754	46.6
Estimated unique article references	23,184	36.3
Undetermined unique references	10,852	17.1
Unique cited references	63,790	100

Source WoS

historical books. In this respect, HET is similar to other humanities fields belonging to the area of history (Nederhof 2006; Hellqvist 2010).

To esteem the proportion of books and articles in the *scholarship* references, we limited the analysis to the references published between 2005 and 2018 (17% of the total). It is very unlikely that references published between 2005 and 2018 are historical sources. As Table 3.7 shows, the proportion of books is almost 42% of the references by showing that books are still an important venue of dissemination of HET scholarship.

What are the most used journals in the HET literature? In view of individuating the journals that historians used mostly in their work, it is simply possible to count the number of times that a journal is referenced in the HET corpus. The list of referenced journals contains 102 journals; the total number of references to these journals is 20,664 (23.6% of the total number of references). The average number of references in which a journal appears is 202.6, but references to journals are highly concentrated on a small group of journals. As reported in Table 3.8, the ten most referenced journals cover the 57.4% of the non-unique references to journals, while the four most referenced journals represent the 33.6% of the non-unique references.

In the top ten, three out of ten journals belong to the field of HET, whereas seven out of ten belong to the field of economics. All the so-called Top-Five journals of economics are among the top-referenced paper in HET corpus. With 5923 references, they represented a 28.7% of the total number of references. If it is assumed that all secondary references pointed to HET journals, a rough estimate of the references to primary sources published in journals can be obtained as the difference between

Table 3.7 Estimation of the proportion of books and serials in the HET references published from 2005 to 2018

	Number	*Percentage*
Estimated unique book references	4432	41.6
Estimated unique article references	6208	58.4
Undetermined unique references	0	0.0
Unique cited references	10,640	100.0

Source WoS

Table 3.8 Most cited journals in the corpus. In italics journal belonging to the corpus

Rank	*Journal*	*Non-unique references*
1	*History of Political Economy*	2192
2	American Economic Review*	1836
3	Economic Journal	1572
4	Journal of Political Economy*	1349
5	Econometrica*	1142
6	Quarterly Journal of Economics*	1131
7	*European Journal of the History of Economic Thought*	926
8	*Journal of the History of Economic Thought*	738
9	Economica	538
10	Review of Economic Studies*	482

* = top-five journal
Source WoS

the total number of references and the number of references to HET journals (4230). The estimated number of references to primary sources published in economic journals is 16,434 and the Top-Five represented the 36% of the total; *The Economic Journal* is referenced only a bit less than the *American Economic Review* but much more than the four remaining Top-Five.

By focusing attention on references to HET journals, it is possible to estimate the use of HET journals inside the HET field. They represent less than the 5% of the total number of references. Indeed it is possible to estimate the 'market share' of each HET journal when historians wrote for a professional audience. This estimate represents also a proxy of the degree of auto-referentiality of HET journals. In Table 3.9, the number of non-unique references to HET journals is reported together with the percentage of references received by each journal on the total references in the corpus. The last column is the estimate of the disciplinary market share of each HET journal (percentage of each journal on the total number of references pointing to HET journals). HOPE is the most referenced journal, representing 10.6% of the total references to journals and more than a half of the total references to HET journals.

Data about referenced journals can be explored by using journal co-citation analysis (White and Griffith 1981; McCain 1991). In co-citation analysis (Small 1973), the similarity between two documents is proxied by

Table 3.9 References to HET journals from HET journals

Rank	*Journal*	*Non-unique references*	*% of non-unique references*	*% of non-unique references to journals*	*% of references to HET journals*
1	*History of Political Economy*	2192	2.5	10.6	51.7
2	*European Journal of the History of Economic Thought*	926	1.1	4.5	21.8
3	*Journal of the History of Economic Thought*	738	0.8	3.6	17.4
4	*History of Economic Ideas*	167	0.2	0.8	3.9
5	*Research in the History of Economic Thought and Methodology*	141	0.2	0.7	3.3
6	*History of Economic Thought and Policy*	75	0.1	0.4	1.7

Source WoS

the number of times they are cited together in a given set of documents. The idea is that two documents frequently cited together are intellectually similar, because they share common themes or methods (van Eck and Waltman 2010). In the case at hand, the similarity between two journals is proxied by the number of times they are cited together by the articles of HET corpus. Figure 3.2 shows the co-citation relationship among the journals cited in the HET corpus. Nodes of the network are journals and edges between nodes are co-citations: the closer journals are, the more frequently they are cited together. The dimension of the nodes is proportional to the number of times a journal is referenced. The network is realized by using VOSviewer (van Eck and Waltman 2010), with full

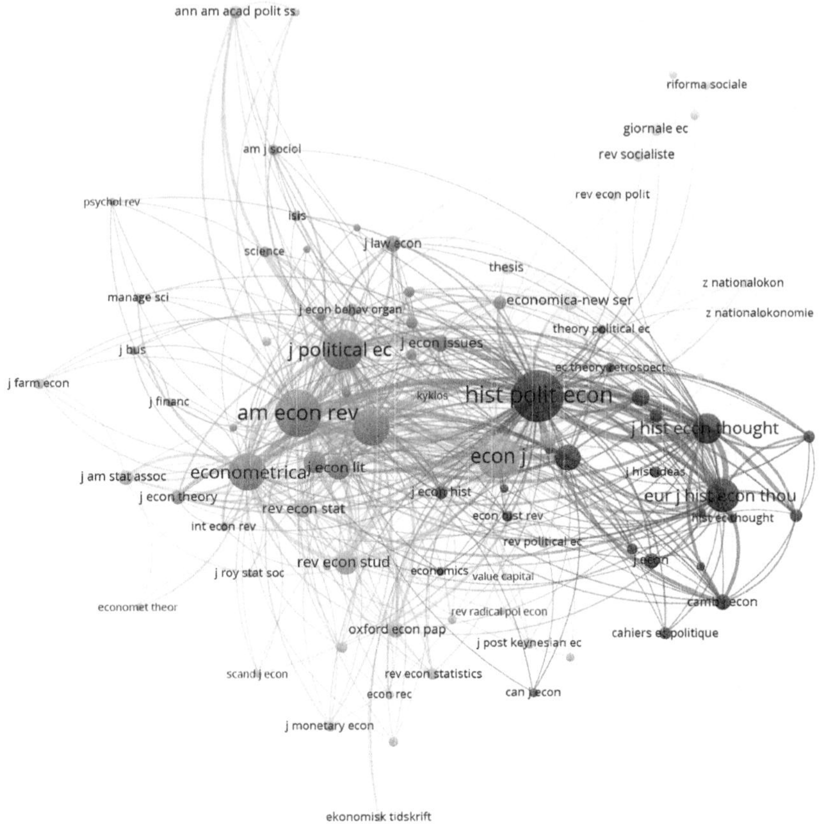

Fig. 3.2 Co-citation map of referenced journals in HET

counting method, a minimum number of citations fixed to 50, and a resolution parameter of 0.9.

Journals are clustered by using the VOS community detection algorithm (van Eck and Waltman 2010). Five clusters can be detected. The first cluster contains mainly the outlets hosting the literature produced by HET scholars, i.e. the journals on which the HET debate takes place, the six HET journals here considered.

The other clusters contain instead economic journals representing the sources used by historians for their work. A second cluster contains the most influent journals in contemporary economics such as *Quarterly Journal of Economics*, *American Economic Review*, *Journal of Economic Literature*, *Journal of Political Economy*. It contains also multidisciplinary journals, such as *Science*, and sub-field journals such as *Public Choice* or *Journal of Law and Economics*. Probably these journals represent the main sources for historians interested to mainstream economics and especially to microeconomic oriented HET. A third cluster contains econometrics and statistical journals. They may represent the main sources of articles devoted to history of econometrics and statistics. A fourth cluster contains macro-oriented journals, including non-mainstream and economic history journals. Hence, HET journals and economic history journals are classified in different clusters. This confirms the conjecture of Annalisa Rosselli (2013, p. 867) according to which 'the more closely the economic history and HET journals pursue specialised issues, the greater grows the distance between the two subjects'. Finally, the fifth cluster contains peripheral journals useful for historians interested in Italian and German HET.

The journals on the map belong mainly to the area of economics. In particular, in the map there are only a few of history of science journals (*ISIS*, *Science in Context*) or of general history. In every case these last journals are in very peripheral position, despite the explicit research program of 'coming together' proposed by Margaret Schabas (Giraud 2019). Hence, it can be argued that HET continues to be a self-contained discipline, at most a sub-area of economics, with a low degree of openness towards other disciplines, namely philosophy of science, history and economic history. A result that may be considered coherent with the conclusions of Yann Giraud (2019, p. 603) surveying five decades of HOPE: 'while some individuals or groups of individuals have suggested bolder inflections for the field over the years, their attempts, while sparking debates and, at times, controversies, have had limited effect on a vast portion of the journal's content'.

Who are the most cited authors in the HET literature? The next step of the analysis consisted in producing the list of the most cited authors in the HET corpus and in visualizing their co-citation relations. It is worthwhile to recall that WoS includes only the first author of a cited document; hence, other authors are not considered in this analysis. Table 3.10 shows the top ten of the most cited authors. Indeed it represents the list of the most studied authors in HET journals.

Table 3.10 Top ten most cited authors

Rank	*Author*	*Number of citation*
1	John Maynard Keynes	928
2	Paul A. Samuelson	720
3	Friedrich von Hayek	548
4	Adam Smith	505
5	Milton Friedman	503
6	Karl Marx	402
7	Joseph Alois Schumpeter	391
8	Alfred Marshall	355
9	John Stuart Mill	343
10	Arthur Cecil Pigou	309

Source WoS

Figure 3.3 represents authors' co-citation map by using the colour density visualization technique. It is built by considering only authors ($n = 58$) with more than 100 citations. The VOS clustering technique, applied with full counting method and a resolution parameter of 0.8, detects clusters of authors, i.e. authors frequently co-cited. Lines enclose the four detected clusters of authors. Parts of the figure with darker shades of grey indicate stronger co-citation relationships among the authors.

Each cluster contains both primary source authors, and historians of economic thought active in the study of the primary source authors. The bottom cluster contains classical economists and Sraffa. It includes also historians working on these authors and frequently co-cited together with classical economists. Analogously, the right cluster contains economists working on macroeconomics and historians working mainly on the history of macroeconomics. The cluster at the top collects authors and historians working on the history of contemporary microeconomics. The left cluster contains the authors of the marginalist revolution.

What are the most cited articles or books in the HET literature? If we focus on the basic units of intellectual production, namely the single work, it may be of interest to explore what are the most cited articles or books in HET. Table 3.11 shows the top ten most cited works in HET corpus. They are all books. As it was for the most cited authors, also this list contains the classics of economic theory.

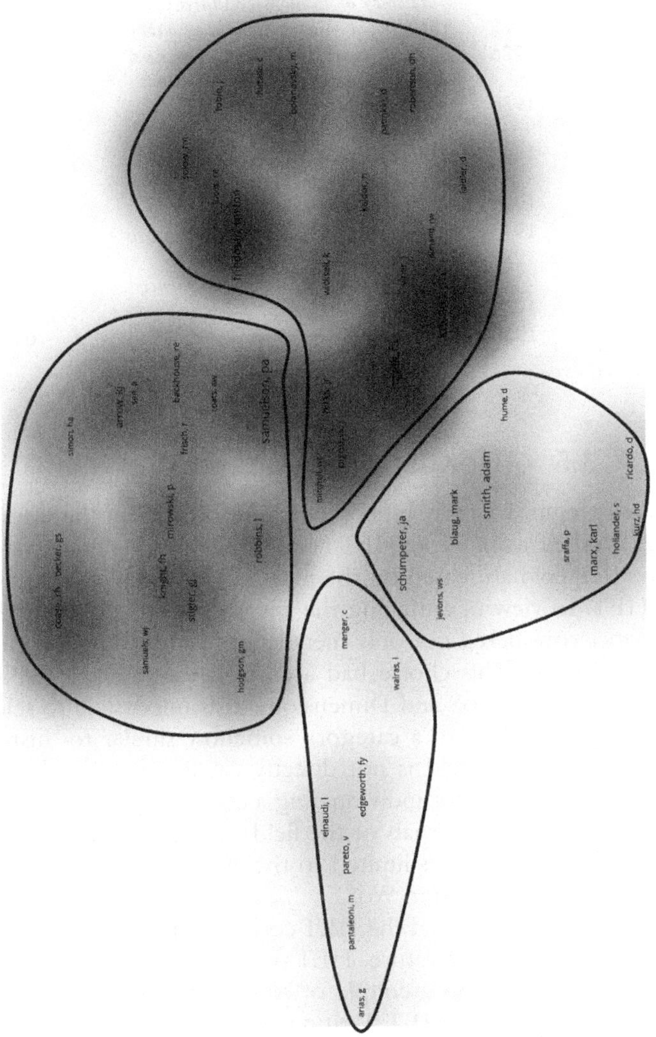

Fig. 3.3 Authors' co-citation density map

Table 3.11 Top ten most cited documents

Author	*Year*	*Title*	*Citations*
Schumpeter, J.A.	1954	*History of Economic Analysis*	202
Marx, K., Engels, F.	1975	*Collected Works (Gesamtausgabe)*	158
Smith, A.	1776	*An Inquiry into the Nature and Causes of the Wealth of Nations*	155
Keynes, J.M.	1936	*General Theory of Employment, Interest and Money*	148
Marx, K.	1867	*Das Kapital. A Critique of Political Economy*	121
Marshall, A.	1920	*Principles of Economics*	111
Samuelson, P.A.	1947	*Foundations of Economic Analysis*	71
Robbins, L.	1932	*Essay on the Nature and Significance of Economic Science*	68
Hicks, J.R.	1939	*Value and Capital*	67
Keynes, J.M.	1930	*Collected Writings*	64

Source WoS

3.5 Concluding Remarks

This paper is an attempt to apply bibliometrics for describing the ways in which scholars do their work in the HET field. Other existing quantitative studies of the HET field are based on the metadata of the research items produced in HET. In view of enriching the already available quantitative analysis, this paper considered not only metadata of articles but also their references and citations. This choice had a cost: in the available bibliometric databases (Scopus, WoS and Dimensions) it is impossible to select a corpus of papers according to a category somehow similar to 'history of economic thought'. If a field is not directly categorized in a bibliometric database, the best way for individuating a corpus of papers consists in selecting the professional journals of the field. As a matter of fact, the HET corpus used in this paper is limited to the articles published in the six professional journals indexed in WoS.

This paper has documented that the HET corpus represents a small and stable niche in the economic literature. HET production is relatively concentrated in few countries, and a couple of countries (Italy and France) have a relative specialization in HET. Writing HET is still a male individual enterprise, and collaboration in the form of multi-authored papers is rather uncommon, as in the big part of arts and humanities.

The analysis of references contained in the articles of HET corpus permitted, maybe for the first time, to have information about articles, journals and books used by the historians of economic thought. Books still represent a big part of the primary sources used by historians of economic thought. As for references to journals, the most relevant issue is that historians cite a relatively small number of journals, and references are relatively concentrated. In particular, results showed that references pointing to source articles published in the Top-Five journals of economics represent more than a third of the total number of references to journal articles. Trivially enough, it follows that two thirds of the references to source journal articles points to other economic journals. It appears therefore that a substantial share of source articles appeared in non-Top-Five journals. Note that a source article is an article that a historian judged for whatever reason, influential or important for economics, and nonetheless relevant for her/his work. It may be conjectured that the role of the Top-Five journals is not (yet) so central in a HET perspective.

The analysis of references in a corpus of papers is very different from the analysis of the topics of these papers. The analysis of references says something about 'the use of pre-existent knowledge' by authors of a corpus of papers; the analysis of topics instead says something about the research produced by these authors. For instance, a paper containing a reference to Adam Smith is not necessarily a paper about Adam Smith. This is the reason why it is very difficult to compare results presented here about the most cited authors and works with evidence drawn from other works. For example, Zacchia and Marcuzzo (2016) showed an increased interest for minor economists from the recent past. This result is completely compatible with the list of top-cited authors discussed above, that includes only some giants of the past. It is well known that citation distributions are highly skewed: a few authors receive many citations and the big part of scholars receives very few citations. So it is hardly probable that a minor economist of the past may appear at the top of a list of the most referenced authors in a big corpus of HET articles.

The HET corpus here analysed represents the stream of contemporary HET literature produced by historians and published for readers of HET journals, i.e. mainly for an audience of HET scholars. As a consequence, the results for the HET corpus cannot be considered as representative also for the stream of HET literature directed to an audience that includes also or above all the economists, such as the articles covered by Duarte and Giraud (2016), or other non-professional readers. The comparisons of the two streams of HET literature would be not only possible but also of great interest for verifying if and how historians of economic thought adapt their work to different audiences, in terms, for example, of references to authors and journals. Another comparison of great interest would be with the general stream of HET literature, analysed by Zacchia and Marcuzzo (2016), that includes journal articles not indexed in bibliometric databases, books and books chapters. Unfortunately, this last comparison is yet impossible precisely because of the lack of coverage of books in the existing bibliometric databases.

Results presented in this paper are only a step towards a quantitative historiography of HET. Many other relevant questions remain unanswered and need further analysis. How back in time do HET scholars cite? Where do the HET knowledge flow? Does it remain confined within the borders of the field or does it flow to other economic disciplines? What is the degree of autonomy and self-referentiality of HET within the larger ecosystem of economic literature? Hopefully, results presented here may suggest that bibliometrics and scientometrics are useful instruments for addressing these questions.

Acknowledgement Eugenio Petrovich's research assistance is gratefully acknowledged.

Note

1. Data retrieved on 12.06.2019.

References

Ambrosino, A., Cedrini, M., Davis, J. B., Fiori, S., Guerzoni, M., & Nuccio, M. (2018). What Topic Modeling Could Reveal About the Evolution of Economics. *Journal of Economic Methodology, 25*(4), 329–348.

Baccini, A., De Nicolao, G., & Petrovich, E. (2019). Citation Gaming Induced by Bibliometric Evaluation: A Country-Level Comparative Analysis. *PLoS One, 14*(9), e0221212. Available at https://doi.org/10.1371/journal.pone.

Backhouse, R., Middleton, R., & Tribe, K. (1997). *'Economics Is What Economists Do', But What Do the Numbers Tell Us?* Paper for Annual History of Economic Thought Conference, University of Bristol, 3–5 September 1997. https://doi.org/10.2139/ssrn.2942733.

Catherine, H., & Doehne, M. (2018). Five Reasons for the Use of Network Analysis in the History of Economics. *Journal of Economic Methodology, 25*(4), 311–328.

Cherrier, B., & Svorenčík, A. (2018). The Quantitative Turn in the History of Economics: Promises, Perils and Challenges. *Journal of Economic Methodology, 25*(4), 367–377.

Claveau, F., & Gingras, Y. (2016). Macrodynamics of Economics: A Bibliometric History. *History of Political Economy, 48*(4), 551–592.

De Bellis, N. (2014). History and Evolution of (Biblio)Metrics. In B. Cronin & C. R. Sugimoto (Eds.), *Beyond Bibliometrics: Harnessing Multidimensional Indicators of Scholarly Impact* (pp. 23–44). Cambridge, MA: The MIT Press.

Duarte, P. G., & Giraud, Y. (2016). The Place of the History of Economic Thought in Mainstream Economics, 1991–2011, Viewed Through a Bibliographic Survey. *Journal of the History of Economic Thought, 38*(4), 431–462.

Edwards, J., Giraud, Y., & Schinckus, C. (2018). A Quantitative Turn in the Historiography of Economics? *Journal of Economic Methodology, 25*(4), 283–290.

Giraud, Y. (2019). Five Decades of HOPE. *History of Political Economy, 51*(4), 601–669.

Hansen, W. L., & Weisbrod, B. (1972). Toward a General Theory of Awards, or, Do Economists Need a Hall of Fame? *Journal of Political Economy, 80*, 422–431.

Heckman, J., & Moktan, S. (2018). *Publishing and Promotion in Economics: The Tyranny of the Top Five* (NBER Working Paper, no. 25093). Cambridge, MA: National Bureau of Economic Research.

Hellqvist, B. (2010). Referencing in the Humanities and Its Implications for Citation Analysis. *Journal of the American Society for Information Science and Technology, 61*(2), 310–318.

Jovanovic, F. (2018). A Comparison Between Qualitative and Quantitative Histories: The Example of the Efficient Market Hypothesis. *Journal of Economic Methodology, 25*(4), 291–310.

Larivière, V., Archambault, É., Gingras, Y., & Vignola-Gagné, É. (2006). The Place of Serials in Referencing Practices: Comparing Natural Sciences and Engineering with Social Sciences and Humanities. *Journal of the American Society for Information Science and Technology, 57*(8), 997–1004.

Lucio-Arias, D., & Leydesdorff, L. (2009). The Dynamics of Exchanges and References Among Scientific Texts, and the Autopoiesis of Discursive Knowledge. *Journal of Informetrics, 3*(3), 261–271.

McCain, K. W. (1991). Mapping Economics Through the Journal Literature: An Experiment in Journal Cocitation Analysis. *Journal of the American Society for Information Science, 42*(4), 290–296.

Mingers, J., & Leydesdorff, L. (2015). A Review of Theory and Practice in Scientometrics. *European Journal of Operational Research, 246*(1), 1–19.

Nederhof, A. J. (2006). Bibliometric Monitoring of Research Performance in the Social Sciences and the Humanities: A Review. *Scientometrics, 66*(1), 81–100.

Oliveira, T. D. (2018). *From Modelmania to Datanomics: The Top Journals and the Quest for Formalization* (STOREPapers, no. WP 2-2018). Italian Association for History of Political Economy.

Rosselli, A. (2013). Economic History and History of Economics: In Praise of an Old Relationship. *The European Journal of the History of Economic Thought, 20*(6), 865–881.

Small, H. (1973). Co-citation in the Scientific Literature: A New Measure of the Relationship Between Two Documents. *Journal of the American Society for Information Science, 24*(4), 265–269.

Todeschini, R., & Baccini, A. (2016). *Handbook of Bibliometric Indicators: Quantitative Tools for Studying and Evaluating Research.* Weinheim: Wiley-VCH Verlag.

van Eck, N. J., & Waltman, L. (2010). Software Survey: VOSviewer, a Computer Program for Bibliometric Mapping. *Scientometrics, 84*(2), 523–538.

Wais, K. (2016). Gender Prediction Methods Based on First Names with genderizeR. *The R Journal, 8*(1), 17–37.

White, H. D., & Griffith, B. C. (1981). Author Cocitation: A Literature Measure of Intellectual Structure. *Journal of the American Society for Information Science, 32*(3), 163–171.

Zacchia, G., & Marcuzzo, M. C. (2016). Is History of Economics What Historians of Economic Thought Do? A Quantitative Investigation. *History of Economic Ideas, 24*(3), 29–46.

CHAPTER 4

Moving Boundaries with Gender Budgeting: From the Margins to the Mainstream

Elisabeth Klatzer and Angela O'Hagan

4.1 Introduction

This chapter reflects on conceptual approaches to gender budgeting (GB), and especially gender analysis of public spending and its implications for practical implementation in public finance. Our reflections are based on our own work and our work with colleagues across Europe through the European Gender Budgeting Network (EGBN) which from its start in the early 2000s has been a network of feminist economists, practitioners and activists engaged with GB across Europe. In Italy, Annalisa Rosselli, together with Francesca Bettio, has been at the forefront of work on developing conceptual approaches and providing practical evidence, and as an active member of the EGBN.

E. Klatzer
Independent Researcher-Activist, Feminist Economics and Gender Budgeting, Vienna, Austria

A. O'Hagan (✉)
Glasgow Caledonian University, Glasgow, UK
e-mail: Angela.OHagan@gcu.ac.uk

M. C. Marcuzzo et al. (eds.), *New Perspectives on Political Economy and Its History*, Palgrave Studies in the History of Economic Thought,
https://doi.org/10.1007/978-3-030-42925-6_4

Gender budgeting, or gender budget analysis, is the examination, from a gender perspective, of the potential impacts of benefits of public spending and revenue decisions, including at the macroeconomic level. It incorporates a gender equality perspective in economic policies and budget processes and aims at restructuring these in order to promote gender equality. In theorizing economic policy and gender policy, Rosselli and other feminist economists, have demonstrated not only that gender is relevant to economic policy, but also that gender analysis is central to the formulation of economic policy and the implementation of gender equality outcomes as public policy objectives at programme and project level. In practice, this has meant deconstructing established economic theory and practice to reveal its inherent weaknesses when gender considerations are excluded. Demonstrating the deficiencies of 'gender-blind' economic policy has provided evidence and demand for improved gendered analysis in public policy and the need to integrate questions of resource allocation into policy rationale and objectives.

At its core, the concept of GB is a radical and transformative proposition from feminist economists such as Rosselli who has described it as 'a powerful instrument for feminist transformation'.[1] As GB has moved from the margins to the mainstream of public finance over more than 30 years, the understanding and situating of gender responsive budgeting (GRB) has changed considerably. This includes a gradual shift whereby the radical nature of GB is potentially being lost to increasingly bureaucratized processes of 'doing GRB' within institutionalized process which themselves do not change. The current challenge is around how to maintain its transformational character as GB gains increasing validation as a tool of modern Public Finance Management (PFM) and becomes more implemented widely.

This chapter expands on some of the specific activities and favourable conditions that are integral to creating, activating and sustaining the practice of gender budget analysis and implementation of gender budgeting. Following the discussion on learning from more recent experience and the wider literature on gender knowledge, feminist policy change and the exchange of knowledge and practice on gender budgeting in Europe (O'Hagan and Klatzer 2018), this chapter offers an updated version of the Framework of Favourable Conditions (O'Hagan 2015) for sustainable and transformative gender budgeting.

4.2 Developments of Gender Budgeting and Conceptual Debates

Feminist economics analysis has consistently critiqued and challenged established economic models for their failure to account for the unpaid contribution, mainly by women, to the productive economy. Unpaid care and work have been disregarded as productive activities in economics, even though they are essential for the functioning of market based activities. Over many years, feminist economics scholars have critiqued systems of national accounts (Waring 1989), male bias in economic policymaking bias and 'gender-blind' policy processes (Elson 1995, 1997; Elson and Cagatay 2000), and the failure to make visible the centrality of unpaid care work (Himmelweit 2002; Sharp 2003). Budget processes and public finance management have long been treated as somehow separate or at one remove from the process of formulating government policy. Taking a perspective that government budgets 'reflect societal, social, and economic priorities and power relations in society' (BEIGEWUM 2002, p. 12), gender budgeting challenges the established characterization of budgetary processes as being about managing abstract financial information that is not directly relevant to the everyday lives of women and men. More recently, feminist political science has increasingly reflected on and engaged in the political and institutional character of budgetary processes, with contributions characterizing GB as feminist policy change (O'Hagan 2015), and an increasing focus on understanding how gendered knowledge is developed—and resisted—in political institutions (Cavaghan 2017).

Gender budgeting emerged at the confluence of work by feminist economists to engender macroeconomic and budgetary theories and policies, and feminist movements challenging negative impacts of economic policies on social and gender relations. Based on these theoretical contributions and feminist advocacy, the Fourth World Women's Conference in Beijing in 1995 adopted GB as part of the Beijing Platform for Action. This international commitment created a broader momentum for engendering macroeconomic and budgetary policies across the globe (Budlender et al. 2002; Budlender and Hewitt 2002; Khan and Burn 2017). In Europe, a broad range of experimentation started with feminist economists taking a lead in building methodologies for GB, clarifying concepts, developing analytical tools and indicators for measuring progress and engaging with public institutions to promote its implementation (UNIFEM 2002; Klatzer and Neumayr 2006).

As Rosselli reminds us, 'Gender budgeting is a powerful instrument for feminist transformation of our societies because it addresses the crucial economic issue of how resources are allocated'.[2] Thus, engagement with the budget is a crucial entry point for change towards gender equality. By using gender analysis of budgets and policies as a key instrument, impacts of budgets and policies on women and gender relations, and in particular impacts on the care economy, are made visible. Results of gender analysis provide a basis for designing more effectively targeted policies and budget allocations to ensure better outcomes and greater accountability of governments. The objective of GB is to make the diverse lived realities of women's and men's lives visible in policy analysis that informs decisions on spending and revenue decisions. It follows then that at the core GB is the feminist economics focus on the centrality of care to the economy. Thus, it enlarges conventional analysis of budget proposals and economic policies by focussing attention on gendered roles in paid and unpaid work, especially the provision of care and the implications of gendered social roles for budget impacts.

Another founding proposition of gender budgeting is to change budget processes to make them more participatory and open. This is an integral part of GB as a transformational strategy; transforming institutions and decision-making processes to fully integrate gender equality perspectives and actors. It is also an aspect of GB practice that has remained the least developed and most resistant to change. The inspiring work of feminist economists, combined with continued advocacy of feminist actors inside and outside government, has achieved a gradual transfer of gender budgeting into government processes at different levels. However, the gradual adoption of GB by governments and international institutions often involves a narrowing of conceptual approaches. O'Hagan highlights the widely used definition of GB by the Council of Europe (2005) that defines gender budgeting as an application of gender mainstreaming in the budgetary process as resulting in 'a rather technocratic approach with a focus on institutional processes rather than a transformation in those processes of who participates in them, how those people and processes seek to transform gender relations by making alternative decisions about resources' (O'Hagan and Klatzer 2018, p. 29).

Over time, the understanding and situating of GB has gradually changed as the concept of GB has developed from a radical and transformative proposition from feminist economists into the increasingly bureaucratized process of 'doing GB' within institutionalized process which themselves do not change. In addition to the International Monetary Funds and the World Bank interest in gender budgeting in the context of public finance management reforms, the OECD is doing important work in facilitating exchange of experience and debates among public finance management and gender equality officials. However, as GB becomes 'part of the policy toolkit for modern governance and inclusive growth',[3] its ambitions and conceptual focus potentially become more narrow, and certainly gain some distance from the orignial feminist intent. This is evident, for example, in the OECD definition of gender budgeting, framed as 'integrating a clear gender perspective within the overall context of the budgetary process, through the use of special processes and analytical tools, with a view to promoting gender-responsive policies' (Downes et al. 2016, p. 7). This definition does not include gender equality as a central objective of gender equality and GB is limited to a technical tool of adding gender perspectives.

The adoption of the 2030 Agenda and the Sustainable Development Goals in 2015, with a clear goal on gender equality and a specific indicator on gender budgeting, has marked a new level of international commitment and provides a basis for more ambitious GB implementation. The gender budgeting indicator (SDG indicator 5.c.1.) defines an international standard for GB and a reference for measuring progress along three dimensions:

(i) intent of a government to address well-identified gender equality goals by identifying whether policies, programmes and adequate resources are in place and executed;
(ii) Public Financial Management systems promoting gender-related or gender-responsive goals and mechanisms to track resource allocations towards these policy goals; and
(iii) existence of mechanisms to make resource allocations for gender equality and women's empowerment publicly available.

While GB is being increasingly adopted internationally as an approach to public finance management, maintaining its broader feminist ambitions and conceptualizations in the process of implementation depends on continuous work and engagement of feminist scholars as much as it ever has. For example, in Italy feminist economists organized the first international workshop in 2000 (Rosselli 2006), effectively promoting interest in and dissemination of knowledge about GB in Italy.[4] Rosselli has contributed significantly to the conceptual development of the stages of how gender budgeting can become embedded in institutional practice, as policy change, as well as the wider conceptual debates around purpose and character of GB. Among these, Rosselli's configuration (with Francesca Bettio) of policy-based, women-centred, and holistic approaches[5] to the practical implementation of gender budgeting (Bettio and Rosselli 2018, p. 210) has had significant practical utility for policymakers. This formulation has been consistently revisited by members of the European Gender Budgeting Network in their work at country, regional and European level, as well as internationally (for an overview of GB approaches and methods see Klatzer et al. 2018).

Policy-based gender budgeting approach. In a policy approach, such as that attempted at municipal and regional level in Modena and Siena for example, there is an explicit *focus on policy objectives* agreed as priority actions from a gender perspective. These can include closing gaps in employment, wages or political representation, improving work-life balance, and reducing violence against women. Local-level indicators, developed from an analysis of the local context, assess actual conditions against ideal benchmarks and objectives set to achieve priority goals. Key policies are selected in priority policy areas in line with available resources and the final step is the auditing exercise. In Modena and Siena, expenditure items or programmes were selected for audit if they could be expected to further progress gender equality outcomes in the key policy areas, based on the available evidence.

Account-based gender budgeting approach. An account-based approach reclassifies *expenditure* with the ultimate aim of assessing the alignment between the gender-relevant objectives identified by government and the actual budget allocations. Bettio and Rosselli (2018) recall the important caveat originally raised by Sharp (2000) of maintaining a focus on the overall budget and government activity rather than considering GB as a focus on women-only or gender-specific spending.

The policy- or account-based approaches opened up a way of thinking not only about how public money is allocated within specific programmes or to support policy objectives, but how gender equality objectives are structured as central and core aims of policy, or as among a set of project outcomes. This analytical divide reveals the extent to which public policy interventions are clearly conceived as actions to advance gender equality or not.

4.3 Gender Budgeting at Crossroads: Overcoming Current Challenges

In 'moving from the margins to the mainstream', GB developments have arrived at an important conjuncture. Methodology and methods are available and well developed, commitments at national and international level are in place—to varying degrees—and there are numerous promising indications and examples of practice available. However, alongside these developments over the past two decades of significant progress, major challenges have emerged at different levels which can be grouped into seven themes:

1. Feminist policy change. As GB gains increasing validation as a tool of modern Public Finance Management (PFM) and has become implemented more widely, a key challenge is how to maintain its transformational character to achieve feminist policy changes, especially regarding the progressive realization of women's rights and human rights.
2. Micro: macro challenge. In spite of the continued engagement of feminist economists and policymakers and some progress at the level of specific budget items and policies, gender-blind macroeconomic and budget policies, with a focus on austerity and restrictive fiscal policy rules and reducing democratic spaces, are still limiting effective progress towards gender equality and social justice (O'Hagan and Klatzer 2018, p. 364). Thus, '[c]hallenging the idea that macroeconomic policy is a gender neutral, technical process; and challenging EU economic governance rules, as well as the policies of national governments' (Elson 2018, p. viii) is a key requirement for enlarging the potential effectiveness of GB implementation. Elson's proposition for the EU is largely relevant for other global institutions and regions as well. As Seguino (2017) argues, the development of new economic paradigms with 'the centrality of care, democratizing of economic policy institutions and rebuilding strong emancipatory public sectors and social security systems' as central tenets presents a way forward and an adequate frame for gender budgeting to be advanced as a key strategy for progress.
3. Tax injustice and tax policies that limit fiscal space on the revenue side. From a human rights perspective, maximizing available resources to enable progressive realization of human rights as

well as gender equality is a legal obligation. Long-standing trends of eroding public revenue due to fiscal systems of tax competition, international arrangements facilitating profit shifting and tax avoidance need to be challenged. Similarly, the trends towards undermining progressive taxation of capital, income and wealth, and increasing reliance on consumption taxes which are regressive in their effect, need to be revisited for their impacts on increasing inequalities. Gender budgeting as a concept equally addresses the revenue and expenditure side of budgets. An invigorated focus is needed on gender budget analysis of tax systems and individual tax schemes to reverse negative impacts in practice and the challenges to gender equality they represent.

4. Limited implementation of gender budgeting. Rosselli, together with Bettio, argues that in implementing GB, gender budgeting needs to follow a common protocol, enhancing its effectiveness through coordination across different policy and programme initiatives, moving towards full implementation. Gender budgeting applied as monitoring of policy proposals and ex-post monitoring is a 'must-do' (Bettio and Rosselli 2018, p. 218). However, even in public finance systems where gender budgeting is implemented, the actual change in gender equality outcomes may remain limited. This is due, in part, to several shortcomings in implementing gender budgeting. These can include, claiming full implementation while in practice there is a partial focus on selected aspects of programmes or services with limited transformative potential; a lack of translation of findings from gender budget analysis into policy and budget changes; a lack of effective monitoring for results; or a failure to follow an integrated approach between different departments and levels of government limits its effectiveness.
5. Divergence between political commitments and actual investments in gender equality and women's rights. Interestingly, while the key motivation for gender budgeting from the beginning was to change public resource allocations—and public revenue raising—the implications of gender budgeting practice in relation to major shifts in reallocating public expenditures towards more gender responsive public services and investments are limited: especially investments in care infrastructure. The gap in financing for gender equality and women's rights is still significant across the globe. The challenge for gender budgeting implementation still remains: How to move

beyond incremental changes and use the approach to effectively increase public resource allocation to advance gender equality and women's rights.

6. Enabling civil society and researcher involvement in gender budgeting. A central aim of gender budgeting was the intention to change budget processes by taking macro-fiscal priorities and decisions about budget allocations into more open and democratic decision-making spaces. The demand for greater access and more gender equal participation in decision-making has been a core concept in gender budgeting. However, practice again reveals weaknesses in implementation. Opportunities and access to spaces for feminist voices to be heard in gender budgeting practice—especially from independent feminist economists and feminist advocacy groups—are limited, with some notable exceptions. Challenges remain to enable equal participation, democracy and transparency as a central element of any gender budgeting work.
7. Institutional transformations and institutional practices. Gender budgeting practice shows that in spite of well-established methods of GB analysis and processes of implementation, overcoming male-dominated and gendered power structures in public institutions, especially in public finance is an ongoing challenge. A wide range of institutional practices exists. However, transforming budget systems and decision-making processes towards gender budgeting, not as a more or less marginal add-on, but as an integral part of public finance management systems and practice is key to reaping the full benefits of gender budgeting. Enabling institutional and personal learning towards gender equality as an integral part of institutional culture and practice is an ongoing process which needs further innovation and systemic transformation (Cavaghan 2017).

Thus, in order to realize the potential of gender budgeting as a transformative approach towards effective public policies and finance to achieve gender equality and women's rights, continued work by researchers and feminist advocacy is needed. In this context, the exploration of favourable conditions and methodological refinements to achieve feminist policy change and transform public policy institutions is a collaborative learning process between academic researchers and activists, civil society activists and policymakers.

4.4 Favourable Conditions for Sustainable and Transformative Gender Budgeting

In her work on gender budgeting, Rosselli has been clear on the need for well-defined operational objectives and conceptual approaches to gender analysis in policy and spending commitments, and the need for gender aware and informed officials and practitioners, and institutional arrangements that will sustain gender budget analysis beyond the life of specific projects or programmes.

In a similar vein, O'Hagan (2015) proposed a range of conditions—contextual, political and institutional—that require to exist and to some degree co-exist in order for a policy innovation like gender budgeting to be considered for formal adoption and implementation as an approach to policymaking and particularly as an approach to public finance decision-making. These conditions, presented as a Framework of Favourable Conditions (FFC), have been applied at national and sub-national government level, for example, in Scotland, in a proposed approach for Wales, and used as a reference point in gender budgeting advocacy and agenda-setting by, for example, the European Women's Lobby Group on gender budgeting.

The FFC initially aimed to capture the dynamic nature of the phases of agenda-setting, adoption and implementation, as well as of the relationships of critical actors within government institutions and between government and non-governmental organizations and potentially academics or other 'external' stakeholders. The framework can also be used as a diagnostic of actions taken to advance gender budgeting and to identify a plan of action to create receptive conditions and appropriate institutional practice. The FFC has usually appeared in summarized, diagrammatic form (O'Hagan 2015, 2017; O'Hagan and Klatzer 2018) as represented here (Fig. 4.1).

In the updating and expanding of the FFC that follows here, we draw on the learnings and reflections offered by Bettio and Rosselli's chapter in O'Hagan and Klatzer (2018) on approaches to gender budgeting in Italy and other contributions to that volume. In the revised version of the FFC, we focus on some of the specific activities that are integral to creating, activating and sustaining practice of gender budget analysis and implementation of gender budgeting. From the analysis of efforts to

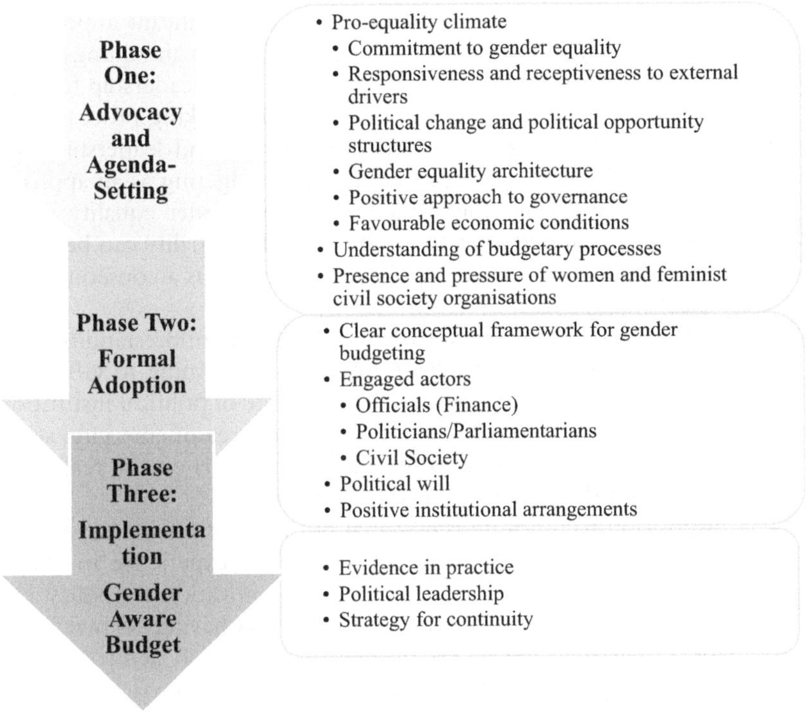

Fig. 4.1 Framework of favourable conditions (*Source* O'Hagan [2015])

implement gender budgeting over different levels of government and different time frames, a series of generalizable factors emerge, relevant to effective implementation of gender budgeting in different contexts.

- Reliance on individuals reinforces the need for political will and leadership, and the need for building confidence and competence in gender analysis among policy officials and analysts. The historic Italian experience demonstrates that advancing gender budgeting requires a concerted and sustained investment in political interest and in building the knowledge of officials. Bettio and Rosselli (2018) clearly highlight that the stop-start approach to gender budgeting due to the short-term funding of ESF projects, and the instability and lack of durability both of national governments and the commitments to gender equality of those governments, was a significant impediment to sustainability. This underpins the centrality of maintaining a political commitment to gender equality and political leadership to direct and resource gender competence in the policymaking process.

- Clearly articulated and sustained political will and leadership from elected politicians need to protect gender budgeting as an approach to policymaking from the vulnerabilities of gender equality policy. Commitments and actions to advance gender equality can be lost in changes of administration or political leadership as a consequence of the electoral cycle.
- Thinking about gendered knowledge as a way of understanding institutional resistances and applying institutional learning to GB implementation. Building the gendered knowledge of political institutions (Cavaghan 2017; Elomäki et al. 2019) is an area of emerging scholarship that speaks directly to the FFC in its focus on the realities of actors within the policy process in institutions.
- A disposition to innovate is essential but innovation and experiment should not become a permanent state. The experience in Italy—and elsewhere—usefully describes policy innovation by policy officials and project leads in short-term projects having to invent and adapt, rather than follow established procedure on gender budgeting because up to that point there had been no approach to gender analysis in the allocation of funds. These reflections offer useful caution about balancing the necessity to innovate and learn from experimentation in policymaking, and the need to maintain innovation in process and practice as the flip-side to institutionalizing practice in a way that intentionally limits practice, thereby producing stasis rather than transformation.
- Learning and knowledge transfer between levels of government and across institutions, as well as learning from other countries. Comparative policy learning and transfer has been a characteristic of how gender budgeting has travelled the globe. 'Pioneer' governments have sought to showcase their efforts, serving to demonstrate their innovation but also to nurture conceptual and practical developments elsewhere. Epistemic and activist communities such as the EGBN have consistently sought means to bring together interested scholars, and community and academic activists.[6] Governments and international organizations, such as the IMF, World Bank and OECD, have increasingly engaged with GB, including through a

number of high level international meetings and conferences promoting GB and contributing to moving GB from the margin to the mainstream of public finance. Has this led to an advance in transformative gender budgeting or merely a longer list of governments publicly expressing their commitments to progress while achieving little? While these supra-national bodies have augmented their spend on gender budgeting, civil society organizations have struggled to keep up and to maintain and critical analysis of the development of gender budgeting given the inequalities and imbalances in resources between the different organizations.

- Part of the dissemination of gender budgeting has included the development of practical tools and transferrable methodologies. Bettio and Rosselli in 2018 usefully highlighted three elements of practice that are replicable in different political and geographic contexts and which could, or should, reasonably be part of the early evidence gathering and populating the conceptual understanding/approach of GB in a particular area.
- A principle of ensuring context-specific analysis was established as essential by McKay et al. (2002) and is reaffirmed in Bettio and Rosselli's (2018) analysis of experience in Italy as they argue for
  - context analysis—identification and calculation of a set of demographic, social and economic indicators of gender equality and women's well-being in the reference area;
  - analysis of local gender equality practices within and for the administration being audited; and
  - gender impact analysis of the administration's expenditure and taxation (Bettio and Rosselli 2018).

Governments at different levels and in different geographic contexts have their own structures and characteristics; this in turn requires appropriate institutional and context-specific adaption of GB approaches.

More recent reviews of international practice (O'Hagan et al. 2019; Kolovich 2018; O'Hagan and Klatzer 2018) have re-confirmed some key elements that are essential components of the favourable conditions for adoption and implementation. These include

- Leadership by the Ministry of Finance is consistently demonstrated internationally to be an essential element of successful adoption of gender budgeting. The engagement of officials and Ministers from the Ministry of Finance with delivery and spending departments, as well as aligning institutional commitment to gender equality and spending commitments across government departments, is essential for GB implementation.
- Legal requirements for gender budgeting are important as they provide guidance for compliance as well as protection from dismantling of policy or institutional structures as a consequence of electoral change.
- Gender budgeting goals should be aligned with national gender equality plans and international gender equality commitments such as the SDGs.
- Gender budgeting can be implemented successfully at the national, state, and/or local levels, as well as within individual institutions such as universities, health boards, and other public bodies.
- The need to build the knowledge and capacity of policymakers—at all levels—is consistently reiterated across international experience, as identified so clearly by Bettio and Rosselli in the Italian experience.

4.5 Revised Framework of Favourable Conditions

The revised version of the FFC, proposed in this chapter, seeks to emphasize the importance of the range and engagement of actors inside and from outside government at the different phases of adoption and implementation. The dynamic nature of policy learning inside government and from the relations with external stakeholders have been important dimensions of advancing gender equality at different levels of government. Engaged officials, who bring their knowledge and experience about gendered dimensions of policymaking to the process and are disposed to alter established practices and respond to the tenacity and learning from epistemic communities, academics, activists and practitioners external to government, are essential dynamics for advancing gender budgeting.

The range of voices and actors around gender budgeting has grown, with the IMF, OECD and World Bank also advocating for gender budget analysis as well as NGOs, activists and academic researchers. The political and conceptual starting point of these different actors is not likely to be the same. For the international institutions, women's economic participation and public finance to support economic growth programmes are of greater concern than women's emancipation and economic independence. These tensions and differences require to be understood and adapted by governments and public institutions, framing gender equality as a legitimate and integral political goal, rather than as an element of economic development, dislocated from the social, economic and structural change necessary to empower women and dismantle the constraints of gendered relations. These dynamic tensions can also vary at different stages of policy learning and transfer whether the idea of gender budgeting is still being pushed on to political or institutional agendas or whether it has been adopted. The concept of gender budgeting has been in play for over 30 years and has become increasingly adopted conceptually, but has not yet been universally adopted operationally. That is why we have retained phase one around advocacy and agenda-setting while recognizing that it is perhaps a less prominent stage of the process than in earlier iterations of the framework.

Originally, the FFC highlighted a commitment to gender mainstreaming as a condition. It is clear from practice over many years that an institutional commitment to gender mainstreaming is not a guarantee of transformation or transformational practice. Too often, gender mainstreaming has been used as a tactic for inaction or limited change. We continue to argue that gender budgeting *activates* gender mainstreaming as it is a whole systems approach to policymaking and related decisions on resource allocation and revenue raising.

Finally, we are proposing a fourth phase of gender budgeting in this revised framework (see Fig. 4.2). The intention is to reflect the need not only for gender *aware* budget documentation as originally proposed, but rather that the decision-making process and policy and budgetary cycle require to be sighted on

- how gender equality is being advanced,
- how gender budgeting is being resourced as a practice of government, and
- what arrangements are in place to ensure robust monitoring and evaluation of outcomes in relation to gender equality and women's economic status.

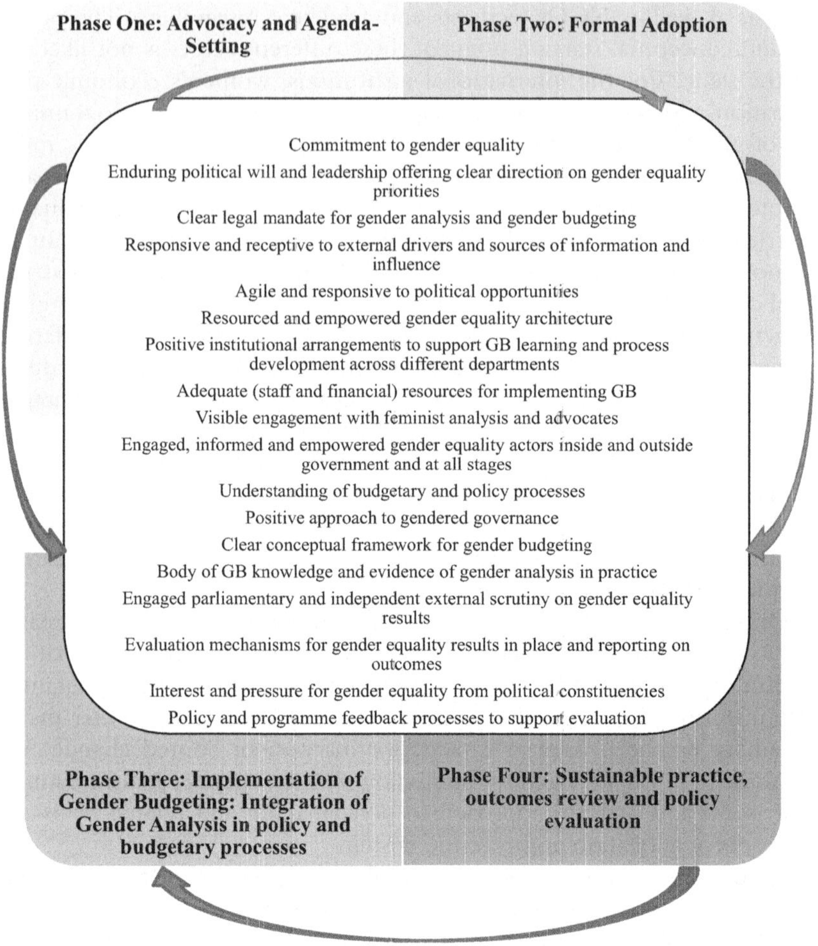

Fig. 4.2 Revised framework of favourable conditions for sustainable and transformative gender budgeting (*Source* O'Hagan [2015]. Authors' elaboration [2019])

The revised Framework of Favourable Conditions for sustainable and transformative gender budgeting presented in Fig. 4.2 clearly highlights the range of conditions and arrangements to be promoted in order to provide for sustainable practice with tangible results and progress on gender equality. Only when these are in place, can GB fully develop its potential within mainstream public finance.

4.6 Conclusion

In our revision of the Framework of Favourable Conditions, we have sought to integrate the lessons and critiques from Rosselli's work on gender budgeting. Her insights have consistently highlighted the need for engagement across government departments and with external stakeholders, sustained political commitment and operational implementation, informed by robust gender data and analysis and an understanding of the gendered dimensions of policy impacts. The goal of gender budgeting is transformative, producing systemic change in how policy is formulated and programmes designed and delivered, moving beyond beneficiary analysis to delivering improved economic analysis and above all improved, more equal outcomes for women and men.

In the policy and accounts model, Rosselli has offered a useful diagnostic for approaches to gender budget analysis that consider the political and institutional environments in which policy and resource decisions are made, and highlights the pitfalls and lessons for ensuring sustainability and enduring commitments to advance gender equality. Rosselli's contribution includes signposting the directions for future research, advocacy and policy development.

Analysis of and commitment to gender equality in economic policymaking and institutional practice have consistently sought to challenge established approaches to economic analysis and policymaking. In this constant process of seeking to move gender equality from the margins of economic policymaking and economic theory to the mainstream of policy processes, Rosselli has sought and encouraged others to push the boundaries of the discipline of economics to which she has been so committed. The revised framework presented here and the wealth of experience and comparative analysis of developments in Europe that underpin it support and aim to drive forward the intention to move consideration of gender equality from the margins of policymaking to the mainstream.

Notes

1. Email exchange (2017) in preparation of the chapter 'Gender Budgeting as Feminist Policy Change: Feminist Advocacy and Alliances' (in O'Hagan and Klatzer 2018).
2. Email exchange previously cited.
3. Ronnie Downes, endorsement of the book by O'Hagan and Klatzer (2018).
4. Thereafter, political conditions at the local and national levels meant that it was not until 2016 that practical GB implementation began at the central government level. In the intervening years, as Bettio and Rosselli (2018) describe extensive work on developing and implementing different approaches and pilot projects had been taking place at regional and local level.
5. Among Rosselli's contributions to knowledge, is the approach developed with Francesca Bettio of distinguishing policy based or accounts-based gender budgeting.
6. In many countries, conferences, workshops and practice exchanges at national and sub-national level have given important impetus for GB implementation, e.g. Junta de Andalucía, Spain, UK 'Pan Islands', and EGBN meetings in Vienna, Austria and OECD Expert meetings, including in Iceland.

References

BEIGEWUM. (2002). *Frauen macht Budgets. Staatsfinanzen aus Geschlechterperspektive*. Vienna: Mandelbaum Verlag.

Bettio, F., & Rosselli, A. (2018). Gender Budgeting in Italy: A Laboratory for Alternative Methodologies? In A. O'Hagan & E. Klatzer (Eds.), *Gender Budgeting in Europe* (pp. 199–220). Cham: Palgrave Macmillan.

Budlender, D., Elson, D., Hewitt, G., & Mukhopadhyay, T. (2002). *Gender Budgets Make Cents*. London: Commonwealth Secretariat.

Budlender, D., & Hewitt, G. (Eds.). (2002). *Gender Budgets Make More Cents: Country Studies and Good Practice*. London: Commonwealth Secretariat.

Cavaghan, R. (2017). *Making Gender Equality Happen: Knowledge, Change and Resistance in EU Gender Mainstreaming*. Abingdon: Routledge.

Council of Europe. (2005). *Gender Budgeting: Final Report of Group of Specialists on Gender Budgeting (EG-S-GB)*. Strasbourg: Equality Division, Directorate General of Human Rights, Council of Europe.

Downes, R., von Trapp, L., & Nicol, S. (2016). Gender Budgeting in OECD Countries. *OECD Journal on Budgeting, 16*(3), 71–107.

Elomäki, A., Kantola, J., Koivunen, A., & Ylöstalo, H. (2019). Affective Virtuosity: Challenges for Governance Feminism in the Context of the Economic Crisis. *Gender, Work & Organization, 26*(6), 822–839.

Elson, D. (1995). *Male Bias in the Development Process*. Manchester: Manchester University Press.

Elson, D. (1997). *Gender-Neutral, Gender-Blind, or Gender-Sensitive Budgets? Changing the Conceptual Framework to Include Women's Empowerment and the Economy of Care*. Preparatory Country Mission to Integrate Gender into National Budgetary Policies and Procedures in the Context of Economic Reform. Background Paper. London: Commonwealth Secretariat.

Elson, D. (2018). Preface. In A. O'Hagan & E. Klatzer (Eds.), *Gender Budgeting in Europe: Developments and Challenges* (pp. vii–viii). Cham: Palgrave Macmillan.

Elson, D., & Cagatay, N. (2000). The Social Content of Macroeconomic Policies. *World Development, 28*(7), 1347–1364.

Himmelweit, S. (2002). Making Visible the Hidden Economy: The Case for Gender-Impact Analysis of Economic Policy. *Feminist Economics, 8*(1), 49–70.

Khan, A., & Burn, N. (Eds.). (2017). *Financing for Gender Equality: Realising Women's Rights Through Gender Responsive Budgeting*. London: Palgrave Macmillan.

Klatzer, E., Addabbo, T., Alarcon-García, G., & O'Hagan, A. (2018). Developments in Practice: Methodologies and Approaches to Gender Budgeting. In A. O'Hagan & E. Klatzer (Eds.), *Gender Budgeting in Europe: Developments and Challenges* (pp. 109–133). Cham: Palgrave Macmillan.

Klatzer, E., & Neumayr, M. (2006). *Gender Budgeting in Europa*, Conference Documentation. Vienna: Arbeiterkammer.

Kolovich, M. L. L. (Ed.). (2018). *Fiscal Policies and Gender Equality*. Washington, DC: International Monetary Fund.

McKay, A., Fitzgerald, R., & O'Hagan, A. (2002). Scotland: Using Political Change to Advance Gender Concerns. In D. Budlender & G. Hewitt (Eds.), *Gender Budgets Make More Cents: Country Studies and Good Practice* (pp. 134–151). London: Commonwealth Secretariat.

O'Hagan, A. (2015). Favourable Conditions for the Adoption and Implementation of Gender Budgeting: Insights from Comparative Analysis. *Politica economica/Journal of Economic Policy, 31*(2), 233–252.

O'Hagan, A. (2017). Gender Budgeting in Scotland: A Work in Progress. *Administration, 65*(3), 17–39.

O'Hagan, A., Christensen, E., Tilley, H., & Newsom, S. (2019). *Tackling Inequality Through Gender Budgeting*. Wales Centre for Public Policy. Available at https://www.wcpp.org.uk/wp-content/uploads/2019/09/Tackling-Inequality-Through-Gender-Budgeting.pdf. Accessed 21 Jan 2019.

O'Hagan, A., & Klatzer, E. (Eds.). (2018). *Gender Budgeting in Europe: Developments and Challenges*. Cham: Palgrave Macmillan.

Rosselli, A. (2006). Gender Budgeting—European Models and Initiatives: Local Gender Budgeting Projects in the Tuscany, Italy. In E. Klatzer & M. Neumayr (Eds.), *Gender Budgeting in Europa, Conference Documentation* (pp. 17–22). Vienna: Arbeiterkammer.

Seguino, S. (2017). Financing for Gender Equality: Reframing and Prioritizing Public Expenditures to Promote Gender Equality. In Z. Khan & N. Burn (Eds.), *Financing for Gender Equality: Realising Women's Rights Through Gender Responsive Budgeting* (pp. 5–21). London: Palgrave Macmillan.

Sharp, R. (2000, September 15–16). *Gender Responsive Budget: The Australian Experience*. Paper prepared for the International Workshop on Gender Auditing of Government Budget, Rome.

Sharp, R. (2003). *Budgeting for Equity: Gender Budget Initiatives Within a Framework of Performance Oriented Budgeting*. New York: UNIFEM.

UNIFEM. (2002). *Gender Budget Initiatives: Strategies, Concepts and Experiences*. Papers from a High Level International Conference Strengthening Economic and Financial Governance Through Gender Responsive Budgeting, Brussels, 16–18 October 2001. New York: UNIFEM.

Waring, M. (1989). *If Women Counted: A New Feminist Economics*. London: Macmillan.

CHAPTER 5

Family, Gender Inequality and Growth: History Matters

Paola Villa

The family is a key socio-economic unit in society.[1] The nature of its organization is shaped by cultural values and gender norms that change slowly over time. Cultural traits are transmitted across generations via the family and they interact with other institutions, reinforcing prevailing cultural norms (Giuliano 2010; Farré and Vella 2013; Alesina and Giuliano 2014). This implies that history matters in the sense that social institutions (e.g. the family, values, norms) tend to reproduce themselves over time, revealing a certain inability to make the necessary adjustments to new challenges. The expression 'too much family' is used here to identify those societies in the industrialized world where family ties are strong, playing a predominant role in the organization of the social and economic life of all its members. This implies, first of all, that nowadays many activities are still being performed directly (and to a large extent) by family members as unpaid work, limiting the scope of the market. Secondly, it means that a disproportionally large share of economic production—in

P. Villa (✉)
University of Trento, Trento, Italy
e-mail: paola.villa@unitn.it

M. C. Marcuzzo et al. (eds.), *New Perspectives on Political Economy and Its History*, Palgrave Studies in the History of Economic Thought,
https://doi.org/10.1007/978-3-030-42925-6_5

services and manufacturing—is still being organized by small family firms, unfit to compete through technological innovation (e.g. digitalization) in a globalized world. With regard to the first point, in familistic societies family ties are strongly rooted in traditional values and gender norms; women bear the burden of unpaid work, with negative effects in terms of both gender equity and fertility decisions. As for the second point, economic growth—hence more job opportunities for women—tends to be constrained in societies where the family still plays a strong economic role—e.g. where there is a disproportionally large share of small family firms.

The aim of this paper is to elaborate on the two points made above in order to offer policymakers some guidelines on the direction and design of the policies to be implemented. The goals of policy intervention should be to reduce the material burden falling on families in terms of home production, as well as care services supplied by women (e.g. mothers, wives and daughters) and grandparents, but also to support young people entering working life and to promote gender equity. The final goals to be pursued by policies should be to allow families, and women in particular, to have the desired number of children and to promote women-friendly economic growth, with high numbers of mothers happily engaged in paid work. Some empirical evidence on European countries is provided to support the hypothesis advanced here, though more detailed information focuses on Italy, a country characterized by strong family ties and long-term economic decline.[2]

The chapter is organized in three sections. Section 5.1 presents some background evidence on female employment, gender gaps in unpaid and paid work, and fertility in European countries. Section 5.2 discusses the hypothesis that fertility decisions tend to be constrained in societies where the family plays a strong central role in the organization of all its members' daily life. Section 5.3 focuses on the hypothesis that economic growth tends to be constrained in societies where the family still plays a strong economic role in the functioning of the economy.

5.1 Gender Inequalities, Gender Norms and the Role of the State

Equality between women and men is a fundamental right and a common principle of the European Union (EU).[3] The EU can be seen as one of the main actors in this field. Since the 1970s, an extensive body of equal treatment legislation has been adopted. Thirteen directives have been introduced in areas including equal pay, equal treatment in employment and occupation, social security and parental leave.[4] This body of law is among the world's most extensive legislation promoting gender equality. Along with this legislation, the EU has developed other instruments to fight gender inequality more generally: gender mainstreaming, gender budgeting (Klatzer and O'Hagan, Chapter 4 in this volume; Bettio and Rosselli 2018) and specific measures for the advancement of women.

Throughout the past decades, significant progress has been made regarding gender equality in the EU; however, gender inequalities persist, predominantly to the disadvantage of women, with significant differences across countries. If gender equality is to be fully realized, and all Europeans are to enjoy equal opportunities, further action is required. And countries characterized by poor long-run performance in terms of female employment and fertility should learn from the experience of the best performing countries.

5.1.1 Paid and Unpaid Work: Differences Between Men and Women

Gender inequalities persist in all areas of social and economic life and across countries. Young women generally enjoy more years of schooling than young men, but women are less likely than men to engage in paid work. The gaps widen with age, as motherhood typically has marked negative effects on gender pay gaps and career advancement. Women are also less likely to be entrepreneurs and are underrepresented in private and public leadership positions (OECD 2017).

Gender inequality in the labour market is closely linked to gender inequality in the work-family balance, especially in the division of paid and unpaid work. Women continue to spend far more hours than men on unpaid childcare and housework, and in most countries women spend more total time on paid and unpaid work than men do. In a recent publication on the pursuit of gender equality in OECD countries, it is highlighted that across countries, at the aggregate level, women show fuller participation in the labour market when their male partners take on more unpaid work (ibid.). For the working-age population (15–64 years), women in countries with high employment rates also spend fewer minutes (on average, per day) on unpaid work than women in countries with lower employment rates (see Fig. 5.1). Of the OECD countries (with data

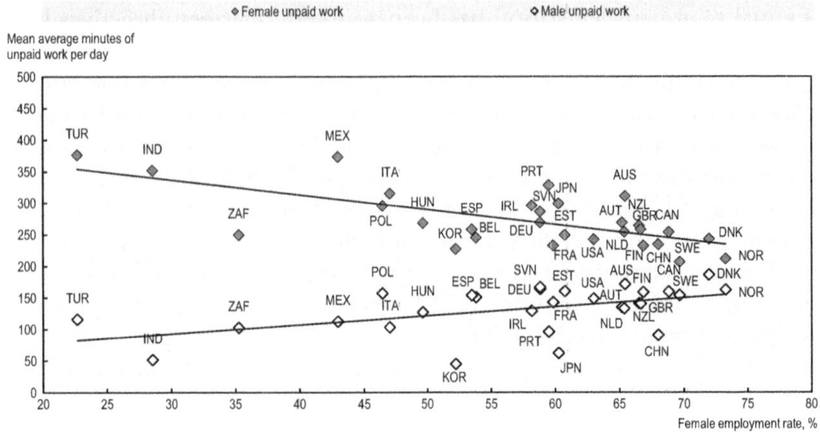

Fig. 5.1 Gender balance in unpaid work correlates with greater female employment rate in OECD countries (Reference year varies across countries). Mean average minutes per day in unpaid work, by gender and female employment rates (15–64-year-olds) (*Source* OECD Gender Data Portal, http://www.oecd.org/gender/data/, and OECD Employment Database, http://www.oecd.org/employment/emp/onlineoecdemploymentdatabase.htm)

available on time-use survey around 2010), Norway, Denmark and Sweden are the best performers, registering both the highest female employment rates and the smallest gender gaps in unpaid work (on average, less than one hour per day).

Time-use surveys for OECD countries present some shortcomings (i.e. heterogeneity in methodology, definitions adopted, year of survey). Moreover, time-use patterns across countries differ as a result of differences in the use of part-time work, their prevailing gender norms and gender stereotypes. The Eurostat harmonized time-use survey (EHTUS) allows for cross-country comparison for men and women employed full time, a more homogeneous group. Paid and unpaid work is measured in average hours per day (based on the EHTUS daily diary).

Table 5.1 shows that in 2010 the paid work patterns between men and women employed full time are fairly similar (6.4 and 5.6, respectively) for the average of the 16 countries considered, with a gender gap of less than one hour per day. Italy is one of the countries registering high numbers of paid working hours for both men and women (7.4 and 6.3,

Table 5.1 Average daily paid and unpaid-work hours among women and men employed full time (2010 wave)

	16 European countries			*Italy*			*Norway*		
	Men	*Women*	*Gender gap*	*Men*	*Women*	*Gender gap*	*Men*	*Women*	*Gender gap*
Paid	6.4	5.6	−0.8	7.4	6.3	−1.1	5.5	4.9	−0.6
Unpaid	1.9	3.2	+1.3	1.3	3.3	+2.0	2.6	3.2	+0.6
Total work	8.3	8.8	+0.5	8.7	9.6	+0.9	8.1	8.1	No gap

Source Eurostat EHTUS
Note The sample is restricted to countries with data available for the year 2010 and includes men and women employed full time. Work (paid work and unpaid work) is measured in hours per day (based on the EHTUS daily diary). The 16 countries considered are: Belgium, Germany, Estonia, Greece, Spain, France, Italy, Hungary, the Netherlands, Austria, Poland, Romania, Finland, UK, Norway and Serbia

respectively), while Norway is characterized by lower figures (5.5 and 4.9, respectively). In short, in all countries men work longer hours on paid work than women, but the gender gap is relatively small. The picture changes for unpaid work patterns: as expected, of the full-time employed individuals, men spend less time on unpaid work than women. For the 16 countries as a whole, of the full-timers the men spend a little less than two hours per day, against over three hours for women. Thus, the gender gap in unpaid work is well over one hour per day, almost twice as large as that in paid work. Across countries, there are notable differences in the size of the gender gap in unpaid working hours per day. Italy registers a two hour-gap in unpaid work between men and women employed full time (given 1.3 and 3.3, respectively), while Norway registers a mere half-hour gender gap (given 2.6 and 3.2, respectively).

This is a notable result, casting doubt on the claim that men specialize in the market and women in the household: when they work full time, both provide similar amounts of paid work, but unequal amounts of unpaid work. The asymmetry in unpaid work cannot be accounted for with the hypothesis that men specialize in market work, women in household work. On the contrary, the fact that, on average, the extra hours of unpaid work done by women exceed the extra hours of paid work performed by men is reflected in the finding that men spend, on average, more time on leisure activities than do women (with the one exception of Norway).

It follows that, in most countries (for which data are available) women's 'total work', defined as the sum of paid and unpaid work, exceeds men's total work (by about half an hour per day, for the 16 countries considered), with the one exception of Norway, where the amount of total work is identical by gender. Thus, of the Europeans with a full-time working week, men work, on average, 4 more paid hours per week than women, but they also enjoy about 3.5 extra hours of leisure activities, as they perform much less unpaid work than women employed full time. As for cross-country differences, Italy stands out among the countries with the largest gender gaps in total work among full-time workers, with 6.3 hours difference per week. This is in sharp contrast with Norway where men and women spend exactly the same total amount of time in paid and unpaid work: the little extra time spent by men on paid work is offset by the little extra time spent by women in unpaid work. Moreover, both men and women enjoy some additional time for leisure activities, unlike the other countries.

5.1.2 *Gender Norms Are Sticky, but They Can Change*

Women's hours in unpaid work restrict the time they can spend in the labour market, a pattern observed both within households and at the cross-national level in European countries. Norms, attitudes and behaviour concerning care and housework are sticky, as they are slow to change over time. Adult offspring, both daughters and sons, tend to replicate the behaviour of their parents (observed during adolescence), perpetuating an unequal distribution of unpaid and paid work behaviour.

Gender norms play an important role in women's decisions to participate in the labour market. Traditional social norms may restrain participation for women. But the contrary effect—that female labour participation can affect social norms—is also possible. This raises the question of whether the participation of women in the labour market is capable of changing cultural norms. Stephanie Seguino (2007) argues that cultural norms and stereotypes that perpetuate inequality are deeply embedded in social and individual consciousness and, as a result, are resistant to change. But women's control over material resources can enhance their bargaining power to leverage change in key institutions, prompting a shift to more equitable norms. By extension, policies that promote women's paid employment should serve as a fulcrum for gender-equitable change. Using some key questions of the *World Values Survey* (for over 70 countries) to capture gender norms and stereotypes at the societal level that span a twenty-year period, Seguino finds evidence that increases in women's paid employment promote gender-equitable norms and stereotypes (with a time lag).

The policy implication is that policymakers have an important role to play in favouring the diffusion of gender-equal norms. This implies, on the one hand, favouring the expansion of female employment both directly (through the strengthening of those sectors able to create good employment opportunities for young women) and indirectly (through policies supporting working parents). On the other hand, they have a role to play in favouring the diffusion of norms supporting gender equality in society at large, from education to family life.

5.1.3 *Gender Inequalities, Maternal Employment and Fertility Decisions*

In familistic countries, the family-employment system is based on rather traditional gender roles, with adult men employed full time throughout their working life, mainly responsible for earning enough for the economic well-being of the whole family, while women have the responsibility for family care and domestic work. Of course, the realities are more diversified than this stylised model, but this is the model around which labour market policies and personnel management practices are constructed and implemented. In short, the male breadwinner model of the family remains dominant. On the one hand, there is pervasive discrimination against maternity, reflected gender inequalities in the labour market: access to secure jobs is more difficult for young women than for young men, and the unemployment rates for young women are consequently higher. On the other hand, support for combining motherhood and paid work remains weak: services for the family are insufficiently developed, family-friendly organizations are few, and gender roles in the family lead to a decidedly asymmetric distribution of unpaid work. This accounts for the large share of inactive mothers and, on the other hand, the pervasive discrimination against maternity reflected in gender inequality: young women are caught in the intergenerational solidarity trap: because of the lack of adequate family policies and the unfavourable context for working mothers (and in general, for women with family responsibilities) they have to choose between the family (taking care of children, elderly and/or frail family members) and employment. In some countries, the choice is less clear-cut, and high numbers of women are employed in part-time jobs. And the price women pay for entering the labour market is being employed in part-time dead-end jobs, poorly paid with low pension rights in old age.

As already argued, women are still the main providers of domestic services and care work; therefore, childbearing is seen to exacerbate an already heavy and unbalanced division of household labour. And this not only makes difficult for working mothers to remain active, but it also tends to limit their fertility intentions.

It has been suggested in the literature that gender inequality is a key factor behind the phenomenon of the lowest-low fertility typical of familistic countries (McDonald 2000, 2013; Mills et al. 2008). The paradox of the Mediterranean model, with low female employment rates associated with low fertility rates, already pointed out in the late 1990s (Bettio and Villa 1998), proves to be persistent. And the explanation for this persistent paradox is the lack of progress towards equal treatment in society, in the labour market and in the family.

5.2 'Too Much Family' Hurts Fertility Decisions

In the post-war decades, in almost all the developed countries fertility measured by the total fertility rate (TFR, the average number of children per woman) fell below the replacement rate (TFR = 2.1), i.e. the rate necessary to ensure generational replacement. But the fall in fertility became an increasing concern in those countries (e.g. the Mediterranean countries) where it dropped well below the replacement level for a longer period, with serious long-term consequences, including more rapid population ageing and contraction in the working-age population. In particular, 'lowest-low fertility' (i.e. TFR < 1.5) has been experienced by Italy, Spain and Greece since the 1990s and by Portugal in more recent years. Conversely, other European countries (Denmark, France, Sweden, UK, Norway and Iceland) which experienced falling fertility in the 1970s and 1980s later recovered or maintained considerably higher levels of fertility, close to replacement rate. Somewhat surprisingly, this resumption of fertility was observed in conjunction with high and/or increasing female employment rates. Table 5.2 reports the female employment rate (population aged 15–64) and the total fertility rate in 2013 for a large number of European countries. The data show that 'virtuous' countries have been able to include large numbers of women into the labour market without negative effects on fertility. For descriptive purposes, countries are ranked by a combination index of the two dimensions (obtained by multiplying the two indicators, employment rate and TFR).

This section discusses a point made in the literature a long time ago (Bettio and Villa 1998), but which still holds. The point is that fertility decisions tend to be constrained in societies where the family plays a strong central role in the organization of all its members' daily lives. There are three main reasons that account for this: (i) traditional gender roles tend to prevail within the family; (ii) both housework and childcare standards are set at too high a level; and (iii) the evolution in family formation patterns is relatively sticky.

Table 5.2 Female employment rate (ER), total fertility rate (TFR), share of births outside marriage and a combination index (ER*TFR), in 2013[a]

		ER (%)	*TFR*	*% births outside marriage*	*Index (ER*TFR)*			*ER (%)*	*TFR*	*% births outside marriage*	*Index (ER*TFR)*
1	Greece	39.9	1.29	7.0	51.47	16	Austria	66.9	1.44	41.4	96.34
2	Spain	50.3	1.27	40.9	63.88	17	Latvia	63.4	1.52	44.6	96.37
3	Italy	46.5	1.39	26.9	64.64	18	Germany	69.0	1.42	34.8	97.98
4	Malta	48.8	1.36	25.9	66.37	19	Lithuania	62.8	1.59	29.5	99.85
5	Poland	53.4	1.29	23.4	68.89	20	Estonia	65.7	1.52	58.9	99.86
6	Portugal	57.9	1.21	47.6	70.06	21	Belgium	57.2	1.76	49.5	100.67
7	Croatia	48.5	1.46	16.1	70.81	22	Ireland	57.1	1.93	35.3	110.20
8	Hungary	52.6	1.35	45.6	71.01	23	Netherlands	69.0	1.68	47.4	115.92
9	Slovakia	53.4	1.34	37.0	71.56	24	Denmark	70.0	1.67	51.5	116.90
10	Cyprus	56.9	1.30	20.2	73.97	25	Finland	67.8	1.75	42.1	118.65
11	Romania	52.6	1.46	31.4	76.80	26	France	60.4	1.99	57.2	120.20
12	Bulgaria	56.8	1.48	59.1	84.06	27	UK	65.8	1.83	47.5	120.41
13	Czechia	59.6	1.46	n.a.	87.02	28	Norway	73.5	1.78	55.2	130.83
14	Luxemb.	59.1	1.55	37.8	91.61	29	Sweden	72.5	1.89	54.4	137.03
15	Slovenia	59.2	1.55	58.0	91.76	30	Iceland	79.0	1.93	69.0	152.47

Source Eurostat database; Eurostat Demo

Note [a]A more recent year could not be considered for lack of information on the TFR for several countries

5.2.1 *Traditional Gender Roles Within the Family and Fertility Decisions*

As already shown, the empirical evidence on the total amount of unpaid work done by women and men within households shows that women continue to spend far more hours than men on unpaid housework and childcare, but with significant variation across countries in the differences between women and men in the average total time spent on unpaid work. In this scenario, Italy is the country with the widest gender gap in unpaid work among the European countries (see Fig. 5.1 and Table 5.1).

Gender relations within *familistic* households—both with and without children—are shaped to a large extent on traditional gender roles. This implies that women take on the responsibility for a substantial share of housework (cleaning, cooking, laundry, ironing, down to a variety of small tasks, like mending and sewing on buttons) and care work (childcare, but also elderly care and care for frail family members). This holds not only in male breadwinner families, but also in dual-earner families, as discussed in Sect. 5.1.

As noted above, norms, attitudes and behaviours regarding childcare and housework are slow to change over time. Moreover, on considering the evolution over time in the distribution of unpaid work between men and women, the stickiness of gender norms within households stands out (Sayer 2005). As shown by several studies (Cunningham 2001; Farré and Vella 2013; Olivetti et al. 2018), adult offspring tend to replicate their parents' paid and unpaid work behaviour observed during adolescence. This suggests that the parental division of unpaid work when their children were adolescents tends to shape their adult behaviour, perpetuating gender norms. As the gender gap in unpaid work is on average smaller in countries experiencing a high (and increasing) involvement of women in paid work, this helps to explain why countries with low female employment rates also show a more unequal division of unpaid work in the households, perpetuating over time an unequal distribution of total work (paid and unpaid).

As pointed out above, of the European countries, Italy is characterized by a particularly large amount of unpaid work done by women. This holds true for working-age women, but also for women employed full time. Unsurprisingly, Italy is also the country in Europe registering one of the widest gender gaps in unpaid work (see Fig. 5.1), one of the lowest employment rate (only 46.5% in 2013, the second lowest after Greece, see Table 5.2) and a 'lowest-low' fertility rate (around 1.3 children per women) from the mid-1990s (Istat 2016).

Time is a finite resource. The unpaid work burden for women increases significantly when children enter a family. Long hours spent cooking, cleaning and caring for family members not only set a limit to the amount of time women can spend on paid work, preventing some women from entering the labour market or discouraging them from remaining in the labour market after childbirth, but they can also discourage women from having children.

The case of the Mediterranean countries, but also of some CEE countries, shows that an increasing number of women in childbearing age may choose to have only one child. The case of these countries suggests that the lowest-low fertility rate[5] registered since the mid-1990s has to be explained taking into account the very high cost of living with a partner and having children in terms of time spent in unpaid work. Since gender norms are sticky, low fertility persists over time.

5.2.2 Housework and Childcare Standards Are Set at Too High a Level

Many factors influence the total amount of time devoted to unpaid work in the household and the distribution of responsibilities between women and men. Clearly, the level of standards can play an important role.

In a now classic article on the time women spend on housework, Joan Vanek (1974) provided evidence for the USA showing that when labour-saving appliances found wide circulation (between 1925 and 1966) the housework time for non-employed women had remained relatively constant. Her article is still relevant today for the hypothesis put forward to explain the paradox of the constancy of domestic work in the presence of relevant technological labour-saving innovations. She remarked that 'the amount of time spent doing the laundry has increased …' presumably because 'people have more clothes now than they did in the past and they wash them more often' (Vanek 1974, p. 117). This suggests that culture plays a role in setting the standards, and these standards may rise over time, increasing the amount of unpaid work performed by women. More recent research, conducted with detailed information on time spent by women in Australia (Bittman et al. 2004), found similar results. Domestic technology rarely reduces women's unpaid working time and, paradoxically, produces some increases in household work. The empirical evidence for Australia suggests that households behave in this way. The concept of rising standards implies a greater quantity or quality of unpaid work. For example, more or better cooked meals, cleaner houses, cleaner and better-ironed cloths, a new emphasis on childcare extending parent's investment in the quantity and quality of 'human capital'.

High standards applied to children imply a substantial investment in human capital not only in terms of education but also in all sorts of additional activities performed outside the school—from sports to music—that involve parents driving their children at the right time from school to the location where these activities are performed. As mother's time is less valued in the household because of gender segregation and discrimination in the labour market, this means additional time devoted to children (or better, to the only child), recalling the thesis advanced by Ariès (a well-known French historian), to interpret the 'first demographic transition',[6] the decline in fertility being brought on by an enormous sentimental and financial investment in the child. Ariès (1980) referred to this period as the 'child-king era', when the fertility transition was driven by the altruistic investment in child quality made by the parents. Nowadays, this is no longer the dominant motivation in most countries, though it has not disappeared. However, in familistic countries, for a large proportion of households investment in child quality is set very high, absorbing not only a large amount of economic resources but also a great deal of the parents' time (especially the mothers'), thereby limiting fertility.

Unfortunately, the lack of detailed data on time use in domestic tasks and childcare translates into wanting research. However, the differences observed across countries in the total amount of unpaid work done by women, in female employment rates and in total fertility rates suggest that standards in traditional familistic countries are set to excessively high levels, constraining fertility choices.

5.2.3 Evolution in Family Formation Patterns Is Relatively Sticky

Marriage is no longer the main (or only) channel for family formation processes and parenthood in European countries. An increasing number of children are born outside marriage, suggesting that the cultural concepts of marriage, family and parenthood have been changing over time. The hypothesis advanced (but not developed) here is that the societies more open to accepting a multiplicity of family models are also those favouring fertility.

The empirical evidence presented in Table 5.2 shows a positive association between the share of children born outside marriage and the TFR in European countries in 2013. Iceland emerges as an emblematic case. It registers one of the highest female employment rates (almost 80%), associated with one of the highest fertility rates in Europe (around 1.8) associated with the highest share of children born outside marriage (69%). This outcome is in contrast with the experience of Greece, Italy, Malta and Poland.

5.3 'Too Much Family' Limits the Growth of the Economic System

The second hypothesis advanced here is that the growth of the economic system tends to be constrained in societies where the family still plays a strong economic role. There are three main arguments supporting this proposition: (i) a traditional family organization prevents the development of a large number of service activities produced in the market to supply goods and/or personal services; (ii) strong family ties used to support family members in overcoming difficulties faced in the labour market may prove inefficient solutions; and (iii) the diffusion of micro-family firms in manufacturing, as well as other family-based organizational structures (home-based elderly care), constitutes a brake on innovation and growth.

5.3.1 'Too Much Family' Limits the Market

The point to highlight is very simple, but at the same time crucial. Of the European countries, Italy is well known for its strong traditions rooted in the family's ability to satisfy the many consumption needs of its members. Homemade Italy has its roots in the gastronomic traditions handed down from mothers to daughters. This applies across the country, from the rich and developed Emilia-Romagna (in the North) to the poor and under-developed Sicily (in the South). What changes are the recipes, not the tradition of good housewives who prepare long and elaborate (time-consuming) dishes, as their mothers and grandmothers did. Even today, in Emilia-Romagna (one of the most developed regions of the country),[7] tradition entails that for feast days women prepare homemade 'tortellini'. It is a task that requires high manual skills and much time: preparing the dough, making the filling, rolling out the dough and then fashioning the 'tortellini' by hand, one by one.

As is well known, the extent of the market tends to increase as long as some of the home production activities are externalized and provided by private firms or the public sector. What cannot be externalized are human relations, attention, and love, as is the case in every society. But there are several activities that can be provided via the market, in exchange for money, freeing women from tight time constraints and reducing the gender gap in unpaid work. As long as these activities are affordable in terms of money and provide services of good quality, it is a solution that helps not only to reduce unpaid work (inside the household) but also to stimulate employment growth, transforming unpaid work into paid work through some entrepreneurial activity. Many examples could be considered: laundrettes (instead of home washing and ironing) and flexible public childcare services (instead of using grandparents as babysitters) are two good examples. There is lack of comparable data on the diffusion and use of laundrette services (and the like) in familistic societies, but we all know the deplorable habit of many university students (both sons and daughters), taking their dirty laundry home at the weekend to be washed and ironed by mum.

The home economy extends outside the kitchen, from homemade bread and cooked meals to childcare, elderly care and care or frail family members. And this calls into question the role of grandparents and the provision of childcare services in familistic societies. Evermore small children are cared for by grandparents, especially in countries where public services for children are insufficient and/or not flexible enough. And their availability has even decreased, or they have become more expensive, because of austerity. Mothers are increasingly present in the labour market—and they also would like to be—because economic independence is perceived by young women as a value in itself and because the experience of the Great Recession has made it clear that women's employment plays a crucial role for the economic well-being of the family when traditionally male jobs are at risk (Karamessini and Rubery 2013).

Some evidence on Italy helps to highlight the central role played by grandparents in a familistic society. According to the information collected by the Labour Inspectorate (Ispettorato Nazionale del Lavoro 2019, p. 7) on resignations of parents of young children (<3 yrs.), the most frequent reason for voluntary resignation is the unavailability of relatives to support the working parent (27%). The excessively high costs of alternative solutions (e.g. babysitter, nursery school fees) and unavailability of childcare services play a marginal role (7 and 2%, respectively). Comparison between two national surveys on Italian families shows that between 1998 and 2009 the active role of grandparents in the care of their grandchildren actually grew, despite the reduction in the average number of grandchildren (Istat 2016). Entrustment of grandchildren (<14 yrs.) to the care of grandparents came to 86.9% of cases in 2009 (compared to 85.7% in 1998). The reasons provided for looking after their grandchildren show both the multiple needs of parents and the flexibility of grandparents: they look after grandchildren when parents work, have occasional commitments, in emergency situations, when the child is sick, and during holidays. The strong intergenerational support—characterizing the parent/child/grandchildren links—is facilitated by the widespread tendency to live close together. 43% of grandparents live less than one kilometre (km) away from the nearest grandchild, 40% 1.6 km away and only 17% more than 16 km away (Zamberletti et al. 2015).

The contribution of grandparents as family support figures in the care of grandchildren is certainly still very important in countries lacking childcare services (i.e. Mediterranean and some CEE countries). However, the growing proportion of divorcees among the elderly and the recent pension reforms increasing retirement age could stand in the way of their full involvement in the near future. Moreover, given the increasing average age of the population, a large share of elderly people have to care for their very old parents/relatives, the overall care burden tends to increase. Finally, given that today grandparents are on average older than a few decades ago, worsening health conditions could undermine their ability to play their role fully.

Some claim that the contribution of the elderly population to the care of grandchildren should be recognized, protected and valued. If there were no grandparents, mothers (and fathers) would have even more difficulty reconciling family and work, and this could yet further depress the fertility rate of young couples. But this is not the solution to the problem of insufficient and inflexible childcare services. In fact, it could be argued that it is the ample availability of unpaid and extremely flexible grandparents—typical of familistic societies—that weakens the social demand for childcare services sufficient in quantity, flexible in organizational structure and affordable in terms of costs for parents. In other words, this private and very valuable resource may to some extent limit the pressure on local governments to respond to this basic crucial need for families with small children.

Neither families nor the welfare system should take grandparents for granted. It is neither feasible nor efficient. Substantial modification of the public intervention would be appropriate, with a decisive strengthening of care services for children, at sustainable costs for families and organized in a flexible way (in a sense, imitating the grandparent model). At the same time, this is a policy to expand employment. The unpaid work of the grandparent-babysitters can give way to the paid work of qualified personnel. Moreover, the large share of children growing up as only child will learn how to interact with other children.

5.3.2 *'Too Much Family' Limits the Scope for Efficient Solutions*

It is widely acknowledged that informal networks play a key role in job search processes and their employment outcomes. The circulation of job-related information through informal networks is thought to account for the large range of employment outcomes across similar socio-demographic groups. The basic intuition is that if jobseekers have connections with employed individuals who have privileged access to information on available employment opportunities, this will positively affect their job search.

The degree to which jobseekers become aware of available employment opportunities depends on the quality (and extent) of their informal networks. In other words, the speed and quality of the job-matching process through informal networks depend, to a large extent, on the quality of job-related information. It can reasonably be assumed that jobseekers with sufficiently long employment experience tend to rely on former fellow workers, who have privileged access to information on available employment opportunities. In contrast, first-jobseekers and unemployed people with weak contacts in the labour market tend to rely on family networks. And the role of family informal networks is all the stronger the weaker the public employment services turn out to be.

The use of informal job search methods through social networks is prevalent in many countries, and it has prompted several studies. The available evidence indicates that the use of informal networks speeds up the matching process (Cingano and Rosolia 2012) and shortens job search time (Pellizzari 2010). The results in terms of the quality of jobs filled through such methods, however, are much more controversial.

In familistic countries, strong family ties are typically used to support family members facing difficulties in the labour market, such as first-jobseekers, unemployed young people and women with discontinuous careers. Recent research on the role of informal networks in job searching focused on Italy has confirmed that jobseekers relying on informal networks, mainly friends and family members, may find employment faster; however, in the medium-long term, the matching turns out to be poorer (i.e. lower wages and scant career prospects). This is especially true of women, who often limit their search to a given geographical area for family reasons (i.e. to take advantage of grandparents looking after their children, or to be able to take care of elderly parents).

A large body of literature considers the advantages of using informal networks to match workers to jobs. However, Meliciani and Radicchia (2016) argue that the informal recruitment channel (with family ties playing a major role) may increase job-education mismatches both directly (by inducing some workers to undertake careers in industries, professions or firms where their comparative productive advantage is not fully exploited) and indirectly by negatively affecting spatial flexibility.[8] Moreover, family ties may interfere with a genuine process of worker selection, favouring people with connections over more talented workers. Ponzo and Scoppa (2010) propose a simple model of favouritism to analyse these risks in Italy. They find that informal networks tend to be used by low-educated individuals, in small firms, in low-productivity jobs and in less developed regions.[9] Moreover, informal networks have a negative impact on wages (controlling for individual and firm characteristics).

These findings suggest that family networks may help jobseekers into employment and reduce family members' unemployment spells. But the role played by the family is not necessarily efficient (it may result in job-education mismatches) or indeed equitable (some more talented people will remain unemployed). To conclude, it would be better to develop efficient public employment services to favour job match quality (i.e. when the skills of workers are suited to their job tasks).

5.3.3 'Too Much Family' Limits Growth and Innovation

The strength of the family in shaping some structural features of the productive structure may result in weaknesses, limiting economic growth and innovation, and so also employment. The case of Italy fits well into this stylized interpretation. It is a well-known fact that the success of the Italian economic model in the post-war period, up to the mid-1980s, was rooted in the strength of the industrial districts, based on a network of highly specialized and innovative small family firms. Globalization and technological innovation (associated with digitalization) changed the scenario within which these micro- and small family firms interact, produce and compete on the international markets. In short, the structural features of the Italian productive system—with a large proportion of family firms—appear to have turned from a strength into a weakness, limiting technological innovation and growth. In what follows, I will outline some evidence to support this hypothesis.

The fragmentation of the productive system is evident in Italy, where the average enterprise is much smaller than the European average. In 2016, there were approximately 47.8 private enterprises (in industry and services) per 1000 inhabitants in the EU28, but with extremely different densities from one country to another (Istat 2019). Italy was among the countries with the highest density of private enterprises (72.4), in contrast with Germany and the UK (30 and 32.3, respectively). The fragmentation of the Italian productive structure is reflected in the very low number of employees per enterprise (industry and services): 3.8, as against 11.8 in Germany and 9.4 in the UK.

It is widely acknowledged that low productivity is the main factor holding back long-term economic growth in Italy. Since the early 1990s, productivity growth has been feeble both by historical standards and compared with the other main euro area countries (Bugamelli et al. 2018). The productivity growth gap between Italy and the rest of the EU remains very large (Istat 2018b). Behind the underperformance of Italy's aggregate productivity lies a considerable heterogeneity across firms. Micro- and small firms in Italy are less productive than in peer countries, even taking into account the specialisation in traditional sectors, and have a much greater weight.[10]

An in-depth analysis of the factors behind the underperformance of Italy's aggregate productivity (Bugamelli et al. 2018) explained it as the consequence of a highly polarized productive system. The many micro- and small enterprises, mostly family-managed, are on average old and have a limited aptitude for innovation, adoption of advanced technologies and internationalization. They are ineffective in their management skills and practices (the recruitment of external managers is limited) and show a vulnerable financial structure. Their poor productivity performance is also due to the quantitative and qualitative shortage of human capital.

These small family firms lag behind in innovation, despite the fact that process and organizational innovation is particularly relevant for smaller firms. Their ability to benefit from synergies along the value chain, following innovative investment, is limited by the high degree of vertical fragmentation of the production chain and the low degree of formal cooperation among firms (Istat 2019; Bugamelli et al. 2018). The fragmentation of the productive system into small firms slows digitalization down, as isolated investment of small firms cannot benefit from economies of scale or a coordinated approach (Istat 2019). This results in a polarization between many micro- and small firms—with limited resources, skills, propensity to export to foreign markets and innovation—and few larger, highly innovative, productive firms active on international markets.

In short, Italy's poor growth performance in the long run is determined, among other factors, by its innovation and technology gap. This negative gap reflects underinvestment by a great majority of firms, especially those of a micro- and small size. Small family firms are less able to face the risks and costs of undertaking innovative projects, hiring and training skilled workers, adopting organizational innovations, and benefiting from knowledge spillovers. In short, the large share of small family firms in the Italian economy is at present one of the structural weaknesses that help to account for the slow economic growth registered since the early 1990s. Unsurprisingly, both the total and the female employment rate in Italy are among the lowest in the EU. In 2018, for the population aged 20–64 the total employment rate was 63% (compared to 79.9% in Germany and 78.7% in the UK), while the female employment rate was 53.1% (compared to 75.8% in Germany and 78.7% in the UK) (Eurostat database).

5.4 Concluding Remarks

Family structures and family cultural values, including gender norms, are sticky institutions that tend to reproduce themselves over time. This implies that in familistic societies the family continues to play a key role in the economy, affecting social and economic outcomes. This paper draws attention to the fact that history matters, in the sense that 'too much family' may over time limit the possibilities for adjustments to new challenges. Familistic societies show high levels of home production, limiting the extent of the market and employment growth; the degree of economic independence enjoyed by women through paid work is low; the division of paid and unpaid work between women and men is unequal; and finally, fertility is very low. But 'too much family' also has negative implications in terms of the efficiency of the labour market (the job-matching process), innovation and growth. In short, the pervasiveness of the family in the productive structure turns out to be a limit to economic growth and high employment rates.

Gender norms play an important role for economic outcomes, as they affect both gender relations within the family and in society at large. In societies with strong family ties, there is a risk of lack of social pressure for stronger and more efficient public policies able to reduce the material burden falling on families (and in particular on the women) in terms of home production and care activities, but also for developing efficient public employment services and devising integrated strategies able to help small family firms to grow and transform.

Notes

1. The idea that the role of the family needs to be considered in analysis of the poor long-run performance of familistic economies was first discussed by Francesca Bettio in Ferrara, at the Festival organized by *Internazionale* in October 2019, in a special session chaired by the editorial board of the web journal www.inGenere.it. Francesca and I were unable to finalize a joint contribution for various reasons: the overlapping of too many commitments, the difficulties we faced in planning our agendas in advance and the inadequate train connections between Siena and Trento (where our universities are located). The good ideas presented here are the result of joint discussion based on the original hypothesis advanced by Francesca. The weaknesses of some of the arguments put forward are due to the problems encountered in producing a thoroughgoing joint contribution.
2. The economic decline of Italy has been documented extensively before the Great Recession of 2008–09 (see Ciocca 2004; Daveri et al. 2005; Pellegrino and Zingales 2017, among others).
3. Gender equality is an important goal of the European Union, included in TEU (Treaty on European Union, art. 2 and 3) and TFEU (Treaty on the Functioning of the European Union, art. 8 and 9).
4. WikiGender.org, 'Gender Equality Law in the European Union', available at https://www.wikigender.org/wiki/gender-equality-law-in-the-european-union/ (accessed 20 Jan 2020).

5. The lowest-low fertility rate was introduced by demographers (Kohler et al. 2002) to point out the risk of a low-fertility trap where falls in fertility could be self-reinforcing. This was identified with a TFR under 1.5. The persistence over time of a lowest-low fertility rate raises the possibility of dramatic, rapid population ageing and population decline.
6. The first demographic transition refers to the historical declines in both mortality and fertility as witnessed from the eighteenth century on in Europe (and continuing at present in most developing countries). The second demographic transition refers to the observed decline to sub-replacement fertility, as observed in the post-war period (in Europe and Japan).
7. Emilia-Romagna also registers one of the highest female employment rates in Italy (66.9% in 2018 for women aged 20–64 years) and a very low TFR (1.17 for women with Italian citizenship, in 2017) (see Istat 2018a, p. 8).
8. They test these hypotheses (using ISFOL Plus survey data on Italy) and find a robust positive impact of the use of the informal channel on over-education and a robust negative effect of the use of this channel on migration.
9. They empirically investigate the determinants and consequences of using informal networks in Italy using the Bank of Italy Survey (SHIW).
10. The productivity of medium and large firms is in line with peer countries, but their weight is smaller (respectively, 0.5% and less than 0.1% compared to 0.9 and 0.2% in the EU) (European Commission 2019, p. 47).

References

Alesina, A., & Giuliano, P. (2014). Family Ties. In P. Aghion & S. N. Durlauf (Eds.), *Handbook of Economic Growth* (Vol. 2A, pp. 177–215). Oxford: Elsevier.

Ariès, P. (1980). Two Successive Motivations for the Declining Birth Rate in the West. *Population and Development Review, 6*(4), 645–650.

Bettio, F., & Rosselli, A. (2018). Gender Budgeting in Italy: A Laboratory for Alternative Methodologies? In A. O'Hagan & E. Klatzer (Eds.), *Gender Budgeting in Europe* (pp. 199–220). Cham: Palgrave Macmillan.

Bettio, F., & Villa, P. (1998). A Mediterranean Perspective on the Breakdown of the Relationship Between Participation and Fertility. *Cambridge Journal of Economics, 22*(2), 137–171.

Bittman, M., Rice, J. M., & Wajcman, J. (2004). Appliances and Their Impact: The Ownership of Domestic Technology and Time Spent on Household Work. *The British Journal of Sociology, 55*(34), 401–423.

Bugamelli, M., Lotti, F., Amici, M., Ciapanna, E., Colonna, F., D'Amuri, F., et al. (2018, January). *Productivity Growth in Italy: A Tale of Slow-Motion Change*. Questioni di Economia e Finanza (Occasional Papers, No. 422). Rome: Bank of Italy.

Cingano, F., & Rosolia, A. (2012). People I Know: Job Search and Social Networks. *Journal of Labor Economics, 30*(2), 291–332.

Ciocca, P. (2004). L'economia italiana: un problema di crescita. *Rivista italiana degli economisti, 9*(1), 7–28.

Cunningham, M. (2001). The Influence of Parental Attitudes and Behaviors on Children's Attitudes Toward Gender and Household Labor in Early Adulthood. *Journal of Marriage and Family, 63*(1), 111–122.

Daveri, F., Jona-Lasinio, C., & Zollino, F. (2005). Italy's Decline: Getting the Facts Right. *Giornale degli economisti e annali di economia, 64*(4), 365–421.

European Commission. (2019). Country Report Italy 2019. *Staff Working Document*, no. SWD(2019) 1011 final, 27.02.2019. Brussels: European Commission.

Farré, L., & Vella, F. (2013). The Intergenerational Transmission of Gender Role Attitudes and Its Implications for Female Labour Force Participation. *Economica, 80*(318), 219–247.

Giuliano, P. (2010). Ties That Matter: Cultural Norms and Family Formation in Western Europe. In C. Brown, B. Eichengreen, & M. Reich (Eds.), *Labor in the Era of Globalization* (pp. 211–239). Cambridge: Cambridge University Press.

Ispettorato Nazionale del Lavoro. (2019). *Relazione annuale sulle convalide delle dimissioni e risoluzioni consensuali delle lavoratrici madri e dei lavoratori padri ai sensi dell'art. 55 del Decreto Legislativo 26 marzo 2001. Anno 2018*. No. 151. Rome: INL.

Istat. (2016). La dinamica familiare nella fase adulta e anziana. In Istat, *Relazione annuale 2016* (pp. 80–83). Rome: Istat.

Istat. (2018a, novembre 28). *Natalità e fecondità della popolazione residente. Anno 2017* (Statistiche Report). Rome: Istat.

Istat. (2018b). *Rapporto sulla competitività dei settori produttivi*. Rome: Istat.

Istat. (2019). *Noi Italia: 100 Statistics to Understand the Country We Live in* (2019 ed.). Rome: Istat.

Karamessini, M., & Rubery, J. (Eds.). (2013). *Women and Austerity: The Economic Crisis and the Future for Gender Equality*. New York: Routledge.

Kohler, H.-P., Billari, F. C., & Ortega, J. A. (2002). The Emergence of Lowest-Low Fertility in Europe During the 1990s. *Population and Development Review, 28*(4), 641–680.

McDonald, P. (2000). Gender Equity in Theories of Fertility Transition. *Population and Development Review, 26*(3), 427–439.

McDonald, P. (2013). Societal Foundations for Explaining Low Fertility: Gender Equity. *Demographic Research, 28*, Article 34, 981–994.

Mills, M., Mencarini, L., Tanturri, M. L., & Begall, K. (2008). Gender Equity and Fertility Intentions in Italy and the Netherlands. *Demographic Research, 18*(1), 1–26.

Meliciani, V., & Radicchia, D. (2016). Informal Networks, Spatial Mobility and Overeducation in the Italian Labour Market. *The Annals of Regional Science, 56*(2), 513–535.

OECD. (2017). Gender Inequality in Unpaid Work. In OECD, *The Pursuit of Gender Equality: An Uphill Battle* (pp. 189–98). Paris: OECD Publishing.

Olivetti, C., Patacchini, E., & Zenou, Y. (2018). Mothers, Peers, and Gender-Role Identity. *Journal of the European Economic Association*, jvy050. https://doi.org/10.1093/jeea/jvy050.

Pellegrino, B., & Zingales, L. (2017). *Diagnosing the Italian Disease* (NBER Working Paper, No. 23964). Cambridge, MA: National Bureau of Economic Research.

Pellizzari, M. (2010). Do Friends and Relatives Really Help in Getting a Good Job? *Industrial and Labor Relations Review, 63*(3), 494–510.

Ponzo, M., & Scoppa, V. (2010). The Use of Informal Networks in Italy: Efficiency or Favoritism? *The Journal of Socio-Economics, 39*(1), 89–99.

Sayer, L. C. (2005). Gender, Time and Inequality: Trends in Women's and Men's Paid Work, Unpaid Work and Free Time. *Social Forces, 84*(1), 285–303.

Seguino, S. (2007). PlusÇa Change? Evidence on Global Trends in Gender Norms and Stereotypes. *Feminist Economics, 13*(2), 1–28.

Vanek, J. (1974). Time Spent in Housework. *Scientific American, 231*(5), 116–120.

Zamberletti, J., Tommasini, C., & Cavrini, G. (2015, February 25). Quando mamma e papà lavorano… ci sono i nonni. *Neodemos*. Available at https://www.neodemos.info/articoli/quando-mamma-e-papa-lavorano-ci-sono-i-nonni/. Accessed 23 Jan 2020.

CHAPTER 6

Money, Banking and Politics in Early Nineteenth-Century Portugal

José Luís Cardoso

6.1 Introduction

This contribution seeks to present the main political debates and proposals presented on the subject of money, credit and public debt in the context of the Portuguese liberal revolution of 1820. The first Portuguese bank (*Banco de Lisboa*) was founded in 1821, in a period of significant economic and political change. The new political situation, which marked the end of the absolutist regime and the beginning of a constitutional monarchy, created an opportunity for lively debates in the public sphere on topics relating to monetary theories and policies. The control of the issue of paper money and the management of public debt were particularly relevant matters that were subject to scrutiny in parliamentary debates and public opinion making (pamphlets and journals). These matters were closely linked to the formation of the Bank of Lisbon.

For a better understanding and contextualization of the public debate about the motives for the creation of the Bank of Lisbon, in the first

J. L. Cardoso (✉)
Instituto de Ciências Sociais, Universidade de Lisboa, Lisbon, Portugal
e-mail: jcardoso@ics.ulisboa.pt

M. C. Marcuzzo et al. (eds.), *New Perspectives on Political Economy and Its History*, Palgrave Studies in the History of Economic Thought,
https://doi.org/10.1007/978-3-030-42925-6_6

section I shall briefly deal with the antecedents of banking organization in Portugal, paying special attention to the attempts to create a national bank in the early nineteenth century.

By focusing on the political conditions inherent in the public discussion about monetary problems and banking solutions, I shall argue that the close links between money, credit, banks and politics constitute an important starting point when analysing the history of banking in the early nineteenth century. Therefore, the Portuguese case serves as a useful illustration of a global issue relating to the links between economic and financial institutions, banking activities and political change.

6.2 The Early Beginnings of the Banking System in Portugal

The first consistent and well-grounded attempt to create a banking institution in Portugal occurred in 1797, the year when the Minister Rodrigo de Sousa Coutinho presented his project for the constitution of a national bank, which he named *Banco Nacional Brigantino* (Coutinho [1797] 1993).

The development of banking activities—such as money counting, deposits, loans and the discounting of bills of exchange—had naturally increased as a result of the process of commercial expansion that Portugal had been experiencing, especially since the second half of the fifteenth century. Notwithstanding the regularity of such practices, their size never made it necessary to institutionalize banks or banking services, with their own autonomy and specialization. Portugal did not keep pace with the creation of specialized banking institutions in the main European markets (Roover 1974), especially in Italy and the Netherlands. The efforts to create banking institutions began relatively late on and were finally materialized in the form of two events of special political significance: in October 1808, the creation of the *Banco do Brasil* (following the transfer of the king and his court from Lisbon to Rio de Janeiro in the context of the Napoleonic wars), and, in December 1821, the establishment of the first Portuguese bank, the *Banco de Lisboa*, created by a decision of Parliament, meeting after the Portuguese liberal revolution of 1820.

The fact that there were no banking institutions in Portugal and its empire before 1808 does not mean that the sort of financial transactions normally conducted through banks had not been taking place before that time. In fact, individual borrowing and lending practices, conducted on a personal basis or through private institutions that centralized lending operations, are well known and well documented (Rocha 1996, 1998). The involvement of rich merchants in the profitable operations of discounting bills of exchange and lending money by charging an interest rate has also been carefully analysed (Madureira 1994; Pedreira 1996).

In this network of credit and finance operations prior to the establishment of an organized banking system, it is also important to bear in mind the role played by religious organizations, such as the poor-relief institutions known as *Misericórdias* (Holy Houses of Mercy), brotherhoods and convents, which were approached by high-ranking social groups, namely nobles and merchants, looking for the means to pay their current and future investment expenses (Monteiro 1992). This involved a network of agents who shared mutual rights and obligations, arising from their simultaneous participation as debtors and creditors.

The creation of institutions specially dedicated to the operations of deposit-taking and financing is a subject referred to in various opinions and *arbitrios* written in the years 1796 and 1797 by Domingos Vandelli, an Italian naturalist who had lived in Portugal since 1764.[1] In his proposals for setting up banking institutions, he explicitly advocated the participation of foreigners in the bank's capital, namely Jews of Portuguese origin who had become established in England and the Netherlands, and mentioned the name of the minister Sousa Coutinho as the person best qualified to promote the organization of a bank. However, his mistrust of the local management of the bank led him to admit the possibility of 'welcoming people from London or Amsterdam to direct this new establishment' (Vandelli [1796–97] 1994, p. 382). His main concern, however, was the difficulty of setting up a bank due to the distrust of the shareholders about receiving 'discredited paper' in exchange for the funds invested (ibid., p. 402).

It was certainly these difficulties and the dubious credibility of the system of public finance that explained the inability of Sousa Coutinho to find the financial support necessary for his National Bank project, dated July 1797, when he was in charge of the Ministry of the Navy and Overseas Dominions. The capital of the bank would be 1600 *contos* (c. £400,000),[2] distributed equally between the State and private shareholders. Under the terms of its bylaws, the bank proposed to fulfil several objectives for the issue of banknotes, the deposit of metallic money, payment advances and the discounting of bills of exchange. However, the crucial problem underlying the proposal for the bank's formation was the loan to the State of the amount necessary for the amortization of the internal public debt, arising from the loan of 4000 *contos* taken out in November 1796.[3]

Sousa Coutinho's banking solution was designed to make the State appear credible and to reassure public opinion regarding the process of public debt management. However, what prevailed was another solution linked to the issue of new debt securities of a very low nominal value (small *apólices*). These bonds began to circulate as inconvertible paper money and, due to their uncontrolled and fraudulent issue, caused inflationary effects and disturbances to the monetary circulation.[4] As we shall see later on, it was the negative consequences of this issue of paper money, which replaced the previous bonds (*apólices*) that were supposed to serve as debt securities and whose discounting resulted in huge losses (about 25% of the initial value) for their owners, that lay behind the creation of the Bank of Lisbon in 1821.

The failure to implement Sousa Coutinho's project could be explained by the lack of commitment on the part of the great merchants who had been contacted for this purpose. The initiative of creating a bank did not deserve their consideration, certainly because they could not expect it to provide them with a profitable capital investment, when compared with the gains to be made through informal lending. This also meant that, as far as the performance of their own business was concerned, credit practices were carried out through an informal structure of bank-like operations, namely payment delays and deferrals, as well as through personal borrowing operations at low interest rates (Pedreira 1996). The same thing happened in situations of lesser economic impact, but perhaps greater social significance, which involved daily credit operations conducted among low income social groups. Thus, at the dawn of the nineteenth century, economic activities took place in Portugal with the aid of parabanking instruments, but without an institution specifically conceived for this purpose.

It is in this context that we can understand how, during the period under analysis, several projects had been presented for the formation of banks whose functions did not expressly involve the specific needs of financing the State, managing the public debt or reorganizing the circulation of paper money. Their objective would be, above all, to aid the development of economic activities and to serve the private economic agents.[5]

Taken together, these different proposals provide a very significant testimony to the monetary and financial problems that were under debate in Portugal in the early years of the nineteenth century, thereby anticipating the type of solutions that would later be encountered in the debates on the creation of the Bank of Lisbon in the new political climate of the liberal revolution of 1820. It should be emphasized, however, that the theoretical framework of bank projects viewed in the light of the teachings of political economy was certainly not one of the most important features of the proposals that were narrowly disseminated in the early years of the nineteenth century. José Acúrsio das Neves was one of the rare authors who, in the period before the liberal revolution of 1820, discussed the problems of banking organization based on the arguments and principles of political economy (Neves [1814–17], pp. 403–471).

Acúrsio das Neves presented the wide range of different forms that existed for the circulation of paper money, in order to establish a clear distinction between the convertible banknotes, which were used like money and complemented the circulation of specie, and the debt securities and credit paper issued by the State (*apólices*) or by private individuals (bills of exchange and land bills). The latter were not intended to be used as currency, but were technical instruments placed at the service of the expansion of productive and mercantile activities, provided that they were carefully managed.

Acúrsio das Neves' concern was to warn of the negative consequences of an excess of paper money circulating in Portugal, using the approaches of Adam Smith and J.-B. Say, who recommended prudence and control over the quantity issued, taking into account the level of wealth created and represented.

The theme also served as a pretext for Acúrsio das Neves to undertake a brief survey of the process that had been followed in setting up the main European banks, explaining their distinct vocations: in some cases, they had the priority objectives of withdrawing inconvertible paper money from circulation and managing the public debt system; in other cases, their purpose was to take deposits and make loans and advances, with the aim of fostering the development of agriculture and manufactures. He also paid special attention to the case of savings banks, which were designed to capture significant amounts of small private savings and could play an important role in boosting investment in productive economic sectors.

The panorama presented by Acúrsio das Neves anticipated and heralded the discussion about the need for a banking institution in Portugal that was to occur after the liberal revolution of 1820. When Acúrsio das Neves published his book, the Bank of Brazil was already in operation, to which he made a short reference. This bank had been established in Rio de Janeiro on October 1808 and was part of the set of economic and financial measures associated with the move of the Portuguese court to Brazil at the end of 1807, when Portugal was invaded by the Napoleonic army. Those measures included the inaugural Royal *Carta* (28 January 1808), which established new rules opening Brazilian ports to international trade, the new legislative framework accepting the installation of manufactures in Brazil (1 April 1808) and the creation or adaptation of royal institutions—such as the Board of Trade or the Royal Exchequer—to the new political environment resulting from the court's expected lengthy stay in Rio de Janeiro. The lack of specie in circulation, the excessive demand for money due to the opening of the ports and the consequent increase in transactions, which were, in turn, related to the increase in public services and the greater expenditure involved in establishing the court in Brazil, were all factors that justified the devising of new solutions designed to improve monetary circulation. However, this experiment was to fail when the main reasons for its creation no longer existed, i.e. when the king and his court returned to the European continent. Meanwhile, a revolution had taken place in Porto and Lisbon, significantly altering the political make-up of economic and financial institutions.[6]

6.3 The Liberal Revolution of 1820: The Debates About Debt and Money in the Public Sphere

The Portuguese liberal revolution of 1820 was possible thanks to the combination of a variety of short-term conditions and structural factors. Among these, emphasis should be given to the dissatisfaction that several social sectors felt towards the political fragility of the kingdom and its colonial dominions and what they considered to be the continuation of obstacles that impeded the full development of national capacities. Portugal was then a European country with the seat of its imperial power in Brazil, in the hands of a regency controlled both politically and militarily by its British ally, who had played a prominent role in the liberation of Portugal after the French invasions between 1808 and 1811.

The establishment of a constitutional monarchy and a new form for the exercise of sovereignty (based on the legislative power) created the appropriate institutional and political conditions for dismantling the *ancien régime*'s economic and social structure. Although its fundamental purpose was the elaboration of a constitutional code, the first Portuguese Parliament discussed and legislated on a wide range of matters relating to social, economic and political life, seeking to give the form of law to everything that lacked regulation, as well as to respond to the various requests emanating from an effervescent civil society eager for solutions to its individual and collective problems.

Freedom of expression and freedom of the press were among the first concerns to merit the attention of liberal politicians who did not hesitate in establishing the conditions for the formation of an active public sphere committed to the exercise of free and responsible citizenship. The proliferation of newspapers and pamphlets dedicated to a wide range of topics considered to be of public interest, as well as the abundant flow of petitions, *manifestos* and proposals to the deputies and to the parliamentary committees, were eloquent signs of the strength of a public opinion that claimed the right to play an important part in building a new society.

It is therefore not surprising that, among the issues that caught the attention of anonymous citizens or competent public officials and intellectuals, we find matters relating to the economic and financial situation of the country and the specific problems of public credit, as well as to the necessary remedies for redeeming public debt and for stabilizing the credibility of institutions that had been designed for that purpose.

In the months following the revolutionary movements of 1820, strong public pressure was exerted, demanding that a solution be found to the problems that had long afflicted both the holders of increasingly depreciated paper money and the public and private institutions forced to accept payments in the form of paper. In some cases, solutions were presented for the consolidation of the public debt and for the extinction of inconvertible paper money, which required the occurrence of one of the following conditions: the existence of an institution already prepared for this mission, such as the Royal Exchequer, or the creation of a new institution specifically designed for that purpose. It was in this last context that the urgency of setting up a bank was discussed.

The political climate created by the liberal revolution allowed for the presentation of solutions that involved a criticism (and ultimately the loss) of the privileges held by members of the *ancien régime*'s social orders, aiming at a diversification of the sources for funding debt repayment, namely by selling off chapels and ecclesiastical benefices, auctioning public lands and enclosures, and creating a special tax on urban buildings (Moniz 1820).

The solution by means of taxation policies, thus providing the State with an increase in revenues for debt repayment, met with the approval of another participant in this public debate (Pinto 1820). The *Cortes* (Parliament or Constitutional Assembly) were not yet assembled, and therefore the suggestions presented in this pamphlet were addressed to the government, particularly regarding the allocation of existing taxes to the amortization of debt securities. The theme also mobilized merchants and manufacturers, as was the case with Francisco Azevedo, who published two pamphlets in 1822 dedicated to the subject of discounting paper money (Azevedo 1822a, b). In one of these pamphlets, he proposed technical measures that would prevent the counterfeit issue of paper money and allow for the replacement of old paper bonds. In this way, the State needed to be rigorously aware of the amount of debt securities that should be redeemed and could define a tax-guaranteed plan for the allocation of funds.

State creditors kept hoping that the revolution initiated in 1820 would resolve the default situation in which the State found itself, paying off the public debt and its interest. It was vital that the State should gain the confidence of the holders of debt securities and maintain its good reputation with the political body of the nation.[7]

Among the various pamphlets published at the time, it is worth mentioning Vicente da Costa's proposal for the creation of a bank specifically designed for overseeing the process of public debt management (Costa 1822). The author acknowledged from the start that, due to an unexpected delay in publication, his proposal had lost momentum, since the *Cortes* had already approved the constitution of the Bank of Lisbon. But the problem he was discussing did not fail to give rise to contributions that served to keep people thinking about the role of a bank in the new constitutional political conjuncture. Costa's main concern was to reactivate what he considered to be a 'stalled circulation' that prevented a normal relationship between sellers and buyers in the market.

The difficulty of finding shareholders for such a venture could be resolved by resorting to the holders of public debt, through the conversion of their interest-bearing debt securities into the bank's capital.

In this way, the former public debt was extinguished and the new capital would appreciate thanks to the bank's income-generating operations. Shareholders would therefore receive an interest payment (corresponding to the debt securities converted into shares) and dividends, based on the results of the bank's operations.

Costa gave special attention to the need to distinguish between different types of fiduciary circulation (paper money issued by the State and banknotes issued by a private bank). Furthermore, he warned of the inflationary risks of an excessive monetary circulation (mainly in the form of banknotes) and asked for a rigorous selection of qualified people for the bank's management. Finally, we should note Vicente da Costa's insistence on a political dimension that was not always made explicit in the technical literature on financial and banking matters: the bank rendered a service to the Constitution, the State and the political revolution, so that the Constitution and the State therefore had to repay and compensate the bank for the importance of its mission.

The contents of these proposals and messages were extended to other areas of the public sphere, particularly in the newspapers dedicated to the current national and international political debates that had proliferated in Lisbon and Porto since September 1820. Accompanying the public debate on technical solutions relating to the debt amortization process, the newspapers opened their pages to the collaboration of authors who presented and discussed proposals for the payments owed to private creditors.

6.4 Parliamentary Papers and the Creation of the Bank of Lisbon

The *Cortes* and their specialized committees also received many expressions of concern about the state of the country in a wide range of fields, including naturally the domain of public credit and the credibility of financial institutions. In the years 1821 and 1822, the Public Finance Committee received a total of 63 memoranda and reports on the financial situation, in addition to some 330 letters and petitions relating to the private problems of citizens and institutions who complained of tax evasion, abuses of power and contract cancellations, or claimed some of the rights and benefits facilitated by the new political regime.[8] Among the reports whose content was of greatest analytical interest, the most noteworthy were the observations and proposals on the circulation of paper money, the amortization of public debt, the elimination or creation of taxes and, in general, the problems relating to the reform of the system for the administration of public finance. Of course, the question of the creation of a banking institution was the main focus of many of these texts (namely Gallard 1821; Jordão 1821), in which the positive expectations about the political conditions offered by the new liberal regime were directly invoked.

Thus, when the details of the proposal for the creation of the Bank of Lisbon were discussed in Parliament between 13 and 29 December 1821, its members could not ignore the multiple contributions originating from an enlightened public sphere that was aware of the important opportunity that the political moment provided. They were also fully acquainted with the language of political economy and could therefore argue in terms that proved the relevance of Parliament as a place for enhancing the links between economic doctrine and the course of political events. Throughout the parliamentary debates taking place on the formation of the bank, opinions were often expressed about the autonomy of its decision-making processes, with a clearly majority position prevailing over the need for its independence from the executive and legislative powers.

The creation of the Bank of Lisbon was inseparable from a broadly shared concern for financial equilibrium, as was clearly expressed in the preamble to the Law that set it up, 'taking into account the public advantage resulting from the establishment of a Loan, Deposit and Discount Bank, which banishes usury, and promotes the convenience of transactions between individuals, and is simultaneously applicable to the amortization of paper money' (*Regulamento* 1822, p. 3).

In order that this aim of amortizing the large amount of paper money in circulation could be realized, the Bank was legally obliged to lend the State the sum of 2000 *contos* in banknotes, at an interest rate of 4%, which would gradually replace the debt securities (*apólices*) that circulated as currency and whose uncontrolled issue had begun in 1796. The capital stock of the Bank of Lisbon was 5000 *contos* (10,000 shares of 500,000 *reis* each)[9] and its subscription would be made by individual shareholders, without any restrictions in terms of nationality. Consequently, it was a private bank with a public mission established by the political will of the *Cortes*, which regarded the Bank of Lisbon as an instrument of credibility that would guarantee the proper functioning of the mechanisms of fiduciary circulation.

The compulsory loan to the State had as its counterpart the benefits received by the Bank of Lisbon, namely those referring to the total exemption from taxes on banking operations and the State's obligation to accept banknotes issued by the bank in public offices. The issuing of these banknotes enjoyed a monopoly of 20 years. The bank was thus protected against competition in the various profitable areas of business that could be dedicated to it, namely the discounting of bills of exchange, loans against pledges and mortgages, deposits, transfers and payments of services requested by its customers.[10]

As an institution, the Bank of Lisbon displayed similar characteristics to other private banks created in Europe at the same time, with its multiple purposes being linked by two primary functions serving the needs of the modern fiscal state: the amortization and management of the public debt and the issuing of banknotes, in order to guarantee the efficiency of monetary circulation (Pohl 1994; Atack and Neal 2009). The Portuguese experience benefited greatly from the lessons provided by the trajectories of the Bank of England, created in 1694 (Temin and Voth 2013), and the Bank of San Carlos, established in Spain in 1782 (Tedde de Lorca 1999).

During the early years of its activity, the Bank of Lisbon performed well in the aftermath of the absolutist counterrevolution that had occurred in Portugal in April 1823, also withstanding the political changes that were subsequently introduced.[11] The revocation of the Constitution of 1822 and all the liberal legislation produced since the beginning of the 1820 revolution had no effect on the situation of the Bank of Lisbon, which, curiously, was the only institution created by the liberal regime to keep its status unchanged. The operating results of the Bank of Lisbon and the dividends distributed to the shareholders allow us to conclude that the contemporary political vicissitudes did not affect the bank's overall performance or the fulfilment of its basic activities (Reis 1996). The bank's highly coveted technical independence from the legislative and executive powers thus seemed to be a factor in the bank's survival, regardless of the changes taking place in the political regime.

However, at the end of 1827, a critical situation of some importance was declared, which led the bank's management to suspend the conversion of paper money (originally issued in the context of the first public loan of November 1796) and banknotes (issued by the bank) into metallic money (silver and gold). This decision was opposed by the government that called on the Bank of Lisbon to re-establish its commitments and obligations to the public, thus challenging the desired political neutrality of the bank.

This positioning clearly demonstrated the attention given by the government to the activities of the Bank of Lisbon, whose solvency and credibility were fundamental for ensuring the stability of the financial system. In fact, the government's dependence on borrowing from the Bank of Lisbon to sustain public debt, as well as the advances made on regular payments to the different sectors of public administration, justified the political warning concerning the breach of statutory obligations.

This context of a banking crisis served as an opportune pretext for the analysis and debate that José Ferreira Borges, one of the most important liberal politicians, produced on the subject (Borges 1827). For Ferreira Borges, the explanation for the crisis was not the one presented by the bank's directors, who claimed that the unfavourable balance of trade required payments abroad in bullion, thus giving rise to a run on the bank by traders who needed to carry out their transactions. This excess demand for liquidity in bullion would have given rise to cash-flow difficulties which, in turn, would have provoked fear and panic from holders of paper money, who suddenly demanded its conversion into specie.

Irrespective of whether these situations might have occurred, Ferreira Borges diminished their significance, on the one hand, by explaining that commercial crises could not be treated like simple short-term episodes, and, on the other hand, by demonstrating his knowledge of the automatic mechanisms of regulation between specie flows, price determination and the balance of trade.[12] For those who were frightened by the outflow of money, he offered the explanation that this short-term effect would generate an increase in future competitiveness due to the reduction in domestic prices that would make export products more attractive. Furthermore, he was also inspired by the doctrinal conviction that 'nothing will better prove what can be attained from the absolute freedom of trade than the study of our situation without it compared to the one we have with it' (Borges 1827, p. 28).

As far as the display of panic was concerned, Ferreira Borges considered it momentary and insignificant, compared to banking crises in other countries. In his opinion, the craving for bullion concealed the main reason for the suspension of convertibility that the bank's directors had approved, namely the excess of banknotes in circulation. He was careful to explain that the issue of banknotes by the Bank of Lisbon had been justified by the need to withdraw and replace the paper money (initially equivalent to public debt securities) in circulation. And he was also concerned about explaining that the evil was not in the issue of banknotes, which were a fundamental resource for guaranteeing monetary circulation, but rather in the excess amount that was issued.[13]

One of the appeals of this text by Ferreira Borges is the way in which he develops his argument by comparing the situation experienced by the Bank of Lisbon with the examples given by recent European banking history, namely the Bank of England and the Bank of France. Recalling that the institutional nature of the Bank of Lisbon was similar to that of the Bank of England (a private bank engaged in circulation and deposit activities, but also fulfilling the role of state lender and the agency administering the public debt), Ferreira Borges relied on the Bank of England's experience to show that the magnitude of the situation which led to the suspension of the convertibility of its notes in 1797 (and which lasted until 1821), as well as the institutional reputation of the Bank of England, were not comparable to the episode which afflicted the directors of the Bank of Lisbon in 1827.[14]

In addition to historical evidence, Ferreira Borges also relied on the theoretical arguments provided by political economists attentive to monetary phenomena and banking crises, such as Heinrich Storch, Thomas Joplin, David Buchanan, John R. McCulloch and, above all, the 'wise economist and financier David Ricardo' (Borges 1827, p. 16). Borges explicitly cited the text by Ricardo (1816) in which he presented the concept of a money market with a secure currency. Although he was not interested, nor even prepared, to discuss the analytical contents of Ricardo's proposal, Borges made typical use of the argument of authority, provided by his reference to the name of the 'wise economist and financier', to sustain his own broad vision of a money market that is not self-regulated and requires the assistance and control of a single (central) bank with a monopoly over the issue of banknotes.[15]

Finally, it is also worth noting how Ferreira Borges condemned the lack of transparency and reliable information provided by the Bank of Lisbon about its operations, calling for the need for public scrutiny, to which the bank's activities necessarily had to be subject: 'Without this publicity, the bank's credit will always be more subject to the shocks inherent in similar institutions than if their frank and open march presents the public with its regularity. It is a great mistake to suppose that in this case the mystery is the foundation of its existence' (Borges 1827, p. 14).

6.5 Concluding Remarks

Studies in banking history offer a diversity of themes and perspectives to be explored. The role of banks in the issue of banknotes and the acceleration of monetary circulation, their place within the political system, especially in the definition and implementation of monetary policies, the instrumental nature of their economic functions in raising savings and investments, their contribution to balancing the financial system, are common generic features that make banks indispensable for the stability of contemporary capitalist economies. It was only at the beginning of the nineteenth century that this indispensability began to be clearly discerned.

This contribution towards the history of the early years of the Bank of Lisbon and its immediate antecedents allows us to illustrate, as a case study, some of the more general and common characteristics of the banking history of the period under analysis. But the specificity of the Portuguese case suggests that special attention should be paid to the relationship between public debt, banking organization, political process and the formation of the public sphere.

The creation of the Bank of Lisbon took place at a particularly fertile historical moment for the explanation of how economic circumstances, the political context and the public sphere interfered with the decision-making processes that justified its establishment at the end of 1821. The history of the Bank of Lisbon is an integral part of the history of the Portuguese liberal revolution and of the dismantling of the old economic and financial system.

The analysis of failed attempts to set up banks in the early years of the nineteenth century, as well as the unsuccessful experience of the creation of the Bank of Brazil in 1808 (serving the Portuguese court residing in Rio de Janeiro between 1808 and 1821), makes it possible to understand the essential features that the Bank of Lisbon displayed: a private bank with a mandate to issue banknotes for the purposes of regularizing monetary circulation, and with the function of financing the State for current payments and for the amortization and consolidation of the public debt. Furthermore, the Bank of Lisbon also had the opportunity to develop other business areas that demonstrated, in its first years of activity, how it was possible to reconcile the shareholders' particular interests and the general interest supposedly represented by the State.

Those who, in Portugal, most actively participated in the public debate on these matters in the early decades of the nineteenth century did not reveal any particular enthusiasm for theoretical and analytical approaches, namely those relating to the monetary controversies that took place in England on the occasion of the parliamentary debates on the Bullion Report (1810–11) and on the resumption of convertibility (1819–21). Nevertheless, they bear fundamental witness to the understanding of how an enlightened public sphere, deeply aware of the importance of the state of confidence and trust in the public debt and credit system, is an indispensable condition for the success of public policies in monetary and financial issues.

Acknowledgements This is a preliminary outcome of a research project on the history of the Bank of Lisbon and the liberal revolution of 1820, conducted with the financial support of *Banco de Portugal.* I am grateful to comments made by Antoin Murphy, Nuno Palma, Jaime Reis, Ulas Sener and the editors of this book. The usual disclaimer applies.

Notes

1. Vandelli played a major role in the enlightened reform of the University of Coimbra in 1772 and the creation of the Royal Academy of Sciences in Lisbon in 1779. He was one of the most important contributors to Portuguese economic and financial thought in the late eighteenth century (Cardoso 1990).
2. Around 1800, 1 *conto* = 1 million *réis* = £275 sterling (source: Reis 1836, pp. 22–23).
3. This amount corresponds to roughly half of the total annual average revenue of the Portuguese Exchequer throughout the period from 1797 to 1803 (Costa 2016, p. 606).
4. The theme has received attention and debate in Portuguese historiography. For an overview, see Silveira (1987), Cardoso (1989), Madureira (1994), and Costa (2016).
5. This different typology applied to three bank projects sent to Sousa Coutinho, from 1801 to 1803. On the content and meaning of these bank projects, including their full transcript, see Cardoso (1997). It was also at the initiative of Sousa Coutinho that the Portuguese translation of a brief history of the Bank of England (Fortune 1801) was published in 1801, with the obvious intention of clarifying public opinion on the advantages of creating a similar institution in Portugal.
6. On the history of the Bank of Brazil, with an emphasis on the period corresponding to the Portuguese court's stay in Rio de Janeiro, see Cardoso (2010).

7. The creation of a climate of confidence, in relation to both the debt system and the monetary system, was crucial for the authors participating in this public debate. This positioning revealed the understanding of a fundamental link between the high levels of confidence on the part of the economic agents and the possibilities of economic development. For the English case, see Capie (2004).
8. *Arquivo Histórico Parlamentar, Comissão de Fazenda* (Parliamentary Historical Archives, Public Finance Committee). A selection of these petitions and memoranda was published in Pinheiro (1991).
9. Corresponding in 1821 to £1,250,000 (1 *conto* = £250).
10. The history of the Bank of Lisbon has attracted the attention of several scholars, especially from the viewpoint of studying the background of the Bank of Portugal established in 1846 after a merger between the Bank of Lisbon and the financial company *Confiança Nacional*. See Peres (1971), Reis (1996), Valério (2007), and Nunes (2018).
11. Portugal then experienced a period of some political instability, culminating in the civil war of 1832–1834, which ended in the definitive victory of the liberal forces.
12. Although there is no textual evidence confirming his reading of David Hume's *Essays*, it is clear that Borges was aware of the meaning of Hume's famous price-specie flow mechanism.
13. The Board of Directors of the Bank of Lisbon did not accept José Ferreira Borges' approach to the problem and immediately published a pamphlet showing that the issue of paper money was within the conventional limits (*Breve Ensaio* 1828).
14. On the explanation of the restriction policy pursued by the Bank of England following the decision of non-convertibility of paper money in 1797, stressing the role of its institutional reputation, see O'Brien and Palma (2019).
15. This Ricardian topic has been brilliantly addressed by Annalisa Rosselli (1999), to whom this chapter is dedicated. On Ricardo's ideas on money and banks, see also Arnon (2010), Deleplace (2013), and Diatkine (2013).

References

Arnon, A. (2010). Ricardo Versus Bosanquet. In *Monetary Theory and Policy from Hume and Smith to Wicksell: Money, Credit, and the Economy* (pp. 127–151). Cambridge and New York: Cambridge University Press.

Atack, J., & Neal, L. (Eds.). (2009). *The Origins and Development of Financial Markets and Institutions: From the Seventeenth Century to the Present.* Cambridge and New York: Cambridge University Press.

Azevedo, F. Gomes Veloso de. (1822a). *Método de evitar a introdução do falso papel-moeda, e extinguir o que atualmente circula*. Lisbon: Tipografia Rollandiana.

Azevedo, F. Gomes Veloso de. (1822b). *Indicação de projeto sobre a amortização da dívida pública, oferecido à iluminada consideração do Soberano Congresso*. Lisbon: Tipografia Rollandiana.

Borges, J. Ferreira. (1827). *Do Banco de Lisboa*. Lisbon: Tipografia de António Rodrigues Galhardo.

Breve Ensaio para servir à História do Banco de Lisboa. (1828). Lisbon: Impressão Régia.

Capie, F. (2004). Money and Economic Development in Eighteenth-Century England. In L. Prados de la Escosura (Ed.), *Exceptionalism and Industrialization: Britain and Its European Rivals, 1688–1815* (pp. 216–232). Cambridge and New York: Cambridge University Press.

Cardoso, J. L. (1989). *O Pensamento Económico em Portugal nos Finais do Século XVIII (1780–1808)*. Lisbon: Editorial Estampa.

Cardoso, J. L. (1990). Economic Thought in Late Eighteenth-Century Portugal: Physiocratic and Smithian Influences. *History of Political Economy, 22*(3), 429–441.

Cardoso, J. L. (1997). *Novos Elementos para a História Bancária de Portugal. Projetos de Banco, 1801–1803*. Lisbon: Banco de Portugal.

Cardoso, J. L. (2010). A New Contribution to the History of Banco do Brasil (1808–1829): Chronicle of a Foretold Failure. *Revista Brasileira de História, 30*(59), 165–189.

Costa, F. Dores. (2016). A 'nova dívida' - 1796–1803. A difusão de uma nova política financeira. *Análise Social, 51*(3), 598–627.

Costa, V. J. Ferreira Cardoso da. (1822). *Os bons desejos de um português, ou a sua receita para se animar a circulação paralisada, acudindo-se aos males do papel-moeda e à miséria pública* .... Lisbon: Tipografia de António Rodrigues Galhardo.

Coutinho, D. R. de Sousa. ([1797] 1993). Projeto de Banco Nacional Brigantino. In A. Diniz Silva (Ed.), *Textos Políticos, Económicos e Financeiros (1783–1811)* (Vol. 2, pp. 110–119). Lisbon: Banco de Portugal.

Deleplace, G. (2013). The Role of the Standard in Ricardo's Theory of Money. In Y. Sato & S. Takenaga (Eds.), *Ricardo on Money and Finance: A Bicentenary Reappraisal* (pp. 115–123). London and New York: Routledge.

Diatkine, S. (2013). Interest Rates, Banking Theory and Monetary Policy in Ricardo's Economics. In Y. Sato & S. Takenaga (Eds.), *Ricardo on Money and Finance: A Bicentenary Reappraisal* (pp. 124–146). London and New York: Routledge.

Fortune, T. (1801). *História Breve e Autêntica do Banco de Inglaterra* (H. J. da Costa Pereira, Trans.). Lisbon: Tipografia do Arco do Cego.

Gallard, D. M. (1821). Memória sobra a utilidade e fáceis meios para estabelecer em Lisboa um Banco Nacional com caixa de desconto anexa do papel-moeda circulante (manuscript). *Arquivo Histórico Parlamentar*, Cortes Constituintes 1821–22, Comissão de Fazenda, Cx. 117, mç 80, doc. 25.

Jordão, J. Lineu. (1821). Meio fácil natural, e proveitoso de sobreviver às fatais consequências do papel-moeda tornado e descrédito pelo estado infeliz das Finanças (manuscript). *Arquivo Histórico Parlamentar*, Cortes Constituintes 1821–22, Comissão de Fazenda, Cx. 117, mç 80, doc. 20.

Madureira, N. L. (1994). Crédito e mercados financeiros em Lisboa. *Ler História, 26*, 21–43.

Moniz, J. de Sousa. (1820). *Plano para se extinguir a dívida nacional tanto antiga como moderna, oferecido ao Supremo Governo do Reino*. Lisbon: Tipografia de Bulhões.

Monteiro, N. G. (1992). O endividamento aristocrático (1750–1832): alguns aspetos. *Análise Social, 27*(2/3), 263–283.

Neves, J. Acúrsio das. ([1814–17] 1984). *Variedades sobre objectos relativos às artes, comércio e manufacturas, consideradas segundo os princípios da economia política*. In A. Almodovar & A. Castro (Eds.), *Obras Completas de José Acúrsio das Neves* (Vol. 3). Porto: Edições Afrontamento.

Nunes, J. A. (2018). Contributo para um estudo histórico-jurídico do Banco de Lisboa. *Revista de Direito Das Sociedades, 9*(1), 79–133.

O'Brien, P., & Palma, N. (2019). Danger to the Old Lady of Threadneedle Street? The Bank Restriction Act and the Regime Shift to Paper Money, 1797–1821. *European Review of Economic History*. https://doi.org/10.1093/ereh/hez008.

Pedreira, J. M. (1996). Tratos e contratos: atividades, interesses e orientações dos investimentos dos negociantes da praça de Lisboa. *Análise Social, 31*(2/3), 355–379.

Peres, D. (1971). *História do Banco de Portugal (1821–1846)*. Lisbon: Banco de Portugal.

Pinheiro, M. (1991). *Os Portugueses e as Finanças no Dealbar do Liberalismo*. Lisbon: Edições João Sá da Costa.

Pinto, A. J. de Gouveia. (1820). *Memória em que se mostra a origem e progresso do papel-moeda em o nosso reino, e apontam os meios de verificar a sua amortização*. Lisbon: Impressão Régia.

Pohl, M. (Ed.). (1994). *Handbook on the History of European Banks*. Aldershot: Edward Elgar.

Regulamento do Banco de Lisboa precedido das leis, ofícios do Presidente da Assembleia Geral e Resolução das Cortes relativas ao mesmo Banco. (1822). Lisbon: Tipografia Maigrense.

Reis, D. L. C. Moura. (1836). *Repertório Comercial ou Novo Tratado das moedas efetivas, e conta, pesos e medidas, preço e curso de câmbios das 36 praças da Europa mais comerciantes ....* Porto: Tipografia Comercial Portuense.

Reis, J. (1996). *O Banco de Portugal. Das origens a 1914.* Lisbon: Banco de Portugal.

Ricardo, D. (1816). *Proposals for an Economical and Secure Currency.* Reprinted in P. Sraffa (Ed., with the collaboration of M. H. Dobb), *The Works and Correspondence of David Ricardo, Vol. 4: Pamphlets and Papers 1815–1823* (pp. 43–141). Cambridge: Cambridge University Press for the Royal Economic Society, 1951.

Rocha, M. M. (1996). Atividade creditícia em Lisboa (1770–1830). *Análise Social, 31*(2/3), 579–598.

Rocha, M. M. (1998). Crédito privado em Lisboa numa perspetiva comparada. *Análise Social, 33*(1), 91–115.

Roover, R. de. (1974). New Interpretations of the History of Banking. *Business, Banking and Economic Thought in Late Medieval and Early Modern Europe* (pp. 200–238). Chicago and London: University of Chicago Press.

Rosselli, A. (1999). The Origin of the Political Economy of Money. *Review of Political Economy, 11*(4), 443–454.

Silveira, L. Espinha. (1987). Aspetos da evolução das finanças públicas portuguesas nas primeiras décadas do século XIX (1800–1827). *Análise Social, 23*(3), 505–529.

Tedde de Lorca, P. (1999). Los primeros ciento cincuenta años del Banco de España (1782–1931). In P. M. Aceña & M. T. Martínez (Eds.), *El Sistema Financiero en España. Una síntesis histórica* (pp. 53–82). Granada: Universidad de Granada.

Temin, P., & Voth, H.-J. (2013). *Prometheus Shackled: Goldsmith Banks and England's Financial Revolution After 1700.* Oxford and New York: Oxford University Press.

Valério, N. (Ed.). (2007). *História do Sistema Bancário Português* (Vol. 1). Lisbon: Banco de Portugal.

Vandelli, D. ([1796–97] 1994). Alvitrismo económico e financeiro. In J. V. Serrão (Ed.), *Aritmética Política, Economia e Finanças (1770–1804)* (pp. 273–421). Lisbon: Banco de Portugal.

PART II

The Classical Perspective: Distribution of Income and Accumulation of Capital

CHAPTER 7

Considerations on the Development of Quesnay's *Tableau Économique*

Paolo Trabucchi

7.1 Introduction

In this chapter, I want to go over the main stages in the development of Quesnay's *Tableau Économique* (1758–66). My main purpose shall be to see whether a significant change in Quesnay's position ought to be identified at a certain point in this development, or whether this should be considered as a substantially continuous process of clarification and elaboration.

That (at least as far as the basic 'simple reproduction' *Tableau* is concerned) no such relevant change would have occurred, is taken very much for granted in most modern interpretations, and this view evidently underlies the reconstruction by Meek (1962) who, by referring rather freely to different versions of the *Tableau*, presented practically for the first time a demonstration of its internal consistency that was largely based on Quesnay's own explanations. But though we shall find reasons to confirm this view, we shall also find that the opposite view, which has

P. Trabucchi (✉)
Department of Economics, Roma Tre University, Rome, Italy
e-mail: paolo.trabucchi@uniroma3.it

M. C. Marcuzzo et al. (eds.), *New Perspectives on Political Economy and Its History*, Palgrave Studies in the History of Economic Thought,
https://doi.org/10.1007/978-3-030-42925-6_7

been held from time to time, is still worth discussing: particularly so (for the light it indirectly throws on the question) when the discontinuity in the development of the *Tableau* is argued on the basis of the difficulties that Quesnay would have met on account of his lack of a well-developed theory of prices.

A brief account of the different versions of the *Tableau* will help explain the plan of the chapter. The first appearance of the *Tableau économique* dates from the years 1758–59, when Quesnay circulated privately its first three 'editions'.[1] The first *public* appearance of the *Tableau* occurred then only in 1760, when it was published in Mirabeau's *Ami des hommes.* In all these cases, the *Tableau* is presented in its so-called zigzag diagrammatic formulation. This will be introduced in Sect. 7.2 by looking at the connections between the zigzag and Quesnay's previous writings on economic subjects from the years 1756–58; while the (often perplexing) explanations of the working of the zigzag given by Quesnay between 1758 and 1760 will be the object of Sect. 7.3. This will be sufficient to discard (while at the same time incorporating some of its aspects) a first version of what we might call the discontinuity view of the development of the *Tableau Économique*: namely the thesis put forward by Herlitz (1996), according to which at a certain point Quesnay would have changed his mind as to the *purpose* to be assigned to the *Tableau.*

The year 1763 saw a new appearance of the *Tableau* (again under the name of Mirabeau alone) in the *Philosophie rurale.* Here the zigzag is still present, but a new formulation, the *précis*, is introduced and extensively used. Finally, a further change in formulation from the *précis* to the *formule* will mark the *Tableau*'s last appearance in Quesnay's *Analyse* (1766). These two works will be taken into consideration in Sect. 7.4. This will lead us in Sect. 7.5 to discuss a second version of what we have called the discontinuity view of the development of the *Tableau Économique*: namely the reconstruction proposed by Gilibert (1977), which, we shall argue, though not acceptable in itself, contains elements that should not be lost in *formulating* the question of the role of a price theory in Quesnay's thought.[2]

7.2 The Zigzag and Quesnay's Early Economic Writings

In its original formulation, the *Tableau Économique* presents itself as shown in Fig. 7.1.

This is the famous zigzag showing 'the order of the regular circulation' of the 'annual revenue' (*Tableau I–III*, p. 420; KM, 3, p. 31).[3] Here the figures are those (drawn for simplicity by Quesnay for a single landowner, but in fact referred to the entire economic system) of the last zigzag in order of appearance, i.e. of the zigzag reproduced in the *Philosophie rurale*. Since the frequent changes in the absolute value of the magnitudes appearing in the different versions of the *Tableau* are of no real consequence, I shall always refer to a *Tableau* with a revenue of 2000 livres. To facilitate comparison, the same will be done when reporting

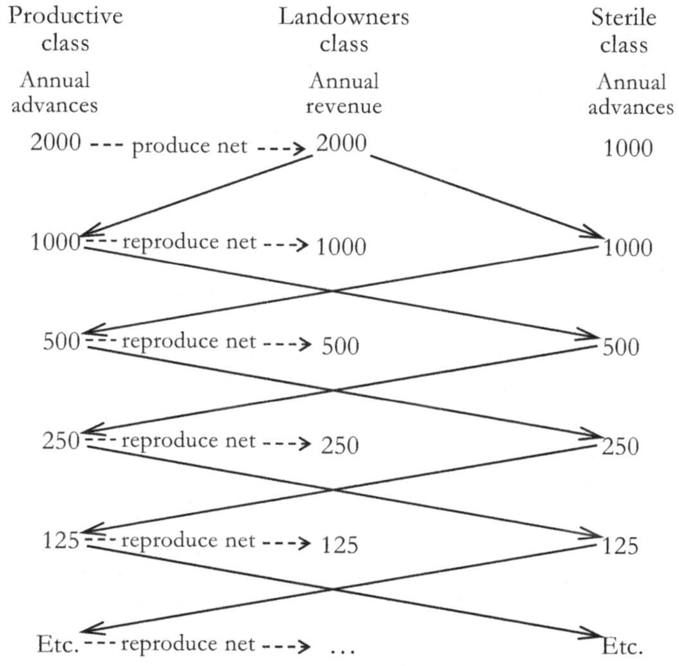

Fig. 7.1 The zigzag

passages from Quesnay's writings. (For the same reason, it will be sometimes convenient to take one half of the revenue as a single 'unit' and to measure the other magnitudes accordingly.)

The *Tableau Économique* was not Quesnay's first work as an economist. Between 1756 and 1758, Quesnay had in fact already written four entries for the *Encyclopédie* directed by Diderot and d'Alembert, which, starting from a predominantly (though by no means exclusive) agronomical concern (*Fermiers*), soon developed into the sketch of a new economic theory (*Grains*, *Hommes* and *Impôts*). It was only natural, then, that for Quesnay the most important, if only implicit, purpose of the *Tableau* was *to give evidence* to the two main conclusions he had reached in those writings: namely, on the one hand, the doctrine of the existence of a surplus (*produit net*), and, on the other, the doctrine (in his mind inextricably linked to the first) of the exclusive capacity of the agricultural sector to generate such a surplus.

This is directly reflected in the *structure* of the zigzag. This is in fact built, on the one hand, on the distinction between two classes engaged in production (appearing on the left-hand and right-hand columns) and a class that merely receives and spends a certain revenue (the landowners' class appearing in the central column), and, on the other hand, on the fact that it is only one class (the 'productive' class, which appears on the left-hand column and whose product consists of 'corn, drink, wood, livestock, raw materials for manufactured goods, etc.'; *Tableau I–III*, p. 413; KM, 3, p. 7) that, as is shown by the first horizontal line connecting the left-hand column to the central one, reproduces and hence pays the revenue, while no such payment occurs from the other 'active' class (the 'sterile' class, which appears on the right-hand column and whose product consists of 'manufactured commodities, houseroom, clothing, interest on money, servants, commercial costs, foreign produce, etc'; ibid.).

A most striking aspect of the zigzag has, however, no counterpart in Quesnay's early writings. If, as we just said, the implicit purpose of the *Tableau* was to give evidence to the doctrine of the exclusive capacity of the agricultural sector to generate a surplus, its explicit purpose was, as we have seen, to represent the 'order' of its 'regular circulation'. Now, in what has been considered the first verbal sketch of the *Tableau*, Quesnay had assumed manufactured commodities to be purchased only by landowners.[4] But this is not what we see in the *zigzag*. Indeed, the very essence of the zigzag appears to lie in the fact that, at least with respect to consumption, *all* classes *equally* divide their expenditure between agricultural and manufactured goods.[5]

There are some other aspects of the *Tableau* that stem from the *Encyclopédie* articles, but that do not emerge directly in what in the zigzag is *shown*. In contrast with the symmetrical view of the expenditure of the three classes that we have just seen, those writings presented an eminently asymmetrical view, not only of the French economy as this actually presented itself at the time, but also (and possibly to a greater extent) of the ideal state that, under the circumstances then prevailing, that economy could aim at—which is what the *Tableau* was in fact meant to portray.

Such an asymmetrical view of the economy had to do in the first place with the distribution of the population between the two 'active' classes. In an 'agricultural nation' such as France was at the time and, Quesnay thought, ought to remain in the future, this should involve a population in the agricultural sector twice as numerous as that in the manufacturing sector.

The second aspect of this asymmetrical view had to do instead with the extension to the entire agricultural sector of those modern techniques that at the time were in use only in one-third of the French agriculture, and that in Quesnay's view involved what were essentially new social relations of an eminently capitalistic nature. The contrast here is between what Quesnay called the *grande* and the *petite culture*. Now, since the time of *Fermiers*, two points had been fairly clear to Quesnay in this regard. The first was that, when compared with the *petite culture*, the *grande culture* yielded a higher net product in proportion to its advances. This happened, Quesnay argued, because in the *grande culture* advances per unit of land were higher, these higher advances being in turn needed in order to pass from a two-year rotation system of cultivation, with extensive recourse to fallow land and working animals fed by pasturage (and hence little direct expenses for the feeding of livestock, but at the same time only scarce possibility of collecting its manure to fertilize land), to a system based on a three-year rotation, with livestock fed in stables on fodder raised in one of the two cultivated portions of land (and consequently a higher availability of manure). The second point was that these higher advances could only be the result of land being cultivated by *rich farmers* and not by poor sharecroppers. It was this outright technical as well as social revolution in agriculture (and *exclusively* in agriculture) that, according to Quesnay, provided the first necessary condition for the specific quantitative ratio between the agricultural advances and the net product, which is shown at the top of the zigzag reproduced in Fig. 7.1.[6]

The second necessary condition for such a ratio had to do instead for Quesnay with what was perhaps the most radical change that in his opinion had to be introduced in the French economy: namely the unrestricted freedom to export corn. For this would have established, or at least *maintained*, the 'good price' (*bon prix*) for corn without which Quesnay believed that the net product could not rise to the level that is assumed in the *Tableau*.[7]

Summing up, we arrive then at a set of five propositions that characterize the ideal state at which, according to Quesnay, the French economy of the time could aspire—which in turn give us as many *conditions* that every *Tableau*, aimed as it was at portraying that ideal state, ought to satisfy:

(i) agriculture being the only productive activity, its annual advances reproduce a revenue in a 1:1 proportion;
(ii) all three classes equally divide their consumption between agricultural and manufactured goods;
(iii) the population in the agricultural sector is twice as numerous as the population in the manufacturing sector;
(iv) as a consequence of the general passage to the *grande culture*, half of the annual advances of the agricultural sector go to the feeding of working animals; and
(v) as a consequence of free trade in corn, corn is sold at its 'bon prix'.

7.3 From the 'First Edition' to the *Ami des hommes*

Though there can hardly be any doubt that all the conditions we have just seen were equally present to Quesnay's mind, I think it can be safely said that he only gradually became aware of the difficulties that arise in connection with the attempt at bringing them all under the same consistent representation.

To see this, let us start by giving a look at what can be gathered from a simple inspection of the zigzag. As we said before, what we see in the first place is, at the top of the diagram, the landowners receiving a rent of 2000 livres from the productive class. As we already know, the rent is spent half in the purchase of agricultural goods and half in the purchase of manufactured goods. Summing up the various exchanges that are shown in the zigzag, we then learn that the productive class buys manufactured goods for 1000 livres, while the sterile class buys agricultural goods for 1000 livres. Now, since both classes receive 2000 livres and spend only 1000 livres, they both must retain 1000 livres in money. What we see in this regard is that the productive class seems to use the sum of money it retains in order to circulate its advances within itself. If, then, we suppose by analogy that the sterile class too uses for its own internal circulation the sum of money it has retained, and if we remember that, since this class is sterile, the value of its product must equal its costs, we shall see that, as far as the distribution of the social product is concerned, the results of the zigzag should be summarized as shown in Table 7.1 (where figures are all in livres).

There are clearly at least two problems with these results. In the first place, while apparently the system needs more manufactured goods than it seems able to produce, the agricultural product does not appear to be entirely absorbed. Nor is it clear how our conditions (iii) and (iv) can both be satisfied: for the two classes appear to receive the same share of the social product, so that, if part of the product going to the agricultural sector has to be set apart for the feeding of working animals, there would seem to be no room left for an agricultural population twice as numerous as the manufacturing population.

The brief explanatory notes added by Quesnay to the first two 'editions' of the *Tableau* seem to go some way towards the solution of the *first* problem (the disproportion between the two sectors). Here we find it asserted that, of the 2000 livres that 'the process of circulation sends' to the sterile class, '[1000] livres have to be kept back for the annual advances', the remaining 1000 livres being used, in the 'first edition', for an otherwise unspecified 'expenditure' (*Tableau I*, p. 397; KM, 6, p. 3), but being expressly destined in the 'second edition' 'for wages' (*Tableau II*, p. 405; KM, 7, p. 5). Now, if the 1000 livres which are 'kept back' are

Table 7.1 Distribution of the social product as shown in the zigzag

	Productive class	*Landowners' class*	*Sterile class*
Agricultural product 4000	1000	1000	1000
Manufactured product 2000	1000	1000	1000

needed for the annual advances, ***and if these do not include wages***, then at least a relevant portion of those 1000 livres must go, not to the internal circulation of the sterile class, but to the purchase of raw materials from the agricultural sector.

A first obstacle to this ***relative*** increase in the demand for agricultural goods would be represented by the fact that this appears to be possible only at the cost of limiting the consumption of the manufacturing class to agricultural goods, thus contradicting our condition (ii). This obstacle can be however held to be removed already in the explanatory notes to the 'third edition' of the *Tableau*, where one half of the 1000 livres that the sterile class spends for its wages are 'taken for external trade' (*Tableau III*, p. 415; KM, 3, p. 9). For, if the reference here is to the exportation of agricultural products against the importation of manufactured products (and not against the importation of ***different*** agricultural products),[8] external trade, by increasing the amount of these goods that may be consumed within the economy, would allow to satisfy the need of manufactured goods for the consumption of the artisans by means of the exclusive ***domestic*** purchase of agricultural goods.[9]

But a second obstacle to the increase in the demand for agricultural products arises from the need to meet the two 'asymmetry' conditions (iii) and (iv). This emerges in Quesnay's attempt, repeated in the explanatory notes to all three 'editions', to determine the population that would be implied in the *Tableau*. Multiplying by one million the results that can be derived from the zigzag drawn for a single landowner, Quesnay states that, since 'the proprietor subsists by means of the [2000] livres that he spends' and since 'the [1000] livres distributed to each expenditure class ... can support one man in each', '[two million] of revenue can enable three million families to subsist'. To this, however, he adds that the annual advances of the productive class ('of which about one half is spent on the feeding of livestock and the other half in paying wages') would 'add [one million] that can enable another million head of families to subsist' (*Tableau I–II–III*, p. 416; KM, 3, pp. 11–13[10]). Since there is no reason why this 'addition' should not take place also for, on the one hand, that part of the agricultural advances that go to the feeding of livestock and, on the other, the manufacturing advances, according to this account we would have the situation summarized in Table 7.2, where both condition (iii) and (iv) are satisfied, but the system requires a total product in excess of what it is capable of generating.

Table 7.2 Distribution of the social product in the notes to the first three 'editions'

	Productive class	*Landowners' class*	*Sterile class*
Agricultural product 4000	1000 w 1000 f	1000	1000
Manufactured product 2000	1000 w	1000	1000

w = wages; f = fodder

Clearly, in order to solve the problems of the zigzag, external trade is not sufficient: what is needed is, in addition, an increase in the agricultural product. And it is probably for this reason that, in the 'third edition' of the *Tableau*, the agricultural product is raised from a value of 4000 livres to a value of 5000 livres (*Tableau III*, p. 413; KM, 3, p. 5). At least this is what one is led to think by a new account of the population, where, of the *five* units of which the agricultural product is now composed, one goes to 'that half of the reproduction of the annual advances which is employed in feeding livestock', while the value of all the other four would go 'for men's expenditure' (*Tableau III*, p. 417; KM, 3, pp. 19–20). The fact is, however, that the increase in the agricultural product occurs in order to make room for the *interests* on the original advances of the agricultural sector, and that these interests are in Quesnay's view nothing more than an insurance and an amortization allowance: so that they also involve an increase in costs, thus leaving the terms of our problem totally unaffected.

The definitive step towards a correct solution will have to wait until the publication of the *Tableau* in the sixth part of Mirabeau's *Ami des hommes*. Going back to the account of the distribution of an agricultural product of the value of 4000 livres, here we are told that, of the 2000 livres that remain after the consumption of the landowners and the artisans, only 'one half is consumed within the productive expenditure class by the men who cause the product to be generated', while '*the product of the other half is employed to complete the payment of the rent to the proprietor*'. As far as '[t]he fodder for livestock' is concerned, we are instead told that 'although [it is] derived from the products of the land, [it] *is not brought into the reckoning* ... since the sale of the livestock itself forms a part of the revenue' (*Ami des hommes*, p. 452; Meek 1973, p. 131; emphasis added).

It is in connection with this passage that we can discuss the thesis put forward by Herlitz (1996, p. 10) according to which there would have been 'a rupture in the development of the *Tableau économique*' connected with the ***purpose*** for which the *Tableau* itself would have been conceived. For it is Herlitz's (1996, p. 9) contention that in such a development the need to 'close the flow of money' would have shown its 'first sign' precisely in the passage from the *Ami des hommes* we have just seen. More specifically, Herlitz maintains (a) that in the first three 'editions' of the *Tableau* 'neither the manufacturers' need for raw materials, nor the farmers' need for money to pay the rent to the landlord is considered', and (b) that this would have happened because 'the purpose of the zigzag' would have been, on the one hand, 'more limited' than the one that the *Tableau* will only gradually assume later, and, on the other, more 'genuinely dynamic'.

As we have seen, 'raw materials for manufactured goods' are in fact mentioned among the products of agriculture since the 'first edition' of the *Tableau*, and, at least in the 'second edition', the purchases of agricultural goods by the sterile class which are shown in the zigzag are said to consist solely of 'wages'. This should be sufficient to say that the ***problem*** of the reintegration of the raw materials used up in the manufacturing sector belongs to the *Tableau* from its very beginning. The same can be said for the 'farmers' need for money to pay the rent' on account of statements by Quesnay such as the one pointing at a 'reproductive expenditure [which] *renews* the same revenue *from year to year*' (*Tableau III*, p. 414; KM, 3, p. 5; emphasis added) as the cornerstone on which the *Tableau* itself is built: at least if Quesnay's repeated warnings in the first 'editions' of the *Tableau* that no 'monetary fortunes' (i.e. no hoards) are formed 'to the detriment of the reproduction of the revenue' (*Tableau I–II–III*, p. 421; KM, 3, p. 31) is to make any sense.[11]

But the question is simpler than that. The fact is that the doctrine of the sterility of the manufacturing class clearly requires that the value of the purchases of agricultural goods by this class be equal to that of the manufactured products this class sells to the other two classes. Now, since no possible 'purpose' assigned by Quesnay to the *Tableau* could omit to confirm *this* doctrine, the equality between those two magnitudes must hold in any *Tableau*. But this equality implies that the receipts of the agricultural class from the manufacturing class exceed its expenditure on that class by an amount equal to the value of that part of the revenue which is not spent on agricultural products, and this is precisely what is needed in order 'to complete the payment of the rent'.

The particular 'closure' that is required by Quesnay's *Tableau* (the inflow, at the end of the year, of the entire sum of money to the agricultural sector) is in other terms nothing more than the other side of the doctrine of the exclusive productivity of agriculture. It seems therefore that Herlitz's thesis as to the existence of 'a rupture in the development of the *Tableau économique*' cannot be accepted. What has instead to be accepted from his reconstruction is the importance given to the role played in this development by the *Ami des hommes*: this being not that of setting a new purpose to the *Tableau*, but that of clearly indicating, on the one hand, the problem that affected the *Tableau* since its 'first edition' and, on the other hand, the road along which that problem *had* to be solved.

7.4 The *Philosophie rurale* and the *Analyse*

Indeed, the suggestion given in the *Ami des hommes* was clear enough. Once the consumption of manufactured goods is assured to the sterile class by external trade, the remaining problems of the *Tableau* can be solved: (a) by getting somehow rid of the need to account for the feeding of livestock in the *Tableau* itself; and (b) by allowing the productive class to sell to the sterile class the unit of agricultural product that is thus made available.

This is precisely what we find in the *Philosophie rurale*. First of all, things are made here definitely clear as regards the exact destination of the annual advances of the sterile class. Almost from the outset it is in fact stated that the annual advances of this class constitute 'a fund ... for the purchase of raw materials' (*Philosophie rurale*, p. 116). Indeed, we also find it stated that by its very nature a *Tableau* would *not be able* to account explicitly for such a purchase, so that here 'the understanding must make up for the organ [the eye]' (ibid., p. 101)—certainly an acknowledgement of the fact that, in this regard, something was after all missing in the first *Tableaux*. As for a justification of the exclusion of fodder, we must wait until the seventh chapter of the *Philosophie rurale*, where Quesnay is engaged in the detailed estimation of the value that the magnitudes involved in the *Tableau* would actually take if the ideal conditions that are there assumed prevailed in France. In the course of these lengthy calculations (ibid., pp. 259–280), we are told, on the one hand, that the breeding of livestock involves a product of a value only slightly inferior to *one unit* out of a total product of the value of *six*, and, on the other, that this unit of product would have not entered the explicit representation of the zigzag on account of the fact that the breeding of livestock *would not produce a net product*. This apparently surprising result would in turn occur only because the net product that *is* in fact generated in the profit livestock sector (*bestiaux de profit*) would be equal to the costs for working animals—this exact compensation emerging rather clearly as an absolutely ad hoc assumption introduced by Quesnay himself.[12]

We thus arrive at the situation represented in Table 7.3, where the proportion between the magnitudes involved in the *Tableau* is, on the one hand, the one presented by Quesnay at the end of Chapter VII of the *Philosophie rurale* (with the inevitable approximation involved in the nature of the calculations Quesnay presents in that chapter), and, on the other, the one that Meek (1962) applies to the *Tableau in general*.

But, as we know, the *Philosophie rurale* did not include the last version of the *Tableau*. This was to appear only in 1766 in Quesnay's *Analyse*. Now, from a diagrammatical point of view, the *Tableau* of the *Analyse* must be traced back to the diagram that, along with the original zigzag, is introduced in the *Philosophie rurale*, namely the *précis des résultats de la distribution représentée dans le tableau*, that is a 'shortened and summarily explained tableau' aimed at showing 'from a single simpler and more compact point of view' (*Philosophie rurale*, p. 133) the results of the zigzag. This presents itself as shown in Fig. 7.2.

As can be seen, the main differences with the original version of the *Tableau* are two. On the one hand, the zigzag is summarized in only two lines connecting the two 'active' classes; on the other, these lines

Table 7.3 Distribution of the social product in the *Philosophie rurale*

	Productive class	*Landowners' class*	*Sterile class*
Agricultural product	1000 w	1000	500 w
6000	1000 f		500 et
	1000 i		1000 rm
Manufactured product	1000 w	1000	
2000			

w = wages; f = fodder; i = interests; et = external trade; rm = raw materials

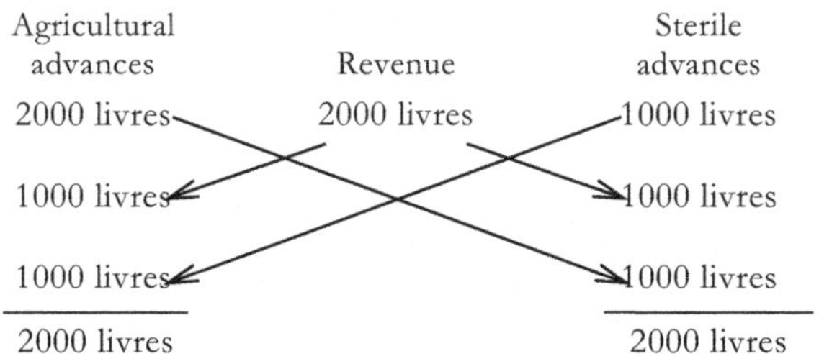

Fig. 7.2 *Précis* of the *Tableau*

start from their annual advances and not from their respective receipt of the expenditure of the revenue by the landowners. We can however disregard the latter difference, which in itself is in fact quite relevant, but only becomes so when it comes to the representation of situations where agricultural advances do not 'reproduce a hundred per cent'.[13] What from our point of view needs to be underlined is rather that the former difference—the disappearance of the zigzag—does not seem to have any *necessary* analytical consequence. For instance, it is not from the new diagram, but only from the 'summary explanation' added at the foot of the diagram, that we are informed of the fact that, in addition to the 1000 livres spent by the sterile class on agricultural goods that are explicitly shown, other 1000 livres must be counted, equal to the annual advances of this class 'used for the purchase of raw materials from the productive class' (ibid., p. 135).

It is at any rate precisely the explicit representation of the purchase of a second unit of agricultural product by the sterile class—certainly *made easier* by the more compact form of the *précis*—that characterizes the *formule* of the *Analyse*. This presents itself as shown in Fig. 7.3.

With the *précis* in mind, it is not difficult, then, to see the *Analyse* as the lineal descendent of the first zigzags *from a diagrammatical point of view*, and hence to establish a clear relation between these different versions of the *Tableau* with reference to those magnitudes that in the *Tableau* itself are explicitly *shown*. Things turn out to be less clear, however, when it comes to those magnitudes that, as we know, receive no such explicit representation. It is true that on this point Quesnay warns the reader (*Analyse*, p. 537; Meek 1962, p. 162) that, 'if a more detailed examination of the distribution of a nation's expenditure' is desired, this

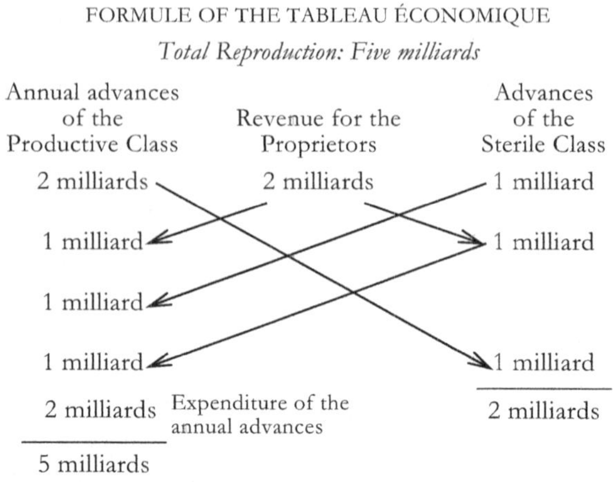

Fig. 7.3 *Formule* of the *Tableau*

'will be found in Chapter VII of the *Philosophie rurale*'. In this way, we are for example explicitly allowed by Quesnay to consider for the *Analyse* as well a *sixth* unit of agricultural product 'for the fodder of the labouring animals employed in cultivation'.

But on another point the *Analyse* raises a question. As we have seen, in the seventh chapter of the *Philosophie rurale* reference was still made to the exportation of agricultural goods for a value equal to half the wages of the artisans. Now, instead, *while for the first time no reference is made to the composition of the consumption of the 'active' classes*, it is clearly stated that 'it has been assumed that the nation trades only with itself' (*Analyse*, p. 537; Meek 1962, p. 162).

7.5 The *Tableau* and the Sterility of the Artisans

The question then is whether the exclusion of external trade that we find in the *Analyse* can be viewed as a simplification aimed at presenting the results of the *Tableau* in a more readily comprehensible and manageable form, which is the idea we find in Meek (1962, p. 282), or whether it reflects a deeper change in Quesnay's position.

To discuss this point, we must now turn to a second version of the discontinuity view of the development of the *Tableau*: namely the thesis put forward, in his first reconstruction of the development of the *Tableau*, by Gilibert (1977, pp. 43–49). In essence, the problem for Gilibert would have been that, precisely because thanks to external trade in the first versions of the *Tableaux* manufactured goods are included among the inputs of the manufacturing sector, artisans could not there be considered as mere 'transformers of agricultural produce' (ibid., p. 43), this being the 'substantial' notion of sterility that would have been 'preferred by the Physiocrats' (ibid.). According to Gilibert, it would have been to avoid *this* problem that Quesnay would have progressively modified the *Tableau*, the final outcome of this process being the *Analyse*, where the exclusion of external trade would simply reflect the abandonment of the assumption that artisans consume both agricultural and manufactured goods.

On Gilibert's reconstruction, the crucial step in the process would have occurred, however, already in the *Philosophie rurale*. Here, on the one hand, the abandonment of the zigzag in favour of the *précis* would have been the inevitable consequence of the abandonment of the assumption allowing for the consumption of manufactured goods by the artisans, and, on the other, the increase in the agricultural product from four to five units would have been there to meet the additional demand for such goods that would have followed from the abandonment of that assumption.

This, however, cannot be true, and not only because, as we know, the increase in the agricultural product occurred already in the 'third edition' of the *Tableau*, that is four years before the *Philosophie rurale*. The fact is that, as we have seen in particular by looking at the *Ami des hommes*, the internal consistency of the original *Tableau* requires that, within the economy, the sterile class *purchases* agricultural goods for a value equal to the purchase of manufactured goods by the other two classes, *whether or not* these agricultural goods are all directly consumed by this class. No additional demand for agricultural goods can then follow from a change in an assumption concerning exclusively the *consumption* of the sterile class.

The idea that the need to reaffirm the sterility of the artisans would have determined a discontinuity in the development of the *Tableau* cannot, therefore, be accepted. This does not mean, however, that it did not play *any* role in that development.

This is indeed the impression one gathers from Gilibert (2007). Here external trade is never given a role in the *Tableau*. As a consequence, the *Tableau* is said to have been internally inconsistent up to 'the last version (1763) of the *Tableau à zigzag*' (Gilibert 2007, p. 33), that is up to the *Philosophie rurale*. The correction consisting in allowing the sterile class to purchase two units of agricultural produce is said then to occur only in the *Analyse* and to be one and the same thing with Quesnay's abandonment of his original view admitting the consumption of manufactured goods by the sterile class. Thus the fundamental continuity in the development of the *Tableau* is reaffirmed, with the stress on the 'purely transformative (i.e. sterile) nature of manufacture' appearing merely as an 'agreeable side-effect' (ibid.).

This result depends, however, on that identification between the consumption of the manufacturing class and its domestic purchases that already appeared in Gilibert's first reconstruction. But once this identification is dropped (as must be done in interpreting the *Tableau* up to the *Philosophie rurale*) and once as a consequence the correction consisting in allowing the sterile class to purchase two units of agricultural produce is said to have occurred well before the *Analyse*, a conclusion on the role of the question of the sterility of the artisans somehow closer to the spirit of Gilibert's first reconstruction can, I think, be proposed.

In order to do this, we have to go back to the question of the possible implications of the change from the zigzag to the *précis*. Now, save for the fact that the purchase of the second unit of agricultural product by the sterile class is shown only in the *formule*, what can be said in general is that no necessary connection can be established between the diagrammatic form of the *Tableau* and the assumption on the composition of the consumption of the manufacturing class. That being said, it is true that the zigzag, (a) by showing, at each new step in the geometrical progression, what appear to be single acts of self-consumption by the agricultural class, and (b) by giving the same representation for the sterile class, strongly suggests that this class consumes the manufactured goods it has produced. With the disappearance of the zigzag, though not contradicting our condition (ii), the *précis* becomes then relatively *more free* not to refer to it. As a consequence, it is particularly well suited to represent situations in which not only the sterile class limits its *domestic purchases* to agricultural goods (which is what must happen in any *Tableau*), but in which this class *consumes* only such goods.[14]

The question then is what need Quesnay may have had to lend credit, at least to a certain extent, to this 'restrictive' interpretation of the *précis* and *hence* of the *formule* of the *Analyse*. And to do this we must return to Gilibert's observation according to which the notion of sterility as the mere transforming role attributed to the manufacturing class was the one 'preferred by the Physiocrats'.

The reason for this preference can be clarified by a remarkable passage, which is likewise quoted by Gilibert, but is generally overlooked. The passage occurs in the letter prefacing an article with which Quesnay intervened *in incognito* in the debate on the sterility of manufactures. What is important from our point of view is that here Quesnay declares in advance the provisional nature of his contribution, arguing that 'in order to put an end to the controversy' it would be 'indispensable' to compose an '*Essay on prices*' which, on the other hand, 'cannot but be meditated for a long time before it is published' (*Réponse au Mémoire de M.H. sur les avantages de l'industrie et du commerce*, p. 836; my translation).

The passage seems to show an acute awareness both of the need of a price theory in order to substantiate the notion of surplus, and of the enormous difficulties posed by the construction of such a theory. In the light of this awareness, it does not seem too unlikely, then, that Quesnay, who had initially conceived the *précis* as a mere simplified presentation of the zigzag, may have looked at its 'restrictive' interpretation (where the most urgent question of the sterility of the artisans was apparently directly solved by means of the 'substantial' notion of sterility) as a useful temporary retreat. The construction of a theory of prices, however, proved to be much harder than Quesnay had suspected, and the temporary retreat ended up being definitive: so that it can be said that the need to reaffirm the sterility of the artisans, while not directly determining the development of the *Tableau*, determined its point of arrest.

It is this particular reformulation of the thesis put forward by Gilibert in 1977 that, if confirmed, should, I think, be kept in mind when formulating the question of Quesnay's price theory. For what we know from Gilibert's own works as well as from the works by Cartelier from the 1970s is that there is a price theory that can be held to be *implicit* in the *Tableau*.[15] This theory, however, is arrived at by looking at the doctrine of the exclusive productivity of agriculture as that particular rule for the distribution of the net product that would distinguish Quesnay's theory among the class of 'classical system[s] of price' (Cartelier 1976, p. 57; 2015, p. 808). It seems then that it would not be without interest to find out that Quesnay may have looked at the 'substantial' notion of the sterility of the manufacturing sector—which in effect should have provided a proof of the exclusive productivity of agriculture—as a temporary alternative to a price theory, and not as an essential component of such a theory. And not because this should suggest to go back to the idea that Quesnay had no theory of prices, or that the classical theory implicit in the *Tableau* is irrelevant; but because it suggests the existence in this regard of a number of alternatives between which Quesnay *struggled*: a fact that may be important not only to place Quesnay exactly in the history of economic thought, but also, by this means, to reach a better understanding of the internal logic of a theory of prices based on the notion of a social surplus.

Notes

1. For the term 'edition', humorously used by Quesnay himself, and more in general for the complex 'private history of the *Tableau Économique*', see Meek (1972).
2. A different reconstruction, discussed in Sect. 7.5, is offered in Gilibert (2007).
3. All references to Quesnay's writings will be given as follows: (i) the title of the work, (ii) the page reference to Quesnay (2005), save in the case of the *Philosophie rurale*, where the page reference is to Mirabeau and Quesnay ([1763] 2014); (iii) the English translation used (when available) and (iv) the page reference to the English translation (in this case, KM stands for Kuczynski and Meek 1972, where pagination is given indicating the section and the page number internal to the section). In the case of the same passage occurring in different 'editions' of the *Tableau*, only the page reference to the last 'edition' is given.
4. The relevant passage is in Quesnay (2005, p. 288). See the comment in Gilibert (2007, p. 30).
5. The point is underlined by Quesnay in a letter to Mirabeau (*Dossier Correspondance*, pp. 1182–1183).
6. For the debate triggered by Quesnay's distinction between *petite* and *grande culture*, see Groenewegen (1983). On the interweaving of the strictly technical and the more generally social elements involved in the distinction, see also Serrano and Mazat (2017).
7. For a discussion of the debates on Quesnay's price theory see van den Berg (2004).
8. Indeed, here Quesnay explicitly states that '[a]n agricultural nation should facilitate an active external trade in raw produce, by means of a passive external trade in manufactured commodities' (*Tableau III*, p. 421; KM, 3, p. 56).

9. This possibility was first pointed out by Meek (1962, pp. 282–283) who applied it to the *Tableau* in all its versions. As we shall see in Sect. 7.5, it is possible to doubt that this is correct for the last version of the *Tableau*. Naturally, foreign trade would not be necessary to supply the manufacturing class with manufactured goods if the product of this class could rise above the 2000 livres that are required for the consumption of the other two classes. But this would go against Quesnay's statement to the effect that those 2000 livres are equal to the sum of the annual advances and the wages of the manufacturing class (*Tableau III*, p. 417; KM, 3, p. 11). Besides, an increase in the manufactured product would be compatible with our condition (iii) only by increasing either the per capita income of the sterile class, or the ratio of raw materials to wages in the production of manufactured goods, and neither appear to have a sufficient textual basis.
10. The reference to 'the feeding of livestock' appears only in the 'third edition'.
11. Herlitz (1996, p. 9) maintains that in the zigzag 'revenue is reproduced in kind, not repaid in money', presumably on the ground that the horizontal lines in the zigzag refer to production and reproduction of the revenue. Since the revenue is spent in money, this however is clearly unacceptable.
12. See the passage (*Philosophie rurale*, p. 263) where the same relation between the net product related to the profit livestock and the costs for working animals is said to hold in that part of agriculture that is essentially related to corn-growing and in the remaining part which, as far as animal breeding is concerned, 'is largely destined for the profit livestock', 'in order for the product of these animals [...] to compensate for the same costs'.
13. See Mirabeau and Quesnay ([1763] 2014, pp. 390–393). The point is made by Pressman (1994, pp. 31–32).
14. For an instance of this use of the condensed formulation of the *Tableau*, see the *précis* appearing in Mirabeau and Quesnay ([1763] 2014, p. 399), where the entire expenditure of the sterile class above its purchases for raw materials is referred to as the expenditure 'to feed itself'.
15. See Gilibert (1972, 1977), and Cartelier (1976). For a recent presentation, see Cartelier (2015).

References

Cartelier, J. (1976). *Surproduit et reproduction*. Grenoble: Maspéro et Presses Universitaires de Grenoble.

Cartelier, J. (2015). Early Classics and Quesnay After Sraffa: A Suggested Interpretation. *Cambridge Journal of Economics, 39*(3), 807–824.

Gilibert, G. (1972). Una formulazione algebrica del *Tableau économique*. *Studi Economici, 27,* 1–11.
Gilibert, G. (1977). *Quesnay. La costruzione della 'macchina della prosperità'*. Milano: Etas libri.
Gilibert, G. (2007). From Cantillon to Quesnay: Birth and Evolution of the *Tableau Économique*. *Annali Della Fondazione Giangiacomo Feltrinelli, 43*(1), 21–34.
Groenewegen, P. D. (1983). *Quesnay: Farmers, 1756 and Turgot: Sur la Grande et la Petite Culture, 1766*. Sydney: Department of Economics, University of Sidney.
Herlitz, L. (1996). From Spending and Reproduction to Circuit Flow and Equilibrium: The Two Conceptions of *Tableau économique*. *European Journal for the History of Economic Thought, 3*(1), 1–20.
Kuczynski, M., & Meek, R. L. (Eds.). (1972). *Quesnay's Tableau économique*. London: Macmillan.
Meek, R. L. (1962). *The Economics of Physiocracy: Essays and Translations*. London: George Allen & Unwin.
Meek, R. L. (1972). Introduction. In M. Kuczynski & R. L. Meek (Eds.), *Quesnay's Tableau économique*. London: Macmillan.
Meek, R. L. (Ed.). (1973). *Precursors of Adam Smith*. London: Dent.
Mirabeau, V. R., & Quesnay, F. ([1763] 2014). *Philosophie rurale* (R. Dupuy & P. Le Masne, Eds.). Geneva: Slatkine Érudition.
Pressman, S. (1994). *Quesnay's Tableau économique. A Critique and Reassessment*. Fairfield: A.M. Kelley.
Quesnay, F. (2005). *Œuvres économiques complètes et autres textes* (2 Vols., C. Théré, C. Loïc, & J.-C. Perrot, Eds.). Paris: INED.
Serrano, F., & Mazat, N. (2017). Quesnay and the Analysis of Surplus in the Capitalist Agriculture. *Contributions to Political Economy, 36,* 81–102.
Van den Berg, R. (2004). 'Un état de pleine concurrence': Old and New Controversies About the Physiocratic Theory of Value. *Économies et Sociétés, 35,* 1431–1457.

CHAPTER 8

Classical Roots of the Criticisms of John Stuart Mill's Wage-Fund Theory

Antonella Stirati

8.1 Introduction

The purpose of this contribution is to discuss the analytical contents of the criticisms levelled at J.S. Mill's theory of the wage fund and accepted by him in his famous recantation of 1869. I will therefore disregard other important aspects of that debate, of a historical-political nature, particularly in relation to the controversy on the role and legitimacy of the trade unions.

The reasons for the interest in the analytical issues that emerged in the criticisms of the wage-fund theory lie in the fact that they take up and revive many aspects of Smith's approach to wage determination. In so doing, they show its inconsistency with the wage-fund theory presented by Mill; that is, they show the existence of a conflict between Smith's views, representative of the theory of wages proper to the classical political economy (from Petty to Ricardo) and the subsequently established theory of the wage fund. The arguments advanced by the

A. Stirati (✉)
Roma Tre University, Rome, Italy
e-mail: antonella.stirati@uniroma3.it

M. C. Marcuzzo et al. (eds.), *New Perspectives on Political Economy and Its History*, Palgrave Studies in the History of Economic Thought,
https://doi.org/10.1007/978-3-030-42925-6_8

critics support the interpretation of classical political economy, which refutes the wage-fund theory in contributions by major figures of the classical period such as Smith and Ricardo, and underlines the different analytical structure of their approach compared to concepts developed at a later stage in the history of economics—an interpretation that I have labelled elsewhere the 'alternative interpretation' (Stirati 2011). Thus, the arguments presented in this chapter link-up with the controversy over the interpretation of Ricardo's wage theory and by implication over the classical approach more generally: an important aspect of the controversy was assessment of the similarities and differences between the classical approach to income distribution and neoclassical supply and demand determination (for surveys of this controversy, see Rosselli 1985; Stirati 1995, 2011). Scholars taking a view of the entire classical period as characterized by the wage-fund theory find quite marked similarities with the neoclassical approach, since both neoclassical theory and wage-fund theory involve full employment, and no substantial role for institutional and social forces in the determination of wages. By contrast, according to the 'alternative interpretation', a central feature of the *distinct* character of the classical approach *vis à vis* subsequent developments lies precisely in the way in which the real wage was explained, and particularly in the absence of a systematic decreasing relationship between real wage and employment, such as will be maintained later on in the wage-fund theory and (based on different premises) in marginalist theory. Indeed, in Stirati (2011), as well as in earlier contributions (Stirati 1994), it is stressed that in order to correctly interpret the distinctive features of the classical wage theory, as opposed to the wage-fund theory and neoclassical theory, it is of paramount importance that the expression 'demand for labour' in the writings of the classical economists be understood as a given quantity of labour (i.e. the employment level). Interestingly enough, this theme is also prominent in the controversy over the wage-fund theory.

Also of interest is the fact that the absence of the notion of an inverse relationship between employment and wage levels and of the associated tendency towards full employment is accompanied both in the Classics and in the critics of the wage-fund theory by a view of competition on the labour market as *necessarily* limited by conventional elements, and the role of social norms and institutions such as workers' and employers' associations as an integral and natural part of the wage-setting process.

In the critical discussion of the wage-fund theory, some peculiarities of the labour market as compared to other commodity markets appear as a direct and necessary consequence of the absence of supply-side adjustment mechanisms comparable to those existing for produced commodities, since the adjustment of labour supply to the employment level is regarded as taking place through a slow and to some extent uncertain demographic process. At the same time, in the labour market, like other commodity markets, there is no decreasing demand curve with respect to price which could adjust demand to existing supply. Consequently, in the labour market, the gap between the employment level and labour supply (working-age population) may be large and persistent.

The theory of the wage fund proposed by major figures such as McCulloch, Senior and J.S. Mill in the decades following Ricardo's death can therefore be regarded as one of the symptoms of the progressive decline of the Ricardian approach (Meek 1950). Indeed, the reactions of the critics show that the wage-fund theory appeared to contemporaries as introducing a new approach and novel definitions. With the wage-fund theory, concepts appear for the first time that will then play—albeit with different analytical foundations—a central role in the subsequently developed marginalist theory, and in particular the notion of a systematic decreasing relationship between employment and real wages and the associated tendency to full employment of labour in the presence of real-wage flexibility. When such ideas emerged, they provoked reactions among some contemporaries based on the arguments that closely reflect the approach found in Adam Smith and in the classical tradition in general, showing on the one hand that the latter had distinct features, and on the other that it had not yet completely lost its influence.

In the following sections, I will first present a summary of Smith's wage theory, regarded as representative of the classical tradition (Sect. 8.2), and of Mill's wage-fund theory (Sect. 8.3), in order to contextualize the subsequent discussion of the criticisms to Mill put forward by Longe and Thornton (Sect. 8.4).

8.2 The Explanation of the Natural Wage in Smith

Here, I will summarize some aspects of the interpretation of Smith's theory of wages that has been supported in other works (Stirati 1994, 1995)—a theory that can be considered representative of the dominant view in the classical period, before Ricardo's death. Only afterwards did the theory of the wage fund become prevalent (Stirati 1999).

In the *Wealth of Nations*, Smith indicates three main factors in determining wages: (i) the workers' usual living standards, which determine the minimum subsistence consumption, seen as that wage 'below which it is impossible to reduce, for any considerable time, the ordinary wages even of the lowest species of labour' (Smith [1776] 1976), hereafter *WN*, I.viii.14); (ii) the advantage employers have in setting wages; and (iii) the relative rates of growth of population and capital. This has often led to interpreting Smith as proposing three or more different theories of wage determination, and some scholars have argued that all of these explanations are simultaneously present in the *Wealth of Nations*, although they are logically inconsistent with each other (Blaug 1985, p. 44; Cannan 1893, pp. 235, 379–383; Hollander 1973, pp. 185–186; Knight [1956] 1963, pp. 80–83; Schumpeter [1954] 1982, pp. 268–269). The three different explanations associated with the argument listed have been interpreted respectively as: (i) a theory of subsistence wages in which subsistence is a 'social datum' (Schumpeter [1954] 1982, p. 665); (ii) an explanation based on monopsony in which wages are arbitrarily fixed by employers (Knight [1956] 1963, p. 81; Hollander 1973, p. 185); and (iii) the wage-fund theory, on the basis of which the evolution of wages over time depends on the respective growth rates of population and capital (Cannan 1893, pp. 235–237; Skinner 1979, pp. 164–166, among several others).

However, the three factors affecting wages pointed out by Smith are part of a fully consistent explanation of natural wages, which—unlike the wage-fund theory and the subsequent marginalist theory—is not based on the existence of a decreasing systematic relationship between wages and employment but attributes a central role to the bargaining position of the parties. The apparent contradictions between Smith's 'three theories' are no longer such once the demand for labour to which he often refers is interpreted as a given quantity—that is, a given number of employed workers, determined by the existing level and composition of production and the techniques in use—or in other words, by the stage reached by accumulation. The demand for labour, by analogy with the demand for a commodity or 'effectual demand', is a given quantity (of labour, or of the commodity) and not a function of the price, nor a given 'fund' destined to the employment of labour. Therefore, there is no spontaneous tendency of the system towards full employment. On this basis, the role of population growth and accumulation in influencing wage developments can clearly be seen not to clash with other parts of Smith's analysis. The tendency of the natural wage towards the minimum subsistence is caused by the bargaining advantage of employers in the conflict over income distribution; this advantage in turn is accounted for by several factors: the urgency of workers' need to find employment—since they have nothing to live on if they are not working—a need much stronger than that of employers to obtain their services (*WN*, I.viii.12); institutional circumstances, such as the laws prohibiting workers' 'combinations' (i.e. collective organizations); and also 'the constant scarcity of employment' that exists in declining or stagnant economies, where 'the hands ... multiply beyond their employment' (*WN*, I.viii.24), which forces workers to compete with each other accepting lower wages. But on the other hand, in fast-growing economies, employment is growing faster than the population, and accordingly, there is a persistent 'scarcity of hands' that will cause employers to compete with each other, so that the natural wage will be higher than the subsistence minimum (*WN*, I.viii.17). The relative growth of population and capital in Smith's theory therefore influences the level of the normal or natural wage because the proportion between employment (in turn determined by the pace of economic growth) and population is an important factor affecting the bargaining power of the parties.

Like other classical economists, Smith believed that the existence of large reserves of unemployed labour would tend to push the natural wage to its subsistence minimum level, but not below it, and that situations of scarcity of hands would by contrast help to fix the natural wage at a higher level, but not determine its indefinite growth. The writings of Smith and other classical economists suggest that the same social norms and conventions that define the subsistence minimum also have a role in setting limits to wage variations and in preventing wages from falling below that minimum. In Smith (as in other classical economists), the pursuit of the individual interest appears limited by the norms and conventions prevailing in society or in specific social groups. These do not prevent or substitute competition but define the boundaries within which it normally operates.[1]

In short, therefore, in the classical approach, the normal or natural wage depends on the (historically determined) subsistence consumption of the workers and their bargaining strength *vis-à-vis* the employers. The latter in turn depends on social and institutional factors as well as more strictly economic factors, among which importance is given to labour market conditions, gauged by the ratio between employment and population (i.e. in modern terms, the employment rate)—a measure of what in modern terms would be indicated as 'labour market slack'.

Since the classical approach is quite different from the picture suggested by present-day economic analysis framed in terms of neoclassical supply and demand functions, it has often been and is still being misinterpreted. In order to make the classical framework described above as clear as possible, I propose below a formal and simplified summary, to be then compared with the wage-fund theory.

In a given period, understood as a classical and Marshallian 'long-period' framework of analysis, i.e. ignoring short-term transitory disturbances as well as the 'secular' evolution of the variables taken as the initial data (Marshall [1890] 1920, pp. 314–315), and hence while taking as given the acquired consumption habits and the associated historically and socially defined subsistence, the stage reached by accumulation and population size:

$$w_n = su + B(Z; EMP/POP) \tag{8.1}$$

$$POP = POP_0 \tag{8.2}$$

$$EMP = SP_0/q_0 \tag{8.3}$$

$$WF_{expost} = w_n * EMP \tag{8.4}$$

where

w_n is the natural (normal) wage expressed by the Classics in nominal terms, but under the assumption of a constant value of money, i.e. in modern language, a given general price level. Hence, it measures the natural wage in real terms, with the caveat, however, that increases in the natural price of wage-goods ('corn') relative to the general price level would cause the natural wage in money to increase so as to leave the purchasing power of the natural wage in terms of wage-goods unchanged.

su is the historically and socially defined subsistence minimum;

B is a non-negative function;

Z indicates the socio-institutional set-up affecting the bargaining position of workers, particularly the division between labour and ownership of the means of production, the rules concerning workers 'combinations' and collective actions, the poverty of the workers and lack of means to subsist if unemployed. Clearly, these can hardly be measured numerically (although nowadays there exist numerical indexes constructed to measure labour protection institutions). The variable is, however, there to remind us of the importance of such factors in affecting the wage level in the classical approach;

EMP is the employment level measured in heads;

POP is the population size (the labour force) measured in heads, and POP_0 indicates that the size of population is given;

SP_0 is the given social product which, like wages, may also be regarded as measured in nominal terms but under the assumption of a given general price level;

q_0 is social product per worker, also assumed as given;

WF_{expost} is the wage fund, in this framework merely an accounting *ex post* variable equal to the wage rate times the employment level. The actual wage rate will tend to be at or around the natural level in the long-period framework adopted here, although it may temporarily differ from it owing to transitory events, such as bad harvests causing short-term alterations in prices, employment and wages;

EMP/POP is the ratio of employment to the population (labour force). While the existing labour force represents an upper limit to total employment, the classical authors regarded the existence of an excess of population over available jobs as a normal feature of the economic system, and thus the ratio as generally lower than one, its size affecting the bargaining position of the workers. Only over a longer time span (the 'secular' evolution in Marshallian terms), according to the classical economists, is there the possibility that changes in the natural wage and in the employment level *may* affect population growth, gradually bringing it *roughly* in line with employment.

8.3 The Theory of the Wage Fund in Mill

In the wage-fund theory, the full employment equilibrium wage is determined as the ratio of a *given* 'wage fund' to the entire labour supply, identified with the working-age population (Mill [1848] 1987, pp. 343–344; McCulloch [1864] 1965, pp. 316–317; Senior [1836] 1965, p. 153). Competition between workers and employers is seen as the force ensuring that 'If the supply [of labour] is in excess of what capital can at present employ, wages must fall. If the labourers are all employed, and there is a surplus of capital still unused, wages will rise' (Mill [1869] 1967, p. 643; also [1848] 1987, p. 362). Since the wage fund is given *ex ante* (i.e. independently of the wage level and the numbers employed), there is a decreasing relationship between wage and employment levels of elasticity equal to one: 'In this doctrine it is by implication affirmed, that the demand for labour not only increases with the cheapness, but increases in exact proportion to it, the same aggregate sum being paid for labour whatever its price may be' (Mill [1869] 1967, pp. 643–644).

Changes in the equilibrium wage over time will result from changes in the proportion between population and the wage fund. Any attempt to raise the normal level of wages that does not change the ratio of the population to the wage fund is doomed to failure (Mill [1848] 1987, pp. 344, 350, 360–362; see also McCulloch [1864] 1965, pp. 317, 320). It is precisely on this basis that Mill, even before his recantation, did not oppose the legalization of trade unions, since he maintained that they could not alter the outcome of the forces of competition.

Mill saw the 'wage fund' as consisting of capital, i.e. savings, intended for the remuneration of workers as decided by the capitalists: 'The distinction … between Capital and Not-capital does not lie in the kind of commodities, but in the mind of the capitalist … all property, however ill adapted in itself for the use of labourers, is a part of capital so soon as it, or the value received from it, is set apart for productive reinvestment' (Mill [1848] 1987, p. 56).

Once there has been an increase in the capital allocated to the employment of labour, it is possible that the corresponding wage-goods may not *immediately* be available and that the total consumption of the workers cannot therefore *immediately* increase, but this is a short-run, transitory phase, since: 'the consequence of this change in the demand for commodities, occasioned by the change in expenditure of capitalists from unproductive to productive, is that next year more food will be produced' (Mill [1848] 1987, p. 56).

Thus, in Mill's theory, it is very clearly stated that the physical composition of the national product is only 'a temporary accident' (ibid.) and can be quickly modified to adjust to the composition of the demand—the size of the wage fund therefore depends solely on the capitalists' decisions on its use.

Mill's theory of the wage fund is therefore not based on a notion of the wage fund as given in physical terms, i.e. as a set of goods that can be used for the subsistence of workers, the quantity of which cannot be modified until a new production cycle is completed, but is identified with that part of 'income and wealth' that capitalists intend to allocate to the acquisition of labour. This contrasts with a—frequently postulated—different characterization of the theory of the wage fund as linked to a concept of 'advances' to employees of goods that must have already been produced in the previous production cycle—the agricultural 'year' (see, e.g., Blaug 1985, pp. 44–45). This notion of 'advances' in physical form is indeed sometimes found in other authors, particularly McCulloch. However, it is Mill's exposition that can be regarded as 'canonical' because it shows greater internal coherence than McCulloch's. The latter, in fact, when he applies the theory, comes to conclusions that are the same as Mill's, and do not appear to be consistent with a conception of the 'wage fund' as a given quantity of wage-goods ('corn') already produced and usable only for the sustenance of the workers. For example, like Mill, he believes that an increase in the relative price of corn *vis-à-vis* other commodities implies, all other things being equal, a decrease in real wages (i.e. it implies a reduction in the purchasing power of money wages in terms of wage-goods, with the latter largely made up of corn)—a conclusion that would *not* apply were the wage fund conceived as a *given* amount of corn already available for workers' consumption.[2] There are also passages in McCulloch, as well as, even more explicitly, in Senior, which clearly point to the wage fund as the result of decisions by the capitalists concerning the amount of savings and their destination: 'it is ... on the amount of its capital applicable to the employment of labour, and on the *disposition* of the owners of capital so to apply it, that the capacity of a country to support work-people at any given period, and the amount of their wages, wholly depend' (McCulloch [1864] 1965, p. 316); 'all savings go to swell, directly or indirectly, the amount of the fund for the employment of labour' (ibid., p. 318; on this point see also Senior [1836] 1965, pp. 189–193).

This conception of the wage fund as an amount of savings implies that the period during which the wage fund can be assumed as given is the same for which circulating capital in general can be taken as a datum. Although net savings can continually alter such amount, it is generally reasonable to assume that the yearly change is relatively small and can therefore be overlooked. In view of this, ignoring the accumulation (or decline) of the capital stock is a characteristic of what Marshall defined as long-period analysis, in which the initial data of the theory (including precisely the amount of capital and gross savings) are assumed unchanged, while transitory factors causing short-run alterations are neglected in order to focus on the underlying major tendencies of the economic system (Marshall [1890] 1920, pp. 314–315). In this sense, therefore, again in contrast to the characterizations frequently made of it, the theory of the wage fund is *not* a short-run theory but stands as an explanation of the *normal* level of the wage rate (i.e. what Smith had called 'natural wage').

To sum up, below is a formal representation of the wage-fund theory.

In a given period, i.e. assuming both population size and the wage fund as given, we have:

$$WF_{exante} = WF_0 \tag{8.5}$$

$$w_n = WF_0/POP \tag{8.6}$$

$$POP = POP_0 \tag{8.7}$$

Hence, implicit in the above:

$$EMP = EMP(w) = WF_0\ /w \tag{8.8}$$

and

$$EMP(w_n) = WF_0\ /w_n = POP_0 \tag{8.9}$$

where the symbols have the same meaning as before but now the wage fund WF_{exante} is an *ex ante* given variable, meaning that it determines the natural wage (given population) rather than being determined by it as in the earlier approach. The equilibrium natural or normal wage w_n is equal to the ratio between the given wage fund and the given labour supply (population); when it prevails, the economy is at full employment (Eq. 8.9). $EMP(w)$ indicates that employment is a function of the wage rate (of elasticity equal to one) and the normal wage rate w_n is the rate that brings the employment level into equilibrium with the given population. Competition among the workers (if w is higher than w_n and hence there is unemployment) or among the employers (if w is lower than w_n and hence employers demand more workers than are available) is what ensures that the actual wage w will tend towards w_n and employment will tend to be equal to population. Equations (8.8) and (8.9) are actually implied by (8.6), but it may be useful to restate them in explicit form. Note that employment is a decreasing function of the wage rate only because of the assumption that the wage fund is given *ex ante* (i.e. it is given *before* the wage rate and employment level determination).

As can be seen by comparison with the above summary of Smith's classical approach, in contrast to the latter, here the wage fund is an *ex ante* given variable rather than an *ex post* merely accounting magnitude, employment is a decreasing function of the wage rate while it was independent of it in Smith, and the normal wage rate is a full employment equilibrium wage, in contrast to a classical framework where unemployment was regarded as quite a common feature of market economies and one that would contribute to the bargaining weakness of the workers *vis-à-vis* the employers.

8.4 Criticisms from Longe and Thornton and Accepted by John Stuart Mill

Here, we take only the central and theoretical elements put forward by Longe in 1866 and Thornton in 1869 that were taken up and accepted by Mill in 1869.[3] These arguments concern two fundamental points: the meaning of 'demand for labour' and the legitimacy of considering the wage fund as given before and independently of real-wage determination. Longe and Thornton then advance, in a way that logically follows from those criticisms, some considerations on the forces that determine the normal wage that are strongly reminiscent of Smith's analysis as described above.

8.4.1 The Meaning of 'Demand' for Labour

Both Longe and Thornton observe that in the wage-fund theory, the ratio between demand and supply when labour is concerned is defined by Mill in a different way than in the case of commodities and is inconsistent with the commonly accepted definitions.

Longe quotes some passages by Mill where the latter defines the demand for a commodity as a certain quantity of that commodity: 'a ratio between demand and supply is only intelligible if by demand we mean the quantity demanded, and if the ratio intended is that between the quantity demanded and the quantity supplied'[4] (Mill [1848] 1987 quoted in Longe [1866] 1904, p. 34).

Longe then proceeds to argue that the above definition is at variance with the meaning that Mill himself attributes to the ratio between demand and supply of labour in the wage-fund theory, where it is understood as a ratio between capital (the wage fund) and population:

> The demand for a commodity, then, is not the quantity of money wherewith it is to be purchased, but the quantity of the commodity itself wanted by purchasers. But what is Mr Mill's own law of wages? 'Wages then depend upon the demand and supply of labour or as it is often expressed, *upon the proportion between population and capital*'. (Longe [1866] 1904, p. 34)

According to Longe, the same definitions ought to be used both for commodities and for labour—hence the demand for labour should be understood as the level of employment (the quantity of labour wanted by the employers). In contrast to Mill's analysis, the amount of employment depends on the demand for produced goods that employers can expect, and is completely independent on the one hand of the existing labour force and on the other of the capitalists' available wealth and raw materials (the latter a term generally used to indicate wage-goods or 'corn'):

> ... the existence, or prospective existence of a purchaser, is a condition precedent to the employment of wealth as capital; and the quantity of the products of labour and capital required and the quantity of money for which they will be exchangeable ... govern the quantity of wealth used from time to time in production – whatever may be the quantity of wealth applicable to (or even 'destined' or 'set aside' for) such a purpose, the quantity of labour seeking employment, and the quantity of raw material available to the producer. (Longe [1866] 1904, p. 44)

In a very similar vein, Thornton argues that the amount of labour that an employer will be willing to hire is quite independent of the wage level:

> though as a rule it be true that demand increases with cheapness, it is certainly very seldom, if ever, that demand increases in the same ratio as cheapness. Few of us, if bread or beer became ten times cheaper, would buy ten times as much bread and beer as before. Even in the limited sense, too, in which the rule is true, it is open to very many exceptions, and labour is almost always one of the exceptions. The quantity of labour which an employer needs, depends upon the work he wants to have done ... he will not, merely because labour happens to be cheap instead of dear, hire more than that quantity.[5] (Thornton [1869] 1971, p. 87)

8.4.2 There Is No Such Thing as a Given Wage Fund

If the amount of labour employed by each individual capitalist depends on the demand for its products, there is no reason to believe that there is a wage fund earmarked for the employment of labour, the size of which is determined before and independently of the level of wages and the amount of labour employed.

Longe argues, first, that individual and national wealth cannot be divided a priori into two portions, one of which is intended for productive use while the other is not. In addition, the total amount of wealth available in the country does not limit the total amount of wages that can be paid. In fact, the resources for the employment of labour need not be available in advance, since they can also come from the value of what the workers produce: 'the wealth or capital available for the purchase of their work ... may even be taken out of the very goods which the labourers produce, or their money value' (Longe [1866] 1904, p. 47).

Thornton, while accepting the idea that wages are paid from capital advanced by the capitalists, denies the existence of a wage fund given *ex ante*, regardless of the wage level (employment, as we have seen above, being determined by the production decisions of individual capitalists, which are independent of the wage). Thornton asks, rhetorically:

> Is there any specific portion of any individual's capital which the owner must necessarily spend upon labour? ... is there any law fixing the amount of his domestic expenditure, and thereby fixing likewise the balance available for his industrial operation?... If he could get as much labour as he wanted at a cheap rate, would he voluntarily pay as much for it as he would be compelled to pay if it were dearer?... if in the case of individual employers there be no wages funds – no definite or definable portions of their capitals which, and neither more nor less than which, they must severally apply to the hiring of labour – clearly there can be no aggregate such funds, clearly there can be no national wages fund. (Thornton [1869] 1971, pp. 84–85)

It is therefore clear that when the 'demand for labour' is defined as a given number of workers, which does not vary inversely with the wage, there is no longer the logical possibility of conceiving of a wage fund determined *ex ante*, independently of the level of the wage: 'If, at a given rate, he [the capitalist] can obtain all the labour he is in a position to employ, he will not, merely because that rate happens to be a low one, either hire additional labour for which he has no employment, or voluntarily raise that rate, instead of retaining the difference for himself …' (Thornton [1869] 1971, p. 88).

As Thornton himself points out, the wage fund is an *ex post*, accounting magnitude, equal to labour employed times its remuneration, and as such is totally irrelevant from the point of view of the *explanation* of wage and employment levels. In a passage where he ironically responds to the observations of a reviewer of the previous edition of his work, Thornton makes the point clearly:

> He [the reviewer] admits … 'the idea that every such a person regularly sets apart a fixed sum to be expended, neither more nor less, in wages, would doubtless be found unsupported by the fact.' Having thus quietly surrendered all that I have contended for, he proceeds: 'Still it remains true … that at any given time a definite sum is being actually employed in payment of wages' … We all see at once, now that the reviewer has been good enough to enlighten us, that the sum actually expended on wages in a given period must be a definite sum. And by dint of further reflection the reviewer himself may further perceive that if, on making up his accounts at the end of the year, he discovers how much his potatoes have cost him altogether, he may, if he pleases, denominate their aggregate cost a 'potatoe fund'; and if then, recollecting how many potatoes he has bought in the year, he divides the potatoe fund by the number bought, he will learn how much on average each potatoe has cost him. And no doubt he will be all the wiser for the knowledge. (Thornton [1869] 1971, p. 89, footnote)

8.4.3 *Some Specific Features of Labour Compared to Other Commodities, in the Views of Thornton and Longe*

As we have seen, these authors' critique starts from the need for coherence between analysis of the market of any commodity and of the labour market in order to show the inconsistent and groundless nature of the wage-fund theory. However, moving on from the fundamental analogy in the definition of supply and demand for any produced commodity and supply and demand for labour as given quantities, they identify some specific characteristics of the labour market—already highlighted in Smith's discussion of the matter—which tend to differentiate it from that of a commodity. For both Longe and Thornton, these differences consist in the fact that in the labour market (unlike the case of produced commodities) competition generally tends to be on the supply side, that is between workers, rather than between employers. Longe attributes this to the fact that in the labour market (unlike the market for other commodities) conditions of oversupply normally prevail: 'the quantity of labour capable of being employed is ever somewhat in excess of the demand for it at a sufficient price or wage ... competition is on the side of the labourers; and such competition can never have the effect of bringing the whole supply of labour into employment, however low it may reduce its price' (Longe [1866] 1904, pp. 66–67).

Thornton underlines a different aspect of the relative weakness of labour, which is that of the 'urgency' of the workers' need to work, which, according to Thornton, is different from the need of those who sell not labour but any other commodity. A first peculiarity of labour is that: 'labour, differing in this from every other commodity, will not *keep* ... To-day's labour cannot be sold after to-day, for tomorrow it will have ceased to exist' (Thornton [1869] 1971, p. 93). Thus, Thornton notes that labour cannot be kept and saved for future sale: any postponement in its sale entails the complete loss of the income that could have been obtained during that time interval. The other cause of urgency of the need to work is the extreme poverty in which the workers generally find themselves, since: 'extreme poverty virtually disables them from bargaining' (ibid.).

According to Longe, a consequence of the bargaining weakness of the workers (which in his view is due to constant 'oversupply', that is, unemployment) is that normally wages are not regulated by the quantities of labour demanded and supplied but tend to be fixed at their subsistence minimum: 'supply and demand ... would never ... reduce wages below the minimum rate at which they would be able and willing to continue working as well as they did on the higher wages' (Longe [1866] 1904, p. 61).

Starting from this perspective, Longe develops some interesting considerations concerning competition, and particularly competition in the labour market: 'The competition of industrious men, whether traders or labourers, is the life of trade, but it is no less true that unrestrained competition is its destruction' (ibid., p. 65).

Hence, according to Longe, institutions such as trade unions or employers' associations, which have the purpose of keeping in check the damaging effects of competition, must be regarded: 'as a force by which wages may be regulated, of the same natural and normal character as competition itself' (ibid., p. 17).

At any rate, Longe continues, social conventions and acquired habits set the boundaries within which competition and bargaining over wages can take place: 'this problem [sufficiency of wage], as it arises from time to time in actual life ... offers no wider field for doubt, dispute or error than such as lies between two figures, not far apart in the numerical scale, one of which would be admitted by both parties to be too high, and the other too low' (ibid., p. 18).

It will readily be seen that there are strong similarities between the views summarized above and some prominent themes in Smith's discussion in the chapter on wages concerning the masters' advantage in bargaining over wages, owing among other things to the workers' urgent need to find employment and the 'constant scarcity of employment' characteristic of economies that are not growing at a high rate. And as in Smith, this advantage, together with the competition among workers, does not cause an indefinite fall in wages, but fixes them at the minimum, historically determined subsistence level, defined by widely shared social norms, which Smith had described referring to subsistence as a minimum floor 'consistent with common humanity'.

8.4.4 *The Arguments Accepted by J.S. Mill in His Recantation*

As we know, in 1869, Mill accepted the criticisms made by Thornton. Mill accepts the view that for every individual capitalist the demand for labour is a given number of workers which depends on the demand for his products. Since a reduction in wages does not necessarily increase the demand for products, employment does not necessarily increase as wages fall. However, according to Mill, this fact alone is not enough to refute the theory: actually, the amount of capital left free by the reduction of wages can be used by the capitalist himself or by others, giving rise to additional employment. But here comes the other objection put forward by Thornton and accepted by Mill: there is no clearly identifiable 'wage fund' of a precise amount—no more nor less—that will be spent on employing labour. The only thing that can be said, according to Mill, is that this fund:

cannot exceed the aggregate means of the employing classes ... the wages fund ... is co-extensive with the whole proceeds of his business, after keeping up his machinery, building and materials and feeding his family; and it is expended jointly upon himself and his labourers .... *The price of labour, instead of being determined by the division of the proceeds between the employer and the labourers, determines it.* If he gets his labour cheaper, he can afford to spend more upon himself. If he has to pay more for labour, the additional payment comes out of his own income. (Mill [1869] 1967, pp. 644–645, emphasis added)

Thus, Mill accepts the view that the wage fund is an *ex post* variable jointly determined by the wage rate and the given employment level required by the capitalists. Higher wages, with a given employment level, can be financed simply through a reduction in the capitalists' income.[6] These analytical changes in Mill's view lead him to change his position, not on the *legitimacy* of the trade unions (which he had always recognized) but on their *role*: in 1869, departing from what he had maintained before, he concluded that they can indeed, all other things being equal, change the distribution of income in favour of the workers. In other words, institutional factors can play a full role in determining the distribution of the product, with a given level of employment:

The doctrine hitherto taught by all or most economists (including myself), which denied it to be possible that trade combinations can raise wages, or which limited their operation in that respect to the somewhat earlier attainment of a rise which the competition of the market would have produced without them, – this doctrine is deprived of its scientific foundation, and must be thrown aside. The right and wrong of the proceedings of Trades' Unions becomes a common question of prudence and social duty, not one which is peremptorily decided by unbending necessities of political economy. (ibid., p. 645)

8.5 Concluding Remarks

According to the 'alternative interpretation' (Sect. 8.2 above and Stirati 2011) of the classical theory of wages, the emergence of the wage-fund theory in major figures such as McCulloch, Senior and J.S. Mill in the decades following Ricardo's death can be regarded as one aspect of the decline of Ricardian economics. However, it is often not perceived as such, since many historians of economic thought have (erroneously) attributed the wage-fund theory to Smith and Ricardo as well. In contrast to the latter view, and in support of the 'alternative interpretation', the criticisms levelled at J.S. Mill show that contemporary economists like Longe and Thornton saw the wage-fund theory as introducing new definitions and concepts that were criticized as inconsistent. In addition, the critics explicitly proposed a view of the labour market and wage-setting which came extremely close to that of Smith and Ricardo as portrayed by proponents of the 'alternative interpretation'. Hence, the analytical arguments advanced against J.S. Mill discussed in this paper provide further support to the view that the wage-fund theory represents a break with the earlier classical tradition and was perceived as such by contemporaries.

As mentioned above, in the criticisms of the wage-fund theory, there re-emerge several elements of Smith's treatment of wage determination and, more generally, of the approach that had been dominant up to Ricardo. In particular, it is stressed that the proportion between labour demand and population must be understood, as for any other commodity, as the ratio between two given quantities (number of workers wanted by employers and population)—a proportion which, in the case of the labour market, tends to be favourable to the employers, as normally there is an excess of available labour force over the opportunities for employment.

This view is naturally accompanied by a conception of competition as *necessarily* limited by customary and conventional factors and, more generally, by the idea that institutions such as workers' and employers' associations are not an obstacle or an alternative to the action of competition, nor indeed a 'distortion' of market outcomes, but are a 'natural' part, as Longe says, of the process of wage determination. This is so since, without the boundaries constituted precisely by norms and institutions, unconstrained competition over wages would prove destructive according to the classical analytical framework. It may be maintained, therefore, that an often recognized peculiarity of the classical approach, consisting in the important role attributed to social norms and institutional factors in the labour market, is the direct consequence of a more general analytical difference between the classical approach and the subsequently developed wage-fund and marginalist theories, that is, the absence in the former of the notion of a decreasing relationship between real wages and employment.

Mill's acceptance of the two main arguments advanced by Longe and Thornton in turn shows that the departure from the classical tradition was still flimsy, as a new, general analytical framework alternative to the classical approach was yet to become available. The absence of analytical foundations for a decreasing relationship between real wages and employment other than the simple and arbitrary assumption of a given wage fund led to rejection of the wage-fund theory.

Acknowledgements I wish to thank the referees and the editors of the volume for their comments on an earlier draft of the paper.

Notes

1. On this point, see Stirati (1994, pp. 194–198) and Levrero (2011).
2. For further elements in support of the 'canonical' character of Mill's theory and his conception of the wage fund as savings rather than as a given quantity of wage-goods, see also the discussion of the theory of the incidence of taxation in Stirati (1999, Appendix A).
3. Neither Thornton nor Mill mention Longe's criticisms; but here we are not so much interested in historically ascertaining the possible influence of that contribution as in the substantial similarity of many arguments.
4. These definitions are similar to and reminiscent of Smith's discussion of market price deviations from natural price as affected by the ratio between 'effectual demand' and the 'quantity brought to market' (*WN*, I.vii.7–8; cfr. Stirati 1994, pp. 6–7).
5. This passage by Thornton echoes a passage by Ricardo: '... in proportion to the work to be done will be the demand for those who are to do it' (Ricardo [1821] 1951, p. 95).
6. For further discussion of this point, see Stirati (1994, pp. 184–186).

References

Blaug, M. (1985). *Economic Theory in Retrospect* (4th ed.). Cambridge, UK: Cambridge University Press.

Cannan, E. (1893). *A History of the Theories of Production and Distribution in English Political Economy from 1776 to 1848*. London: Percival and Co.

Hollander, S. (1973). *The Economics of Adam Smith*. London: Heinemann.

Knight, F. H. ([1956] 1963). *On the History and Method in Economics*. Reprint. Chicago: Chicago University Press.

Levrero, E. S. (2011). Some Notes on Wages and Competition in the Labour Market. In R. Ciccone, C. Gehrke, & G. Mongiovi (Eds.), *Sraffa and Modern Economics* (Vol. 1, pp. 361–384). London and New York: Routledge.

Longe, F. D. ([1866] 1904). *A Refutation of the Wage-Fund Theory of Modern Political Economy as Enunciated by Mr Mill and Mr Fawcett*. Reprint: J. H. Hollander (Ed.). Baltimore, MD: Johns Hopkins Press.

Marshall, A. ([1890] 1920). *Principles of Economics* (8th ed.). Reprint 1982. London: Macmillan.

McCulloch, J. R. ([1864] 1965). *Principles of Political Economy, with Some Inquiries Concerning Their Application* (5th ed.). Reprint. New York: A. M. Kelley.

Meek, R. L. (1950). The Decline of Ricardian Economics in England. *Economica, 17*(65), 43–62.

Mill, J. S. ([1848] 1987). *Principles of Political Economy with Some of Their Applications to Social Philosophy*. Reprint. New York: A. M. Kelley.

Mill, J.S. ([1869] 1967). *Thornton on Labour and Its Claims*. As reprinted in: J. M. Robson (Ed.), *Collected Works of John Stuart Mill* (Vol. 5). Essays on Economics and Society, Part II (pp. 633–668). Toronto: University of Toronto Press.

Ricardo, D. ([1821] 1951). *On the Principles of Political Economy and Taxation* (3rd ed.). In P. Sraffa (Ed.), with the collaboration of M. H. Dobb, *The Works and Correspondence of David Ricardo* (Vol. 1). Cambridge: Cambridge University Press.

Rosselli, A. (1985). The Theory of the Natural Wage. In G. Caravale (Ed.), *The Legacy of Ricardo* (pp. 239–254). Oxford: Basil Blackwell.

Schumpeter, J. ([1954] 1982). *History of Economic Analysis*. London: Allen and Unwin.

Senior, N. W. ([1836] 1965). *An Outline of the Science of Political Economy*. Reprint. New York: A. M. Kelley.

Skinner, A. S. (1979). A Conceptual System. In *A System of Social Science: Papers Relating to Adam Smith*. Oxford: Clarendon Press.

Smith, A. ([1776] 1976). An Inquiry into the Nature and Causes of the Wealth of Nations. In R. H. Campbell & A. S. Skinner (Eds.), textual editor W.B. Todd), The Glasgow Edition of *The Works and Correspondence of Adam Smith* (Vols. 2a & 2b). Oxford: Oxford University Press.

Stirati, A. (1994). *The Theory of Wages in Classical Economics: A Study of Adam Smith, David Ricardo, and Their Contemporaries*. Aldershot, UK: E. Elgar.

Stirati, A. (1995). Smith's Legacy and the Definitions of Natural Wage in Ricardo. *Journal of the History of Economic Thought, 17*(1), 106–132.

Stirati, A. (1999). Ricardo and the Wages Fund. In G. Mongiovi & F. Petri (Eds.), *Value, Distribution and Capital: Essays in Honour of Pierangelo Garegnani* (pp. 184–209). London: Routledge.

Stirati, A. (2011). Interpretations of Ricardo and the Classics: The Theory of Wages. In R. Ciccone, C. Gherke, & G. Mongiovi (Eds.), *Sraffa and Modern Economics* (Vol. 1, pp. 349–360). Abingdon: Routledge.

Thornton, W. T. ([1869] 1971). *On Labour, Its Wrongful Claims and Rightful Dues, Its Actual Present and Possible Future* (2nd ed.). Reprint (1870). Shannon: Irish University Press.

CHAPTER 9

Classics Today: Smith, Ricardo, Marx

Christian Gehrke, Heinz D. Kurz, and Richard Sturn

9.1 Introduction

The interest of the modern reader in the key authors of classical economics should not be of a purely historical nature. The reasons for this claim are manifold. In this piece, we are trying to shed light on some of them, all related to the fact that the classical approach to studying an economic system in motion under a cumulative process of division of labour offers a superior starting point for analysing salient properties of capitalist market economies. We discuss three thinkers, each of whom offered an original and unique combination of ideas and concepts—and whose

C. Gehrke (✉) · H. D. Kurz
Department of Economics and Graz Schumpeter Centre, University of Graz, Graz, Austria
e-mail: christian.gehrke@uni-graz.at

H. D. Kurz
e-mail: heinz.kurz@uni-graz.at

R. Sturn
Department of Public Economics and Graz Schumpeter Centre, University of Graz, Graz, Austria
e-mail: richard.sturn@uni-graz.at

M. C. Marcuzzo et al. (eds.), *New Perspectives on Political Economy and Its History*, Palgrave Studies in the History of Economic Thought,
https://doi.org/10.1007/978-3-030-42925-6_9

very different backgrounds and characters as individuals, scholars and political beings need not be stressed here. What we want to emphasize is rather the unity in their theoretical approach and their common concern with studying the dynamic evolution of a market system with inherently changing technological conditions, taking into account the existence of distributional conflicts that are not resolved in the domain of competitive markets. It is these aspects, we submit, that the modern reader will have difficulties finding in the contemporary mainstream economic literature, and that make it worthwhile to study the contributions of the classical authors today.[1]

9.2 Adam Smith

Adam Smith is considered a pioneering figure by different currents of economics, including modern mainstream economics. Indeed, the tradition of classical economics as inaugurated by Adam Smith put forward a number of ideas and concepts making perfect sense to readers educated in the principles of modern mainstream economics. It may suffice to mention a few exemplary topics developed by Smith in an eloquent and persuasive way:

- Interdependence and unintended consequences;
- Emphasis on free trade and exchange;
- The role of incentives in socio-economic mechanisms;
- The private-property market economy as a sphere of specific interest with a logic of its own.

And over and above all:

- The proposition that all this can and ought to be studied in a systematic way by the new economic science.

If interested in history, modern economists will moreover find the 'philosophical history' of the period from the fall of the Roman Empire to the rise of cities and trade (Smith [1776] 1976, hereafter *WN*, III) stimulating, as it is used to illustrate the unplanned effects of institutional arrangements on the economy and the repercussions on the institutions themselves. The key message of Smith's critical discussion of the theoretical foundations and economic policy views of the mercantile system and physiocracy is easy to grasp. The same applies to the more general critique of unnatural interventionism. Smith's enlightened counter-project (the legally ordered competition in the system of natural liberty of *WN*, IV.ix) appears as a plausible and forceful expression of economic liberalism.

By contrast, Smith's in-depth discussion of the practical role of the scientific 'system' inaugurated by himself as 'the science of the legislator' belongs to a *second group* of Smithian insights, tenets, topics, and agenda: the topics of that second group may be expected to have some superficial appeal to modern economists, even though upon closer inspection some gaps between Smith and the understanding of the modern mainstream become evident. That is, some aspects and implications of the Smithian view are not particularly close to pertinent aspects of mental models in the economic mainstream. In addition to the (i) mentioned vision of the practical-political role of economics, (ii) Smith's recurrent talk about 'the wretched spirit of monopoly', (iii) the antecedents of behavioural economics which nowadays are highlighted by some authors, this second, more ambivalent group of topics notably includes (iv) the endogenous developmental ('growth') potential of specialization processes and the theory of the division of labour, which (according to Stigler 1976, p. 1210) 'almost no one used or uses'.

However, there is a *third group* of tenets where the discontinuity is still more marked. They include discussions of price, value, distribution, scarcity and class. Smith's pertinent writings may be considered under *two aspects: first*, they include some of the most prominent instances of flawed reasoning and unsatisfactory theorizing in Smith's oeuvre, as diagnosed by Ricardo and subsequent authors in the classical tradition, as well as (from a quite different background with different main thrust) by Whiggish readers viewing Smith as an early and rude forerunner of modern economics. As those 'flaws' have been widely discussed in the literature, there is no point in reiterating them here—also because the discontinuity between Smith and the moderns may be seen under a *second* aspect, which is less widely discussed and more interesting in that it offers some insights regarding characteristic weaknesses of mainstream economics implied by two related features: (i) the way in which distribution is located within the theoretical architecture; (ii) scarcity-theoretic reductionism, connoting inter alia the conceptualization of labour (and capital) as just another case of a scarce resource.

Before sketching some of the specificities of Smith's theorizing rendering it incongruous to deeply entrenched mental models, a remark is in order. Theorizing in the neoclassical tradition is not in general committed to disregard the importance of distribution, and it may develop specific models in order to accommodate contextually relevant properties of labour and capital markets which are not captured in the canonic scarcity-theoretic framework, such as efficiency wage models enriched by politico-economic perspectives or Zingales's (2017) political theory of the firm. However, there is a certain tendency to treat the canonic case as a theoretical (and sometimes practical) ideal or benchmark. Inter alia, this is conducive to the dominant modelling strategies where distribution gets out of sight.[2] The more far-reaching and deeper implications come to the fore in a perceptive passage from Abba Lerner's (1972, p. 259) AEA-presidential address. According to Lerner, the domain of economics is related to the solution of political problems in a peculiar way: '... the solution is essentially the transformation of the *conflict* from a political *problem* to an economic *transaction*. An economic transaction is a solved political problem. Economics has gained the title of queen of the social sciences by choosing *solved* political problems as its domain' (italics by Lerner).

In a nutshell, this summarizes a powerful vision of a rigorously depoliticized, aseptic kind of pure economics. Unfortunately, this vision could prove an illusion, not least because its translation in applied contexts tends to end up in technocratic approaches including a bunch of problems of their own. Nonetheless, most modern mainstream economists do not feel obliged to engage in scrupulous disquisitions such as those accompanying Smith's case for the science of the legislator, which (for systemic reasons) does not and cannot provide unambiguous recipes guaranteeing success on the great chessboard of human society (see, e.g., Smith [1759] 1976, VI.ii.2, 16–18). In their view, such disquisitions seem all the less necessary in view of the ever-improving econometric/experimental toolboxes progressively eliminating the drawbacks of ill-conceived technocratic policy interventions. Smith certainly would stress pertinent caveats: the protagonist of the 'system of natural liberty' believed that a meticulous discussion of the limits of 'systems' applied in politics is indispensable.

To be sure, theorizing in the neoclassical tradition can do better than that. From Walras's *économie sociale* to Solow (1990) and beyond, its best protagonists knew that distribution matters and that for 'factor markets' further considerations beyond the scarcity-theoretic framework may be relevant. However, some of the architectonic features of Smith's theory (which mutatis mutandis are also relevant for the subsequent classical tradition) determine the way in which key aspects such as the role of distribution are located within the theoretical framework such that they appear centre stage. A framework as the one sketched by Lerner is preparing the ground for eventually getting issues such as distribution out of sight, creating a situation in which they have to be brought back in 'from the cold', as Tony Atkinson (1997) put it.

The rest of this section focuses on the third group of Smith's tenets: *those which are difficult to grasp, given these architectonic properties of modern mainstream economics.* Three related moments of Smithian economic progress are the increasing division of labour, the expansion of markets, and the accumulation of capital. In and beyond this economic context, largely spontaneous processes of specialization and division of labour (introduced at the beginning of the *WN* as an overarching theoretical perspective) are characteristic for the specific thrust of his oeuvre: his philosophical writings already deal with social, cognitive and normative division of labour. The phenomenon of the economic division of labour and its welfare effects had long been known at Smith's time. Therefore, it is sometimes argued that Smith's original argument in this context is only the extraordinarily strong weight attributed to the division of labour among the driving forces of growth. This assessment is wrong for two reasons: (1) It fails to recognize the decisive progress Smith has made in the conception of firm-specific and societal division of labour and specialization as a process with dynamically increasing returns to scale and cumulative causation, a process whose progression is *limited only by the extent of the market.* Little of these dynamic elements can be seen in Smith's immediate predecessors, while Rae, Babbage and Marx built on them in the nineteenth century. (2) Smith does not place the discussion on the division of labour at the beginning of his treatise without reason. The purpose of this is to specify the general problem setting of the new science (as also advertised in the long title of the *WN*): The systemic environment to be explored with regard to 'the nature and causes of wealth' is a growth process with interdependent, co-developing subsystems including the politics, government and family-based reproduction. The early drafts of the *WN*, which demonstrate Smith's preoccupation with economic problems in the early 1760s, already provide a good illustration of how Smith uses these complex process-related interdependencies to establish the central systemic role of competitive-market coordination and price-based incentives, making coordination in great societies possible by exonerating people from cognitively and psychologically excessive demands on their agency. Morally coded coordination of expectations is inexpedient and dispensable in the core of the economic system: the price mechanism ensures that we are not dependent on the moral virtues or goodwill of the butcher, baker or master brewer for our meal, but can rely on their self-interest. Following the discussion of the basic structure of the coordination problems of the economy based on the division of labour and the role of unplanned and unexpected effects and feedbacks, the early draft formulates price and wage theory as the primary research agenda. Here, another central concept of Smith's political economy comes to the fore: competition. This is also the linchpin of the regulatory mechanism of the system of natural liberty, which however requires sustained political effort combatting the 'wretched spirit of monopoly'.

Issues of allocation theory are dealt with in a development-related framework: Smith is interested in the conditions of a growing economy. It follows that Smith's thought *cannot be seen as a prelude to the modern scarcity-theoretical view of allocation problems.* In the following sketch, we restrict ourselves to highlighting reasons for this incongruity without invoking further issues of a critical discussion of Smith's value theory.

Forms and causes of division of labour as well as their relation to market-based coordination are discussed in the first three chapters of the *WN*. The differentiation of a specific good as money and of relevant institutions (Chapter 4) results as a co-evolutionary process of the progressive division of labour. This motivates Smith's inquiry into the laws governing exchange relations. However, Smith does not immediately turn to the determination of relative prices: following the chapter on money, he finds it necessary to correct mercantilist misjudgements, according to which a larger money supply expresses higher welfare and dynamic prosperity, an issue already dealt with by David Hume (1752) in his essay 'Of Money'. This challenge motivates the introduction of labour as the 'ultimate and real' standard of value, leading to the much-criticized labour theory of value. After the appropriation of land and the accumulation of stock, the determination of the relative exchange ratios follows the natural recompense of labour (wages), capital (profit) and land (rent). Smith's three-component theory of price corresponds to a sociological perspective based on three classes (workers, capitalists, landowners) with three different types of income, stressing *institutional* features (property) and *accumulation*. The natural price to be derived from adding-up these three components is the centre of gravity, the equilibrium to which market prices under competitive conditions constantly tend. Market prices never remain below natural prices for long periods of time, whereas there are institutional circumstances (e.g., monopolies) that may stabilize them above natural values for longer periods of time or permanently.

But how are the natural rewards determined? At the centre of Smith's wage theory is a socioculturally extended family reproduction wage influenced by demographic feedbacks in the long term, supplemented by a variety of considerations that anticipate compensating wage differentials as well as elements of efficiency wage theory (cf. Sturn 1990). In particular, the latter, together with socio-demographic considerations, are integrated into his considerations that economic growth, increases in labour productivity and higher wages are mutually dependent. The profit rate, too, albeit with a different sign, is related to the dynamic conditions of the economy, namely the increase or decrease in the wealth of society (*WN*, I.ix.1): the larger the increase in the capital stock, the smaller the profit rate tends to be due to the intensifying competition among capital owners, which Smith tries to explain with a questionable partial-analytical analogy to the decline of sectoral profit rates when the stocks of many rich merchants are turned into the same trade. Similar to compensating wage differentials, Smith also discusses differences in profit rates caused by different risks, etc. Notice that Smith's theory as sketched so far does not envisage perspectives abstracting from distributive considerations. Quite to the contrary, it is suggested that there is no unique rate of wages or profits determined by allocative considerations. However, certain patterns of wages and profits are associated with the progressive, regressive or stagnant condition of the economy. The rent is derived from an institutional fact, namely private ownership of land (considered as a distributional norm: *WN*, I.vi.8). Scarcity is not systematically incorporated here. In the notorious passages claiming that rents participate in the composition of commodity prices in ways other than wages and profits, as high and low wages and profits are the causes of high or low prices, whereas high or low rents are their effect (*WN*, I.xi.a.8), no coherent scarcity-theoretic explanation of rents becomes visible. This is not even the case in Smith's detailed discussion of Bordeaux wines, where a high price results from the interplay of a specifically high effective demand with land of a specific quality making it uniquely suitable for the production of Bordeaux wine (*WN*, I.xi.b.31). When Smith then introduces the term pair scarcity/plenty in the justification of diamond prices, he explicitly stresses the socio-psychological function of scarcity with regard to the conspicuous consumption of the rich (*WN*, I.xi.c.31). For Smith, a natural price system is not one that efficiently regulates the use of scarce resources. This is partly conditioned by his diffuse conceptualization of scarcity—and partly by his alternative view: prices are part of the conditions of reproduction/development of the system. In a development-related context, price systems support income distributions, which reflect the respective socio-economic positions and powers of the different social classes. Insofar prices are signals; they are signals for the adjustment of self-interested individual actions to pertinent development paths, not indicators of relative scarcities in the modern sense.

9.3 David Ricardo

In the Preface of his *Principles*, Ricardo announced that he would 'advert more particularly to those passages in the writings of Adam Smith from which he sees reason to differ' (Ricardo 1951–73, vol. 1, p. 6). By implication, he thus made it clear that there was much in Smith's economic analysis with which he was in agreement. This included in particular also the following aspects. First, he shared with Smith the concentration on 'natural' or 'normal' prices in conditions of universal free competition and on the associated levels of the three distributive variables—wages, profits and rents. Second, he declared that all that concerns the distinction between 'natural' and 'market' prices had been 'most ably treated' in the *Wealth of Nations* (Ricardo 1951–73, vol. 1, p. 91). Third, he appreciated Smith's recognition of the inherent dynamism of the modern economic system and fully endorsed his view of the overwhelming importance of dynamically increasing returns that emanate from the social division of labour. This latter aspect has often been lost sight of because of the great emphasis that Ricardo put on diminishing returns in agriculture and its impact on the general rate of profits. However, passages like the following one clearly indicate that Ricardo agreed with Smith in attributing an important role to an always deeper social division of labour:

> The natural price of all commodities, excepting raw produce and labour, has a tendency to fall, in the progress of wealth and population; for though, on one hand, they are enhanced in real value, from the rise in the natural price of the raw material from which they are made, this is more than counterbalanced by the improvements in machinery, by the better division and distribution of labour, and by the increasing skill, both in science and art, of the producers. (Ricardo 1951–73, vol. 1, pp. 93–94)

In order to focus attention on those Smithian topics which have been noted above as being particularly difficult to reconcile with the scarcity-related mental models prevalent in today's economic mainstream, we will concentrate in the following on the assessment of Ricardo's analysis of income distribution in the 'natural course of economic development', his treatment of dynamically increasing returns and his analysis of different forms of technical change.

9.3.1 Income Distribution

In the Preface of his *Principles,* Ricardo famously placed the problem of income distribution at centre stage, and insisted on the necessity of analysing this problem in the context of a *dynamic* economic system:

> The produce of the earth – all that is derived from its surface by the united application of labour, machinery, and capital, is divided among three classes of the community; namely, the proprietor of the land, the owner of the stock or capital necessary for its cultivation, and the labourers by whose industry it is cultivated.
>
> But in different stages of society, the proportions of the whole produce of the earth which will be allotted to each of these classes, under the names of rent, profit, and wages, will be essentially different; depending mainly on the actual fertility of the soil, on the accumulation of capital and population, and on the skill, ingenuity, and instruments employed in agriculture. (Ricardo 1951–73, vol. 1, p. 5)

Ricardo shifted the focus of political economy from the production of wealth to distribution, because he was convinced that the capitalist economic system entails definite 'laws' with regard to the development of income distribution. He sought to determine those laws by first concentrating attention on a growing economic system in which capital accumulates and the population increases, but in which all forms of technical progress are deliberately set aside. In this 'natural course' scenario of economic development the rate of profits must decline, because the increasing difficulties in the production of food and necessaries imply that money wages must rise in order to prevent real wages from falling below the subsistence level (where the latter was defined not by minimal physiologically necessary requirements, but as formed by 'habits and conventions'). In his *Essay on Profits* (Ricardo 1951–73, vol. 4, pp. 9–42), Ricardo was able to show that rent did not enter into the determination of production costs at the agricultural margin by means of the theory of extensive differential rent. This had several important implications. First, by 'getting rid of rent', the analysis of the problem of distribution between wages and profits was considerably simplified. Based on the simplifying device of 'corn-ratio' reasoning, Ricardo was able to demonstrate the inverse wage-profit relationship, and thus to dispel the idea, occasionally present in Adam Smith's reasoning, that the wage rate and the rate of profit can be determined independently of each other. Second, he was able to dispel Smith's erroneous view—clearly a remnant of physiocratic thinking—that rent formed a component part of price and arose from nature's generosity. Third, he placed the explanation of rent on a new basis by relating it to the non-reproducibility of natural resources, which allowed the owners of such resources to extract a part of the surplus. With its focus on diminishing returns and the production conditions at the agricultural margin, the theory of differential rent was especially well disposed for converting it into an analysis based on marginalist reasoning. It could in fact be argued that 'the law of diminishing returns was the thin end of the wedge by which marginal analysis was introduced and generalized' (Bharadwaj 1986, p. 41) and that the 'marginal revolution' in economic analysis essentially consisted in little more than the extension of intensive rent theory, which Ricardo and the classical economists had applied to non-reproducible inputs like land only, indiscriminately to all 'factors of production', including a factor called 'capital'. It is no wonder, then, that today the 'Ricardian' theory of differential rent (besides the principle of comparative advantage in international trade theory and the so-called Ricardian equivalence theorem) is widely considered as one of Ricardo's main contributions to the development of economic analysis.

In his *Principles*, Ricardo then demonstrated in a more general framework that the general rate of profits is related inversely to the level of wages by adopting the labour theory of value. Today, it is clear that the latter can be dispensed with, and that the inverse wage-profit relationship, or constraint binding changes in the two distributive variables, must rigorously hold true for an economic system *in a given state of technical knowledge*. However, in his *Essay on Profits* and in his correspondence with Malthus, Ricardo had maintained that this relationship must also apply in the presence of productivity-enhancing technical progress. In order to counter Malthus's criticism that in a technologically changing system rising commodity wages could well go together with a rise in the general rate of profits, Ricardo introduced the novel concept of 'proportional wages' in Chapter 1 of his *Principles* (Ricardo 1951–73, vol. 1, pp. 64–65). This ingenious device of expressing wages simply as a percentage of the value of the social product allows for a changing commodity composition of the wage basket, and even for entirely new products entering into it—features that render the concept particularly suitable for the analysis of a dynamically changing economic system. However, Ricardo believed—wrongly, as we now know (see Sect. 9.4 below)—that it would also allow him to demonstrate the inverse wage-profit relationship in conditions of changing technical environments.

9.3.2 Dynamically Increasing Returns

It has not been widely recognized that when Ricardo proposed to concentrate attention on the *proportional* distribution of income, this involved not only a novel conceptualization of wages that is congenial to an economic system incessantly in motion, but also a (partial) departure from Adam Smith's research focus. This becomes clear from the following passage in a letter to Malthus, who closely followed Smith in this regard:

> Political Economy you think is an enquiry into the nature and causes of wealth – I think it should be called an enquiry into the laws which determine the division of the produce of industry amongst the classes who concur in its formation. *No law can be laid down respecting the quantity, but a tolerably correct one can be laid down respecting proportions. Every day I am more satisfied that the former enquiry is vain and the latter only the true objects of the science.* (Ricardo 1951–73, vol. 8, pp. 278–279, emphasis added)

In Ricardo's view, the attempt to determine *endogenously* not only prices and income distribution, but also the size and composition of the social product and its development over time, that is, the levels of the quantities annually produced and consumed, was far too ambitious and inevitably bound to fail. In order to ascertain relative prices and the proportional division of the annual product 'in different stages of society', quantities rather had to be taken as given magnitudes at a particular moment of time in the enfolding of the development process. With given quantities, reflecting the needs and wants of society at a given stage of social and economic development, the set of methods that are available to cost-minimizing producers could then be supposed to vary with the levels of the quantities produced. In this way, (firm-external) scale economies or increasing returns can be accommodated, and can be conceptualized as being dependent on, and varying with, the 'extent of the market'—as Smith had suggested. The inherent dynamism of the modern economic system was thus proposed by Ricardo to be captured in terms of a comparative static analysis, which shows the relative prices and the distribution of income corresponding to different levels of outputs. Dynamically increasing returns thus provide the connecting link between the two notions of 'effectual demand' (which Smith and Ricardo use in relation to the determination of prices) and 'extent of the market' (which they use in the determination of quantities). The idea in both Smith and Ricardo is that a greater 'extent of the market' allows for an increasing 'division of labour', that is, for an expanded set of methods from which cost-minimizing producers can choose. This leads to the introduction of improved production methods, which lower prices and raise real incomes, and thus increases the 'effectual demand'. This in turn implies that the 'extent of the market' increases still further, and so on.

9.3.3 Different Forms of Technical Change

In his *Principles*, Ricardo also provided a sophisticated analysis of different forms of technical change. Introducing the distinction between 'land-saving' and 'labour-saving' agricultural improvements, he showed that the impact of such improvements on rents depends both on the specific type of technical progress and on how it affects the cost differentials between the methods under consideration and those at the extensive or intensive margin. In addition, Ricardo also studied various other types of technical progress in order to evaluate their possible impact on income distribution, and even contemplated the case (which for him was a purely hypothetical one) of a fully automated production: 'If machinery could do all the work that labour now does, there would be no demand for labour. Nobody would be entitled to consume anything who was not a capitalist, and who could not buy or hire a machine' (Ricardo 1951–73, vol. 8, pp. 399–400). In the chapter 'On Machinery', which he added to the third edition (1821) of his *Principles*, Ricardo also put forward an intricate analysis of a particularly important form of technical change: the replacement of labour by machinery.

By means of numerical examples based on a set of precisely specified hypotheses, Ricardo showed that 'the opinion entertained by the labouring class, that the employment of machinery is frequently detrimental to their interests, is not founded on prejudice and error, but is conformable to the correct principles of political economy' (Ricardo 1951–73, vol. 1, p. 392). Moreover, he explained the predominance of this particular form of technical progress—the substitution of machinery for labour—by demonstrating that it did not derive from some incidental technological trends but was rather induced by economic incentive mechanisms that are endogenously generated in an expanding economic system with limited amounts of lands. It needs to be stressed that Ricardo's machinery substitution argument is not identical with the standard capital-labour factor substitution argument: For Ricardo, wages and profits do not reflect relative scarcities, and capital is not considered as a single (and often ill-specified) 'factor of production'. Ricardo's argument is rather that in the course of economic development money, wages are bound to rise in order to keep the level of real wages constant in the face of rising food prices from diminishing returns in agriculture. With rising money wages, however, there are incentives for cost-minimizing producers to substitute long-lasting machines—or, more generally, technologies that are embodied in fixed capital—for labour-using methods requiring annual capital advances for *ante-factum* wage payments. The machinery substitution argument thus refers to the substitution of *fixed* for *circulating* capital: it is a substitution not of 'capital' for 'labour', but of one form of capital for another one. Ricardo further demonstrated that with higher money wages, a machine can be profitably introduced even if the *annual* gross produce is thereby reduced. This is so because fixed capital, as opposed to circulating capital, does not need to be replaced on an annual basis, and thus from the proceeds of a single year (Gehrke 2003). Accordingly, Ricardo concluded that the dominant form of technical change in a growing economic system that is subject to land scarcity will 'naturally' be of a labour-saving and gross produce-reducing form. What is driving the direction of technological change are not changing relative 'factor prices' of capital and labour, as in modern (neoclassical) theories of induced technical change (Acemoglu 2002). The labour-saving bias is rather induced by the interplay of diminishing returns in the production of food and raw materials and the impact that rising money wages exert on the profitability of industrial production methods that use fixed capital.

9.4 Karl Marx

Marx stands on the shoulders of Smith and Ricardo and many others, especially Aristotle and Hegel, but repeatedly his body weighs heavily on them and is meant to somewhat diminish their greatness. He is keen to absorb everything that is convincing and valuable in their contributions and replace what he considers to be dubious or wrong. He does not always succeed in this endeavour and occasionally substitutes something flawed for something fundamentally correct. But in a number of respects he was able to improve our knowledge above and beyond where Smith and Ricardo had left it. This concerns in particular an analysis of the interdependence of economic industries in terms of a multi-sector analysis and an attempt to discuss the dynamics of the economy—its 'law of motion'—within such a framework.

9.4.1 Marx and Smith

Marx shares Smith's idea that the socio-economic system is possessed of properties that can be studied in a systematic fashion by political economy. He also subscribes to the Scotsman's view that the system is bound to transform itself from within, endogenously, from (using his concept) one 'mode of production' to another one. Marx puts forward a new version of the doctrine of the unintended consequences of human action. However, while Smith was optimistic that mankind was in principle capable of bettering its lot, but relegated the idea that a paradise-like state could be reached in the here and now to the world of pure fiction, Marx instead saw history as geared towards the establishment of a classless society, in which the exploitation of man by man would vanish and possessive individualism end: the high level of labour productivity then attained would make the scarcity of goods and distributive justice fade away. Marx shared Smith's view that capitalism developed the powers of social productivity within an incessantly growing social division of labour, with the emergence of an *R&D* sector as a part and parcel of this process. And he saw more clearly a thing that Smith glimpsed only vaguely, namely, that the modern economy was subject to dynamically increasing returns and processes of cumulative and circular causation. The manufacturing industry turned out to be an engine of growth, which Marx understood well, being exposed to a much richer empirical evidence than Smith, who mistook it as essentially concerned with producing trinkets for the rich and not productivity-enhancing tools and machinery for the system as a whole.

Marx accuses Smith time and again of his blunders, contradictions, repeated superficiality and even vulgar point of view, and the classical economists in general for conceiving capitalism not as a transitory, but as a permanent system, viz. the subtitle of *Capital*, 'A Critique of Political Economy', meaning, of course, classical political economy from William Petty to David Ricardo. Marx's 'law of the falling tendency of the general rate of profit' was supposed to do away with this view and establish 'scientifically' the evanescent nature of the capitalist mode of production.

As Schumpeter ([1942] 2008, p. 162) insisted, Marx's neglect to study carefully socialism and identify both its potentialities and the dangers to which it is exposed from within, is among the 'most serious shortcomings' of his analysis. Apart from incidental remarks, Marx does not investigate the political, sociological, juridical and institutional prerequisites that have to be met in order to avoid the danger of the system degenerating to one form or another of despotism; he does not discuss in sufficient depth and breadth the means and ways of centrally planned production and allocation of productive resources, the role of democratic political structures and of the rule of law, the features of a system of incentives capable of effectively replacing the profit-loss scheme of capitalism and so on. In several of these regards, he could have benefited from Smith's analysis in *The Wealth of Nations*, but also in the *Theory of Moral Sentiments*, especially as regards the latter's sophisticated anthropology, his knowledge about the light and dark sides of man, which must not be forgotten when building a new society. The hope that new people ideally suited for the new society will emerge he considered as utterly naive. Smith's 'science of the legislator' sought to answer the age-old question of what constitutes a society that allows, and preserves, the 'good life' of all of its citizens. Smith approached the question in a sober and pragmatic way, leaving the distribution of property and wealth untouched. He refrained from engaging in utopian plans and focused attention on what he felt was both reasonable and feasible, his main concern being the improvement of the living conditions of the 'labouring poor'.

The desire to establish not just a better, but a genuinely good society was the driving motive behind the socialist movement, whose main intellectual architect was Marx. Yet, as the proverb says, the opposite of well meant is occasionally badly done. Not having seriously investigated the opportunities and dangers of such a project and not having taken effective precaution to exploit the former and avoid the latter, is to a large extent responsible for its failure. But ignoring Smith's insights cannot only be blamed on Marx and his followers. The profession of modern economists can be accused of not taking seriously, for example, Smith's warnings about contagion, herd behaviour and the ensuing instability of the financial system and its impact on the 'real' part of the economy.

9.4.2 Marx and Ricardo

While Marx held Smith (wrongly) in relatively low esteem, he thought very highly of Ricardo, his numerous criticisms notwithstanding. He praised Ricardo's 'scientific impartiality and love of truth' (Marx 1954, p. 412) and the 'honesty which so essentially distinguishes him from the vulgar economists' (Marx 1959, p. 555). Yet despite all the praise he ushered upon Ricardo and the many insights and concepts he adopted from him, in some important respects he parted company with Ricardo, keen to demonstrate his own originality. This concerned first and foremost the theory of value and the 'law' of the falling tendency of the rate of profits.

Marx studied the law of motion of modern society in terms of an input-output system developed in his theory of simple and extended reproduction in volume 2 of *Capital*.[3] He had access to much larger empirical evidence than Ricardo, which showed impressively that capitalism revolutionized continually the system of production from within. How to grasp the technological dynamism of capitalism and its implications for the long-term trend of the general rate of profits?[4] Marx felt that this was possible by starting from the premise that abstract labour was the source and measure of value.

He praised Ricardo for rejecting Adam Smith's view that the domain of the labour theory of value was exclusively the 'early and rude state of society' prior to the appropriation of land and the production and accumulation of produced means of production. But he criticized Ricardo for not having succeeded in determining the general rate of profits and 'prices of production' in conditions of free competition in a consistent way in terms of what he dubbed the 'law of value'. Ricardo had indeed adopted the labour theory of value as a makeshift solution that approximated, or so he thought, the correct prices of production, but despite many advances into the field he lacked a coherent theory. Marx sought to make good the lacuna in terms of that 'law', which, while not valid with regard to single commodities, applied, he surmised, to the sum total of commodities employed and produced during a year.

We know today that Marx's solution cannot generally be sustained and that normal prices and the general rate of profits can be determined without any recourse to labour values (see Sraffa 1960). We also know that for a given real wage rate, the general rate of profits is determined exclusively with regard to those industries producing wage goods and industries directly or indirectly producing means of production needed in the production of wage goods, whereas other industries (producing luxuries, for example) don't matter. This Ricardo had already grasped well, but not so Marx, who wrongly criticized his respective view. When Marx identified labour to be the sought 'common third' of two commodities that are exchanged for one another at a given rate, he insisted that exchange values do not contain any 'atom of use value'. However, this flies in the face of his statement that the value of a particular type of labour power resolves itself in the value of a certain 'sum of means of sustenance' (Marx and Engels 1976–2012, II/10, p. 156) needed to support the worker and his family, that is, a certain basket of use values. The values of the different types of labour power employed in the economy therefore presuppose the knowledge of the values of commodities. The latter, however, presuppose the knowledge of the former. In short: the two have to be determined simultaneously. The data on the basis of which this can only be done are the data describing the social metabolism under consideration, that is, the production of commodities by means of commodities, as a famous book title has it. These data suffice to determine the system of prices in the case of an economy that is just capable of reproducing itself, the no-surplus case, and the system of prices and the general rate of profits in the case in which the system produces a social surplus that is appropriated at a uniform rate of return on capital in conditions of free competition.

As regards the 'law of the falling tendency of the rate of profits', Marx insisted that it was the most important law of political economy because it showed conclusively that capitalism was not an eternal, but a transitory mode of production. He also insisted that commodities are produced by means of commodities and rejected the view entertained by Ricardo, who, for simplicity, envisaged production as a unidirectional process of finite duration leading from a series of dated labour inputs to a final output. In Marx's reproduction schemes, this is reflected by a 'constant capital' needed in each line and at each stage of production. The important implication of this is that the maximum rate of profits of the system, R, which corresponds to a real wage that is hypothetically nil, is finite and not infinite: even with vanishing wages and thus a vanishing 'variable capital', the rate of profits would have an upper limit given by the inverse of the 'organic composition of capital' of the system as a whole. The organic composition, k, is equal to the ratio of 'dead' (C) to 'living labour' (L):

$$k = \frac{C}{L} = \frac{1}{R}.$$

The actual rate of profits, r, is instead given by:

$$r = \frac{M}{C+V} = \frac{M/L}{(C/L)+(V/L)} = \frac{1-\omega}{(1/R)+\omega} = \frac{R(1-\omega)}{1+R\omega}.$$

M/L is the ratio of surplus value to total labour employed, which translates into the share of profits in the social product, which equals unity minus the share of wages, $1-\omega$.

According to Marx, the long-run trend of the rate of profits thus depends on two magnitudes, instead of only one, as Ricardo had wrongly contended: in addition to the share of profits, it also depends on the organic composition of capital or its inverse, the maximum rate of profits. The second determinant reflects the circular flow character of production in the modern economy. The capacity of the economic system to generate a surplus product over and above what is being used up in production is expressed by R.[5]

It cannot come as a surprise, then, that Marx focused attention on what happens to k and therefore R as the system is affected by technological change and the corresponding reorganisation of the labour process. Differentiating r partially with respect to R gives:

$$\frac{\partial r}{\partial R} = \frac{1-\omega}{(1+R\omega)^2} > 0.$$

If the maximum rate of profits happens to fall (rise) and if proportional wages (the rate of surplus value) remains constant, the actual rate of profits is bound to fall (rise). The question regarding the long-term development of profitability thus boils down to how technological change will affect R. In other words, which form of technical progress can be expected to dominate capitalist development?

In Ricardo's chapter 'On Machinery', added to the third edition of the *Principles* (1821), Marx found the clue to an answer that apparently appealed to him. Ricardo had argued that the introduction of machinery involves a substitution of the fixed part of constant capital for direct labour, or variable capital (using Marx's concept). Accordingly, the capital-output ratio will increase together with labour productivity (see Ricardo 1951–73, vol. 1, Chapter 31). Ricardo identified a particular variant of this form as being especially detrimental to the interests of labourers: it is the production and introduction of machinery that reduces society's 'gross produce'. Such a reduction of the gross produce means, however, that total employment (L) is bound to shrink, giving rise to (additional) unemployment. This kind of progress Marx took to be the form congenial to the capitalist mode of production: it was characterized by an increase in the organic composition of capital and a refilling of the 'industrial reserve army of the unemployed', which kept workers' aspirations at bay.

Marx sought to underpin the 'law' under consideration in terms of this form of technological progress. As the formula of the rate of profits shows, contrary to Ricardo's doctrine, the general rate of profits can fall, even if the rate of surplus value (proportional wages) remains constant. This is necessarily the case, when the organic composition of capital rises (see Marx 1959, pp. 212–213). However, Marx's argument is not conclusive. He was aware of the fact that a rising labour productivity implies falling (labour) values of means of production and means of subsistence of workers. For a given length of the working day, this implies a rising rate of surplus value and it also implies a stunted increase in the organic composition of capital. The overall impact of this on the rate of profits is not immediately clear. But we know from Sraffa (1960) and Okishio (1961) that the rate of profits will remain constant, if technical change affects only the production of luxuries (or of 'non-basics' in Sraffa's case), and it will rise, if it affects means of subsistence of workers or means of production needed directly or indirectly in their production (or 'basics').

9.5 Concluding Remarks

This chapter argues that while modern mainstream economics has adopted, but variously narrowed some of the ideas contained especially in the works of Adam Smith and less so in the works of David Ricardo and Karl Marx, its historical development involved a growing distance and even opposition to the concerns, methods and analytical approaches of the classical economists. This implied a remarkable loss of the huge analytical potentialities offered by the classical economists, which has only gradually and rather incompletely been made good in recent times, viz., for example, the rise of behavioural economics, the attempt to understand economic development and growth in terms of multi-disciplinary studies and the view that the financial sector is unstable. The crises of the first decades of the twenty-first century request the economics profession to reconsider its doctrines, abandon views that can no longer be sustained, return to views that can or create new ones appropriate to the current situation. The elaboration of modern versions of some of the viewpoints of the classical economists appears to us to be a promising way out of the impasse.

Notes

1. This chapter has many points of contact with the important contributions of Annalisa Rosselli dealing with the classical authors and especially Ricardo, which the reader will easily recognize. We see our chapter as a tribute to her very fine work in the field under consideration and our long friendship and cooperation with her.
2. The assumption of quasi-linear preferences as a modelling strategy (which makes life easier by eliminating complications caused by wealth-effects) is just the tip of an iceberg.
3. We now know, thanks to the MEGA^2 edition (Marx and Engels *Gesamtausgabe*, 1976–2012) that Marx even developed a system with six interrelated sectors in order to study the properties of the system that is exposed to technological change, see Gehrke (2018).
4. The fact that Marx did not succeed in preparing volumes 2 and 3 of *Capital* for the printer indicates inter alia that he got doubts about parts of his argument—doubts that Friedrich Engels brushed aside in his edition of the two volumes by a judicious selection of manuscripts he included and by occasionally interspersing remarks without telling the reader.

5. In linear multi-sector analysis, it is related to the dominant eigenvalue of the matrix of coefficients of produced means of production, see Kurz and Salvadori (1995, Chapter 5).

References

Acemoglu, D. (2002). Directed Technical Change. *Review of Economic Studies, 69*(4), 781–809.

Atkinson, A. B. (1997). Bringing Income Distribution in From the Cold. *The Economic Journal, 107,* 297–321.

Bharadwaj, K. (1986). *Classical Political Economy and the Rise to Dominance of Supply and Demand Theories* (2nd Rev. ed.). Calcutta: Orient Longman.

Gehrke, C. (2003). The Ricardo Effect: Its Meaning and Validity. *Economica, 70*(277), 143–158.

Gehrke, C. (2018). Marx's Reproduction Schemes and Multi-sector Growth Models. *The European Journal of the History of Economic Thought, 25*(5), 859–892.

Hume, D. (1752). *Political Discourses.* Edinburgh: Kincaid and Donaldson.

Kurz, H. D., & Salvadori, N. (1995). *Theory of Production: A Long-Period Analysis.* Cambridge: Cambridge University Press.

Lerner, A. P. (1972). The Economics and Politics of Consumer Sovereignty. *The American Economic Review, 62*(1/2), 258–266.

Marx, K. (1954). *Capital* (Vol. 1). Moscow: Progress Publishers.

Marx, K. (1959). *Capital* (Vol. 3). Moscow: Progress Publishers.

Marx, K., & Engels, F. (1976–2012). *Gesamtausgabe* (MEGA). In International Marx-Engels Foundation (IMES) (Ed.), Second Part: *Das Kapital und Vorarbeiten* ($MEGA^2$). 15 Vols. in 23 separate parts, several editors. Berlin: Akademie Verlag.

Okishio, N. (1961). Technical Change and the Rate of Profit. *Kobe University Economic Review, 7,* 85–99.

Ricardo, D. (1951–73). *The Works and Correspondence of David Ricardo* (P. Sraffa, Ed., with the collaboration of M.H. Dobb, 11 Vols.). Cambridge: Cambridge University Press for the Royal Economic Society.

Schumpeter, J. A. ([1942] 2008). *Capitalism, Socialism and Democracy* (3rd ed., with an introduction by Thomas K. McCraw). New York: Harper Perennial Modern Classics.

Smith, A. ([1759] 1976). *The Theory of Moral Sentiments.* In D. D. Raphael & A. Macfie (Eds.), The Glasgow Edition of *The Works and Correspondence of Adam Smith* (Vol. 1). Oxford: Oxford University Press.

Smith, A. ([1776] 1976). *An Inquiry into the Nature and Causes of the Wealth of Nations.* In R. H. Campbell & A. S. Skinner (Eds., textual editor W. B. Todd), The Glasgow Edition of *The Works and Correspondence of Adam Smith* (Vols. 2a and 2b). Oxford: Oxford University Press.

Solow, R. (1990). *The Labor Market as a Social Institution*. London: Basil Blackwell.

Sraffa, P. (1960). *Production of Commodities by Means of Commodities*. Cambridge: Cambridge University Press.

Stigler, G. (1976). The Successes and Failures of Professor Smith. *Journal of Political Economy, 84*(6), 1199–1213.

Sturn, R. (1990). Natürliche Freiheit und soziale Kontingenz: Individualismus und Kollektivismus der Smithschen Handlungstheorie. In H. D. Kurz (Ed.), *Adam Smith (1723–1790): Ein Werk und seine Wirkungsgeschichte* (pp. 93–117). Marburg/Lahn: Metropolis.

Zingales, L. (2017). Towards a Political Theory of the Firm. *The Journal of Economic Perspectives, 31*(3), 113–130.

PART III

David Ricardo: Utilitarianism, Influence and Money

CHAPTER 10

Bentham and Ricardo's *Rendez-vous Manqués*

Christophe Depoortère, André Lapidus, and Nathalie Sigot

10.1 Introduction

The very suggestion that Bentham had an influence on Ricardo raises a puzzle. Although Stark (1946, p. 583), for instance, wrote in one of his two articles on Bentham published in the *Economic Journal* that '[i]t is not necessary here to furnish concrete proof of the deep indebtedness of Ricardo and his school to Bentham and his philosophy: the identity of outlook is obvious to every reader of the *Principles of Political Economy* or Mill's *Elements*', Hutchison (1956, p. 306), reviewing Stark's edition of Bentham's economic writings, explicitly rejected this statement and claimed that 'Bentham's economic ideas ... run on fundamentally different lines from those of Ricardo'. Such opposing perceptions show how

C. Depoortère
CEMOI, University of Reunion Island, Sainte-Clotilde, France
e-mail: Christophe.depoortere@univ-reunion.fr

A. Lapidus · N. Sigot (✉)
PHARE, University Paris 1 Panthéon-Sorbonne, Paris, France
e-mail: nsigot@univ-paris1.fr

A. Lapidus
e-mail: andre.lapidus@univ-paris1.fr

M. C. Marcuzzo et al. (eds.), *New Perspectives on Political Economy and Its History*, Palgrave Studies in the History of Economic Thought,
https://doi.org/10.1007/978-3-030-42925-6_10

difficult it is to find textual evidence, either in Bentham's writings or in Ricardo's, that would allow one to adopt either of these views.

For an historian of ideas, understanding the relationship between Ricardo and Bentham as regards economic matters calls for dealing with certain vague and often difficult-to-interpret assertions in which economics seems to play a subordinate part. For instance, it is well known that Ricardo wrote to Maria Edgeworth in 1822 that '[his] motto, after Mr Bentham, is the greatest happiness to the greatest number' (Ricardo 1951–73, vol. 9, p. 238). But commentators disagree about the meaning of this statement: while Bonner (1995, p. 2) claimed that it 'was little more than a gesture', Peach (1997, p. 231) took it seriously and defended a view of 'Ricardo as a moderate "radical" in the utilitarian tradition of Mill and Bentham'. But since it seems clear that Ricardo, like many people of his time, 'accepted the *language* of his utilitarian contemporaries' (Peach 1997, p. 220; Peach's emphasis), we have deliberately chosen not to address the interpretation of his few references to the 'happiness of mankind' (Ricardo 1951–73, vol. 4, p. 25), 'the happiness of the people' (Ricardo 1951–73, vol. 5, pp. 486, 499; vol. 7, p. 320) or the 'happiness of the many' (Ricardo 1951–73, vol. 5, p. 498; vol. 7, p. 299). Nor are we concerned with other non-economic issues such as politics: it should be acknowledged that most of those who have addressed the question of the relationship between Ricardo and Bentham did so mainly by asking (i) whether Ricardo was utilitarian in his politics (i.e. whether he adopted Bentham's belief that the government aims at 'rear[ing] the fabric of felicity by the hands of reason and of law'; Bentham [1789] 1996, p. 11), or (ii) whether his politics was influenced by James Mill. Given the role played by Mill in the dissemination of Bentham's utilitarianism, this focus is easily understandable. As Halévy put it, 'Bentham gave Mill a doctrine, and Mill gave Bentham a school' ([1901–04] 1934, p. 251)—the party movement of the Philosophical Radicals.[1] And James Mill urged Ricardo to enter Parliament, to which he was elected in February 1819: according to Snyder (2006, p. 277), Mill 'persuaded [him] to become the spokesperson for the utilitarian radicals'. But such a view has also been challenged, emphasizing instead Ricardo's originality in politics (Milgate and Stimson 1991, pp. 17–18). In this ongoing debate, Ricardo's economics is only granted a modest place in its own right, even if one of the arguments put forward by Snyder (2006, p. 277) was that Ricardo's criticism *vis-à-vis* the landowning classes was viewed by Mill 'as being supportive to the political program of the Philosophical Radicals'.

By contrast, we favour this often neglected economic dimension as a means to investigate the possible relationship between Bentham and Ricardo. Unfortunately, this investigation is far from a success story: rather than a story of meetings, it is a tale of *rendez-vous manqués*. The first (Sect. 10.2) proposed meeting is a mediated *rendez-vous*, in which the possible influence of utilitarianism passed through the action of James Mill, known both as one of Ricardo's closest friends,[2] and, according to Davidson (1916, p. 114), as the 'most strenuous and perhaps ablest … disciple that Bentham had'. Yet, even if one accepts the idea that James Mill might have transmitted the philosophical basis of his economic analysis to Ricardo, we have to acknowledge that such a basis is far from Benthamian. The second two proposed points of contact, in each case an unmediated *rendez-vous* which turns on the respective perceptions by each author of the other's economic works, are not less disappointing. When Ricardo read and commented upon a manuscript on money written by Bentham (Sect. 10.3), or when, according to his executor J. Bowring, Bentham criticized the way Ricardo presented the link between cost and distribution in what we acknowledge to be his *Essay on Profits* (1815) (Sect. 10.4), and leaving aside doctrinal aspects like economic liberalism (on which, by the way, Ricardo's debt to Bentham remains disputable—see Sigot 2015), we see that there is an unbridgeable gap between them on major economic issues such as money, distribution and value.

10.2 The Mediated *Rendez-vous*: From Bentham to Ricardo Through James Mill?

In the *Memoirs of Jeremy Bentham*, Bowring recorded that Bentham used to say that '[he] was the spiritual father of [James] Mill and Mill was the spiritual father of Ricardo, so that Ricardo was [his] spiritual grandson' (in Bentham 1838–43, vol. 10, p. 498), giving James Mill the role of a go-between, connecting Ricardo and himself.

Mill's meeting with Bentham dated back to 1808 and 'marked a turning point in both men's careers' (Winch 1966, p. 10): Mill played a significant role in the spread of Bentham's utilitarianism (Halévy [1901–04] 1934, p. 251; Winch 1966, p. 10), publishing many articles that popularized his principles. He contributed to Bentham's utilitarianism by providing it with a psychological approach, describing the process that led from (painful or pleasurable) sensations to action—i.e. associationism. His writings also dealt with democracy, liberty of the press and education, these being three important topics for utilitarianism, for which a central focus was on how private interests might converge towards public happiness. It was precisely one of these topics which gave rise to most of the correspondence between Ricardo and Bentham: in 1814, the latter sent to the former a draft of a work for the establishment of the 'Chrestomathic School', that is, a school 'for the use of the Middling and Higher ranks in life', modelled on the Bell-Lancaster monitorial system (Itzkin 1978, pp. 308–309). Bentham was hoping that Ricardo would support the proposal, and in fact, this was what Ricardo did (letter by Ricardo to Bentham and Mill, 15 July 1814, in Ricardo 1951–73, vol. 6, p. 112). After various ups and downs, the project was abandoned in 1820–1821, probably due to the 'innumerable conditions' imposed by Bentham for erecting the building in his own garden, the failure to find another site and the shortage of the funds raised (Smith and Burston 1983, p. xvi).

The time at which Ricardo and Mill first met is not clear. Bain's suggestion (1882, p. 74) that 'Mill's acquaintance with Ricardo began in 1811, probably through Bentham' is wrong and we have evidence that in 1811, the two men had already met. Indeed, the first letter of the 'Ricardo–Mill correspondence' in Ricardo's *Works* is dated 25 December 1810 (in Ricardo 1951–73, vol. 6, pp. 13–14). John Stuart Mill wrote in his *Principles* that his father's initial meeting with Ricardo followed the publication of *Commerce defended* in 1808, a pamphlet that James Mill 'prized … as having been his first introduction to the friendship of David Ricardo, the most valued and most intimate friendship of his life' (in Mill 1963–91, vol. 3, p. 576). Jacob Hollander (1910, p. 41) proposed a still earlier date: he stated that the two men first met in 1807 but gave no reason for this claim. Finally, Henderson and Davis (1997, p. 280) contested John Stuart Mill's testimony and supported the view that James Mill and Ricardo 'met in 1810, after Ricardo had published his *Bullion* pamphlet'.

It took some time for Mill to become a disciple of Bentham: when he first met him, he was an admirer of Dugald Stewart's philosophy. As noted by Halévy ([1901–04] 1934, p. 435), when still in Edinburgh, Mill had been a student of Dugald Stewart and had remained his disciple after he moved to London in the beginning of 1802. Stewart followed Thomas Reid in developing common sense philosophy. Furthermore, in addition to his courses in moral philosophy, in the early 1800s he delivered the first *Lectures on Political Economy*. These exerted a great influence over young talented Scots. Among them were James Mill and also the four founders of the *Edinburgh Review*—Francis Horner, Francis Jeffrey, Henry Brougham and Sidney Smith—as well as Macvey Napier, who succeeded Jeffrey as editor of the *Review*. So many names, indeed, that Sir James Mackintosh was induced to declare about Stewart in his *Dissertation on the Progress of Ethical Philosophy* that 'without derogation from his writings it may be said, that his disciples were among his best works' (Mackintosh in Stewart 1854–60, vol. 8, p. ix).

That Mill was deeply impressed by Stewart's teaching appears in a letter he wrote to Macvey Napier in 1821:

> All the years I remained about Edinburgh, I used, as often as I possibly could, to steal into Mr. Stewart's class to hear a lecture, which was always a high treat. ... The taste for the studies which have formed my favourite pursuits and which will be so till the end of my life, I owe to him (in Bain 1882, p. 16).

In contrast to his well-known later positions, this teaching first led Mill to oppose both associationism and utilitarianism. As noted by Winch, it is striking that the first-known article by James Mill—a review of Belsham's *Elements of the Philosophy of the Human Mind* published in 1802 in the *Anti-Jacobin Review*—'took the form of an attack on associationist psychology and utilitarian ethics as put forward by Thomas Belsham. ... Up to his meeting with Bentham in 1808 Mill continued to defend the Scottish philosophy of moral or common sense, and to oppose deterministic, utilitarian doctrines' (Winch 1966, p. 7).

Halévy ([1901–04] 1934, p. 439) stressed the same point and added that four years later, Mill 'was still denouncing a materialism which "whether cast in the mould of Helvetius or Hartley, appears to us equally abhorrent from reason, and mischievous in tendency". Then he became intimate with Bentham [and] became a Hartleyan'.

Both Halévy and, more than half a century later, Winch thus appear to date Mill's adherence to associationism and utilitarianism to his first meeting with Bentham in 1808. According to Halévy ([1901–04] 1934, p. 447), this conversion is apparent from Mill's change of mind with respect to John Horne Tooke's *Diversions of Purley*:

> In 1806, in the *Literary Journal*, James Mill analysed the second edition of Tooke's book: he was still a disciple of the Scottish philosophers, and was alarmed at seeing the philosophy of Tooke leading to the nefarious system of Helvetius and Hartley. ... Two years later, when he had become Bentham's disciple and lieutenant, we find him insinuating that, as regards the nature of the abstract idea, Dugald Stewart and Horne Tooke in the end think very much alike. ... His philosophical conversion seems to date from this same year.

Mill's refusal to oppose Horne Tooke's philological theory of the phenomena of the mind and Stewart's common sense philosophy indicated a significant evolution in his cast of mind which may well be the consequence of Bentham's influence. Yet it would be rather hasty to conclude that Mill was Bentham's 'disciple and lieutenant' as early as 1808 since, at this date, Mill still appeared to consider himself a disciple of Stewart. Indeed, in the article mentioned by Halévy, and published in the *Edinburgh Review* in October 1808, Mill invited readers unacquainted with the demonstration that there can be no such thing as an abstract idea 'to read the elegant and philosophical reasonings of Mr Stewart in his chapter on Abstraction, in the Elements of the Philosophy of the Human Mind' (Mill 1808, p. 44).

Thus, in October 1808, Mill had not yet abandoned Stewart's doctrine for that of Bentham, and the very first writing where Mill clearly broke with Stewart's philosophy was his review of the second volume of Stewart's *Elements* published in the *British Review* in August 1815: it is in this article that Mill described Stewart's recourse to 'fundamental laws of human belief' as a means to explain the phenomena of the human mind as a 'bold assertion, in which that is assumed which ought to be proved' (Mill 1815, p. 189).

Bentham's influence over James Mill and his role in making him evolve from Stewart's philosophy to associationism and utilitarianism seems unquestionable. Yet, the quasi-consensus for claiming that Mill converted to Bentham's doctrine in 1808 should be qualified since, as suggested above, it is likely that Mill's change of mind was more a gradual evolution than a sudden 'conversion'. This process did start in 1808, when Mill got acquainted with Bentham, and was complete in 1815, when Mill reviewed the second volume of Stewart's *Elements.* We have no evidence to answer the question of how long it took Mill to embrace the system he had formerly fought against. However, we can reasonably preclude the idea that Mill became Bentham's spiritual son as early as 1808. Consequently, even if Mill did teach methodological lessons to Ricardo at the beginning of their friendship, these would have been what he had learned from Stewart while still in Edinburgh and not what he later drew from Bentham's utilitarianism and associationism (Depoortère 2008).

Whereas the correspondence between Ricardo and Bentham essentially concerned the Chrestomathia plan and financial matters related to it, that between Ricardo and Mill dealt with economics and politics: it clearly shows that Mill played a crucial role in urging Ricardo to write the *Principles* and in convincing him to enter Parliament. Some commentators, like Jacob Hollander, went so far as to consider that Ricardo's first contact with James Mill was 'destined to become in its intimacy and range the most important influence in his subsequent mental history and personal life' (Hollander 1910, p. 41). And although Halévy ([1901–04] 1934, pp. 281–282) and Hutchison (1978, pp. 26–57) were more moderate when considering the extent of James Mill's influence upon Ricardo, they nevertheless maintained that Ricardo's method was the outcome of Mill's teaching. On the other side, there is a consensus among scholars as different as Sraffa (in Ricardo 1951–73, vol. 10, p. 35), Schumpeter ([1954] 1986, p. 472) and Samuel Hollander (1985, pp. 1–36) that Mill's influence upon Ricardo was close to nil as far as economic analysis and method were concerned.

This last position is corroborated by the lack of signs of any analytical or methodological influence from Mill on Ricardo in their correspondence: Mill gave much advice to Ricardo, but this was limited to the form of his arguments, not their content. A document recently found in John Stuart Mill's library at Somerville College (Oxford, UK) confirmed that Mill's advice concerned only 'ancillary elements of composition: expressive properties of tone and style' (Kerr 2015, p. 543): James Mill, in his notes, attempted first to summarize and understand Ricardo's arguments and then to help him to make his text clearer. Sometimes he suggested developing an argument; at other times, he wanted Ricardo to explain a statement, and so on.[3] How could we, therefore, support the idea of the influence of Mill on Ricardo if neither their correspondence nor the notes of the former on the works of the latter give evidence of such influence?

A possible answer might be that this influence had been exerted earlier, between their first meeting—in case it happened before 1810—and the beginning of their known correspondence, viz., between 1807 or 1808 and December 1810. Such a possibility has to be regarded cautiously, since Ricardo himself considered that his 'intimacy with Mill' was a consequence of the part he took in the Bullion controversy which started in August 1809 with Ricardo's article on *The Price of Gold* (letter to Trower, dated 26 January 1818, in Ricardo 1951–73, vol. 7, p. 246). But even if we deliberately neglect what Ricardo said about the circumstances which gave birth to his relationship with Mill, the idea of an influence of Bentham's utilitarianism on Ricardo's economics mediated by James Mill doesn't seem to have serious basis, for two reasons. The first one is that this coincided with the period in which James Mill was changing his mind from Stewart's to Bentham's philosophy. Hence, even in the case that he exerted a methodological influence upon Ricardo in 1808–1809, it is likely that its content would have been marked at least as much by Stewart's as by Bentham's teaching. The second reason is based on an exchange of letters between the two men, which took place at the end of the year 1817, when Ricardo and Mill discussed philosophy and metaphysics. Ricardo asked Mill: 'I wish to know whether you see no weight in the objections, offered by Reid, and I believe by Dugald Stewart, to the mind perceiving only ideas, and not external objects? Why should we as it is said perceive always the image of an object, and never the object itself?' (Ricardo 1951–73, vol. 7, p. 229).

In this quotation, Ricardo favourably points out the argument upon which Reid and Stewart built their common sense philosophy and opposed associationism. It is therefore to be hoped for Mill's own sake that he had not attempted to make Ricardo a convert, at least with respect to what would become his own contribution to utilitarianism, the associationist theory of the mind. In case he did, he must have been very much disappointed by Ricardo's question.

As a result, the proposed *rendez-vous* between Bentham and Ricardo mediated by James Mill appears to be a will-o-the-wisp. From the probable first meeting between Mill and Ricardo around 1807–1808 and the beginning of their correspondence in December 1810, a non-documented influence might have taken place. But at this time, Mill was Stewartian and not yet Benthamian. And later, that is, after December 1810, their correspondence and notes show no evidence of any philosophical or methodological influence by James Mill over Ricardo, wherein Bentham's utilitarianism could have had a place.

10.3 Unmediated *Rendez-vous* #1: Bentham's *Sur les prix*

In December 1814, in a letter to John Herbert Koe, Bentham reported that 'Ricardo and Say came here yesterday to dinner unexpected', adding that 'both [are] very intelligent and pleasant men, and both seem highly pleased' (Bentham ([1809–16] 1988, p. 441). He was then renting Forde Abbey, a former monastery, in Dorset, but it was in his house in London that, according to John Bowring, the executor and editor of Bentham's works, Ricardo visited him regularly: 'Of Ricardo, Bentham used to say: .... I was often tête-à-tête with Ricardo . ... We used to walk together in Hyde Park, and he reported to me what passed in the House of Commons' (Bentham 1838–43, vol. 10, p. 498).

There is no clear indication of when Ricardo and Bentham first met: Sraffa mentions that it was probably 'not long after the summer of 1811' (Ricardo 1951–73, vol. 6, p. xxviii), while Weatherall (2012, p. 109) states that Ricardo 'had not met Bentham when the scheme of the Chrestomathia was taking shape', but without being more precise (Bentham's involvement in the project of the school dated back to 1814). Sraffa and Weatherall both seem to have based their view on the first letter from Bentham to Ricardo, dated 13 August 1811, when Ricardo thanked Bentham for his invitation to spend some time with him and Mill in his residence of Barrow Green about 45 miles from London—an invitation which he declined, adding: 'I trust that on your return to London, to compensate me for my present disappointment, you will give me your company at Mile End [then Ricardo's house in London]' (Ricardo 1951–73, vol. 6, pp. 46–47). Thanks to letters by Mill and by Bentham, we know that the latter returned to London from Barrow Green between 15 October (letter from Mill to Ricardo, sent from Barrow Green, in Ricardo 1951–73, vol. 6, p. 57) and 30 October (letter from Bentham to James Madison, sent from London, in Bentham ([1809–16] 1988, p. 182): the first meeting between Ricardo and Bentham hence took place after 15 October.

The first mention of Bentham in Ricardo's correspondence dates back to the very end of 1810, that is, before their first meeting in person (in Ricardo 1951–73, vol. 6, p. 13). Interestingly it concerned economics, whereas politics seems to have been the main topic of their '*tête-à-tête*', if we believe Bentham's statement (reported by Bowring) according to which during their walks in Hyde Park, '[Ricardo] reported to me what passed in the House of Commons'.

Before this meeting with Bentham, Ricardo was asked by James Mill to read a manuscript dealing with monetary issues, that Bentham wrote probably from 1797 to 1801—after which date Bentham seems to have lost any interest in this matter.[4] Although the manuscript with Ricardo's annotations was first discovered by Sraffa in 1932 in Dumont's papers in Geneva,[5] part of it and Ricardo's comments were published for the first time by E. Silberner in the *Revue d'Histoire Economique et Sociale* in 1939, under the title 'Un manuscrit inédit de David Ricardo sur le problème monétaire' ('An unpublished manuscript by David Ricardo on the monetary problem').[6] Relying on a (erroneous, see below) statement by Etienne Dumont—Bentham's French translator—according to which he had sent the manuscript to Ricardo in 1808, Silberner (1939, p. 205) emphasized the importance of his 'discovery': it was supposed to prove that 'unintentionally, Bentham directed Ricardo's intellectual focus in a specific direction, that is on monetary issues to which the latter devoted his first publications'.

Unfortunately, it soon appeared that Silberner's assumption was wrong: when Sraffa finally incorporated Ricardo's comments and the corresponding excerpts of Bentham's manuscript in volume 3 of his edition of Ricardo's works in 1951, he could make clear, on the basis of the newly-discovered correspondence between Ricardo and Mill, that Ricardo had read Bentham's manuscript at the end of 1810, hence *after* his first monetary publications (August 1809), so that '[Silberner's] argument loses its basis' (in Ricardo 1951–73, vol. 3, p. 266).

Even though some uncertainties still remain, the story of this manuscript may be reconstructed as follows. It was very likely in December 1802 that Bentham handed Dumont the material for the translation of a manuscript dealing with the causes of inflation and how to combat it. While Dumont had already translated some of Bentham's economic writings, several of which were published in the *Bibliothèque Britannique* in February 1798, he faced serious difficulties understanding the content of Bentham's *Sur les prix*: 'of all the works I have done on Mr B[entham]'s manuscripts, none has caused me so much trouble as this one. .... [t]he manuscripts offered me only an imperfect and often broken thread for guiding me through a labyrinth of independent and at times contradictory essays' (Bentham 1797–1801, f. 31).

As he felt unable to judge their meaning and their importance, Dumont decided later to consult Mill (as he usually did when he did not understand what Bentham wrote), asking his advice about the expediency of publishing the work. Mill's opinion was negative: 'I do not think it will do for publication', he wrote to Ricardo in a letter dated 25 December 1810 (in Ricardo 1951–73, vol. 6, p. 14), asking him to read and comment upon the manuscript. Ricardo did so between 25 December 1810 and 11 January 1811 (Sraffa, in Ricardo 1951–73, vol. 3, p. 261) and confirmed Mill's opinion: the manuscript could not be published as it was, since 'it contains some very able and just views of the subject on which it treats, which I should be sorry should be wholly lost to the public; but at the same time… it contains some radical defects which will prevent it, as a whole, from effecting much good without considerable alterations' (letter to Mill dated 1 January 1811, in Ricardo 1951–73, vol. 6, pp. 14–15).

In this letter, Ricardo summarized his criticisms of Bentham's manuscript. He opposed (i) Bentham's view regarding the absence of any adjustment mechanism which would allow the regulation of the quantity of bank notes; (ii) his belief that no bullion export results from an excess of paper issue; (iii) his assumption that, when it is introduced through commercial purposes, money credit may lead to an increase of capital and production; and (iv) his statement that preventing the depreciation of the value of money requires banks to hold deposits (see Deleplace and Sigot 2012).

Despite these criticisms, Dumont was reluctant to be convinced: 'he seemed adverse to the idea of giving it up, and appeared disposed to work upon it in any way, that it could be rendered fit for the public' (letter from Mill to Ricardo, 4 January 1811, in Ricardo 1951–73, vol. 6, p. 18). Mill then suggested to Ricardo he invited him for dinner, to discuss the manuscript together; Ricardo sent Dumont an invitation on January 6 (p. 20). Ricardo and Mill were probably convincing, because *Sur les prix* was not published[7]: Dumont only inserted an excerpt of 2 pages in volume 2 of the *Théorie des peines et des récompenses* in 1811, with a footnote referring to 'a very great manuscript work of M. Bentham's, *On prices* and upon the causes which *increase prices*' (Bentham 1811, p. 339).

Bentham did not work on the manuscript again; in fact, he did not deal with economics between 1804 and 1820. He would come back to the subject one last time in 1820–21. On this occasion, he wrote a brief outline of a treatise which would have been entitled 'Paper money in Spain' (Stark 1954b, pp. 518–521, see also the letter to Jose Joaquin de Mora dated 13–14 November 1820, in Bentham [1820–21] 1994, p. 149).[8] Maybe Ricardo was involved in this project: a letter which Mill sent him (dated 14 November 1820) shows that Bentham lent some papers to Ricardo 'on the subject of his annuity notes' (in Ricardo 1951–73, vol. 8, p. 293). Ricardo replied to Mill that he did not remember which form the papers took and, at his request, he added that 'M. Bentham's scheme… did not appear to [him] the best mode of establishing a paper money' (p. 295).

We do not know why these papers, written by Bentham from 1796 to 1800—a long time before Ricardo came into possession of them[9]—had been lent to Ricardo, but it may be related to Bentham's offer to assist Spain's finance minister in establishing a new system of paper money; it is likely that he used papers written more than 20 years previously in order to build a new proposal. However, it seems that in 1820, he only outlined his proposal, as shown by the very few pages which Stark reproduced in his volume 3, concluding that they 'contain nothing concrete about "the particular species of paper money to be proposed"' (Stark 1954a, p. 49). Hence, the papers left to Ricardo were the result of several earlier monetary proposals, whose aim was to increase the revenue of the state by the issuance of a public money which would replace banknotes in circulation (see Sigot and Deleplace 2012). Clearly, for Bentham, paper money should be issued for the benefit of the state. He systematized his plan in *Abstract or Compressed View of a Tract Intituled Circulating Annuities*, where the new currency that he imagined was a public bond whose value would regularly increase from the interest it beared. As a consequence, each note would show the current value of it for every date, as computed by the addition of interest to the principal (Bentham 1952–54, vol. 2, p. 210): Bentham gave an illustration of such a note (p. 224), which made obvious to the reader how complicated his project was. Yet, in his answer, Ricardo agreed that the advantage of the use of paper money 'should be enjoyed by the State', but he added 'Mr. Bentham seemed to me to aim at this advantage by a circuitous and intricate course' (in Ricardo 1951–73, vol. 8, p. 295). Again, his comment was overall negative and it may have been one of the reasons why Bentham dropped it. Can we assume, with Hutchison (1956, p. 292) that if Bentham, instead of giving up, 'had devoted a certain amount of time and patience to the task of working his ideas up into a finished, balanced treatise... [he] could have produced a work as outstanding as Thornton's *Paper credit*'? The question remains open. What is clear, however, is that the main manuscript that Bentham devoted to monetary matters, *Sur les prix*, provided a formidable opportunity for a *rendez-vous* between him and Ricardo: yet as regards money it was a *rendez-vous manqué*, since Ricardo was not convinced by Bentham's analysis. As will now be shown, on the issue of value, the *rendez-vous* did not even take place.

10.4 Unmediated *Rendez-vous* #2: Ricardo's *Essay on Profits*

In the *Memoirs of Jeremy Bentham*, Bowring reported something which Bentham apparently had told him: 'in Ricardo's book on Rent, there is a want of logic. I wanted him to correct it in these particulars; but he was not conscious of it, and Mill was not desirous. He confounded *cost* with *value*' (Bentham 1838–43, vol. 10, p. 498).

Of course, one must be cautious with such testimony concerning what Bentham is supposed to have said: the reliability of Bowring's information in what L. Stephen called 'one of the worst biographies in the language' ([1900] 2005, vol. 1, p. 225) has been challenged several times, since what he chose to report seems to have been largely determined by his personal likes and dislikes (see Bartle 1963, p. 29). It is for instance well known that Bentham's negative comments on James Mill that he reported were (at least partly) due to the quarrel Bowring had had with the latter (see, for instance, Atkinson 1905, p. 167; Bartle 1963, pp. 30–31). Regarding Bentham, he was sure of the latter's superiority, and it is likely that he also considered him to have been a better economist than Ricardo.

This quotation might be important, however, insofar as it is—if faithful—till now, the only argued judgement by Bentham on Ricardo's economic analysis. Moreover, though Bentham's comment has been often quoted (Bonar, in Ricardo 1887, p. 55; Taylor [1955] 1993, p. 167; Hutchison 1956, p. 305; Hollander 1979, p. 339), the point raised in it has, to our knowledge, never been investigated.

A first problem lies in what is meant by 'Ricardo's book on Rent'. It seems that Bentham had read at least one of Ricardo's writings: on 5 November 1818, he asked Francis Place to lend him '[his] Ricardo' (in Bentham [1817–20] 1989, p. 288). But he did not specify which book by Ricardo he referred to.[10] We face the same vagueness regarding Bentham's reference to 'Ricardo's book on Rent'. In the absence of any evidence, Hutchison (1956, p. 305) hypothesized that Bentham alluded to Ricardo's *Principles*. This seems quite unlikely since the *Principles* are far from dealing exclusively with rent. We are thus induced to follow Samuel Hollander (1979, p. 339) when he interpreted Bowring's quotation as referring to Ricardo's *Essay on the Influence of a low Price of Corn on the Profits of Stock*. Indeed, as indicated by the first lines of its introduction, the theory of rent was so central in the *Essay* that it could legitimately be called a 'book on rent'[11]: 'In treating on the subject of the profits of capital, it is necessary to consider the principles which regulate the rise and fall of rent; as rent and profits, it will be seen, have a very intimate connexion with each other. The principles which regulate rent are briefly stated in the following pages ...' (Ricardo 1951–73, vol. 4, p. 9).

Bentham's criticism deals with Ricardo's use of the term 'cost' which, in the *Essay*, always refers to the 'cost of production'. There are fourteen occurrences of this locution in the *Essay*: eight in the body of the text, two in the 'table, shewing the Progress of Rent and Profit under an assumed augmentation of capital', and four in the footnotes (two of them belonging to a quotation from Malthus). The difficulty comes from the fact that the same phrase refers to two alternative conceptions of the cost of production, respectively, including and not-including profits.

Ricardo's traditional definition of the cost of production is known to include the profit of the capitalist. It appears in a footnote reading that 'the price of all commodities is ultimately regulated by, and is always tending to, the cost of their production, including the general profits of stock' (Ricardo 1951–73, vol. 4, p. 20 n.). The same conception of the cost of production reappeared a few pages further when Ricardo wrote:

> whilst the use of the machine is confined to one, or a very few manufacturers, they may obtain unusual profits, because they are enabled to sell their commodities at a price much above the cost of production—but as soon as the machine becomes general to the whole trade, the price of the commodities will sink to the actual cost of production, leaving only the usual and ordinary profits. (Ricardo 1951–73, vol. 4, p. 25)

Once again, Ricardo included the general rate of profit in the cost of production.

However, in the *Essay* he also adopted a conception of the cost of production that seems to exclude profits. This second conception appears, for example, in the table: the column 'Neat produce in quarters of wheat after paying the cost of production on each capital' (Ricardo 1951–73, vol. 4, p. 17) shows that this 'neat produce' does include profits. As a result, these profits were not part of the 'cost of production' which Ricardo deduced from the 'total produce' to obtain the 'neat produce'. The same applies to the column 'Total produce in quarters of wheat, after paying the cost of production' (ibid.).

This second conception of the cost of production occurs not only in the table but can also be found in the body of the text, as, for instance, in the following discussion of the distributional effects of the 'progress of the country':

> If the money price of corn, and the wages of labour, did not vary in price in the least degree, during the progress of the country in wealth and population, still profits would fall and rents would rise; because *more* labourers would be employed on the more distant or less fertile land, in order to obtain the same supply of raw produce; and therefore the cost of production would have increased, whilst the value of the produce continued the same. (Ricardo 1951–73, vol. 4, p. 18)

In this discussion, profit is calculated as the difference between the value and the cost of production. Obviously, profit cannot be included in the cost of production.[12]

Thus, as argued by Bentham, there is indeed an issue in the use of the words 'cost of production' in Ricardo's *Essay*. From a Ricardian point of view, the issue is not that serious: despite its dual content, the context clarifies the meaning of the phrase 'cost of production' each time Ricardo used it. But from a Benthamian point of view? It is obvious that one might regret that Bentham's reading of Ricardo's *Essay* (or Bowring's account of this reading) had missed a conception of the cost of production that was sometimes much closer to his own conception. But such selective reading, when Bentham charged Ricardo with confounding '*cost* with *value*', is also significant with regard to his own specific interest.

In this respect, an excerpt from Bentham's manuscript *Sur les prix* deserves special attention. This is the same manuscript as that to which the previous section of our chapter is devoted, but the excerpt is in a part of the manuscript that Ricardo did not read nor comment upon (he only annotated one of the three books that comprise the manuscript). Here, Bentham accused Smith of having confused the term 'cost' with 'price'. This echoes his comment on Ricardo's theory as reported by Bowring, if we accept that 'value' should be regarded as synonymous with 'price'. Today, one can only lament Ricardo's absence of comments on this criticism and speculate on what he might have said had he not skipped it.

The exact meaning of Bentham's criticism is, again, difficult to catch:

> in speaking of price either in money or in labour, he [Smith] does not explain whether he means prime cost or selling price; no more, in speaking of prime cost, does he explain the gradations of which it is susceptible according to the various classes of hands with regard to which the work may be used. Instead of the term costs, which is applicable in all cases because it does not presuppose exchange, he employs the word price, which in its common signification implies the idea of exchange (Bentham 1952–54, vol. 3, p. 112 n.).

It is clear that Bentham's target was Smith's chapter VII, book I of the *Wealth of Nations*, where the latter wrote that 'in common language what is called the prime cost of any commodity does not comprehend the profit of the person who is to sell it again' (Smith [1776] 1976, I.vii.5). In a way, Bentham agreed with this conception but, as we will see, it seems clear that for him, Smith didn't draw all the relevant consequences from this statement.

Such relevant consequences, along with Bentham's comment, should be placed within the context of his concern with the reasons why prices rose—which were the aim of his manuscript *Sur les prix*. Obviously, it could be argued that such a concern was also shared by Ricardo; but the emphasis was not on the same phenomena. Bentham focuses on market price, since his main concern is about inflation. As a result, natural prices as such are of no direct interest to him. They could have denoted a market price but, if so, the way profits are formed by successive layers each time the commodity changes hands would have been ignored. They could alternatively have been seen as prime costs, but here again the operation would have failed. The reason can also be found in Bentham's text: 'the prime cost of an article is what it has cost in labour or in money to the person in whose hands it is at a given time. The same individual article may thus on different occasions have had successively different prime costs' (Bentham 1952–54, vol. 3, p. 112).

This means that, for Bentham, at each step of the commercialization circuit, a new amount of profit, perceived by an intermediary, is added to the current prime cost consisting in the buying price. So that the number of prime costs of a good increases with the number of intermediaries in its commercialization:

> Take for instance a piece of cloth. First prime cost, what is paid to the manufacturer: second prime cost, what is paid to the wholesale dealer: third prime cost, what is paid to the retail merchant. ... In the case of a lot of mushrooms gathered by a woman on a common and sold to the consumer, ... [p]rime cost in money, none. Prime cost in labour, collecting and carrying the article until it has found a buyer. Price paid for the use of the land, none. Materials used for preparation, none. Tools, none. Stores, none. (Bentham 1952–54, vol. 3, p. 112)

This explains his apparently obscure remark about the 'prime cost' and his opposition to Ricardo and to Smith: for Bentham, the prime cost cannot be a cost of production which would include direct profit, as Ricardo argued, since the amount of profit depends on the number of intermediaries, which, in turn, depends on the length of the commercialization circuit. Interestingly, this means that he understands prime costs as determined at the beginning of the process by wage costs, so that they are initially proportional to the amount of labour incorporated directly or indirectly in each good, that is, to labour-values—labour-values which, through the successive layers of profits brought about either by production or by commercialization, determine a market price whose variation determines inflation. Such an understanding of price is consistent with an explanation of inflation which depends on profits generated both by production and by commercialization. And insofar as Ricardo's conception of costs of production and of market prices does not address the same issue, from Bentham's point of view, it is obviously irrelevant.

The disagreement, therefore, rested on the part played by profits in their answers to their respective questions. For Ricardo, at least when the context required it, they are a component of the cost of production as the surplus left on the last cultivated land (which pays no rent) after wages have been paid, contributing as such to the explanation of the secular evolution of the price of corn. For Bentham, profits depend on commercial circumstances whose variations explain why a good is sold to a greater or lesser extent above a cost of production to which they do not belong. Once again, the *rendez-vous* was missed.

10.5 Concluding Remarks

Our conclusion might fairly be viewed as mostly negative. Ricardo, Bentham and James Mill were characters in the same play. To a large extent, they shared the same interests. One of them—James Mill—was a friend of the two others and even considered himself as their disciple. Both Bentham and Ricardo had good reasons not only to exchange ideas, but also to borrow from each other. Yet every potential *rendez-vous*—the one mediated by Mill, and those in which each of them reacted to a work of the other—was missed. What appears from these *rendez-vous manqués* is not only evidence of the distance between the two men; we see also that their intellectual constructions in economics were sufficiently elaborated (which was clear for Ricardo, though not necessarily for Bentham) as to be impermeable to each other. They were doomed to remain side by side, without ever interpenetrating.

Acknowledgements We thank the three editors of this volume for their very helpful and stimulating comments on an earlier version of the paper.

Notes

1. This view has recently been challenged, especially by de Champs (2008, p. 262), who emphasized that '"philosophical radicalism" is to a great extent an entity that postdates Bentham's death'.
2. In a letter that he sent to McCulloch on 19 September 1823, just after the passing of Ricardo, Mill called both of them the 'two and only two genuine disciples' of Ricardo (Ricardo 1951–73, vol. 9, p. 391).
3. Kerr (2015) specifies the content of Mill's notes without reproducing them entirely. We thank Dr. Anne Manuel, Somerville College (Oxford), for giving us access to them.
4. Not only did he turn henceforth to the critique of a pamphlet by Charles Long which argued against a maximum for the price of corn (Dinwiddy 1984, p. xxii), but it seems that he did not even send to the Royal Society the planned letter to ask for publication of the manuscript or part of it (Stark 1954b, pp. 475–476; Bentham [1798–1801] 1984, p. 380 n.4).
5. On 4 November 1932, Friedrich Hayek (who was on the Committee set up at University College, London, for the publication of Bentham's

Economic Writings) wrote to Sraffa: 'I hear about a most marvellous discovery of a manuscript by J. Bentham on Money with annotations by Ricardo which you have made in Geneva. In the first place my sincerest congratulations' (quoted in Ingrao and Ranchetti 2005, p. 394).

6. For more about the history of the publication of the manuscript, see Deleplace and Sigot (2012, pp. 739–740).
7. The English translation of the manuscript was published in full (without Ricardo's comments) by Stark in volume 3 of his edition of Bentham's economic writings in 1954.
8. The full title reads: 'Paper money in Spain. Of paper money in general, its nature, uses and abuses; of the particular species of paper money here proposed, its uses with reference to the commercial world in general and the present situation of Spain in particular; obligations proposed to be attached to the emission of it; particular form proposed to be given it'. The editor of the ongoing publication in five volumes of Bentham's *Writings on Political Economy*, Dr. Michael Quinn, confirmed that this text is the only surviving one dealing with paper money for Spain, except a 'brouillon' (draft), where Bentham was sketching his project (which will be published in vol. 5 of this edition).
9. In a footnote, Sraffa indicated that the papers in question were Bentham's plan of 'Circulating Annuities' (Ricardo 1951–73, vol. 8, p. 293 n.3). Mill's inquiry about the content of the papers confirms it: Bentham, he wrote, 'has mislaid [the papers]. He wishes to know in particular whether the printed papers consisted of two Tables, or of three Tables – the third being the note, in the form intended to be issued – and besides the table, whether there were not two printed sheets, and the half of a third' (Ricardo 1951–73, vol. 8, p. 294).
10. The text reads: 'You are not using your Ricardo: you may as well lend it me'. In a footnote, the editor of Bentham's correspondence referred to Ricardo's *Principles of Political Economy and Taxation*, London, 1817; but no evidence was given. It might be Ricardo's *Principles* (we know that F. Place read and commented on it in 1817—see Ricardo 1951–73, vol. 7, p. 183 n.3), but it might also be one of his monetary writings.
11. On the conflicting interpretations of Ricardo's *Essay* (typically illustrated by Eatwell and Hollander), see Lapidus and Sigot (2001).
12. See also this passage of the *Essay*, where Ricardo explained that 'the extension of commerce', 'the division of labour in manufactures' and 'the discovery of machinery' 'have no effect on the rate of profits, because they do not augment the produce compared with the cost of production on the land, and it is impossible that all other profits should rise whilst the profits on land are either stationary, or retrograde' (Ricardo 1951–73, vol. 4, pp. 25–26).

References

Atkinson, C. M. (1905). *Jeremy Bentham: His Life and Work*. London: Methuen.

Bain, A. (1882). *James Mill: A Biography*. London: Longmans, Green and Co.

Bartle, G. F. (1963). Jeremy Bentham and John Bowring: A Study of the Relationship Between Bentham and the Editor of His *Collected Works*. *Bulletin of the Institute of Historical Research, 36*(93), 27–35.

Bentham, J. ([1789] 1996). *An Introduction to the Principles of Morals and Legislation*. Oxford: Clarendon Press.

Bentham, J. (1797–1801). *The True Alarm*. Ms Dumont 50, Bibliothèque Publique et Universitaire de la Ville de Genève, ff. 30–439.

Bentham, J. ([1798–1801] 1984). *The Correspondence of Jeremy Bentham* (Vol. 6). J. R. Dinwiddy (Ed.). Oxford: Clarendon Press.

Bentham, J. ([1809–16] 1988). *The Correspondence of Jeremy Bentham* (Vol. 8). S. Conway (Ed.). Oxford: Clarendon Press.

Bentham, J. (1811). *Théorie des peines et des recompenses* (Vol. 2). London: Vogel et Schulze.

Bentham, J. ([1817–20] 1989). *The Correspondence of Jeremy Bentham* (Vol. 9). S. Conway (Ed.). Oxford: Clarendon Press.

Bentham J. ([1820–21] 1994). *The Correspondence of Jeremy Bentham* (Vol. 10). S. Conway (Ed.). Oxford: Clarendon Press.

Bentham, J. (1838–43). *The Works of Jeremy Bentham, Published Under the Superintendence of His Executer, John Bowring* (11 Vols). Edinburgh: William Tait.

Bentham, J. (1952–54). *Jeremy Bentham's Economic Writings: Critical Edition Based on His Printed Works and Unprinted Manuscripts* (3 Vols). W. Stark (Ed.). London: Allen & Unwin.

Bonner, J. (1995). *Economic Efficiency and Social Justice*. Aldershot: Edward Elgar.

Davidson, W. L. (1916). *Political Thought in England: The Utilitarians. From Bentham to J.S. Mill*. New York/London: Henry Holt/Williams and Norgate.

de Champs, E. (2008). *La 'déontologie politique' ou la pensée constitutionnelle de Jeremy Bentham*. Geneva, Paris: Librairie Droz.

Deleplace, G., & Sigot, N. (2012). Ricardo's Critique of Bentham's French manuscript: Secure Currency Versus Secure Banks. *European Journal of the History of Economic Thought, 19*(5), 733–764.

Depoortère, C. (2008). On Ricardo's Method: The Scottish Connection Considered. *History of Political Economy, 40*(1), 73–110.

Dinwiddy, J. R. (1984). Outline of Bentham's Life – January 1798 to December 1801. In J. Bentham ([1798–1801] 1984). *The Correspondence of Jeremy Bentham* (Vol. 6, pp. xix–xxvii). J.R. Dinwiddy (Ed.). Oxford: Clarendon Press.

Halévy, E. ([1901–04] 1934). *The Growth of Philosophic Radicalism*. London: Faber and Faber Limited.

Henderson, J. P., & Davis, J. B. (1997). *The Life and Economics of David Ricardo.* Boston, Dordrecht, and London: Kluwer Academic Publishers.
Hollander, J. H. (1910). *David Ricardo: A Centenary Estimate.* Baltimore: The Johns Hopkins Press.
Hollander, S. (1979). The Role of Bentham in the Early Development of Ricardian Theory: A Speculative Essay. In S. Hollander (1995). *Ricardo – The New View* (pp. 323–341). London: Routledge.
Hollander, S. (1985). *The Economics of John Stuart Mill.* Toronto and Buffalo: The University of Toronto Press.
Hutchison, T. W. (1956). Bentham as an Economist. *The Economic Journal, 66*(262), 288–306.
Hutchison, T. W. (1978). *On Revolutions and Progress in Economic Knowledge.* Cambridge: Cambridge University Press.
Ingrao, B., & Ranchetti, F. (2005). Hayek and Cambridge: Dialogue and Contention. The Correspondence with Kahn, Kaldor, J. Robinson and Sraffa. In M. C. Marcuzzo & A. Rosselli (Eds.), *Economists in Cambridge: A Study Through Their Correspondence, 1907–1946* (pp. 392–409). London: Routledge.
Itzkin, E. S. (1978). Bentham's Chrestomathia: Utilitarian Legacy to English Education. *Journal of the History of Ideas, 39*(2), 303–316.
Kerr, M. P. M. (2015). Good Terms: The Style of Ricardian Political Economy. *The Review of English Studies, 66*(275), 540–562.
Lapidus, A., & Sigot, N. (2001). David Ricardo's Contribution to the Constitution of the Canon of Ricardian Economics: A Reconsideration of 1970's Interpretations of the 1815 Debate. In E. Forget & S. Peart (Eds.), *Reflections on the Classical Canon in Economics.* London and New York: Routledge.
Milgate, M., & Stimson, S. (1991). *Ricardian Politics.* Princeton, NJ: Princeton University Press.
Mill, J. (1808). Smith on Money and Exchange. *Edinburgh Review, 13,* 35–68.
Mill, J. (1815). Stewart's Philosophy of the Human Mind. *The British Review, 6,* 170–200.
Mill, J. S. (1963–91). *The Collected Works of John Stuart Mill* (33 Vols). J. M. Robson (Ed.). Toronto: University of Toronto Press.
Peach, T. (1997). The Age of the Universal Consumer: A Reconsideration of Ricardo's Politics. *European Journal of the History of Economic Thought, 4*(2), 217–236.
Ricardo, D. (1887). *Letters of David Ricardo to Thomas Robert Malthus 1810–1823.* J. Bonar (Ed.). Oxford: Clarendon Press.
Ricardo, D. (1951–73). *The Works and Correspondence of David Ricardo* (11 Vols). P. Sraffa (Ed.), with the collaboration of M. H. Dobb. Cambridge: Cambridge University Press for the Royal Economic Society.

Schumpeter, J. A. ([1954] 1986). *History of Economic Analysis*. London: Routledge.

Sigot, N. (2015). Bentham Jeremy and Ricardo. In H. D. Kurz & N. Salvadori (Eds.), *The Elgar Companion to David Ricardo* (pp. 17–23). Cheltenham, UK and Northampton, MA: Edward Elgar.

Sigot, N., & Deleplace, G. (2012). From 'Annuity Notes' to Bank Notes: A Change in Bentham's Theory of Money. *History of Economic Ideas, 20*(1), 45–74.

Silberner, E. (1939). Un manuscript inédit de David Ricardo sur le problème monétaire. *Revue d'histoire économique et sociale, 25*(3/4), 195–259.

Smith, A. ([1776] 1976). *An Inquiry into the Nature and Causes of the Wealth of Nations*. In R. H. Campbell & A. S. Skinner (Eds., textual editor W. B. Todd), The Glasgow Edition of *The Works and Correspondence of Adam Smith*, vol. 2a and 2b. Oxford: Oxford University Press.

Smith, M. J., & Burston, W. H. (1983). Editorial Introduction. In J. Bentham, *Chrestomathia* (pp. xi–xxix). Oxford: Clarendon Press.

Snyder, L. J. (2006). *Reforming Philosophy: A Victorian Debate on Science and Society*. Chicago: University of Chicago Press.

Stark, W. (1946). Jeremy Bentham as an Economist. II: Bentham's Influence. *The Economic Journal, 56*(224), 583–608.

Stark, W. (1954a). Introduction. In J. Bentham, *Jeremy Bentham's Economic Writings: Critical Edition Based on His Printed Works and Unprinted Manuscripts* (Vol. 3, pp. 7–59). London: Allen & Unwin.

Stark, W. (1954b). Appendix III. Systematic Survey of the Surviving Bentham Manuscripts. In J. Bentham, *Jeremy Bentham's Economic Writings: Critical Edition Based on His Printed Works and Unprinted Manuscripts* (Vol. 3, pp. 459–548). London: Allen & Unwin.

Stephen, L. ([1900] 2005). *The English Utilitarians* (3 Vols). New York and London: Continuum.

Stewart, D. (1854–60). *The Collected Works of Dugald Stewart*. W. T. Hamilton (Ed.). Edinburgh: Constable and Co.

Taylor, W. L. ([1955] 1993). Bentham as Economist: A Review Article. In B. Parekh (Ed.), *Jeremy Bentham: Critical Assessments* (Vol. 4, pp. 161–170). London: Routledge.

Weatherall, D. (2012). *David Ricardo: A Biography*. The Hague: Martinus Nijhoff.

Winch, D. (1966). *James Mill Selected Economic Writings*. Edinburgh and London: Oliver & Boyd.

CHAPTER 11

How Ricardo Came to Japan

Masashi Izumo, Yuji Sato, and Susumu Takenaga

11.1 Introduction

The introduction of Western economic thought to Japan can be traced back to 1776, the same year as the publication of Adam Smith's *Wealth of Nations*. Carl Peter Thunberg, a Swedish botanist, taught economics to Japanese scholars of Dutch learning during his short stay in Edo (now Tokyo) in May of that year (Thunberg 1788–93, vol. 3, p. 199). This was probably Japan's first direct contact with Western economic thought.

However, this does not mean that there had been no economic thought in Japan prior to this introduction. In the Edo period (1603–1868), a number of eminent thinkers such as Kumazawa Banzan

M. Izumo
Kanagawa University, Yokohama, Japan
e-mail: izumo@kanagawa-u.ac.jp

Y. Sato
Rikkyo University, Tokyo, Japan
e-mail: ysato@rikkyo.ac.jp

S. Takenaga (✉)
Daito Bunka University, Tokyo, Japan
e-mail: takenaga@qa2.so-net.ne.jp

M. C. Marcuzzo et al. (eds.), *New Perspectives on Political Economy and Its History*, Palgrave Studies in the History of Economic Thought,
https://doi.org/10.1007/978-3-030-42925-6_11

(1619–1691), Ogyū Sorai (1666–1728), Dazai Shundai (1680–1747), Miura Baien (1723–1789), Honda Toshiaki (1743–1821), Kaiho Seiryō (1755–1817), Satō Nobuhiro (1769–1850) and Ninomiya Sontoku (1787–1856) emerged in different parts of the country and analysed the various problems posed by the changes that were occurring in the economic environment due to a monetary economy having taken root in society (Morris-Suzuki 1989, pp. 7–43).[1] This is the background underlying the widespread acceptance and dissemination of Western economic thought which flowed into Japan through a variety of direct and indirect routes—Japanese people studying abroad, economic writings, lectures, translations and textbooks—in parallel with the reform of political and economic systems that began with the arrival of the 'black ships' in 1853 and the Meiji Restoration in 1868.

It should be stressed that Western economic schools such as mercantilism, physiocracy, classical political economy, Marxian economics, the marginal utility school, the historical school and neoclassical economics were all introduced to Japan within a relatively short period of time. This fact suggests that the controversies over the process of transition to a modern Japan must have been quite complicated and confused. Moreover, the opening up of the country to the world in 1859 put Japan on the path to the global market and international relationships with imperialist Western powers. Japan was forced to start trading with Western countries, thereby undergoing a process of changing its social and economic structures dramatically and eventually being incorporated as a part of the global capitalist market economy.[2] It was within this context that the history of the reception of David Ricardo and Ricardo studies in Japan began.

This chapter traces the outline of the reception and diffusion of Ricardo's economic theories in Japan from 1869 to 2019. It describes how Ricardo was introduced in the late nineteenth-century and early twentieth-century Japan (Sect. 11.2), illustrates the development of Japanese Ricardo studies during the interwar period (Sect. 11.3) and examines the controversial interpretations of Ricardo's theories that have been advanced in Japan from 1945 to the present (Sect. 11.4). In doing so, it focuses on several topics such as the theories of value, rent, wages, money and finance that were passed on to later generations of scholars, and particular attention is paid to those Japanese studies that offer original approaches in order to provide interesting comparisons with similar debates in foreign countries.[3]

11.2 The Reception of Ricardo[4]

It was only in 1921 that the first partial translations of Ricardo's *On the Principles of Political Economy and Taxation* appeared—produced independently by Wada Saichirō (1894–1944) and Hori Tsuneo (1896–1981), both professors at Tohoku Imperial University.[5] Kawakami Hajime (1879–1946), Hori's supervisor and de facto co-translator, explains the reason for the translation in his preface: 'Abridged translations of Adam Smith's *Wealth of Nations* and Malthus's *Essay on Population* have already been published in Japan. However, it seemed strange that no one had tried to translate Ricardo's *Principles* into Japanese before, though he is one of the three greatest economists who founded capitalist economics'[6] (Kawakami 1921, p. 2).

Ricardo was unknown in Japan simply because the Japanese translation of his writings did not appear until 1921. Ricardo and his economic theory gradually became known by the late nineteenth century through various types of translations, lectures, journals, textbooks and writings.

11.2.1 Ricardo in the 1860s and the 1870s

Ricardo's name probably first appeared in Japan in a government publication released in 1869, the year after the Meiji Restoration. It was a translation of Arthur Latham Perry's work (Perry 1867) by the bureaucrats Ogata Tadashi (later known as Wakayama Norikazu, 1840–1891) and Mitsukuri Rinshō (1846–1897). In this translation, Ricardo was mentioned as a critic of Adam Smith and J.-B. Say on the theory of value: 'Say mixes up the two ideas even more completely than Adam Smith does; and the errors of the two writers in this respect gave rise to the twentieth chapter of Mr. Ricardo's book, in which the difference between utility and value is pretty clearly unfolded' (Ogata and Mitsukuri 1869, vol. 5, p. 15; translation of Perry 1867, p. 58).[7]

Perry's original English version had been extensively used as a textbook in universities and government offices, but it is not likely that Ricardo received a lot of attention as a result of this translated publication as its circulation was limited to a narrow group of readers.

Ricardo became the subject of special lectures from 1870 to 1873 at a private school called Ikueisha, founded by Nishi Amane (1829–1897), a philosopher and educator (Ōkubo 1981, pp. 599–600). Although it is unlikely that Ricardo was widely known beyond this private school and the transcript of these lectures was not published at the time, it should be noted that Nishi makes specific reference to Ricardo's theory of taxation here (Nishi [1870–73] 1981, vol. 4, p. 239). Undoubtedly, lectures by Simon Vissering, a professor of economics at Leiden University, were reflected in this emphasis. Nishi Amane and Tsuda Mamichi (1829–1903), a legal scholar and statesman, had been sent to the Netherlands by the Edo government and lived in Leiden from 1862 to 1865 where they studied natural law, international law, national law, statistics and economics under Vissering,[8] who was known as an advocate of the laissez-faire principle espoused by Frédéric Bastiat and John Stuart Mill (Sugiyama 1988, p. 59; Morris-Suzuki 1989, p. 49).

11.2.2 Ricardo's Theory of Money and Finance

In 1876, Usagawa Hidejirō (1849–1881), Endō Keishi (1851–1904) and Miwa Shinjirō (1854–1943), bureaucrats in the Ministry of Finance, translated and published (Usagawa et al. 1876) Arthur Crump's work (Crump 1866). In this book, several of Ricardo's passages on banks and currency were quoted from Chapter 27, 'On currency and banks', of his *Principles.* This translated book probably first introduced Ricardo's monetary and financial theory to Japan, but it presumably did not gain a lot of readers because it was not a book intended for the general public.

It was Charles Sumner Griffin (1872–1904) that initiated the study of Ricardo's theory of money and finance based on his original English writings at the Imperial University of Tokyo. Griffin was an American 'employed foreigner' and professor of political economy and finance at the university from 1899 to the year he died, 1904. He edited and published two books (Griffin 1901, 1902).[9] The former consists of five works by Ricardo selected from *The Works of David Ricardo with a Notice of the Life and Writings of the Author by J. R. McCulloch* edited by John Ramsay McCulloch in 1846.[10] In his 'editor's note', Griffin explains the reason for this reprinting of Ricardo's works on money and finance:

> His writings on money and finance... retain at the present day almost as great a value as they had when first published.... The essays here republished are not easily accessible in any other form.... It is thought, therefore, that a reprint of them will be useful to all who are interested in the scientific study of the problems with which they deal. (Griffin 1901, pp. i–ii)

Further details of his lectures are not known; however, Kawakami Hajime, the above-mentioned de facto co-translator of Ricardo's *Principles* in 1921, recorded in a letter to his disciple Kushida Tamizō (1885–1934) dated 27 June 1928 that he had learned about Ricardo as a student from Griffin, and was strongly impressed by Griffin's pronouncing the name of Ricardo as 'Ricar-*dou*' (Kawakami 1983, vol. 24, p. 285).

11.2.3 Ricardo's Theory of Rent

The translation that first drew attention to Ricardo was that of Millicent Garrett Fawcett's work (Fawcett 1876). Undertaken by Nagata Kensuke (1844–1909), a teacher at Keio Gijuku (later Keio University), this translation was published in 1877, the year after the publication of the original text. This text included an explanation of Ricardo's theory of rent:

> The rent of the less productive farm is determined by the pecuniary value of the excess of its productiveness over that of the worst land in cultivation which pays only a nominal rent. This is a short statement of Ricardo's theory of rent.... In every country there is some land so barren or so inconveniently situated that the produce yielded by it is only sufficient to pay the wages of the labourers who till it, and to yield the ordinary rate of profit to the farmer. This land can obviously pay no rent, for if it did pay rent. ... (Nagata 1877, vol. 3, p. 6; translation of Fawcett 1876, p. 97)

This translation was a great success; it was reprinted in several editions and was one of the most widely read beginner's books in Japan between the late nineteenth and the early twentieth centuries (Sugihara 1972, pp. 5–8). It mainly examined Ricardo's theory of rent, and thanks to its early pivotal role in introducing him to Japanese readers the image of Ricardo as a leading rent theorist became widely known in Japan (Mazane 1962, p. 80).

Kita Terujirō (another name for Kita Ikki, 1883–1937)—who was a nationalist and a socialist—published *National Constitution and the Genuine Socialism* in 1906. In this book, Kita mentioned Ricardo's rent theory and used it to criticize the interests of landowners and in particular the concept of rent itself:

> It is a certain fact that rent is a result of an increase in population and a gift of civilization as was revealed by Ricardo's theory of rent.... Therefore, a large amount of the rent which a peasant pays to a landowner is a

> natural consequence of the increase in population today.... All of the rent resulting from the growth of the population is always being plundered by landowners in the name of the sanctity of property rights.... It was not the landowner who created the earth in six days. (Kita 1906, pp. 61–65)

Kita referred to Ricardo to support his ideas and criticism of landowners and rent, and in this sense, he used Ricardo's theory of rent for nationalist and socialist ends. However, he was not the only one who had given this kind of interpretation of Ricardo's theory of rent. Fukuda Tokuzō (1874–1930), a prominent economist and advocate of the right to life and liberty, held exactly the same view. His 1908 lecture at Chuō University, titled 'From the rent theory of Ricardo to Marx' and first published in 1915, pointed out that Marx's theory of exploitation was amplified by Ricardo's rent theory, in which the landowner was viewed as an enemy, and that Ricardian socialists held a position midway between Ricardo and Marx: 'If the point of view of Ricardo's theory of rent is extended, it becomes socialism. But because Ricardo did not go that far, Marx appeared instead.... There are a lot of economists between them, that is, so-called classical economists and "Ricardian socialists"' (Fukuda [1908] 1925, p. 1264).

Fukuda's perspective influenced later Ricardo studies. For instance, Koizumi Shinzō (1888–1966), president of Keio Gijuku in 1933–1947, wrote an article (Koizumi [1920] 1968), and Hori Tsuneo's first publication was on the Ricardian socialists (Hori 1928). It is not difficult to find here a reflection of Fukuda's point of view.

In 1908, Yoshida Kinosuke (1869–1919) translated British economic historian Arnold J. Toynbee's work (Toynbee 1884). In this book, Toynbee pointed out that Henry George, the most influential American advocate of land value tax, was an absolute follower of Ricardo.

11.2.4 Ricardo and Debates Between Free Trade and Protectionism

In 1877, Wakayama Norikazu, the above-mentioned co-translator of Perry (1867) and a pioneer of protectionism in Japan, translated John Barnard Byles (1872) and criticized Ricardo's theory of comparative advantage from the standpoint of protectionism. Interestingly, Taguchi Ukichi (1855–1905), who was called the 'Japanese Smith', also criticized comparative advantage in Taguchi (1878), although he based his arguments on the principle of free trade. Taguchi, however, 'followed Smith only in the theory of free trade' and his approach 'was quite close to that of the Manchester School' (Sugihara 1988, p. 240).

Taguchi began the publication of the fortnightly journal *Tokyo Economics Journal* (in Japanese), the first economics journal in Japan, in 1879, and wrote in favour of free trade influenced by and based on the views of R. Cobden, F. Bastiat, R. Whately, H.D. Macleod and A.L. Perry. In fact, Taguchi's criticism of Ricardo's theory of comparative advantage was based on the explanation of it provided in Perry (1867), not on that given by Ricardo in his *Principles.*

Inukai Tsuyoshi (1855–1932), later a prime minister, argued against the kind of free trade advocated by Taguchi and instead lauded the value of protectionism in *East Sea Economics Courier*, which he founded in 1880 with the cooperation of Wakayama (Chō 1983, p. 4).

It should be stressed that Ricardo's theory of foreign trade, particularly his theory of comparative advantage, did not directly play an important role in the debate among these figures during this period.

11.2.5 Ricardo's Theory of Wages

The sociologist Ōhara Kyūsui (1877–1958) published a journal article (Ōhara 1901), in which he found fault with Ricardo on the basis of the interpretation of his wage theory by the German socialist Ferdinand Lassalle, who referred to it as the 'iron law of wages'. Writing on this issue in the 1900s, numerous scholars engaged in this debate and published many journal articles discussing Ricardo's wage theory in an age marked by urbanization, low wages, high poverty rates and poor living conditions in Japan.

11.3 Interwar Period

11.3.1 How Ricardo Was Recognized by Japanese Economists

It was only after the First World War, the time of diffusion of Marxism in the Japanese academic world under the influence of the Russian Revolution, that Japanese economists came to address the classical works of David Ricardo. The economic theory of Ricardo was now examined in relation to Marx's theory of capitalist economy. Hence, Ricardo was not considered in direct relation to the current problems in Japan; the sole object of examination was his system of abstract theory. The serious research on Ricardo from the 1920s was overwhelmingly carried out by scholars of imperial universities in close relation to research on Marx. Here, Ricardo's theory was regarded as an origin or a shadow of Marx's theory. But this was not the only approach to Ricardo developed during this period. For economists of the private universities like Waseda or Keiō, with a persistent liberal tradition, unlike the imperial universities, and for economists of non-imperial official universities such as the Tokyo Higher Commercial School (present-day Hitotsubashi University), Anglo-American liberal economics since Adam Smith retained its importance during the period of dominance of the German historical school. Here, Ricardo was received mainly in the later historical context of English economics, more precisely in relation to J.S. Mill and Marshall (and their interpretations of Ricardo). For this reason, they did not take up particular theoretical topics contained in the economics of Ricardo in relation to the concrete problems Japan was facing at that time, but they studied the historical progress of the theory as a whole and its systematic character. On the whole, Ricardo's thought came to Japan in the later Taishō era (1919–26) through two distinct intellectual routes with two different aspects, although there existed a degree of interplay between them.

As seen in the previous section, the representative of the first stream was Kawakami Hajime. Hori Tsuneo and Mori Kōjirō (1895–1962) began their studies of Ricardo under the direction and influence of Kawakami and both of them achieved remarkable results in the 1920s. Though not directly related to the three of them, Maide Chōgorō (1891–1961) was equally active during the interwar period as an imperial university researcher. The representative of the second stream was Fukuda Tokuzō, belonging to the same generation as Kawakami and long-time opponent of him. Koizumi Shinzō carried out his studies of Ricardo as a disciple and under the influence of Fukuda, and he proposed his own particular interpretation of Ricardo in opposition to the other four imperial university researchers.

Ricardo attracted much less attention from Japanese economists than Smith and Malthus throughout the entire history of economic research in Japan from the early Meiji era.

After its first full translation in the 1880s, with the Japanese title 'Fukokuron' (enriching nations), Smith's work *The Wealth of Nations* was repeatedly translated, and his name was widely known among the general Japanese readers from early times. In 1923, the Japanese economics profession was busy commemorating the bicentenary of Smith's birth. Although the year 1923 was also the centenary of Ricardo's death, there is no record of similar commemorative events for him. At that time, the economics of Ricardo was not yet well-known in Japan.

As noted above, Malthus's *An Essay on the Principle of Population* was partly and indirectly translated as early as 1876, and his *Principles of Political Economy* was translated in 1934, the centenary of his death. Two years after that, the original English text of his *Principles* was reprinted. This was also the year in which Keynes's *General Theory* was published. Keynes lauded this reprint of Malthus as a 'praiseworthy enterprise' in his short preface to the Japanese edition written in the same year. But similar reprints of Ricardo's works were never published in Japan, either then or later. In 1934, on the occasion of the centenary of Malthus's death, the *Journal of Imperial University* of Tokyo Imperial University published a 'Special Column for the Centenary of the Death of Malthus', to which four economists—Maide Chōgorō, Ōuchi Hyōe (1888–1980), Sakisaka Itsurō (1897–1985) and Yoshida Hideo (1906–1953), all well-known in Japan up to the present day—contributed articles. In particular, Maide, occupied with Ricardo studies, pointed out at the end of his article that in 1923, the centenary of Ricardo's death, 'there was almost no enterprise for commemorating it', in contrast to the case of Malthus. Addressing in detail the problems of population and poverty accompanying industrialization and urbanization, and arguing in favour of protectionism in international trade, Malthus was considered to be more relevant than Ricardo to the problems arising from the process of modernization that was taking place in Japan at that time.

The fact that Ricardo was rather overshadowed by other more popular figures in the history of economic thought, such as Smith and Marx, did not change very much, even after the Second World War. From the fifth year of Meiji (1872), when it is not certain that even the name of Ricardo was known in Japan, till 1972, the bicentenary of his birth nearly 30 years after the Second World War, nothing was done to commemorate him in any of the landmark years relating to his birth or death, or to the publication of his important works.

11.3.2 Methods of Research and Selection of Subjects

As seen above, Ricardo studies in the interwar period proceeded inseparably from the rapid penetration of Marx's influence into the Japanese academic circles of the time. Because of this, Marx's treatment of Ricardo seems to have largely influenced, explicitly or implicitly, the importance that Ricardo scholars attached to specific problems in Ricardo's theory or their selection. The detailed examinations by Marx of Ricardo's theories of value, profit and ground rent in *Theories of Surplus Value* were taken as criteria for either the positive evaluation of these theories or a critical and negative attitude towards them based on Marx's criticism. Ricardo's theory of wages was studied in relation to the theory of surplus value (exploitation) directly following the theory of commodity and money in Volume 1 of *Capital*, and its place in the history of economic theory was determined according to its distance from Marx. As for Ricardo's theory of money, Marx was generally critical. He criticized Ricardo's 'quantity theory of money' only once and rather cursorily in a part of his *A Contribution to the Critique of Political Economy* (1859), on a very partial textual evidence.

On the whole, under the influence of this treatment by Marx, the subjects of Ricardo studies in and after the 1920s (and after the Second World War) were overwhelmingly concentrated on the theory of value and distribution. As for the theory of money and finance, the almost exclusive aim of a small number of research works was, after Marx, to highlight the inconsistency and contradiction between Ricardo's quantity theory of money in *High Price of Bullion* (1810–11) and his theory of value. The other monetary writings of Ricardo were hardly taken into consideration, although a Japanese translation of quality including almost all the main monetary writings of Ricardo was published in 1931 by Obata Shigeo (Obata 1931). It seems that even in English there were, at that time, no such publications of comparable quality in terms of scrupulous text critique and comprehensiveness. But no subsequent research works in Japan undertook any comprehensive study of Ricardo's theory of money, taking all of these writings into account. This is in striking contrast to the situation during the first half of the Meiji era, before about 1890, when the theories of international trade and money and finance were among the preferred topics in the indirect and fragmentary presentations of Ricardo's theory, although most of them were entirely insufficient or at times beside the point (cf. Sect. 11.2 of the present chapter).

11.3.3 Translation of the Original Text of Ricardo

The study of economic theory in Japan after the Meiji Restoration was totally reliant on the importation of economics from the advanced Western countries, written in European languages. Much energy had to be spent on deciphering the economic literature in foreign languages and transferring it into Japanese. The work of translation therefore occupied an important place in research activities. The translation of the essential foreign literature into Japanese as a fundamental resource was the precondition for further research, and conversely, the extent of the translation was an indicator of progress in the research on the original resources. This is of course a preliminary process preceding the production of research results in the strict sense of the term.

First of all, we have to mention the translation of *Principles*, carried out by two pioneering researchers during the 1920s, Hori and Koizumi. Among the works of Ricardo, *Principles* was the first to be translated into Japanese. As in the case of Hori, who started his Ricardo studies at about the same time, Koizumi pursued two inseparable and simultaneous objectives: to present a 'correct and just' interpretation of Ricardo's theory, and to translate Ricardo's texts 'correctly and justly' into Japanese and present them to Japanese readers. While Hori first published in 1921 a partial translation of *Principles* under the direction of Kawakami (cf. Sect. 11.2 of the present chapter), and published in 1928 an entire translation as a sort of variorum edition as completely as possible at that time, Koizumi first published successively the partial translations of *Principles* in the review of Keiōgijuku University and then published them as a book. In 1929, the year after the publication of their respective entire translations of *Principles*, both Hori and Koizumi published the results of their research carried out over nearly ten years (Hori 1929; Koizumi 1929). Hori's translation work finally resulted in the Japanese version of Volume 1 of *The Works and Correspondence of David Ricardo* edited and published in 1951 by Piero Sraffa, published in 1972 from Yushōdō after the several revisions of his earlier translation, and this final translation of his is still in use today. On the other hand, Koizumi's translation of *Principles* was available in the paperback collection of Iwanami for nearly 60 years, from 1928 until 1987. Because of this translation work, Koizumi has also long been remembered as the translator of the chief work of Ricardo, though he had entirely left his earlier Ricardo studies in 1934.

The translations of other works of Ricardo were all published after 1928. Following Obata's translation of a quasi-exhaustive collection of Ricardo's monetary writings in 1931, we have only two: (1) *An Essay on the Influence of a Low Price of Corn on the Profits of Stock* (1815) and *On Protection to Agriculture* (1822), translated by Okawa Kazushi (1938), Iwanami, in its paperback collection and (2) *Letters of David Ricardo to Thomas Robert Malthus 1810–1823*, edited by James Bonar (1887), translated by Nakano Tadashi, in two fascicles (1942 and 1943), Iwanami, in its paperback collection. Of course, there were some other minor translations of Ricardo, but they contained no other original texts than those included in the above given ones.

When the translation work of Nakano appeared, Japan was already engaged in the Second World War, a period particularly difficult for the researchers somehow interested in Marx or classical economics. Instead of continuing to publish their research works, many of them preferred to apply themselves to translating the primary literature in the history of economic thought that had not yet been translated into Japanese. Indeed, a considerable number of classical works, including minor ones, were translated for the first time during this period. The Ricardo translation of Nakano, eminent Marxist economist after the War, may have been conceived like this.

On the other hand, the publication of Sraffa's version of *Principles* in 1951 must have given a great impact on Hori, because he had begun to translate it at the start of his career. So for Hori, the publication of a new edition of *Principles* edited by Sraffa with an impeccable comparison of the three successive original editions might have been an event obliging him to review his previous research. Not only *Principles* but also the new materials made available for the first time in Sraffa's edition may have made him feel the need to revising his earlier research. However, Hori showed no reaction to the particular, meticulous and scrupulous interpretations contained in Sraffa's extensive Introduction to Volume 1 of the *Works*. The impact of the *Works* on Hori was limited to the fact that many new materials were published in it and that Sraffa had performed admirable editorial work on Ricardo's writings. In particular, Hori said nothing about the 'corn ratio theory', which was to become a subject of lasting, animated debates both in Japan and internationally.

This approach to Sraffa's work has been widely shared in Japan by many Ricardo scholars after Hori. There is not one who does not highly esteem Sraffa's edition of *Works*. However, with regard to his 'corn ratio' interpretation, a number of researchers, starting with Hatori Takuya (1922–2012) who was for a long time the leading figure in Ricardo studies in Japan after the War, criticized it or called it into question, mainly on the basis of philological examinations of Ricardo's texts. But these criticisms of Sraffa have remained within the framework of exegetic contests on the subject of Ricardo, never going so far as to examine critically Sraffa's actual idea of measuring the surplus by a physical term (the corn ratio) instead of labour value. For Ricardo scholars, such examinations would have been beyond the scope of their work. It was therefore out of question that Sraffa's 'corn ratio' interpretation should be taken up together with his main work (Sraffa 1960), that systematically developed this idea. For many Ricardo scholars in Japan, this work of Sraffa was not within the scope of their research and probably very difficult to understand.

11.4 Japanese Research on Ricardo After the Second World War

11.4.1 Interest in Marx Between the 1950s and 1960s

Research on the history of economic thought in Japan, a foundation of 'conscientious' investigation, resisted the severe suppression of freedom of thought and speech from the 1930s to the end of the Second World War. Along with the resurgence of academic freedoms after Japan's defeat, investigative interest into social and economic thought increased rapidly, including interest in Marx, which drew considerable attention. At that time, Marxism had an enormous influence on the Japanese academic thought, which is difficult to imagine today, and it included studying Ricardo.

The study of Ricardo incorporated a debate about Japanese capitalism, a topic that interested Japanese Marxists in the 1930s and would continue to influence Japanese social science after 1945. The dispute was divided into two camps. The so-called Koza-ha, or Lectures Faction, followed the precepts of the Communist party, believing that the Great Empire of Japan after the Meiji Restoration was an absolutist state and that a democratic revolution was necessary to modernize Japan. The Rono-ha, or Worker-Farmer Faction, in contrast, defined the Meiji Restoration as a bourgeois revolution and argued that because Japan, after the Restoration, had become a modern capitalist state, a socialist revolution was required. Indeed, some English-language literature has already introduced the debate (i.e. Barshay 2004, chapters 2 and 3). Here, we focus on Japan's post-war research about the history of economic thought, not extensively treated in English literature. The Lectures Faction, revived after a long repression during the war, was characterized by its exclusive focus on Marx's reproduction schema. After the war, 'civil society Marxism', a post-war tributary of the Lectures Faction, attempted to transform the Japanese 'pre-modern' society on the model of the 'advanced Western civil society' depicted by Adam Smith, before proceeding to a socialist revolution based on Marx's theory. This started the history of economic thought in post-war Japan, especially regarding the works of Adam Smith, Marx and the concept of Physiocracy as a pioneering form of reproduction schemas. Research on Marx's theory of capital accumulation and its crises received a great deal of attention. Work on Ricardo proceeded only gradually in the shadow of these studies.[11]

During this period, Ricardo was interpreted largely through the lens of Marx's theory of capital accumulation and crisis. These studies paved the way for the interpretation of Ricardo's economic theory as a system of capital accumulation, a unique framework for Japanese research in the 1970s and 1980s. According to this framework, the key point of Marx's capital accumulation theory was the schematic relationship between capital accumulation and reproduction on an extended scale, from which followed a series of important economic phenomena, such as the rising organic composition of capital, the relative surplus-population, unemployment and crises. And theories of Adam Smith and Ricardo were, it was said, all just the imperfect ones to be completed by Marx. Therefore, studies in classical economics in the 1960s, such as those by Hatori and Tomizuka, must be understood in this context. Mazane (1959), the most comprehensive study about Ricardo's theory of machinery published during the 1950s, accepted Sraffa's annotation that the 'most revolutionary change' in the third edition of Ricardo's *Principles* was regarding machinery. Mazane argued that Marx was greatly inspired by Ricardo's new machinery theory, and that he could build his own theory of 'an industrial reserve army', which rejected Malthus's absolute surplus-population theory. In other words, according to Mazane, Ricardo suggested an 'exclusion theory', where the organic composition of capital would rise with the accumulation of capital, and where workers would be persistently unemployed. However, according to Mazane, while Ricardo certainly recognized that the *rate of increase* in labour demand would decline with capital accumulation, he also noted a 'compensation theory', where *absolute* labour demand would increase with the growth of capital. In 1963, Hatori argued that Ricardo had 'two views' on employment, that the demand for labour depended either on the amount of circulating capital or the volume of gross production. While the former view leads to Marx's rising organic composition of capital, the latter view is very different. In fact, Hatori maintained that it constituted the main idea behind Ricardo's machinery theory. Hatori's allegations were later severely criticized by Tomizuka, a Marxist economist. In Tomizuka's *Studies in the Theory of Capital Accumulation* (1965), he argued that in the new machinery theory in the third edition of his *Principles,* Ricardo understood that the amount of labour employed would decrease proportionally to the increase in capital, as the organic composition of capital rose. This concept greatly influenced Marx's 'theory of relative surplus-population'. However, Tomizuka opined that Ricardo could only grasp capital accumulation from the perspective of the 'circuit of productive capital'. Therefore, Ricardo mistook a decrease in the physical amount of gross production for a reduction in variable capital, which was converted into constant capital. This conversion was indeed the real cause of declining labour demand. This critique of Ricardo was very powerful in Japan during the 1960s.

Of course, many other studies of Ricardo were written during this period (cf. Izumo and Sato 2014, pp. 221–223). Studies about Ricardo's theory of foreign trade were developed in Japan in the 1950s. Among others, Ricardo's theory of foreign trade was originally interpreted in Yukizawa (1974) and this interpretation became well-known.[12] In addition, Kojima, a prominent Japanese scholar of international economics who studied Ricardo, maintained that in the three-goods model of cloth, wine and gold (money), trade terms (the relative prices of cloth and wine) could be determined without introducing reciprocal demand (Kojima 1951). Kojima demonstrated his interpretation, using numerical examples.

Hori moved away from Marxist economics soon after the beginning of 1920s. Having translated Ricardo's *Principles* three times, including the Sraffa edition, Hori was most interested in Ricardo's theory of value and wages. He concluded that Ricardo's theory of value was a 'revised labour theory of value that takes into account an equal rate of profit' (Hori 1958, pp. 68, 72–75). Perhaps Hori implied that Ricardo's theory of value was a system of relative prices, based on production costs that assumed an equal rate of profit. Hori also makes the qualitative difference between the two forms of capital disappear by quantifying the difference between longer and shorter turnover periods (Hori 1958, pp. 62–68). This, in effect, states that Ricardo followed the so-called 'reduction to dated quantities of labour' method.

11.4.2 Criticism of Sraffa's 'Corn Ratio' Theory: A 'Trio' of Ricardo Studies During the 1970s and 1980s

In the 1950s, Sraffa published a complete collection of Ricardo's works, which stimulated a growing interest of researchers in Ricardo in Japan. As an example, a committee urging the publication of a Japanese edition of the *Works and Correspondence of David Ricardo* was formed in 1955, leading to its actual publication in 1969. Importantly, except for Marx and Engels' *Werke*, this was the first attempt to publish a complete Japanese translation of an economist's collected works.

Based on Sraffa's edition of the *Works*, Japanese research on Ricardo expanded to a more thorough textual analysis. Hatori ([1972] 2018), who concluded that a serious gap existed between Sraffa's interpretation of Ricardo and the actual text, was the first Japanese scholar to reject Sraffa's 'corn ratio theory'. The essence of his criticism was as follows. If Ricardo's *Essay on Profits* (1815) had contained something other than corn as an input (with corn nevertheless remaining a measure of value), it could not have been a pure 'corn ratio theory'. Rather, Hatori said that Ricardo's theory of corn as a measure of value was close to Adam Smith's idea of 'labour commanded'. In response to Hatori's assertion, Nakamura (1975) partially agreed with Sraffa that, in the *Essay*, agricultural profit rates, on the margin, determined the general rate of profit, and that corn was used as a measure of value. (This occurred when the exchange ratio of an agricultural product to an industrial product was constant.) On the other hand, Nakamura reasoned that in the *Essay*, a rise in the price of corn would lead to an increase in wages, which in turn would lower profits. (This occurred when the exchange ratio of an agricultural product to an industrial product was variable.) Therefore, he criticized Sraffa (Nakamura 1975, pp. 110–136).

Senga, a relative newcomer, has argued with Hatori and Nakamura over their interpretations of the *Essay* since the 1970s. His work, published as a book at the end of the 1980s, characterized Japanese research on Ricardo during the 1970s and 1980s. He argued (Senga 1989, pp. 27–32) that Ricardo's analysis in the *Essay* was ultimately based on the following:

1. Ricardo's only economic principle was that the mechanism of profit equalization was based on free capital movement.
2. A decrease in agricultural profits signalled a decline in labour productivity, which could be demonstrated without using corn as the estimated input/output measure of value.
3. Agricultural production, which had the lowest labour productivity of any sector, also required capital investment. In other words, agricultural investment would likely to yield the lowest profits. An equal level of profitability would be realized by reducing other industries' profit levels to that of agriculture.

In the 1990s, Hatori, Nakamura and Senga were considered the 'leading trio' of Japanese researchers on Ricardo. Of course, many other interesting Ricardo studies, which have been excluded here because of limited space, were written during this period (cf. Izumo and Sato 2014, pp. 223–225).

11.4.3 Ricardo Research During the 1990s and Later

Since the 1970s, the academic background of scholars studying the history of economic thought has become quite diverse, and those who approach it from the standpoint of Marxist economics have become a minority. Since the 1990s, Ricardo scholars in Japan have explored numerous approaches.

Watarai, a post-Keynesian Japanese scholar of Senga's generation, has made researches on Ricardo and Malthus. Recently, while focusing on social policy, such as relief for the poor and plans for savings banks, Watarai also tried to build a rigorous model of Ricardo. However, because very few of Watarai's works have been translated into English,[13] we comment on an essay he wrote in the Japanese edition of Morishima's *Ricardo's Economics* (Watarai 2003). First of all, Watarai's long-standing interpretation of Ricardo is virtually the same as that of Morishima: that is, according to Watarai, Ricardo must have believed that the real wage rate would tend to decline during the periods of economic growth because of decreasing returns in agriculture. Although Ricardo argued that lower profit rates were caused by higher wages, Watarai believed that explaining wage rate declines using real wages was a specious argument. In the end, Watarai concluded that Ricardo failed, in his *Principles*, to fully explain the consequences of lower real wages (Watarai 2003, pp. 287–295).

Takenaga, a Marxist economist, has written about Ricardo and Keynes. In 2000, he published *Studies in Ricardo's Economics*, in Japanese, in which he maintained that Ricardo's production cost theory presupposed a general rate of profit rather than a Marxian labour theory of value, and that his theory of money was not a 'quantity' theory, because money was produced in the same way as any other commodity. Subsequently, he studied Ricardo's monetary theory exclusively (Takenaga 2013), particularly the question of consistency between Ricardo's monetary theory and his supposed labour theory of value (originally posed by Marx). Takenaga concluded that Ricardo incorporated his quantity theory of money into a concept of inconvertible banknotes, even though it was outside Ricardo's 'normal' monetary theory, where centrally issued banknotes were backed by gold. This would have offset the quantity theory of money.

Although numerous Japanese studies about Ricardo's monetary thought were written from before the Second World War to the 1980s, most were penned by Marxist economists. These studies, along with superficial analyses by a small number of neoclassical scholars, were not very helpful in understanding Ricardo. The work of Marcuzzo and Rosselli (1991), in those circumstances, was very valuable. They believed that the value of a currency relates to its purchasing power over the monetary standard, and that monetary authorities are responsible for wisely managing this value. Currency fluctuation is a change in the exchange ratio between the standard itself and other commodities; it cannot be controlled largely by monetary authorities. Therefore, monetary authorities should keep the demand for the standard as constant as possible. As a corollary note, along with the new research by Marcuzzo and Rosselli, Sato (1999, 2013) made positive statements about Ricardo's monetary policy.

As a concluding note, we may recall that in 2000, the Inaugural Meeting of the Ricardo Society of Japan was held at Rikkyo University in Tokyo. The commemorative speaker was Michio Morishima. As of 2019, the Ricardo Society is the most active group in Japan involved in classical economics research. It holds two regular meetings each year, as well as international conferences. We hope and believe that research about Ricardo in Japan will continue.

Acknowledgments This research was supported by the Japan Society for the Promotion of Sciences (JSPS) KAKENHI Grant Numbers JP16H03602 and JP17H00982.

Notes

1. In this chapter, Japanese names are given in the customary Japanese order, i.e. surname first.
2. Karl Marx points out in his letter to Engels dated 8 October 1858, that 'The proper task of bourgeois society is the creation of the world market, at least in outline, and of the production based on that market. Since the world is round, the colonisation of California and Australia and the opening up of China and Japan would seem to have completed this process' (Marx and Engels 1983, p. 347).
3. Apart from the studies by Mazane (1962, 1965), Izumo and Sato (2014), Izumo (2015) and Takenaga (2016), only a few attempts have been made to consider the reception of Ricardo and Ricardo studies in Japan.
4. This section is based on Izumo and Sato (2014), Izumo (2015), with several errors and mistakes corrected.
5. Wada translated chapters 1–6, 21, and 30, and Hori translated chapters 1–7, 19–21, 24 and 30–32 of Ricardo's *Principles* (Mazane 1975, p. 176).
6. Abridged versions of Smith's *Wealth of Nations* and Malthus's *Essay* had been translated and published respectively in 1884 and 1910.
7. This is an excerpt from the original English text. For the most part, this also applies hereafter to the quotations from translated works.
8. It is not surprising that both Ogata (later Wakayama) and Nishi had a 'Dutch connection' in this period, because Dutch learning had huge appeal for the Japanese intellectuals of the late eighteenth to mid-nineteenth centuries.
9. Intriguingly, Griffin points out in his *Notes and Extracts* that 'Ricardo entitled his work, "Principles of Political Economy, *and Taxation*" clearly implying that taxation is not a part of political economy' (Griffin 1902, p. 5, emphasis in the original).
10. The five selected works are as follows: *The High Price of Bullion: A Proof of the Depreciation of Bank Notes*, 4th edition (1811), *Reply to Mr Bosanquet's Practical Observations on the Report of the Bullion Committee*

(1811), *Proposals for an Economical and Secure Currency; with Observations on the Profits of the Bank of England* (1816), *Plan for the Establishment of a National Bank* (1824), and *Essay on the Funding System* (1820).

11. 'In this period [i.e., between the 1950s and 1960s],... Ricardo was regarded as only a minor theorist relative to Smith and Marx, the giants of economics' (Izumo and Sato 2014, p. 222).
12. See Tabuchi (2017) for the significant impact Yukizawa (1974) has had on studies in the Ricardian theory of international trade. Yukizawa had been already active since the 1950s (e.g. Yukizawa 1952).
13. Watarai (2015) clearly showed that Japanese scholars believed that Ricardo needed to overcome Adam Smith's 'adding-up' theory of prices. Watarai concluded that Ricardo's belief that 'money is a commodity' emancipated him from Smith's erroneous theory of prices.

References

Barshay, A. E. (2004). *The Social Sciences in Modern Japan: The Marxian and Modernist Traditions.* Berkeley and Los Angeles: University of California Press.

Byles, J. B. (1872). *Sophisms of Free-Trade and Popular Political Economy Examined* (9th ed.). Philadelphia: J. Heywood, H.C. Baird.

Chō, Y. (1983). Bibliographical Introduction: Publications. *East Sea Economic Courier, 7*, 1–12 (reprinted, in Japanese).

Crump, A. (1866). *A Practical Treatise on Banking, Currency, and the Exchanges.* London: Longmans, Green.

Fawcett, M. G. (1876). *Political Economy for Beginners* (4th ed.). London: Macmillan.

Fukuda, T. ([1908] 1925). From the Rent Theory of Ricardo to Marx. In *The Complete Works of Fukuda Tokuzō* (Vol. 3, pp. 1259–1264). Tokyo: Dobunkan (in Japanese).

Griffin, C. S. (Ed.). (1901). *Essays on Currency and Finance by David Ricardo.* Tokyo and Osaka: Maruzen.

Griffin, C. S. (1902). *Notes and Extracts to Accompany Lectures on the History of Economic Theories.* Mimeo.

Hatori, T. (1963). *Studies on Classical Theories of Capital Accumulation.* Tokyo: Miraisha (in Japanese).

Hatori, T. ([1972] 2018). Early Period Ricardo's Theories of Value and Distribution. *History of Economic Thought*, JSHET, *59*(2), 118–161 (English translation by R. Chapeskie and S. Senga).

Hori, T. (1928). *Ricardian Socialists.* Tokyo: Nippon Hyoronsha (in Japanese).

Hori, T. (1929). *Theory of Value of Ricardo and History of Its Critiques*. Tokyo: Iwanami (in Japanese).
Hori, T. (1958). *The Formation of Theoretical Political Economy: Ricardo's Theory of Value and Distribution*. Tokyo: Kobundo (in Japanese).
Izumo, M. (2015). Ricardo Studies in Japan 1869–1929. *The Annual Bulletin of the Institute for Economic Studies* (Seijo University), *28*, 133–162 (in Japanese).
Izumo, M., & Sato, S. (2014). The Reception of Ricardo in Japan. In G. Faccarello & M. Izumo (Eds.), *The Reception of David Ricardo in Continental Europe and Japan* (pp. 212–242). London and New York: Routledge.
Kawakami, H. (1921). Preface. In Ricardo, D. ([1821] 1921). *On the Principles of Political Economy and Taxation* (Japanese translation by T. Hori). Tokyo: Iwanami.
Kawakami, H. (1983). *The Complete Works of Kawakami Hajime* (36 Vols.). Tokyo: Iwanami (in Japanese).
Kita, T. (1906). *National Constitution and the Genuine Socialism*. Niikaga: Kita Terujiro (in Japanese).
Koizumi, S. ([1920] 1968). A Socialist Application of the Theory of Rent. In *The Complete Works of Koizumi Shinzō* (28 Vols., Vol. 1, pp. 360–382). Tokyo: Bungei Shunju (in Japanese).
Koizumi, S. (1929). *Ricardo Studies*. Tokyo: Tettō Shoin (in Japanese).
Kojima, K. (1951). Ricardo's Theory of International Balance of Payments Equilibrium. *Annals of the Hitotsubashi Academy, 2*(1), 76–92.
Marcuzzo, M. C., & Rosselli, A. (1991). *Ricardo and the Gold Standard: The Foundations of the International Monetary Order*. London: Macmillan.
Marx, K., & Engels, F. (1983). *Marx & Engels Collected Works*, vol. 40: *Letters 1856–1859*. London: Lawrence & Wishart.
Mazane, K. (1959). *Machinery and Unemployment*. Tokyo: Rironsha (in Japanese).
Mazane, K. (1962). The Reception History of Ricardo in the Meiji Era and Early Taishō Era. *Keizaigakunenpō* (Osaka City University), *16*, 63–168 (in Japanese).
Mazane, K. (1965). The Reception History of Ricardo from the Late Taishō Era to Pre-war Period. *Keizaigakunenpō* (Osaka City University), *22*, 1–61 (in Japanese).
Mazane, K. (1975). *Introduction to Ricardo's Economics*. Tokyo: Shinhyōron (in Japanese).
Morris-Suzuki, T. (1989). *A History of Japanese Economic Thought*. London and New York: Routledge.
Nagata, K. (1877). *Fawcett's Political Economy* (Japanese translation from Fawcett, 1876). Tokyo: Nagata Kensuke.

Nakamura, H. (1975). *The Ricardian System*. Kyoto: Minerva Shobō (in Japanese).

Nishi, A. ([1870–73] 1981). Lectures on Encyclopaedia. In T. Ōkubo (Ed.), *The Complete Works of Nishi Amane* (4 Vols.). Tokyo: Munetaka Shobō (in Japanese).

Obata, S. (Ed.). (1931). *Ricardo's Writings on Money and Banking*. Tokyo: Dōbunkan (in Japanese).

Ogata, T., & Mitsukuri, R. (1869). *The Principles of Economics* (Japanese translation from Perry, 1867). Tokyo: Kaisei Gakko.

Ōhara, K. (1901). A Critical Comment on Ricardo's Theory of Wage and Profit. *Tokyo Economic Journal, 1065*, 138–141(in Japanese).

Ōkubo, T. (1981). Commentary. In T. Ōkubo (Ed.), *The Complete Works of Nishi Amane* (Vol. 4, pp. 591–620). Tokyo: Munetaka Shobō (in Japanese).

Perry, A. L. (1867). *Elements of Political Economy* (2nd ed.). New York: Scribner.

Ricardo, D. ([1821] 1921). *On the Principles of Political Economy and Taxation* (Japanese translation by T. Hori). Tokyo: Iwanami.

Ricardo, D. ([1815; 1822] 1938). *An Essay on the Influence of a Low Price of Corn on the Profits of Stock* and *On Protection to Agriculture* (Japanese translation by K. Okawa). Tokyo: Iwanami.

Ricardo, D. ([1887] 1942–43). *Letters of David Ricardo to Thomas Robert Malthus 1810–1823* (J. Bonar (Ed.), Japanese translation by T. Nakano). (2 Vols.). Tokyo: Iwanami.

Ricardo, D. (1951–73). *The Works and Correspondence of David Ricardo*. P. Sraffa (Ed.), with the collaboration of M. H. Dobb (11 Vols.). Cambridge: Cambridge University Press for the Royal Economic Society.

Sato, Y. (1999). The Politics of the Resumption of Cash Payments: Reconsidering Ricardo's Plans for Bullion Payment and for the Establishment of a National Bank. *Study Series*, no. 41. Tokyo: Center for Historical Social Science Literature, Hitotsubashi University (in Japanese).

Sato, Y. (2013). Old and New Interpretations of Classical Monetary Theory. In Y. Sato & S. Takenaga (Eds.), *Ricardo on Money and Finance: A Bicentenary Reappraisal* (pp. 53–74). London and New York: Routledge.

Senga, S. (1989). *Studies in Political Economy of Ricardo*. Tokyo: Sanrei Shobō (in Japanese).

Sraffa, P. (1960). *Production of Commodities by Means of Commodities: Prelude to a Critique of Economic Theory*. Cambridge: Cambridge University Press.

Sugihara, S. (1972). *Western Economics and Modern Japan*. Osaka: Kansai University Press (in Japanese).

Sugihara, S. (1988). Economists in Journalism: Liberalism, Nationalism and Their Variants. In C. Sugiyama & H. Mizuta (Eds.), *Enlightenment and Beyond: Political Economy Comes to Japan* (pp. 237–253). Tokyo: University of Tokyo Press.

Sugiyama, C. (1988). Nishi Amane and Tsuda Mamichi. In C. Sugiyama & H. Mizuta (Eds.), *Enlightenment and Beyond: Political Economy Comes to Japan* (pp. 59–72). Tokyo: University of Tokyo Press.

Tabuchi, T. (2017). Yukizawa's Interpretation of Ricardo's 'Theory of Comparative Costs'. In S. Senga, M. Fujitomo, & T. Tabuchi (Eds.), *Ricardo on International Trade* (pp. 48–59). London and New York: Routledge.

Taguchi, U. (1878). *Japanese Economy: Free Trade.* Tokyo: Keizai Zasshisha (in Japanese).

Takenaga, S. (2000). *Studies in Ricardo's Economics.* Tokyo: Ochanomizu Shobo (in Japanese).

Takenaga, S. (2013). The Value of Money: Labour Theory of Value and Quantity Theory in Ricardo's Economic Theory. In Y. Sato & S. Takenaga (Eds.), *Ricardo on Money and Finance: A Bicentenary Reappraisal* (pp. 77–114). London and New York: Routledge.

Takenaga, S. (2016). *Ricardo and the Japanese Economic Though: Selection of Ricardo Studies in Japan during the Interwar Period.* London and New York: Routledge.

Thunberg, C.P. (1788–93). *Resa uti Europa, Africa, Asia, förrättad åren 1770–1779* (4 Vols.). Upsala: J. Edman.

Tomizuka, R. (1965). *Studies in the Theory of Capital Accumulation.* Tokyo: Miraisha (in Japanese).

Toynbee, A. J. (1884). *Lectures on the Industrial Revolution of the Eighteenth Century in England.* London: Longmans.

Usagawa, H., Endō, K., & Miwa, S. (1876). *A Treatise on Banking Experiment* (Japanese translation from Crump, 1866). Tokyo: Shiheiryo.

Wakayama, N. (1877). *A Fault-Finding of Free Trade* (Japanese translation of Byles, 1872). Tokyo: Wakayama Norikazu.

Watarai, K. (2003). Professor Morishima's Interpretation of Ricardo and His view on the History of Economic Thought: A Bibliographical Essay. In the Japanese Edition of *Ricardo's Economics*, as vol. 6 of the *Collected Works of Michio Morishima* (pp. 279–302). Tokyo: Iwanami (in Japanese).

Watarai, K. (2015). Ricardo's Emancipation from Smith's Theory of Prices. In H. D. Kurz & N. Salvadori (Eds.), *The Elgar Companion to David Ricardo* (pp. 478–482). Cheltenham, UK and Northampton, MA: Edward Elgar.

Yoshida, K. (1908). *A Treatise on the Industrial Revolution in England* (Japanese translation of Toynbee, 1884). Tokyo: Dainihon Bunmei Kyokai.

Yukizawa, K. (1952). Ricardo's Theory of Comparative Costs and the Labour Theory of Value. In *The International Economy*, the Japan Society of International Economics, 3, 45 (in Japanese).

Yukizawa, K. (1974). The Original Meaning and the Deformed Interpretation of Ricardo's 'Theory of Comparative Cost'. *Shogaku Ronsan*, Chuo University, *15*(6), 25–51 (in Japanese).

CHAPTER 12

From Ricardo to Sraffa: Gold as Monetary Standard in a Classical Theory of Money

Carlo Benetti and Jean Cartelier

Ricardo's theory (or theories) of money and prices has recently (Deleplace 2017) or less recently (Marcuzzo and Rosselli 1991) been revisited. New insights and interpretations have been offered on these occasions. We acknowledge the debt we have to these authors. We do not intend, however, to discuss their interpretations of Ricardo's theory of money. We do not suggest a new view about Ricardo's monetary thought either. The authors mentioned supra are the true experts of it and to establish 'what Ricardo has really said' is not our topic. We have preferred to inquire into what could or should be a Classical theory of money and prices sixty years after Sraffa's *Production of Commodities by Means of Commodities* publication (1960). Needless to say, this is a difficult and debatable question but it may give an opportunity to re-open an interesting debate.

C. Benetti · J. Cartelier (✉)
Université Paris-Nanterre, EconomiX, Paris, France
e-mail: jean.cartelier@parisnanterre.fr

C. Benetti
e-mail: carlo.benetti@orange.fr

M. C. Marcuzzo et al. (eds.), *New Perspectives on Political Economy and Its History*, Palgrave Studies in the History of Economic Thought,
https://doi.org/10.1007/978-3-030-42925-6_12

Three basic propositions are taken as granted and will not be discussed thereafter. They are a starting point for our exploration.

A. The theory of ***natural prices*** does not rely on the quantities of labour but on a ***difficulty of production*** as Sraffa's book makes it clear. It is summed up by:

$$(1+r)A'p = p \tag{12.1}$$

where r is the rate of profit and A' the transpose of A square matrix of the a_{ij}'s, quantity of commodity i used for the production of a commodity j. Natural quantities of commodities q_i are expressed in physical units, each one being equal respectively to total products. As a consequence, the vector of natural quantities is $q' = \left(1 \cdots 1\right)$. A' is assumed to be irreducible and non-negative which means that all commodities are basic in Sraffa's sense (each commodity enters directly or indirectly in the production of each commodity).

Solving system (12.1) gives the rate of profit r and the vector of natural prices p up to a scalar factor. Natural prices are relative ones. Any (simple or composite) commodity may be chosen as a common expression of prices as soon as it is a component of system (12.1). If corn is chosen, system (12.1) becomes:

$$(1+r)A'p = p \tag{12.2}$$

$$p_c^c = 1$$

Solving system (12.2) gives n natural prices expressed in corn and the rate of profit r.

In system (12.2), prices have a common and unique expression; 'the singleness of the standard' is 'the essential feature of money' according to Sraffa (1932, p. 51). A standard has a monetary character as such (see below).

B. The ***monetary standard*** is the central point of a theory of money. Let us choose gold instead of corn and assume that gold is the only non-basic commodity (see infra).

Besides the natural price of gold, expressed in itself $p_g^g = 1$, there is a legal price $\bar{p}_g^{£}$ expressed in £, which is the consequence of the definition of the monetary unit:

$$1£ \equiv \beta gold \rightarrow \bar{p}_g^{£} = \frac{1}{\beta}£ \tag{12.3}$$

Table 12.1 Bank's balance sheet

Assets	*Bank*	*Liabilities*
Gold $= \eta\lambda\bar{p}_g^{£}$		Banknotes issued as a counterpart of gold $\eta\lambda\bar{p}_g^{£}$
Loans L		$L = (\mu - \eta)\lambda\bar{p}_g^{£}$
Total $M^{£}$		$M^{£} = \mu\lambda\bar{p}_g^{£}$

The total quantity of gold is λ. Gold may be used for monetary purposes and for luxury consumption. There is no need that gold effectively circulates. Banknotes convertible in gold at the legal price and issued by a bank may do the job as well.[1] Banknotes of 1 £ are supposed to be the unique means of payment used in the economy. At each period, the bank buys the quantity of gold which is necessary for the circulation of commodities to take place, for a total amount of £ equal to the sum of natural prices $T^{£} = \sum_{i \neq g} p_i^{£}$ (remember that $q' = (1 \cdots 1)$). For the sake of simplicity, the velocity of money is supposed constant and equal to 1. For the same reason, gold is supposed to be a non-durable commodity (see below). Banknotes are issued either as a counterpart of the gold bought by the bank, which is a fraction η of λ, or as a counterpart of the loans of the period (which have to be paid back at the end of the period). The amount of loans is $L = (\mu - \eta)\lambda\bar{p}_g^{£}$, where μ is the ratio of the quantity of issued banknotes to the total value of gold in the vault of the bank at the legal price.

Given our simplifying assumptions, the bank's balance sheet which is also its flow-of-fund account is shown in Table 12.1.

Two cases have to be distinguished depending on whether it is or not necessary to resort to credit for the realization of all transactions. The latter case ($\mu = \eta$) is straightforward. The bank buys only the quantity of gold which is strictly necessary for circulation—$T^{£} \leq \lambda\bar{p}_g^{£}$—and issues convertible banknotes which act as gold certificates circulating at their legal price. The former case ($\eta = 1, \mu \geq 1$) is more interesting. The bank issues convertible banknotes partly as a counterpart of its loans and partly as a counterpart of gold. The total amount of convertible banknotes is now a multiple $\mu > 1$ of the value of the gold in the vault of the bank. The higher μ, the higher the risk of liquidity incurred by the bank (to keep the matter simple we neglect credit risk). In both cases, only banknotes circulate.

Circulation at natural prices is described by Eq. (12.4) which does not pre-suppose any causality direction:

$$M^{\pounds} = \mu\lambda\bar{p}_g^{\pounds} = \sum_{i \neq g} p_i^{\pounds} = T^{\pounds} \tag{12.4}$$

Money (convertible banknotes) is the unique technique of circulation in the economy (the modern question of monetary micro-foundations is not considered). That technique is summed up by a unique exogenous variable, the velocity of circulation of money supposed equal to 1.

C. The third proposition concerns the *market money prices of commodities* (other than gold). In contrast to natural prices which only depend upon production conditions and a uniform rate of profit, market prices depend upon realized transactions in the market. As a matter of fact, 'market money prices' is pleonastic and we will denote them thereafter by 'market prices'.

When Ricardo deals with market prices, he limits himself to approving of Adam Smith's positions. According to Smith, market prices are governed by a general rule which is recalled in Chapter VII of *Wealth of Nations*:

> The market price of every particular commodity is regulated by the proportion between the quantity which is actually brought to market, and the demand of those who are willing to pay the natural price of the commodity .... Such people may be called the effectual demanders, and their demand the effectual demand. (Smith [1776] 1976, I, p. 73)

The rule is borrowed from Cantillon: 'les prix [se] fixent par la proportion des denrées qu'on y expose en vente et de l'argent qu'on y offre pour les acheter' (Cantillon [1755] 1955, p. 7).

If $\tilde{p}_{i\neq g}^{\pounds}$ is the *market price* of commodity, $M_{i\neq g}^{\pounds} = \alpha_i M^{\pounds}$ the amount of money spent in market $i \neq g$, and $\tilde{q}_{i\neq g}$ the quantity of commodity i brought to the market, the rule is expressed as:

$$\tilde{p}_{i\neq g}^{\pounds} = \frac{\alpha_i}{\tilde{q}_{i\neq g}} M^{\pounds} V \rightarrow M_{i\neq g}^{\pounds} V = \tilde{p}_{i\neq g}^{\pounds} \tilde{q}_{i\neq g} \forall i \neq g \tag{12.5}$$

where α_i is the fraction of total expenses $M^{\pounds}$ in market i. Note that quantity $\tilde{q}_{i\neq g}$ of commodity i brought to market is sold not only as an input but also as a component of the surplus. Market prices, given by

Eq. (12.5), depend on the uses of the surplus, in contrast to Sraffian natural prices (see infra).

The market for gold (commodity g) will be considered below. The price which is to be found in that market is critical for the Classical theory of money. We distinguish between ***money depreciation***, which has to do with the quantity of money, and the value of the standard, which has to do with gold production conditions.

From this threefold starting point, three central questions arise:

1. Is it appropriate to speak of a natural price of the standard, here gold? If not, a dichotomy between natural and market prices (and money) would characterize the Classical theory of prices.
2. What is the principle which regulates the market price of gold and what is its relation with its legal price?
3. What is the relation between the quantity of money, the market price of gold, and money depreciation?

Let us see these points successively.

12.1 The Natural Price of Gold

Whether gold has or not a natural price is not a dubious question at first sight. Like any other commodity, gold is competitively produced by capital and the uniformity of the rate of profit applies to its production like to any other. Ricardo is very clear on that point in Chapter XXVII of the *Principles* (Ricardo [1821] 1951). For him, there is no incompatibility between his 'new' and 'general theory of value' (Sraffa 1951, pp. xxx, xxxii) and his monetary theory of the 1810s.

Gold, however, as a standard, is used for circulation. This affects its demand and its position amongst the whole set of commodities. We deal here with a closed economy where gold is produced along with other commodities. A convenient way to consider its specificity is to assume that gold is a non-basic commodity and even the unique non-basic commodity for the sake of simplicity. It would be more appropriate therefore to speak of a production cost of gold rather than of a natural price or value. In Sraffa's terms: 'The price of a non-basic product depends on the price of its means of production, but these do not depend on it. Whereas in the case of a basic product the prices of its means of production depend on its own price no less than the latter depends on them' (Sraffa 1960, p. 9).

While the conditions of production of gold do not influence the prices of basic commodities and the rate of profit, the reverse is not true. Gold may be said neutral in this precise sense.[2]

System (12.2) becomes:

$$(1+r)A'p = p$$

$$(1+r)\lambda \sum_{i \neq g} a_{ig} p_i = \lambda p_g \qquad (12.2*)$$

$$p_g^g = 1$$

where λ is a parameter which applies to the natural quantity of gold (equal to one as for any other commodity).

If the variations of the conditions of production of gold leave prices and the rate of profit unchanged, they affect the circulation.

The system of the first line of (12.2*) determines the rate of profit and the prices of the n basic commodities up to a scalar, while the equation of the second line, which concerns gold, gives the price of gold once the first system has been solved. The last line recalls that gold is the standard used to express commodity prices.

The particularity of the standard as compared with the other commodities, besides being a non-basic commodity, becomes clear when a change in the conditions of production of gold arises (due to a change of technique or to a discovery of a new mine) and prompts some adjustment of the circulation. Ghislain Deleplace (2017) reminds us that two reasons explain why the adjustment is specific (different from that of corn, for example):

- Durability of gold is responsible for a progressive accumulation of available quantities in contrast to corn which is destroyed at each period.
- The demand for corn tends towards its natural quantity and will be equal to it at the end of adjustment while 'the demand for bullion to be transformed into money is not for a definite *quantity* but, with a given aggregate value of the commodities to be circulated, for an aggregate *value*' (Deleplace 2017, p. 182; author's emphasis).

Assuming for the sake of simplicity that gold is no longer durable allows us to get rid of the first difference (we have resorted above to that assumption for simplifying the account of the bank). Absurd as it is from a realistic point of view, that assumption is useful at this level of abstraction. Durability is a feature more or less common to all commodities, while we are interested in gold as specifically used for circulation—which is not the case for all the others. It is that difference only which matters here. We have already dealt with that point in our paragraph (B) above.

Gold, being the standard, is demanded for a special reason—the 'wants of commerce'—not shared by other commodities as Deleplace's quotation above reminds us. Let us make it explicit and note that the 'wants of commerce' at the natural state are:

$$T^g = \sum_{i \neq g} p_i^g \leftrightarrow T^{£} = \sum_{i \neq g} p_i^{£} \tag{12.6}$$

The quantity of gold needed for that circulation is then T^g. The available quantity is λ, the current production, since gold is non-durable and does not enter in the production of basic commodities.

We will consider $\lambda = 1$ as a benchmark where

$$T^g = \sum_{i \neq g} p_i^g = 1 \tag{12.7}$$

The available quantity of gold is precisely equal to the quantity required for circulation. We have reasoned in terms of gold but we could have been reasoning in terms of £ as well on the basis of its legal definition. In this case, the entire production of gold is bought by the bank ($\eta = 1$) which issues as a counterpart an equal amount of convertible banknotes ($\mu = 1$). Expressed in £, the amount of circulation is $\sum_{i \neq g} p_i^{£} = \frac{1}{\beta}£$.

Suppose now that the production (or import) of gold has doubled, the technique being unchanged ($\lambda = 2$). The needs of trade are also unchanged[3] so that the available quantity of gold λ exceeds the quantity needed for circulation: $\lambda > T^g$. A quantity $\lambda - T^g$ is available for consumption. The total quantity of gold is twice the benchmark level but the quantity of gold bought by the bank has not changed.

Here we depart from Ricardo and Deleplace's interpretation according to which double quantity of gold must be associated with double quantity of circulating gold. If the quantity of gold bought by the bank is correlated with the needs of trade, there is no reason for its change in the case we examine. The gold in excess of the needs of trade will be used as a luxury commodity. From the proposition 'The aggregate value of the commodities to be circulated being given, any quantity of money will do' (Deleplace 2017, p. 178), one should not derive that any quantity will do but the opposite: only one quantity of money will do! The aggregate value of the commodities to be circulated being given in gold or in £ (and the velocity of money circulation being constant) determines the amount of means of payment (in gold or in £) the bank has to issue.

Emphasizing that the quantity of money is determined by the needs of trade is not what Ricardo ordinarily maintains. The fear (not unjustified) that the Treasury or the bank could adopt an inflationary behaviour makes him adopt another view: the quantity of money is an independent (or exogenous) variable; consequently, a regulation mechanism has to be implemented in order to deprive the bank of its arbitrary power. But a partially right idea—the Treasury may directly or indirectly influence the quantity of money issued—should not justify a false idea—the total quantity of money is exogenous (of outside type). The monetization of the private debts is endogenous (of inside type).

Assume now, λ being equal to 1, that the price of gold is divided by 2 due to a progress in the technique of production (all a_{ig}'s are divided by 2). The system of the first line of (12.2*) is unchanged: the rate of profit and the vector of natural prices of basic commodities are still the same. But, as a consequence of the decrease in the price of gold, all natural prices of basic commodities are doubled when they are expressed in gold. The quantity of gold the bank should buy has doubled but the quantity available is still 1. We have already noted that gold does not circulate and there is no need to resort to a mechanism of adjustment of gold. The increased needs of trade will be satisfied by additional means of payment issued not as a counterpart of gold but as a counterpart of loans (see above the balance sheet of the bank). It is that quantity of banknotes (and not that issued against gold) which requires to be regulated. This point will be dealt with in Sect. 12.3.

It appears thus that gold (the standard in general), although not having a natural price properly speaking, has a price determined by system (12.2*). Consequently, natural prices may be expressed in money terms (absolute prices) by using the legal definition of the £. *Natural* *money prices* are:

$$p^{\pounds} = p^{g}\frac{1}{\beta}\pounds \tag{12.8}$$

They define what we may dub a complete Ricardian equilibrium, both *real and monetary*.[4]

If gold were not produced in the economy, it would still be possible to define the £ as a weight of gold but it would no longer be possible to express natural prices in £ since it would no longer be possible to determine the price of gold along with the prices of basic commodities.

This would be very harmful to a Classical theory of money since we would have a real equilibrium only, without any monetary expression. Fortunately, this is not the case. It is thus possible to keep searching for a Classical theory of money by dealing now with the market determination of the price of gold.

12.2 Market Price and Legal Price of Gold

According to Deleplace, monetary arbitrage, that is, between the market price and the legal price of gold, is the basis of Ricardo's theory of money. We will first examine the consequences of the unlimited convertibility at the legal price on the working of the gold market and secondly Ricardo's solution to the theoretical difficulties of monetary arbitrage.

12.2.1 The Legal Price of Gold and Arbitrage

When the market price of gold coincides with its legal price, the conversion of £ into gold and of gold into £ is made indiscriminately through the bank or the gold market. Monetary arbitrage implies that there may be a discrepancy between these two prices and that there exist some economic forces which eliminate it. Thus, the economy is protected against a possible arbitrary behaviour of the bank.

Let us suppose that a price different from the legal price is quoted in the gold market. If it is higher than the legal price, individuals could obtain gold at its legal price, bring it to the market in order to sell it at a higher price, but there is no money to buy it since money holders have an interest in obtaining gold at the legal price. If it is lower than the legal price, individuals could obtain £ against gold at the bank in order to buy back gold in the gold market at a lower price, but the gold supply is nil since gold holders have an interest in obtaining £ at the legal price. In each case, there is no transaction. This configuration of the gold market can also be expressed in terms of Cantillon's rule mentioned above. The price quoted is replaced by the expected price. Equation (12.5) shows that there exists no positive and finite market price for gold. This price is either 'nil' or 'infinite'.

But the story does not end here. Gold is in excess supply or in excess demand, so that its price must decrease or increase. Since Cantillon's rule of price formation cannot be applied to the gold market, such equilibrating price changes must be executed by the well-known Walrasian auctioneer. Thus, the Walrasian *tâtonnement* is an implication of monetary arbitrage. We do not see how such an unpleasant conclusion could be avoided since it is directly derived from Ricardo's model based on the convertibility of £.[5]

As a result, when the market price and the mint price of gold differ, the 'gold market' is not, properly speaking, a 'market' in the sense that no exchange relationship between individuals can take place. The arbitrage on gold is as inconceivable as it is on a commodity, the price of which is fixed administratively, and not determined on a market (leaving fraud aside for this case as for gold).

The market price and the legal price of gold cannot differ: the first one is indexed to the second one. Transaction costs being excluded (here they are nil by hypothesis), the equality of both prices is absolutely and instantaneously imposed, i.e.:

$$\tilde{p}_g^{\pounds} = \bar{p}_g^{\pounds} = \frac{1}{\beta}\pounds \qquad (12.9)$$

However, although central in the monetary system, relationship (12.9) is not directly related to the amount of money. This creates a great difficulty since according to Ricardo—as Deleplace reminds us—the amount of money is regulated by the purchasing power over the standard, in other words by the inverse of the market price of gold. But this purchasing power is fixed. Thus, the regulation of the amount of banknotes must be found elsewhere, that is, in the monetary prices of goods except the standard, something which is rejected by both Ricardo and Ghislain Deleplace. We will examine this in Sect. 12.3.

12.2.2 Ricardo and Monetary Arbitrage

According to Ricardo, 'There is no point more important in issuing paper money, than to be fully impressed with the effects which follow from the principle of limitation of quantity' ([1821] 1951, p. 353).

One easily understands the attractiveness of a monetary theory based on arbitrage between the market price and the legal price of gold. The gold market would have the role of regulating the quantity of money since the depreciation of £ would be known by merely observing the money price of gold without bothering about the prices of goods. The question is, therefore, how the market price of gold can deviate from the legal price. Deleplace answers by proposing an interesting interpretation of Ricardo's monetary theory in which the 'debasement' of coins raises the market price of bullion above the mint price (i.e. determines the depreciation of £). 'In practice' (Deleplace 2017, p. 230), the market price of gold lies within a range defined by a price floor given by the mint price minus the minting cost and a price ceiling given by the mint price plus both the melting cost and the rate of debasement.[6] Within these bounds, the price of gold may differ from the mint price and thus play the role of regulating the quantity of money. We have no objection to this position. But it is unsuitable for a possible contemporary Classical theory of a money which entirely consists of paper money convertible into gold at a legal price. According to Ricardo, such money represents the most perfect monetary state: 'A currency is in its most perfect state when it consists wholly of paper money, but of paper money of an equal value with the gold which it professes to represent' ([1821] 1951, p. 361).

In this economy, the factors that allow the market price of gold to deviate from the mint price are irrelevant. The regulation of the quantity of money must then be explained differently as we are going to see in the next section.

12.3 Market Price, Monetary Transactions and Quantity of Money

The monetary system used as a theoretical framework has been sketched out above. Let us consider now the case where the amount of convertible banknotes issued is greater than or equal to the value in £ of the totality of the gold production ($\eta = 1$, $\mu \geq 1$). We also suppose that this production is invariable both in its quantity ($\lambda = 1$) and in its production technique

(a_{ig}). The issue of the value of money therefore does not arise, only its depreciation becomes relevant.

The total amount $M^{£}$ of convertible banknotes issued by the bank is a multiple μ of the value of the gold reserve of the bank:

$$M^{£} = \mu \bar{p}_g^{£} = \mu \frac{1}{\beta} £ \tag{12.10}$$

The transactions carried out using this system determine the market prices according to Cantillon's rule mentioned above

$$\tilde{p}_{i \neq g}^{£} = \frac{\alpha_i}{\tilde{q}_{i \neq g}} M^{£} \rightarrow M_{i \neq g}^{£} = \tilde{p}_{i \neq g}^{£} \tilde{q}_{i \neq g} \forall i \neq g \tag{12.5}$$

The 'wants of commerce' are given by $\sum_{i \neq g} \tilde{q}_i \tilde{p}_i^{£}$, where $\tilde{q}_i$ and $\tilde{p}_i^{£}$ are respectively the quantity and the market price in £ of commodity i. The amount of money issued by the bank is given by equality (12.10). The value of the £, relevant for measuring its depreciation, is, therefore, determined by the adequacy of banknotes to circulation:

$$\frac{\sum_{i \neq g} \tilde{q}_i \tilde{p}_i^{£}}{\mu} = \bar{p}_g^{£} \tag{12.11}$$

It corresponds to the legal definition. This proposal is in line with Ricardo's basic thesis (see the above quotation: Ricardo [1821] 1951, p. 361). This is obviously not surprising since, as shown in the previous section, the market price of gold cannot be different from its legal price.

It should be noted, however, that the adequacy of banknotes to circulation can be interpreted differently depending on whether the amount of banknotes is considered as a cause or a consequence and whether μ is flexible or not.

Equation (12.11) is merely the aggregation of Cantillon's rule Eq. (12.5) over all goods except gold, which gives:

$$\sum_{i \neq g} \tilde{q}_{i \neq g} \tilde{p}_{i \neq g}^{£} = \sum_{i \neq g} \alpha_i M^{£} V = M^{£} V \tag{12.12}$$

Equation (12.12) is the well-known equation of exchange that can be interpreted in many ways,[7] either by denying any causal meaning or by assuming that expenditure or quantities or prices are the independent variable. The only possible assertion at this stage is that there is indeed a close relationship between the amount of money $M^{£}$ and the monetary prices of all commodities except the standard $\tilde{p}^{£}_{i \neq g}$. We have noted (see Eq. (12.5)) that market prices $\tilde{p}^{£}_{i \neq g}$ depend on the sales of commodities not only as inputs but also as components of the surplus. This is true for market quantities $\tilde{q}_{i \neq g}$ as well. The fact that the use of the surplus is not considered in Sraffa's system of natural prices creates an additional difficulty when dealing with the relation between natural and market variables. This would not be the case with Torrens' theory of prices.[8] In any case, relationship (12.12) says nothing about the determination of the amount of money itself.

The convertibility of banknotes at the legal price is, in the Classical theory of money, the regulating mechanism of their quantity. Let us suppose that the issuance of banknotes is higher than what is authorized by the gold reserve of the bank (i.e. a rise in the multiplier μ). The monetary expenditure in various markets increases. In accordance with Cantillon's rule, the money prices of commodities except the standard increase, but not proportionately since the distribution of expenditure amongst the industries is generally not fixed, except in a very particular case. The economy is then in the situation described by Ricardo ([1810–11] 1951, p. 105) when he speaks about gold as 'the cheapest of all ... [exportable] commodities in the English market, in relation to the foreign markets, and therefore the most profitable to be exported'.[9]

Instead of exporting gold, it is also possible to consider its use as a material for ornaments, whose production in the country becomes profitable. Anyway, gold comes out of the bank. The multiplier μ is too high. The need to restore it to an earlier level is the regulating principle of the amount of banknotes. As we have seen, this formulation of the 'principle of limitation of quantity' can be based on some of Ricardo's texts and has the advantage of being more acceptable than arbitrage between the gold market and the bank.

The term 'wants of commerce' could also imply that the banknotes are issued at the initiative of entrepreneurs on the basis of their price expectations. If this were the case, and if the bank were accommodative, the market price expectations by entrepreneurs would be the causal variable which would regulate the amount of money. The variation of multiplier μ would ensure the elasticity of the issue of banknotes in respect to the 'wants of commerce' ($1/\mu$ is the ratio of the gold reserve held by the bank to the banknotes issued as a counterpart of credits).

Owing to the necessary equality of the legal price of gold and its market price, the currency is still in the 'perfect state' pointed out by Ricardo (Equation (12.11)). In this case, as shown by Ghislain Deleplace, Ricardo did not, strictly speaking, support the fixity of μ. It would have been anachronistic and inaccurate for Ricardo to support the *Currency Principle*. That is true. But it would be no less anachronistic and even more inaccurate to include him amongst the defenders of the *Banking Principle*.

The variability of μ, intended to adapt the issuance of convertible banknotes to the 'wants of commerce', is bounded by the liquidity risk. In this context, the idea of a minimum coverage rate—and therefore a maximal μ—is sensible. When the 'wants of commerce' exceed the amount of banknotes that can be issued, the amount of money is no longer determined by the demand for credit but by the constraint on the bank. The maximum amount of banknotes is an exogenous variable, related, through the maximal multiplier μ, to the gold reserve. The modern version of this position is the currency multiplier theory that applies this time to the *high-powered money*. Adopting this view does not require subscribing to the quantity theory of money. It is not necessary, for example, to postulate the fixity of coefficients α_i to conclude that a gold inflow in the reserve of the bank would result in a (not proportional) increase in the market prices of all goods except gold, and thus in a depreciation of money that would occur without any change in the value of the standard.

Such position is on the *Currency* side the supporters of which will claim, rightly or wrongly, to adhere to Ricardo's theory. But it does not follow that the Classical theory of money summarily sketched in this text is incompatible with the *Banking*. This compatibility can be obtained by supplementing that theory with the distinction made by Tooke in 1844 between two money circulations: one of them between consumers and dealers takes place in currency (coins which are the only legal tender for Tooke, and banknotes as gold certificates in this text) while the other one between dealers exclusively uses credit (bills of exchange, cheques for Tooke, here the banknotes issued as a counterpart of credit). The first one concerns the income, the second one the capital. But this would be the subject of another text.

Acknowledgments We are very grateful to Ghislain Deleplace for his critical reading of the first version of this paper. His numerous remarks and observations have been very useful. However, he is not responsible for the remaining errors and insufficiencies. We have also benefited from the suggestions of the editors. The usual disclaimer applies.

Notes

1. We only deal with that regime. Inconvertible banknotes (an important case for Ricardo) will not be considered thereafter.
2. Money neutrality means something totally different in the mainstream theory of money. Money is said to be neutral when a change in its quantity does not affect real variables (prices and market allocations). In the model of system (12.2), variations of the quantities produced do not change the rate of profit and the prices as a consequence of constant returns. That property holds for gold as for basic commodities. There is no specificity of the standard on this point.
3. This is not absolutely exact since the gold used as a luxury good $\lambda - T^g$ is added to the non-basic commodities. To keep the story simple, we neglect this point which does not affect our general argument.
4. If gold were produced abroad and imported in our economy, we could consider a specific industry (foreign trade) buying its inputs λa_{iext} from the other industries and getting its output λ from abroad. This specific industry would yield the uniform rate of profit. System (12.2*) would apply also in this case.
5. It is not the case of Walras' hypothesis of no trade out of equilibrium, the only justification of which is the conception of competitive market as the practical solution of the general equilibrium equations (Walras [1874] 1988, § 116). This hypothesis can therefore be suppressed as shown in particular by the so-called 'non-*tâtonnement* processes' (see Fisher 1983).
6. See also Marcuzzo and Rosselli (1991, p. 107).
7. The quantity theory of money is one of them. By assuming that V and all α_i are fixed, that the quantities of goods brought to the market are the natural quantities $\tilde{q}_{i \neq g} = 1$ that the issuance of banknotes is decided at the initiative of the bank, it can be inferred that the increase in the issuance of banknotes by a factor γ causes an increase in the market prices by the same factor and leaves all other variables unchanged. Under these conditions, the value of the £ is strictly inversely proportional to its quantity.
8. Torrens (1821) emphasized the physical constraints imposed to the reproduction of capital when all profits are reinvested in the sector in which they were generated (see Benetti et al. 2014).
9. In the same vein, see also Ricardo (1951, pp. 57, 208, and 328) about Bentham's interpretation of Smith's monetary theory. On Ricardo's analysis of the export of gold, see Marcuzzo and Rosselli (1991, Chapter 8), according to whom 'there can be only five possible causes for the exportation of gold from a situation of zero gold movements' (p. 132). And they

conclude that 'for Ricardo the export of gold was brought about exclusively by monetary factors' that is, a 'redundancy of currency' (pp. 5 and 141).

References

Benetti, C., Bidard, C., Klimovsky, E., & Rebeyrol, A. (2014). Disequilibrium, Reproduction and Money: A Classical Approach. *Metroeconomica, 65*(3), 524–540.

Cantillon, R. ([1755] 1955). *Essai sur la nature du commerce en general.* Paris: INED, Paris.

Deleplace, G. (2017). *Ricardo on Money, a Reappraisal.* Abingdon: Routledge.

Fisher, F. (1983). *Disequilibrium Foundations of Equilibrium Economics.* Cambridge: Cambridge University Press.

Marcuzzo, M. C., & Rosselli, A. (1991). *Ricardo and the Gold Standard: The Foundations of the International Monetary Order.* London: Macmillan.

Ricardo, D. ([1810–11] 1951). The High Price of Bullion: A Proof of the Depreciation of Bank Notes. In P. Sraffa (Ed., with the collaboration of M. H. Dobb), *The Works and Correspondence of David Ricardo, Vol. 3: Pamphlets and Papers 1809–1811* (pp. 47–128). Cambridge: Cambridge University Press for the Royal Economic Society.

Ricardo, D. ([1821] 1951). *On the Principles of Political Economy and Taxation* (3rd ed.). In P. Sraffa (Ed., with the collaboration of M. H. Dobb), *The Works and Correspondence of David Ricardo* (Vol. 1). Cambridge: Cambridge University Press for the Royal Economic Society.

Ricardo, D. (1951). *Pamphlets and Papers 1809–1811.* In P. Sraffa (Ed., with the collaboration of M. H. Dobb), *The Works and Correspondence of David Ricardo* (Vol. 3). Cambridge: Cambridge University Press for the Royal Economic Society.

Smith, A. ([1776] 1976). *An Inquiry into the Nature and Causes of the Wealth of Nation.* In R. H. Campbell & A. S. Skinner (Eds, textual editor W. B. Todd), The Glasgow Edition of *The Works and Correspondence of Adam Smith* (Vols. 2a and 2b). Oxford: Oxford University Press.

Sraffa, P. (1932). Dr. Hayek on Money and Capital. *The Economic Journal, 42*(165), 42–53.

Sraffa, P. (1951). Introduction. In P. Sraffa (Ed., with the collaboration of M. H. Dobb), *The Works and Correspondence of David Ricardo, Vol. 1: On the Principles of Political Economy and Taxation* (pp. xiii–lxii). Cambridge: Cambridge University Press for the Royal Economic Society.

Sraffa, P. (1960). *Production of Commodities by Means of Commodities: Prelude to a Critique of Economic Theory.* Cambridge: Cambridge University Press.

Tooke, T. (1844). *An Inquiry into the Currency Principle.* London: Longman, Brown, Green and Longmans.

Torrens, R. (1821). *An Essay on the Production of Wealth.* London: Longman, Hurst, Rees, Orme and Brown.

Walras, L. ([1874] 1988). *Eléments d'économie politique pure.* In *Oeuvres économiques completes* (Vol. 8). Paris: Economica.

PART IV

Interpreting Sraffa

CHAPTER 13

Dialogues *Manqués* Between Antonio Gramsci and Piero Sraffa on Ricardo, Classical Political Economy and 'Pure Economics'

Jean-Pierre Potier

The study of the personal and intellectual relations between Antonio Gramsci and Piero Sraffa is always a fascinating experience.[1] Unfailing, Sraffa supported morally and materially his incarcerated friend. He opened for him an unlimited account at a Milan bookshop. By this way, Gramsci had access from the beginning of his imprisonment to a not insignificant documentation on economic matters (books and periodicals) (see Giasi 2017) and had the opportunity to write numerous notes concerning political economy.

In his *Prison Notebooks*, Gramsci asserted that Marxists must study the history of economic thought; a good textbook of 'critical economy' must deal with the history of economic science, precisely because 'the whole conception of critical economy is historicist' (Gramsci 1975, p. 1286, Notebook 10, § 37; English transl. 1995, p. 178). Nevertheless, about this field, Gramsci got access to only one main reference, Charles Gide

J.-P. Potier (✉)
University Lumière-Lyon 2, Lyon, France
e-mail: jppotier@free.fr

M. C. Marcuzzo et al. (eds.), *New Perspectives on Political Economy and Its History*, Palgrave Studies in the History of Economic Thought,
https://doi.org/10.1007/978-3-030-42925-6_13

and Charles Rist's book, *Histoire des doctrines économiques depuis les Physiocrates jusqu'à nos jours* (1926). He did not get the permission to receive Marx's *Theorien über den Mehrwert*, the French translation of which (*Histoire des doctrines économiques*, Marx 1924–25) he had in his possession before his arrestation (see Giasi 2017, p. 167).

Gramsci discarded Luigi Einaudi's assertions according to which economics would be a 'doctrine having the same nature as the mathematical and physical sciences' (Einaudi 1932, p. 310). He could not accept an approach of economic thought conceived as a history of the progressive improvement of 'pure theory', independently of the history of facts, and of philosophical or political trends. Gramsci (1975, p. 1350, Notebook 10, § 57; English transl. 1995, p. 189) pointed out:

> It cannot be denied that it is science and not only in the 'methodological' sense, that is to say not only in the sense that its procedures are scientific and rigorous. It also seems to me that economics cannot be compared to mathematics, although mathematics, among all the various sciences is perhaps the one most closely comparable to economics. In any case, economics cannot be considered a natural science (whatever way one conceives of nature or the external world – subjectivist or objectivist), and neither can it be considered a 'historical' science in the common meaning of the word, etc.

For Gramsci, the birth of economic science is directly linked to the 'bourgeoisie's development as a class "concretely on a world-scale" and to the formation of a world-scale market enough broadened out so that one can isolate and study law of necessary regularity' (Gramsci 1975, p. 1247, Notebook 10, § 9, my translation).

This chapter deals with Gramsci's remarks, questions, and some potential subjects of discussion with Piero Sraffa about Ricardo, classical political economy, then about marginalists' 'pure economics'.

13.1 Classical Political Economy

Gramsci's position concerning classical political economy is intricate because he considered it in two meanings, narrow and large.

In a first meaning, Gramsci understood by 'classical political economy' the economists following the Physiocrats and preceding Marx and 'pure economics': Ricardo, Malthus, and until John Stuart Mill probably.[2] This definition, which does not mention Adam Smith, is different from Marx's approach who included also William Petty and the Physiocrats. Why was Ricardo a departure point?

Perhaps Gramsci was taking into account the importance given to Ricardo by Marx himself. After all, in the *Theories of Surplus Value* (10th chapter), Marx asserted: 'At last, however, Ricardo comes on the stage, and calls to science: Halt! – The foundations, the starting point for the physiology of the bourgeois system – for the understanding of its internal organic coherence and life process – is the determination of *value by labour-time*' (Marx 1951, p. 203; Marx's emphasis). But maybe Gramsci was also influenced by Luigi Einaudi and Piero Sraffa. As a matter of fact, Einaudi considered Ricardo as the 'alfa and omega' of economic science and 'the true founder of economic science, if by founder we mean the one who gave a center to scattered and unrelated theorems, a common reference, creating a first, imperfect but first, scheme of general economic equilibrium' (Einaudi 1930, resp. pp. 271, 273).

Otherwise, from 1927–28, Piero Sraffa was involved in researches into the classical tradition and the building of a theory which will get its end only in 1960 with the publication of *Production of Commodities by Means of Commodities*. Having accepted in 1930 to take charge of the publication of Ricardo's *Collected Works* for the Royal Economic Society, he began to collect his writings and correspondence. Reading an article of Luigi Einaudi in *La Riforma sociale*, Gramsci learned about this project (Einaudi 1931, p. 397); he declared himself very happy and added: 'I hope I shall be in a position to read English with ease when this edition comes out, and so be able to read Ricardo in the original'.[3] This point is important when one knows Gramsci's taste for the main authors' critical editions established according to the most rigorous philological criteria.[4] Sraffa informed him that he hoped his edition 'will be published in a year and a half or two', and he would send him a copy.[5] But in the meanwhile, he did not send him the Italian translation of *On the Principles of Political Economy, and Taxation*, reprinted in 1925, with an introduction by Achille Loria (Ricardo 1925), that Gramsci did not ask. So in prison, Gramsci had to content himself only with incomplete information, sometimes very questionable. He had at his disposal mainly the critical exposition of Ricardo provided by Charles Gide in the *Histoire des doctrines économiques depuis les physiocrates jusqu'à nos jours*. Particularly, Gide asserted: 'His hypothetical method, with the: "let us suppose that..." which comes back very often as his trade-mark, makes its reading a difficult task' (Gide and Rist 1926, p. 155, my translation).

But Gramsci considered 'classical political economy' sometimes in another sense, taking into account furthermore the marginalists' 'pure economics'. So this corresponds to the 'orthodox', 'traditional' or 'liberal school' and includes not only Ricardo and his successors but also contemporary authors such as Luigi Einaudi and Pasquale Jannaccone (see Gramsci 1975, pp. 1076–1078, Notebook 8, § 216 and pp. 1261–1262, Notebook 10, § 23). Why this new definition? One can suggest two arguments.

First of all, for Gramsci, a continuity would exist in the works of these economists as regards methodology. Thus, Charles Gide asserted that the 'abstract method' of the Ricardian motto 'let us suppose that' gave a lasting impulse and remained living today in the 'mathematical school' (Gide and Rist 1926, p. 155, my translation). For his part, in a review published in *La Riforma sociale*, Luigi Einaudi noticed that 'the economist begins always, expressly or tacitly, with *let us suppose that... if we suppose that...*' (underlined by Einaudi 1932, p. 309, note 1, my translation). Gramsci even wished to point out that Luigi Einaudi belonged to 'some authors of classical economy' (Gramsci 1975, p. 1077, Notebook 8, § 216; see also p. 1278, Notebook 10, § 32, my translation).

A second argument can be invoked to understand this other Gramscian definition. Indeed, in the *Histoire des doctrines économiques*, Charles Gide presented marginalism as a 'neo-classical school', which reconnected with the 'great classical tradition' in the defence of free competition; 'pure' economists simply blamed the classics for failing to demonstrate the validity of their conclusions (Gide and Rist 1926, p. 547; see also p. 11, my translation). Otherwise, in *La critica della economia liberale*, written by Ugo Spirito (a follower of Giovanni Gentile and theorist of the so-called leftist corporatism), Gramsci learned about his harsh critic of the 'traditional economic science' and 'pure economics' which took up the classical political economy's 'postulates' (free competition, free trade...) (Spirito 1930, pp. 31, 34, 37, my translation).

However, Sraffa could not have known Gramsci's notes on classical political economy. Only in 1947, on the proofs of the selection of *Notebooks* under the title *Il materialismo storico e la filosofia di Benedetto Croce* for the Einaudi publishing house, he discovered some of them. Sharing his impressions with Felice Platone and Palmiro Togliatti, he recommended to the former not to publish a note belonging to the series 'Punti di meditazione per lo studio dell'economia politica' (Gramsci 1975, pp. 1261–1262, Notebook 10, § 23; English transl. 1995, pp. 168–170), whose planned title was 'Economia classica ed economia critica'. According to him, 'the points mentioned have not been sufficiently considered' and gave an 'impression of superficiality'. Among his critiques, one concerned the second definition of classical political economy. He remarked on this subject: 'What Gramsci calls here "classical political economy" is the contemporary ***bourgeois*** economics: as it is clear from the whole context, and especially the assertion that it comes to the concept of value 'with marginal utility', the latter is notoriously an invention of post-Marxist and anti-marxist ***bourgeois*** economists. ... This terminology naturally creates confusion'[6] (see Sect. 13.2 about the content of this note).

These two different definitions of classical political economy aside, what was there in *Prison Notebooks* about Ricardo's interpretation? The question of the concepts of 'regularity' and 'necessity' in the historical development according to Marx led Gramsci to focus on Ricardian methodology. Particularly he indicated (Gramsci 1975, p. 147, Notebook 11, § 52; English transl., 1971, pp. 755–756; see also Gramsci 1975, pp. 1245–1246, Notebook 10, § 8):

> Concept and fact of 'determined market': i.e. the scientific discovery that specific decisive and permanent forces have risen historically and that the operation of these forces presents itself with a certain 'automatism' which allows a measure of 'predictability' and certainty for the future of those individual initiatives which accept these forces after having discerned and scientifically established their nature. 'Determined market' is therefore equivalent to 'determined relation of social forces in a determined structure of the productive apparatus', this relationship being guaranteed (that is, rendered permanent) by a determined political, moral and juridical superstructure. After having established the character of these decisive and permanent forces and their spontaneous automatism (i.e. their relative independence from individual choices and from arbitrary government interventions), the scientist has, by way of hypothesis, rendered the automatism absolute; he has isolated the merely economic facts from the combinations of varying importance in which they present themselves in reality; he has established relations of cause and effect, of premises and conclusions; and he has thus produced an abstract scheme of a determined economic society [...].

Therefore, Gramsci was thinking that the importance of Ricardo in the formation of Marx's ideas must be reassessed not only from the point of view of the theory of value, but also from the point of view of the world's conception and history. So Gramsci (1975, p. 1247, Notebook 10, § 9; English transl. 1971, pp. 741–742) asserted:

> One could say in a sense, I think, that the philosophy of praxis equals Hegel plus David Ricardo. ... The discovery of the formal logical principle of the 'law of tendency' which leads to the scientific definition of the fundamental economic concepts of *homo oeconomicus* and of the 'determined market', was this not also a discovery of epistemological value as well? Does it not precisely imply a new 'immanence', a new conception of 'necessity' and of freedom, etc.? Translation into these terms seems to me precisely the achievement of the philosophy of praxis, which has universalised Ricardo's discoveries, extending them in an adequate fashion to the whole of history and thus drawing from them, in an original form, a new conception of the world.

For Gramsci, the laws of tendency 'are not laws in the naturalistic sense or that of speculative determinism, but in a "historicist" sense, valid, that is, to the extent that there exists the "determined market" or in other words an environment which is organically alive and interconnected in its movements of development' (1975, p. 1248; English transl. 1971, pp. 742–743). One can note here that Gramsci borrowed without mentioning it the concept of 'determined market [mercato determinato]' from Pasquale Jannaccone, an Italian follower of Alfred Marshall, in a context remoted from the Ricardian problematic, because it designates situations of 'stable equilibrium' of perfect competition or monopoly.[7] Using the concepts of 'law of tendency' and 'determined market', Gramsci elaborated his famous thesis on the sources of Marxism. Ricardo, an innovator in the field of economic method, would be also an innovator from the gnoseological and philosophical point of view. Playing a catalytic role in the transition from Hegelianism to Marxism, he led Marx to go beyond Hegelian philosophy and to develop a new 'historicism', a 'new conception of the world'. In this connection, Gramsci referred to a famous passage of *The Holy Family* about the identity of languages between French politics and German philosophy.

However, very aware of venturing on an unsafe field, on 30 May 1932, Gramsci asked the opinion of Piero Sraffa through Tatiana Schucht. In his letter to Tatiana, he asserted (Gramsci 1996, pp. 581–582; English transl. 1988, pp. 219–220):

> What I would like to know is this: does any special work exist (maybe in English?) on Ricardo's methods of research into economics, and on the innovations which Ricardo introduced into critical methodology?. ... I would base myself on the two fundamental concepts of economics, 'determined market' and 'law of tendency', which I believe we owe to Ricardo, and proceed as follows: it is not possible that these two concepts served as a starting-point when the attempt was being made to reduce the 'immanentist' conception of history (expressed as it was in the idealistic and speculative language of classical German philosophy) to a realistic, immediately historical 'immanence' – an 'immanence' in which the law of causality of the natural sciences has been purged of its mechanistic character, and left free to identify itself systematically with the dialectical reasoning of Hegelianism?

Gramsci concluded his letter by noting that Piero Sraffa, during his editorial work on Ricardo, could collect important materials on this subject.

In a letter to Tatiana Schucht of 21 June 1932, Sraffa (1991, p. 74, my translation) replied that 'Nino cannot imagine how much his observations have interested me' and indicated that he must think about Ricardo's significance for the history of philosophy referring to the writings of Marx and Engels. But he wished to obtain from Gramsci 'some explanations' on the two concepts of 'determined market' and 'law of tendency', to which he 'seems to be giving a technical meaning', since they are placed in quotation marks. He did not understand very well the first concept, and he thought that the second (probably synonymous with law of nature) represented 'more as one of the characteristics of vulgar economics'. In fact, Sraffa was very sceptical about the thesis of a Ricardian historicism. For him (ibid.),

> it is in any case very difficult to evaluate the philosophical importance, if any, of Ricardo's thought, since, unlike the philosophers of praxis, he never subjected his own thought to historical considerations. He rarely placed himself in a historical perspective and, as has been said, he considered the law of the society in which he lived to be natural and immutable. ... But from his writings, it is clear that the only cultural element to be found there is derived from the natural sciences.

Concerning the bibliography, Sraffa noted that it was rather thin on the issues raised. First of all, he mentioned the *Theorien über den Mehrwert* (*Histoire des doctrines économiques*, Marx 1924–25), with this short comment: 'that Nino knows'. Then, he indicated the recent publication in Germany of a collection of Marx's early writings by S. Landhut and J.P. Mayer, *Der historische Materialismus. Die Frühschriften* (Leipzig: Kröner, 1932). In this last book, for the first time, was published especially the *Kritik des Hegelschen Staatsrechts* and the *Ökonomisch-philosophische Manuscript aus den 1844*. He also noted that 'for the centenary of Ricardo's death, were published only few articles of circumstance in English or American periodicals, deprived of any interest'. He therefore indicated two German books, which he did not read, but which he could order for Gramsci: Alfred Amonn, *Ricardo als Begründer der theoretischen Nationalökonomie* (Jena: Fischer, 1924) and Heinrich Borchers, *Das Abstraktions Problem bei David Ricardo* (Jena: Fischer, 1929). Finally, concerning older writings, Sraffa indicated the article of Simon Nelson Patten, 'The Interpretation of Ricardo' (*Quarterly Journal of Economics*, vol. VII, no. 2, April 1893) and Elie Halévy's book, *La formation du radicalisme philosophique* (Paris: F. Alcan, 1901–1904, 3 vols.).[8]

Unfortunately, Gramsci did not receive any book or article from this bibliography and because of his state of physical and moral exhaustion during the summer 1932 (see Vacca 2012, Chapter 12), he would not be able to react to Sraffa's remarks in his letters to Tatiana Schucht or in the *Prison Notebooks*. This attempt at establishing a dialogue on Ricardo was therefore unsuccessful. Now, what about the reflections concerning the marginalist theory?

13.2 The Marginalists' 'Pure Economics'

What about the Gramscian analysis of 'pure economics'? In fact, Gramsci never discussed the writings of the protagonists of the so-called Marginal Revolution (W.S. Jevons, Carl Menger, Léon Walras). When he was sentenced to confinement in the island of Ustica, he wrote to Sraffa to obtain 'a good treatise on economics and finance', 'a fundamental book',[9] and he received Alfred Marshall's *Principles of Economics* (1890), in the Italian translation by Pasquale Jannaccone (Marshall [1905] 1925). Unfortunately, he never commented Alfred Marshall's book, but he discussed Maffeo Pantaleoni's *Principii di economia pura* (*Pure Economics*). We can remind here that in an obituary devoted to the 'prince' of the Italian economists, Sraffa had emphasized Pantaleoni's hostility towards socialism and democracy, which made him qualified by an opponent as 'a reactionary anarchist' (Sraffa 1924, pp. 648, 650), and he considered the *Principii di economia pura* as 'the first organic treatise in which—in accordance with the teaching of Marshall—the doctrines of the classical writers were harmonised with the new theories of Gossen and Jevons' (Sraffa 1924, pp. 650–651). Actually, Pantaleoni was one of the Italian founders of marginalism, in an utilitarian and hedonistic version inspired by H.H. Gossen and W.S. Jevons.

Gramsci commented Pantaleoni's *Principii di economia pura* (1889), the second edition (1931) of which Sraffa had sent him. In the first part of the book, devoted to the theory of utility, the 'hedonistic postulate' was praised. For Gramsci, the intellectual sources of this work were in the eighteen-century sensualist philosophy developed within nineteenth-century positivism. Pantaleoni's *homo oeconomicus* was the abstract 'biological man', that is to say an 'ensemble of painful and pleasurable sensations' (Gramsci 1975, p. 1268, Notebook 10, § 30; English transl. 1995, p. 170); although it was based on human nature in general, and presented in mathematical form, in reality it was not 'outside history'. Indeed, the *homo oeconomicus* was 'the abstraction of the needs and economic operations of a given form of society' (Gramsci 1975, p. 1265, Notebook 10, § 27; English transl. 1995, p. 168); in fact capitalism spread a relatively homogeneous type of economic man. However when reading the *Principii di economia pura*, Gramsci was struck by the possibility of application of the hedonistic postulate, 'not just to economics but to a whole range of human activities that may be termed "economic" only if the notion of economics is extended and made generic to such an enormous extent as to (empirically) empty it of all meaning and make it coincide with a philosophical category, as in fact Croce has sought to do' (Gramsci 1975, p. 1269, Notebook 10, § 30; English transl. 1995, p. 171). Humorously, Gramsci noted that the first part of Pantaleoni's book 'might more properly serve as the introduction to a refined text book on the culinary art or an even more refined manual of love-making positions' (Gramsci 1975, p. 1268; English transl. 1995, p. 170). So the question was whether 'pure economics' is really a science or 'something else', using a method that is intended to be scientific (Gramsci 1975, p. 1277, Notebook 10, § 32, my translation). In any case, Gramsci did not wish to engage in an easy criticism of marginalism. A good example of this last kind was provided by Ugo Spirito's *La critica della economia liberale*, criticizing the Italian marginalists (especially Pantaleoni) and condemning as a whole and without subtlety the *homo oeconomicus* as a category deprived of any scientific or philosophical value. After reading this last book, Gramsci indicated: 'But everything is not to be rejected in Spirito's controversy: there are real demands embedded in the hodgepodge of "speculative" words' (Gramsci 1975, p. 753, Notebook 6, § 82, my translation). Probably, he was referring to Spirito's will to bring out the impossibility to conceive economics as a neutral science free from value judgements (Maccabelli 1998, pp. 84–85). We can imagine how Gramsci would have appreciated a dialogue with Piero Sraffa, who was a critic of marginalism.[10]

However, it should be noted that in the *Principii di economia pura* Pantaleoni put forward an idea that undoubtedly caught Gramsci's attention. He established a link between the marginalist theory of exchange, based on a gap between the marginal utilities of desired goods and available for exchange, and the Ricardian theory of comparative costs, based on the difference between the relative costs of traded goods (Pantaleoni 1931, pp. 192–193, Note 1; see Faucci 2000, pp. 230–231). We recognize here the thesis of the 'convertibility' or the 'translatability' of scientific languages within political economy.

The *Prison Notebooks* discussed the problem of the languages' translatability between political economy and 'critical economy', a question mentioned by Friedrich Engels in his Preface to Book III of *Capital*. In Notebook 7, § 22, Gramsci (1975, p. 870, my translation) asserted: 'Theory of comparative costs [and decreasing]. See if this theory, which is in the foreground of official modern economics with static and dynamic equilibrium's theory, would not be in perfect agreement [or corresponding in another language] with the Marxist theory of value [and of the fall of the profit rate]'. Coming back to this question in Notebook 10, § 23, Gramsci (1975, pp. 1261–1262, English transl. 1995, pp. 168–170) put forward that 'classical political economy' was interested by the formation of 'socially necessary labour' at various levels (local, national, international), from which followed the significance of the 'comparative cost' (comparison of 'particular' labour embodied in various commodities), considered by several theoretical formulations (comparative costs theory, static and dynamic equilibrium theory, etc.). In 1947, while recommending not to publish this note, Sraffa reported to Felice Platone that Gramsci's use of the term 'comparative costs' was 'not very coherent' and recalled that 'in the classical political economy the term has a very specific technical sense, in relation to the international trade'.[11] But this interpretation is very doubtful. Firstly, Gramsci was probably not unaware of the Ricardian theory of international trade. Secondly, he was referring to the 'law of decreasing costs' explained in Ugo Spirito's essay 'I sofismi dell'economia pura', included in *La critica della economia liberale* (1930, pp. 103ff.).[12] In fact, Spirito was summarizing Enrico Barone's arguments ([1908] 1925): the fall of average costs in the firms is stopped by organization problems and by the difficulty to get some factors of production. So the free competition framework can be preserved.[13]

Otherwise in 1933, Gramsci had the opportunity to give cautiously an opinion about the book of another theorist of 'pure economics', *An Essay on the Nature and Significance of Economie Science* by Lionel Robbins (1932), referring to an indirect source, a review signed 'xxx', published in *La Riforma sociale*, whose author was actually Ernesto Rossi (1933).[14] Unfortunately, he did not get this book through Sraffa. Lionel Robbins proposed a technical definition of economic science which became very famous: 'Economics is the science which studies human behaviour as a relationship between ends and scarce means which have alternative uses' (Robbins 1932, p. 15). Gramsci discussed the question of whether this book could correspond to a requirement put by Benedetto Croce in his essays prior to 1900, where he wished 'that economic treatises ought, of necessity, to be prefaced by a theoretical introduction outlining the distinguishing concepts and methods of economics itself' (Gramsci 1975, p. 1802, Notebook 15, § 43; English transl. 1995, p. 174). For him, Robbins did not seem to prove this rigour and he was undoubtedly an '"empiricist" and formal logician'. He also thought that this essay was a good indicator of economists' dissatisfaction with their science and the definition of its field. The author seemed to him having the project 'to free economics from the so-called "pleasure" principle and make a clear distinction between economics and psychology "rejecting the last vestiges of the historical association between utilitarianism and economics"' (ibid.), using perhaps a new concept of utility, 'more comprehensive'. The author's definition paved the way to a full extension of economics and it 'hardly coincides with the concrete problems that economists really study' (Gramsci 1975, p. 1803; English transl. 1995, p. 174). Gramsci formulated the assumption that this new approach would constitute a true 'demolition of marginalist theory' because Robbins was completely discarding the dualism still held by Alfred Marshall for the theory of value, that is to say the duality of marginal utility and cost of production, in favour of an uniting approach based on individual choices.[15] So why separate economics from psychology? (Gramsci 1975, pp. 1803–1804, Notebook 15, § 43). Probably, Gramsci did not welcome this 'demolition' of marginalist theory.[16] But unfortunately his reflections about Robbins's book are not further developed in the *Prison Notebooks* and he did not take the occasion to ask Sraffa's opinion through Tatiana Schucht.

Gramsci understood very well that the Marxists did not know how to fight efficiently 'pure economics' at a theoretical level. Particularly, he noted the serious weaknesses of the *Précis d'économie politique* written by Iosif A. Lapidus and Konstantin U. Ostrovitianov and available in a French translation (1929). For him, this book was a true example of 'economic literature of school popularization', absolutely dogmatic in its content (Gramsci 1975, pp. 1285–1286, Notebook 10, § 37, my translation) and revealing 'an ossified form of thought' (ibid., p. 1806, Notebook 15, § 45, my translation). This kind of textbook never confronted Marxism with the *bourgeois* economic theories of the nineteenth–twentieth centuries and never provided concrete illustration from economic history. Unfortunately, the Marxists did not keep 'the relationship between political economy and critical economy in its organic and historically current forms' (ibid., p. 1805; English transl. 1995, p. 176).

* * *

This investigation, obviously incomplete, into *Prison Notebooks*' reflections in the field of the history of economic thought enables to bring out some interesting results. But it is clear that Gramsci's analysis of classical political economy and Ricardo had no influence on Sraffa's interpretation. And on his side Sraffa did not agree with Gramsci's considerations, who had access only to secondary sources.

As a matter of fact, Piero Sraffa's concerns were not completely irrelevant to those of Gramsci. In his lectures at Cambridge University on *Advanced Theory of Value* (1928–31), he had the opportunity to put forward the thesis according to which economic theories do not appear from the intellectual curiosity of scholars but rather from the necessity to find solutions to concrete questions and to protect the economic interests of certain social classes against those of other classes. For him,

> ... economic theories, whether ancient or modern, do not arise out of the simple intellectual curiosity of finding out the reasons for what is observed to happen in the factory or in the market place. They arise out of practical problems which present themselves to the community and which must be solved. There are opposite interests which support either one solution or the other and they find theoretical, that is universal, arguments in order to prove that the solution they advocate is conformable to natural laws, or to the public interest, or to the interest of the ruling class or to whatever is the ideology which at the particular moment is dominating. (Sraffa Papers, The Wren Library, Cambridge, D2/4/3/2)

Economic theories obtain an independent and unprejudiced scientific status which in turn allows to support or to fight efficiently one or another economic policy. So it is impossible to understand the Ricardian theory of value (and the non-integration of rent into the cost of production) disregarding the class interests expressed during the debate on Corn Laws (1813–15). Likewise, the widespread acceptance after the 1870s of marginal utility theory (discovered before by Cournot, Dupuit and Gossen) cannot be understood taking no account of the 'anti-capitalist' implications of the labour theory of value and of the emergence of Marxism.

Notes

1. Among numerous references, see Naldi (2000, 2012) and Ginzburg (2015, 2019).
2. See, for example, Gramsci (1975, p. 1039 [Notebook 8, § 162]; pp. 1076–1077 [§ 216]; p. 1478 [Notebook 11, § 52]; pp. 1575–1576 [Notebook 13, §13]).
3. Gramsci, letter to Tatiana Schucht, 7 September 1931 (Gramsci 1996, p. 458).
4. Concerning the edition of Marx's works, see Gramsci's reflections in Notebook 16, § 2 (1975, pp. 1840–1843).
5. Sraffa, letter to Tatiana Schucht, 2 October 1931 (Sraffa 1991, p. 36).
6. Sraffa, letter to Felice Platone (March 1947), transmitted to Togliatti (Sraffa 2017, p. 3). See also Badaloni (1992, p. 44). The note in question would be published only in *Prison Notebooks*' edition by Valentino Gerratana (Gramsci 1975).
7. In a polemic against the corporatist Ugo Spirito (reviewing his book, *La critica della economia liberale*), Jannaccone asserted: 'Perhaps our critic

does not know that from now on in economics, the two expressions of free competition and monopoly are only two formulas to express in a synthetic manner the contribution a certain number of conditions, the presence of which renders the market *determined*, while the absence of a single one renders it *indeterminated*. Since the fundamental economic problem is the determination of exchange relations (values, prices), it is natural that economists have given the greatest importance to the state of perfect free competition and absolute monopoly, because only in one or the other hypothesis one finds a determinated situation of stable equilibrium, and therefore a normal price around which real market prices gravitate, just like satellites around their sun' (Jannaccone 1930, p. 524; Jannaccone's emphasis, my translation). See also Potier (1989, p. 119; 2014, p. 166), Maccabelli (1998, p. 94), Guzzone (2018, pp. 296–298).

8. Sraffa, letter to Tatiana Schucht, 21 June 1932 (Sraffa 1991, pp. 74–75). The content of this letter was entirely transmitted by Tatiana Schucht to Gramsci on 5 July 1932 (Gramsci and Schucht 1997, pp. 1039–1041).
9. Gramsci, letter to Tatiana Schucht, 11 December 1926 (Gramsci 1996, p. 13).
10. About this question, see Marcuzzo and Rosselli (2011).
11. Sraffa, letter to Felice Platone, March 1947 (Sraffa 2017, pp. 3–4). See also Badaloni (1992, p. 44).
12. Here we agree with Guzzone (2018, pp. 139–140).
13. During the years 1924–26, in Rome, Sraffa was able to give to his friend some information on the content of his articles of 1925 and 1926. As Naldi (2000, p. 89) points out: 'There are reasons to believe that Gramsci could have been particularly interested in an exposition of Sraffa's research and discussed with him at least some parts of what we find in the two articles'. In a letter to Tatiana Schucht (7 September 1931), interestingly, Gramsci (1996, p. 458, my translation) wrote: 'Each of his writings on economic science was greatly appreciated and gave rise to lengthy discussions in specialized periodicals'.
14. On the identification of the author of this article, see Omiccioli (2018, pp. 144–145).
15. Here, the reviewer said that the subjective evaluations govern at the same time costs and prices of all the commodities (Rossi 1933, p. 220).
16. Obviously, Gramsci was unaware of Sraffa's reflections in progress on the 'degeneration' of the 'cost of production' in classical and marginalist thought (see Fratini 2018).

References

Badaloni, N. (1992). Due manoscritti inediti di Sraffa su Gramsci. *Critica Marxista, 6*(new series), 43–50.

Barone, E. ([1908] 1925). *Principi di economia politica* (6th Reprint). Rome: Atheneum.

Einaudi, L. (1930). Open Letter to Rodolfo Benini. *Nuovi Studi di diritto, economia e politica, 3*(5), 302–314. As reprinted in: U. Spirito. (1970). *Il corporativismo* (pp. 263–274). Florence: Sansoni.

Einaudi, L. (1931). Per una nuova collana di economisti. *La Riforma Sociale, 42*(7–8), 394–399.

Einaudi, L. (1932). Ancora intorno al modo di scrivere la storia del dogma economico. *La Riforma Sociale, 43*(3), 308–313.

Faucci, R. (2000). *L'economia politica in Italia. Dal Cinquecento ai nostri giorni.* Turin: UTET.

Fratini, S. M. (2018). Sraffa on the Degeneration of the Notion of Cost. *Cambridge Journal of Economics, 42*(3), 817–836.

Giasi, F. (Ed.). (2017). *Antonio Gramsci. I quaderni e i libri del carcere.* Cagliari: Arkadia.

Gide, C., & Rist, C. (1926). *Histoire des doctrines économiques depuis les physiocrates jusqu'à nos jours* (5th ed). Paris: Sirey (reprint 1929).

Ginzburg, A. (2015). Two Translators: Gramsci and Sraffa. *Contributions to Political Economy, 34*(1), 31–76.

Ginzburg, A. (2019). Gramsci, Sraffa and Historical Causality. *History of Economic Ideas, 27*(2), 83–117.

Gramsci, A. (1971). *Selections from the Prison Notebooks* (Q. Hoare & G. N. Smith, Ed. and Trans.). London: Lawrence & Wishart.

Gramsci, A. (1975). *Quaderni del carcere* (V. Gerratana, Ed., 4 Vols.). Turin: Einaudi.

Gramsci, A. (1988). *Gramsci's Prison Letters. Lettere dal Carcere. A Selection.* Translated and introduced by H. Henderson. London: Zwan, in association with Edinburgh Review.

Gramsci, A. (1995). *Further Selections from the Prison Notebooks* (D. Boothman, Ed. and Trans.). London: Lawrence & Wishart.

Gramsci, A. (1996). *Lettere dal carcere, 1926–1937* (A. A. Santucci, Ed.). Palermo: Sellerio.

Gramsci, A., & Schucht, T. (1997). *Lettere 1926–1935* (A. Natoli & C. Daniele, Ed.). Turin: Einaudi.

Guzzone, G. (2018). *Gramsci e la critica dell'economia politica. Dal dibattito sul liberismo al paradigma della 'traducibilità'.* Rome: Viella.

Jannaccone, P. (1930). Scienza, critica e realtà economica. *La Riforma Sociale, 41*(11–12), 521–528.
Landhut, S., & Mayer, J. P. (1932). *Der historische Materialismus. Die Frühschriften*. Leipzig: Kröner.
Lapidus, I. A., & Ostrovitianov, K. (1929). *Précis d'économie politique. L'économie politique et la théorie de l'économie soviétique*. Translated from Russian by V. Serge. Paris: Editions sociales internationales.
Maccabelli, T. (1998). Gramsci lettore di Ugo Spirito: economia pura e corporativismo nei Quaderni del carcere. *Il pensiero economico italiano, 6*(2), 73–114.
Marcuzzo, M. C., & Rosselli, A. (2011). Sraffa and His Arguments Against 'Marginism'. *Cambridge Journal of Economics, 35*(1), 219–231.
Marshall, A. ([1905] 1925). *Principi di economia politica*. Turin: UTET, Biblioteca dell'Economista, 4th series, Vol. 9, reprint.
Marx, K. (1924–25). *Histoire des doctrines économiques*. Translated from French by J. Molitor (based on K. Kautsky's edition). 8 Vols. Paris: Alfred Costes.
Marx, K. (1951). *Theories of Surplus Value: A Selection [...]* (G. A. Bonner & E. Burns, Trans.). London: Lawrence & Wishart.
Naldi, N. (2000). The Friendship Between Piero Sraffa and Antonio Gramsci in the Years 1919–1927. *European Journal of the History of Economic Thought, 7*(1), 79–95.
Naldi, N. (2012). Two Notes on Piero Sraffa and Antonio Gramsci. *Cambridge Journal of Economics, 36*(6), 1401–1415.
Omiccioli, M. (2018). *La 'strana' biblioteca di uno 'strano' economista. Viaggio tra i libri di Ernesto Rossi*. Rome: Banca d'Italia.
Pantaleoni, M. (1931). *Principii di economia pura* (2nd ed.). Milan: Trèves.
Potier, J.-P. (1989). Antonio Gramsci lettore degli economisti. Alcune riflessioni dei *Quaderni del carcere* sulla storia del pensiero economico. In G. Baratta & A. Catone (Eds.), *Modern Times. Gramsci e la critica all'americanismo* (pp. 113–125). Milan: Diffusioni.
Potier, J.-P. (2014). Antonio Gramsci et ses tentatives de dialogue avec Piero Sraffa en histoire de la pensée économique. In J.-P. Potier (Ed.), *Les Marmites de l'histoire. Mélanges en l'honneur de Pierre Dockès* (pp. 155–177). Paris: Classiques Garnier.
Ricardo, D. ([1856] 1925). *Principi di economia politica e dell'imposta*. Turin: UTET, Biblioteca dell'Economista, 4th series, Vol. 11, reprint.
Robbins, L. (1932). *An Essay on the Nature and Significance of Economic Science*. London: Macmillan.
Rossi, E. (xxx) (1933). Che cosa è la scienza economica. *La Riforma sociale, 44*(2), 218–226.
Spirito, U. (1930). *La critica della economia liberale*. Milan: Trèves.

Sraffa, P. (1924). Obituary. Maffeo Pantaleoni. *The Economic Journal, 34*, 648–653.
Sraffa, P. (1928–31). *Lecture Notes on the Advanced Theory of Value* (Sraffa Papers, D2/4). Cambridge: The Wren Library, Trinity College.
Sraffa, P. (1991). *Lettere a Tania per Gramsci* (V. Gerratana, Ed.). Rome: Editori Riuniti.
Sraffa, P. (2017). *Lettere editoriali (1947–1975)* (T. Munari, Ed.). Turin: Einaudi.
Vacca, G. (2012). *Vita e pensieri di Antonio Gramsci, 1926–1937*. Turin: Einaudi.

CHAPTER 14

Real and *Apparent* Unknowns and the Origin of Sraffa's Equations

Nerio Naldi

Pierangelo Garegnani, in a paper read at the conference on Piero Sraffa held at the Accademia Nazionale dei Lincei in February 2003, put forward an interpretation of the origin of the research project which led Sraffa to publish his book *Production of Commodities by Means of Commodities* (Sraffa 1960). Some pages of that paper were devoted to a discussion of how Sraffa came to introduce price variables into his equations (Garegnani 2004, pp. 176–178; 2005, pp. 468–470). Even though I agree with Garegnani's idea that Sraffa's earliest equations considered only physical quantities and no price variables, I would like to contribute to this volume in honour of Annalisa Rosselli, who was also among the speakers at that conference, with a reformulation of that part of Garegnani's reconstruction.

Following Garegnani's analysis, we will see that Sraffa's earliest equations included only *things* and no price variables. Furthermore, we will also see that Sraffa still tried to maintain his earliest formulation for the

N. Naldi (✉)
University of Rome La Sapienza, Rome, Italy
e-mail: nerio.naldi@uniroma1.it

M. C. Marcuzzo et al. (eds.), *New Perspectives on Political Economy and Its History*, Palgrave Studies in the History of Economic Thought,
https://doi.org/10.1007/978-3-030-42925-6_14

case of a no surplus economy even after he had decided to introduce price variables into his positive surplus equations.

Highlighting these features of the development of Sraffa's equations will allow us to illuminate some aspects of their origin we already outlined and discussed in other papers (Naldi 2018a, b, 2020).

14.1 Sraffa's Earliest Equations

It is generally accepted that by late November 1927, Sraffa had already formulated the early drafts of the equations that were to appear in *Production of Commodities* (Sraffa 1960). The broad background of the analysis which led him to draft these equations has been indicated in his previous study of contemporary economics, in his critical stance against its subjective foundations, in his study of the epistemological bases of natural sciences, in his interest in Classical political economy and in Marx's contributions, and, in particular, in his search for an approach to the theory of value and prices based on objective magnitudes. Moving from this broad background, two alternative explanations of the origins of Sraffa's equations have been put forward. One stresses the importance of Sraffa's interests in Marx's analysis,[1] while the other emphasizes the importance of his interests in contemporary economics and in recent developments in natural sciences.[2] Neither of these explanations, however, has been able to support its contentions by providing a paper trail showing how, starting from those interests, Sraffa came to develop his own equations. On the contrary, an attempt to explain the origin of Sraffa's equations as an offspring of an endogenous evolution of his analysis of Marshallian economics has allowed a general reconstruction to emerge and a set of manuscripts to be extracted from the Sraffa Papers[3] which may be interpreted as a clear-cut paper trail (Garegnani 2005; Naldi 2018a, b, 2020).

As a result of the latter reconstruction and of the identification of the earliest extant drafts of Sraffa's equations, of what most likely inspired him to formulate them, and of the closest background of that specific development, the path followed by Sraffa appears to be altogether original. His equations turn out to have emerged as an unexpected development of his attempt to counterpose physical costs to psychological costs, distinguishing cost from income and reducing costs to quantities of what he called an ***absolutely necessary commodity***. Indeed, we may point to the schemes laid out in manuscripts D3/12/2/32–35 as the earliest extant drafts of Sraffa's equations, and we may single out a section of the lecture notes written by Sraffa in London in summer 1927 titled 'Physical Real Costs' (D3/12/3/42–8) and, in particular, the note appended on the margin of sheet D3/12/3/44 which pointed to the case (strikingly close to the subsistence economy we will find in the opening chapter of *Production of Commodities*) of 'a community that produces just what is sufficient to keep it going' as the most likely source of inspiration which led Sraffa to write his equations (Naldi 2018a, b, 2020). Sraffa may have perceived that within the confines of a subsistence economy, his attempt to reduce costs to quantities of an absolutely necessary commodity could be successful, and, accordingly, he may have sketched out such an economy in terms of sets of physical inputs. But, once he had actually written that description down, he may have immediately seen it as a simple system of equations, whose straightforward algebraic solution could be used to determine exchange ratios, which would have immediately overshadowed his previous interest in reducing inputs to a single absolutely necessary commodity (see Naldi 2018a, p. 144; 2018b, p. 16; 2020, p. 14).

These results are consistent with the fact that in late November 1927, Sraffa divided his schemes into two different sets: the first set (dubbed *first equations* by Sraffa himself) described the case of an economy producing no surplus product; another set (*second equations*) described the case of an economy producing a positive surplus.

The earliest extant formulations of those equations may be recognized in manuscripts D3/12/2/32–35. Manuscript D3/12/2/32, which presents a no surplus case and shows calculations strewn in a rather haphazard way throughout the page, may be read as Sraffa's earliest attempt to solve such a system of equations. These documents are kept among others dating to the 1940s and 1950s in a folder labelled 'USEFUL (All dates) ex black cover, 1955', but manuscript D3/12/2/32 shows two peculiarities which allow us to state that it was written approximately between the 23rd of November 1927 and the end of that month. On the one hand, on top of it Sraffa annotated '(From folder labelled: "End of Nov. 1927")'.[4] On the other hand, it was written on the back of the second page of a letter which presumably reached Sraffa between the 23rd and the 25th of November.[5] Given that manuscript contains a sketch of a no surplus economy and that Sraffa had a note in his pocket diary which suggests he had shown Keynes his *first equations* on the 26th of November 1927 ('K. approves 1st eq'—E1), we may guess that item D3/12/2/32 was written shortly before the meeting with Keynes. We may apply the same presumption to manuscript D3/12/2/34, which deals with the same no surplus system in a more orderly way,[6] and to documents D3/12/2/33 and D3/12/2/35, where two different positive surplus systems are considered (see Naldi 2018a, pp. 141–145; 2018b, pp. 5–10; 2020, pp. 4–9).

A no surplus production system is described in manuscripts D3/12/2/32 and D3/12/2/34 as follows:

$$\begin{aligned} 10A &= 3A + 7B + 4C \\ 20B &= 6A + 5B + 1C \\ 15C &= 1A + 8B + 10C \end{aligned} \tag{14.1}$$

This scheme—as we shall argue in Sect. 14.2 below—is a simple tabulation of physical inputs and outputs.[7] Obviously, in this case, plus and equal signs cannot be intended to have their ordinary algebraic meaning. Nonetheless, Sraffa read it as a system of equations, which contained proper unknowns (see Sect. 14.2). Accordingly, he solved it by calculating A in terms of B, A in terms of C, and B and C in terms of A (D3/12/2/32, 34; see also Naldi 2018a, p. 141; 2018b, pp. 7–8). These results (even though no price variable was indicated) he quickly interpreted as exchange ratios which allow producers in each sector to exchange their surplus goods with the inputs they need to start production again on the previous scale (see D3/12/11/54, 89, 101; D3/12/6/4 and D3/12/5/2).

Manuscripts D3/12/2/33 and D3/12/2/35—most likely written by Sraffa just after D3/12/2/32 and D3/12/2/34—may be interpreted as attempts at developing the previous analysis by considering the case of a positive surplus scenario. Here, we find two positive surplus systems. Also in this case, they should be interpreted as tabulations that Sraffa tried to solve as ordinary equations:

$$\begin{aligned} 14A &= 3A + 9B \\ 12B &= 7A + 3B \end{aligned} \tag{14.2}$$

and

$$\begin{aligned} 11A &= 3A + 9B \\ 13B &= 7A + 3B \end{aligned} \tag{14.3}$$

These systems (*second equations*), however, proved much more challenging than the *first equations*: Sraffa noted that the solutions he could obtain were contradictory. The first system, for instance, delivered two different values for A: $A = \frac{9}{11}B$ and $A = \frac{9}{7}B$ (D3/12/2/33).[8]

14.2 Real and Apparent Unknowns

That the schemes (14.1)–(14.3) above were indeed simple tabulations and that Sraffa felt he could treat them as systems of equations and solve them as if they contained ordinary unknowns is evident in how he approached the problems posed by the contradictory solutions of the positive surplus case. To this end, Sraffa tried different formulations of his equations and finally introduced an additional variable. This latter attempt can be studied in a manuscript kept in a folder labelled 'Winter 1927–28'.[9] Here, Sraffa, adding a variable (first called R, then r) to his equations to represent the surplus product, came to discuss the following system (D3/12/6/17)[10]:

$$\begin{aligned} A + A_S &= (5a_1 + 6b_1 + 3c_1)r \\ B + B_S &= (4a_2 + 2b_2 + 6c_2)r \\ C + C_S &= (7a_3 + 2b_3 + 3c_3)r \end{aligned} \tag{14.4}$$

According to Sraffa, this system could be solved just like the no surplus case[11]: 'since we have (in the no surplus system) a spare equation, we can use it to determine, simultaneously with values, the ratio that total surplus bears to total initial stocks of the community' (D3/12/6/17).

Obviously, Sraffa was comparing the number of unknowns to the number of equations, and this implies that five magnitudes such as A, A_S, a_1, a_2 and a_3 would be treated as a single unknown (as would B_i, b_i and C_i, c_i). But he also explained that such unknowns were 'only "one unit of measure of each commodity" (1 bushel of wheat, 1 ton of coal etc.)' (D3/12/6/17). This clearly reveals that all his previous schemes were tabulations, which included only physical quantities. And it also reveals that Sraffa was treating their units as unknowns—even while acknowledging that they were 'apparent unknowns' (D3/12/6/17), not 'real unknowns' (D3/12/6/18).

No one would deny that quantities of heterogeneous commodities as such cannot be added together, that units of measure cannot be unknowns, and that *tabulations* are not *equations*. Nevertheless, Sraffa seems to have thought that his tabulations could be treated as systems of equations and that the use of such unusual unknowns would not have been problematic for the structure of his systems or their solutions.

Indeed, in Sraffa's view, the solution of both the no surplus and the positive surplus systems would have provided 'ratios between unknowns' (D3/12/6/17)—i.e., results such as $A = \frac{67}{31}B$ and $C = \frac{63}{67}A$, which, as we have already stated, Sraffa had interpreted as implying that one unit of A was to be exchanged for $\frac{67}{31}$ units of B, and that a unit of C was to be exchanged for $\frac{63}{67}$ units of A.

In the positive surplus case, however, the newly introduced surplus variable (R or r) would have had a slightly different status. Sraffa was aware of this and asked: 'This is satisfactory for values, but is it for R? It will give us the ratios between R and our apparent unknowns, a, b, ...' (D3/12/6/17).

To this question, he provided a positive answer: 'If the equations will give us the ratio $a/r = 10/11$, since we know that a is really 1 bushel, we shall know that $r = 1.1$, i.e., rate of surplus is 10%' (D3/12/6/17).

Yet, even though he did not criticize the above conclusion, he added: 'If this were unsatisfactory, we could put the equations in a form which shows explicitly that our real unknowns are values, and rate of surplus' (D3/12/6/18).

He then modified the previous equations and wrote:

$$
\begin{aligned}
V_{a/b}(A + A_S) &= \left(V_{a/b}a_1 + b_1 + V_{c/b}c_1\right)r \\
(B + B_S) &= \left(V_{a/b}a_2 + b_2 + V_{c/b}c_2\right)r \\
V_{c/b}(C + C_S) &= \left(V_{a/b}a_3 + b_3 + V_{c/b}c_3\right)r
\end{aligned}
\tag{14.5}
$$

$V_{a/b}$ and $V_{c/b}$ are 'the value of A in terms of B [and the value of C in terms of B]' (D3/12/6/18). These we may assume were seen by Sraffa as the 'real unknowns' which had been hidden behind the 'apparent unknowns' of his previous systems.[12]

If the distinction between 'apparent' and 'real' unknowns clearly tells us that Sraffa's earliest systems did not include price variables and that what we recognize as the earliest sketches of Sraffa's equations were intended to be tabulations including only physical quantities and no proper unknowns (yet their structure was read by Sraffa as including unknowns, even though only in *apparent* form), we are led to reconsider the whole story from the beginning: Why was Sraffa interested in tabulating production processes?

In our view, as we have already mentioned, this was the outcome of a line of reasoning focused on the concept of physical real costs whose development could be traced to two folders bearing that very phrase on their label. The first folder ('Physical Real Costs', D3/12/42/32–56) contains notes mainly devoted to identifying physical real costs, or real costs, by discussing the distinction between cost and income. The second folder ('Notes London, summer 1927 (Physical Real Costs etc.)', D3/12/3/1–77) contains a long manuscript prepared in London in the summer of 1927—certainly meant to be used as lecture notes in the following term—where we find a discussion of the conditions which must be fulfilled in order to express cost directly as physical real costs, having no recourse to any kind of common measure of value (D3/12/3/44–7). But the conclusions reached by Sraffa were negative: in general, because of the existence of substitutes—which the reflections collected in the first folder had not been able to sidestep[13]—costs of production of individual commodities could not be directly reduced to a single physical quantity. The summer 1927 manuscript, however, contained a note pointing out an exception: a special case where the physical real costs approach could achieve a direct reduction of heterogeneous physical costs to a single magnitude, with no need to invoke the previous determination of a common measure of value. He was referring to the case of a very poor economy, dominated by bare subsistence and no possible alternative compositions of the wage basket.

In this perspective, we may assume that Sraffa, after having successfully bid to postpone beginning his lectures till Lent term (see Marcuzzo 2005, p. 446, n. 8), tabulated the production processes of a no surplus economy—more specifically, of a special kind of no surplus economy: an economy so poor as to be able to afford only mere subsistence—in order to see how, by a simple numerical example, in this exceptional case, physical real costs could actually be reduced to a single quantity of a most essential wage basket (the hypothetical 'absolutely necessary commodity' he had outlined in his London notes—D3/12/3/44).[14] In his tabulation, plus and equal signs would not have strictly expressed algebraic notions; yet, we may presume that, once he had written it down in the form, we may see in manuscript D3/12/2/32, Sraffa realized that the tabulation could be read as a system of simultaneous equations, where the units of measure of each commodity could be seen as unknowns, and where a solution could easily be calculated. Hence, he solved it and abandoned any attempt to reduce costs to quantities of an absolutely necessary commodity. As he had been able to determine exchange ratios directly from physical real costs, he lost any interest in the less direct route he had originally conceived.[15]

This brief outline confirms that the origins of Sraffa's equations must be sought in the tabulations which Sraffa turned into equations. But it also allows us to establish that to trace the origin of Sraffa's equations, there is no need to invoke any resemblance they may have to any other contemporary economist's system of simultaneous equations (and we may also ask why, since they were all conceived in value terms, Sraffa's consideration of them should have led him to write equations with no price variables). Furthermore, this interpretation also allows us to account for the fact (usually overlooked) that, according to all available evidence, Sraffa originally started his analysis from a no surplus case, while the focus of any major inquiry before his, and also of his own analysis, had been on economies producing positive surplus incomes and positive physical surplus.

14.3 Ramsey on Sraffa's Equations and Their Solution

As we have seen, Sraffa's earliest schemes included only physical quantities and no proper unknown, and he employed addition and equality symbols in a way which did not abide by ordinary algebraic rules. Yet, the resulting tabulations assumed a shape similar to ordinary systems of equations, and Sraffa, ignoring the fact that he had not constructed them as proper equations, treated the units of each commodity as unknowns, and solved them (at least, as we shall see, to the extent that his mathematical abilities allowed him to).

But we have also seen that at a very early stage of the development of his analysis (approximately one or two months after he had first conceived his equations), Sraffa decided that price variables had to be explicitly introduced—at least into his *second equations.*

This latter point must be stressed. Sraffa seems to have felt that satisfactory analysis of no surplus cases could be developed along the lines he had originally conceived. Introduction of price variables could have been restricted to the positive surplus case and to the determination of a variable (R or r) expressing the existence of a surplus product.

In subsequent manuscripts, Sraffa tried to solve his new, real unknowns, positive surplus system.[16] Unlike the no surplus case, he could not complete the process and calculate its solutions, except for systems including only two equations (see D3/12/8/26–29). However, if we may judge from the extant manuscripts, Sraffa does not seem to have spent much time on those attempts. He seems to have been content with the notion he could have formed studying handbooks such as Chini's *Manuale* and Chrystal's *Algebra*, that, in general, such systems could be solved, and price unknowns and the additional surplus variable could be determined.

Most interestingly, we may gather that both questions—the solution of his real unknowns systems and the practicability of treating a tabulation as a system of equations—were submitted by Sraffa to Frank Ramsey in a conversation known to us through notes Sraffa labelled 'F. Ramsey, 26.VI.28' (their catalogue numbers are D3/12/2/28 and D3/12/2/29).[17] The notes were written in part by Sraffa and in part by Ramsey, and Sraffa came to place them in the same folder labelled 'USEFUL (All dates) ex black cover, 1955' which contains the earliest formulations of his equations discussed in Sect. 14.1 above.

Item D3/12/2/29 certainly seems to have been written during the meeting. Item D3/12/2/28, on the other hand, seems to have been written by Sraffa after the meeting as a summary of the answers given by Ramsey to the questions he had asked him.[18] The manuscripts allow us to assume that Sraffa opened the discussion by showing Ramsey the positive surplus system that we find in D3/12/2/29 (v_a and v_b obviously being the values of A and B in terms of C):

$$\begin{aligned} v_a A &= (v_a a_1 + v_b b_1 + c_1)r \\ v_b B &= (v_a a_2 + v_b b_2 + c_2)r \\ C &= (v_a a_3 + v_b b_3 + c_3)r \end{aligned} \tag{14.6}$$

Most likely, Sraffa wrote down this system, which is very similar to the one explicitly including price variables that we know he had first written few months before (D3/12/6/18), to explain the kind of research he was pursuing to Ramsey and to ask his advice on how to solve those equations. As the same document also shows, Ramsey wrote the system once again in matrix form, and we may assume that to have been the basis of the response summarized by Sraffa in manuscript D3/12/2/28 in remarks numbered 1 and 2:

1. Equations with surplus: Exact solutions can be found for up to 4 equations. Approximate solutions can probably be found for any number of equations.

2. It can probably be proved that, whatever the number of equations only one set of solutions is significant.

The most important remark addressing our present concern, however, is number 3 in the same manuscript:

3. Equations without surplus: each quantity must be expressed by two letters, one being the number of units, the other the unit of the commodity. Otherwise, if I use only one letter, this would stand for heterogenous things and the sum would be meaningless.

Its apparent simplicity notwithstanding, the interpretation of this remark, may require some caution: while Sraffa may have condensed it in a way which did not reduce its clarity for him, it may be a bit obscure to others. We will approach its meaning starting with a reading *stricto* sensu.

Given that documents D3/12/2/28–29 do not present any system which may be associated with a no surplus case, we may presume that the third remark had been made by Ramsey after having been shown or otherwise described a system like the following[19]:

$$
\begin{aligned}
a &= a_a + b_a + c_a \\
b &= a_b + b_b + c_b \\
c &= a_c + b_c + c_c
\end{aligned}
\tag{14.7}
$$

Remark no. 3, on the other hand, would imply that Ramsey had argued that system (14.7) had to be written as follows:

$$
\begin{aligned}
aA &= a_a A + b_a B + c_a C \\
bB &= a_b A + b_b B + c_b C \\
cC &= a_c A + b_c B + c_c C
\end{aligned}
\tag{14.8}
$$

The meaning of the magnitudes which appear in systems (14.7) and (14.8) cannot be taken for granted. A strict reading of remark no. 3 would tell us that in system (14.7) a_i, b_i and c_i would stand for given quantities of specific commodities—for instance 3 bushels of corn. In system (14.8), on the other hand, A could stand for a bushel of corn, B for a gallon of water and C for a ton of coal, and a_i, b_i and c_i for the number of such units employed in production or obtained as outputs. System (14.8) would then be equivalent to system (14.1), where the latter could be read following the description Sraffa provided when he stressed the distinction between 'apparent' and 'real' unknowns: A, B and C were 'only "one unit of measure of each commodity" (1 bushel of wheat, 1 ton of coal etc.)' (D3/12/6/17). According to this reading, Ramsey told Sraffa that what Sraffa may have seen as a generalization or a simplification of the original formulation of his systems clashed with simple algebraic rules and directed him back to that original formulation (D3/12/2/32–35) and to his use of *apparent unknowns*. This would also imply that, according to Ramsey, the use of addition and equality symbols in $cC = a_c A + b_c B + c_c C$ or in $15C = 1A + 8B + 10C$, where A, B and C are not values but units of the commodities, would follow the rules of algebraic expressions.

Obviously, these conclusions are unacceptable and our *stricto* sensu interpretation of remark no. 3 must be somehow amended: system (14.8) must be read as different from system (14.1). System (14.8) must contain information which is not found in system (14.1).

Indeed, the algebraic nonsense mentioned above can be turned into meaningful equations if we read the phrase 'each quantity must be expressed by two letters, one being the number of units, the other the unit of the commodity' as lacking some data, whether as intentional shorthand or unintentional oversights: the sentence should be turned into 'each quantity must be expressed by two letters, one being the number of units *of the commodity*, the other the *value* unit of the commodity'.[20]

System (14.8) must then be read as equivalent to the following system:

$$\begin{aligned} av_a &= a_a v_a + b_a v_b + c_a v_c \\ bv_b &= a_b v_a + b_b v_b + c_b v_c \\ cv_c &= a_c v_a + b_c v_b + c_c v_c \end{aligned} \qquad (14.9)$$

In a nutshell: remark no. 3 may be read as stating that the structure of the system employed to describe the no surplus case must be the same that Sraffa had used to show to Ramsey the positive surplus case he had been trying to solve (D3/12/2/29).[21]

14.4 The Importance of the No Surplus Tabulation

This discussion has quite obviously assumed that remark no. 3 could not have been written to summarize Ramsey's answer to a question asked by Sraffa with regard to his own systems in general. As implied by its incipit, the question must have regarded only a no surplus system. In other words, remark no. 3 shows that it was only for the no surplus case that Sraffa was interested in the possibility of maintaining the earliest formulation of his own equations.[22] This is consistent with both what Sraffa had already written before meeting with Ramsey in manuscript D3/12/6/17–18 on real and apparent unknowns (see Sect. 14.2 above) and with the fact that the positive surplus system that Sraffa had written down in front of Ramsey included the relevant price variables.

Given that remarks no. 1 and no. 2 are both concerned with the solution of a system of equations, we may conjecture that the third remark also originated from the same context. In this sense, we formulate the hypothesis that a non-contracted form of the third remark may be reconstructed as follows: 'Equations without surplus: *solutions can be found, but* each quantity must be expressed by two letters, one being the number of units *of the commodity*, the other the *value* unit of the commodity. Otherwise, if I use only one letter, this would stand for heterogenous things and the sum would be meaningless' (italics indicate our additions to the original manuscript).

Whether or not the solution of the no surplus system was part of the discussion, the most fundamental issue remains the same: Why should Sraffa have asked Ramsey's advice on the possibility, with regard to the no surplus case, of treating his own original tabulations, where price variables did not appear, as proper equations and of solving them as if they were ordinary equations? Why—even after he had already written systems including price variables—did he feel that, at least for the no surplus case, sticking to the original formulation could have been so important?

A manuscript most likely dating to winter 1927–1928[23] may help us to answer these questions. In that manuscript, commenting on Torrens' analysis of value, Sraffa had written:

> Torrens knew that the (absolute) value (Torrens calls it natural, as opposed to market, price, Cannan, 208) of the product is determined by (in fact, is) the amount of things that have been destroyed for its production. But

> he did not see his way through without finding a 'common measure' of them: he probably felt a repulsion to, or thought that it could not be done, to sum together quantities of heterogeneous things measured in different units. (D3/12/5/26)

This brings us back to the summer 1927 London notes (D3/12/3), to the discussion of physical real costs they contain (D3/12/3/42–47) and to the tabulation of a subsistence economy that, according to our reconstruction, they prompted. In our view, those developments led Sraffa to perceive that—at least with regard to a no surplus (subsistence) economy—a tabulation of 'quantities of heterogeneous things measured in different units' could lead to a straightforward determination of exchange ratios (see Sect. 14.1 above, and Naldi 2018a, pp. 140–143; 2018b, pp. 12–16; 2020, pp. 11–14). This he may have interpreted as an important result. It meant that exchange ratios could be determined by physical real costs. And it also meant that physical real costs as such *were* the value of the product and that 'heterogeneous things measured in different units' could be added together, in the sense that they directly generated the exchange ratios which, at the end of the process, could also offer a common measure.

But the result was also particularly important in view of the fact that Sraffa had come to see not only that 'physical real costs' could provide the basis for an alternative to contemporary subjective economics; they had also been at the root of the whole Classical approach to political economy, from Petty to Ricardo and Marx. In this sense, Sraffa's initial result (his nonsensical equations) revealed the real root of Classical political economy and established a strict continuity between those authors and his research.[24]

In this sense, Sraffa may have felt that his original treatment of a tabulation of 'quantities of heterogeneous things measured in different units' as if it were a system of equations, leading to a straightforward determination of exchange ratios, even though contradicting elementary algebraic principles, should not be discarded—it was important to convey the full meaning of his own approach.

14.5 Concluding Remarks

In the end, as we can see from Chapter I of *Production of Commodities*, Sraffa followed what we may take to have been Ramsey's advice: he introduced price variables into his no surplus system. But, as shown by Sects. 1 and 2 of the same chapter, he did not completely abandon his earliest formulation. With the exception of replacing equal signs with arrows, he reproduced it exactly as it had appeared in his 1927–1928 tabulations. Indeed, this scheme occupies a most prominent position—it is the first that the reader meets in Sraffa's book[25]:

$$280\,\text{qr.wheat} + 12\,\text{t.iron} \rightarrow 400\,\text{qr.wheat}$$

$$120\,\text{qr.wheat} + 8\,\text{t.iron} \rightarrow 20\,\text{t.iron}$$

Furthermore, just like in his 1927–1928 manuscripts,[26] Sraffa (1960, p. 3) also argued that exchange ratios could be straightforwardly determined from that tabulation:

> There is a unique set of exchange-values which if adopted by the market restores the original distribution of the products and makes it possible for the process to be repeated; such values spring directly from the methods of production. In the particular example we have taken, the exchange-value required is 10 qr. of wheat for 1 t. of iron.

In the following page, however, the scheme was written as suggested by Ramsey:

$$A_a p_a + B_a p_b + \cdots + K_a p_k = A p_a$$

$$A_b p_a + B_b p_b + \cdots + K_b p_k = B p_b$$

$$\cdots\cdots\cdots\cdots\cdots\cdots\cdots\cdots\cdots$$

$$A_k p_a + B_k p_b + \cdots + K_k p_k = K p_k$$

This system was presented by Sraffa as a generalization of the tabulations and propositions he had just put forward. The new equations were described as 'conditions of production' (Sraffa 1960, p. 4), just like the previous tabulation had been labelled 'methods of production' (Sraffa 1960, p. 3). And in introducing the system Sraffa stressed the meaning of its magnitudes exactly as in our reconstructed version of Remark no. 3. On the one hand, A is 'the quantity annually produced of "a"', A_a is the quantity of a 'annually used by the industry which produces A' and so on (Sraffa 1960, p. 4). On the other hand, 'the unknowns to be determined are $p_a, p_b, \ldots, p_k$, respectively the values of units of the commodities "a", "b", ..., "k" which if adopted restore the initial position' (Sraffa 1960, p. 4). Then, the process leading to a general solution was outlined (Sraffa 1960, pp. 4–5).

Quite clearly, the text of *Production of Commodities* shows that Sraffa was convinced that the tabulation was important to a proper presentation of his own research. We may presume that in his eyes it had the merit of emphasizing how material conditions of production—*physical real costs*—lay at the bottom of the whole analysis of prices and distribution and how the existence of a physical net product is a necessary condition to the existence of any distributive variable.

But our reconstruction has also shown that all this directly stemmed from Sraffa's original formulation of his equations and from the original algebraic nonsense which it had prompted: *solving* a tabulation as if it were an ordinary system of equations. Furthermore, the same reconstruction allows us to see that from that tabulation we may go back to the roots of Sraffa's equations and to the conception of *physical real costs* which led him to study the case of a 'community that produces just what is sufficient to keep it going'. This phrase we find embedded in a note appended to the summer 1927 manuscript D3/12/3/44, and it also appears in the very first line of the opening chapter of *Production of Commodities*: 'Let us consider an extremely simple society which produces just enough to maintain itself' (Sraffa 1960, p. 3).

Finally, we may also recall that the wheat-iron tabulation brings us back to the initial problem faced by Sraffa while considering how *physical real costs* could provide an alternative to value determination based on utility or on Marshall's *real costs*: Which common unit could be employed to add together heterogeneous commodities? Sraffa's earliest formulations of his no surplus equations were tainted by algebraic nonsense, but they had allowed him to explore ways to avoid the problem of finding a common unit. In this sense, it may be also worth noting how in Chapter I, Sect. 2, Sraffa stretched the wording of his representation of quantities of commodities:

$$10\,\text{qr.wheat} = 1\,\text{t.iron} = 2\,\text{pigs}$$

This essentially epitomizes exactly what Ramsey had described as meaningless.[27]

Acknowledgements I thank, with no further implication, the institutions mentioned in the chapter and their staff, and Lord Eatwell, who granted his permission to quote from the Piero Sraffa Papers.

Notes

1. See de Vivo (2000, 2003, 2016, 2019) and Gilibert (2001, 2003); this view is criticized in Kurz (2012, 2015) and in Kurz and Salvadori (2015); but see also de Vivo and Gilibert (2013).
2. See Kurz and Salvadori (2004, 2005), Gehrke and Kurz (2006, 2018), Kurz (2006, 2012), Gehrke et al. (2019).
3. Sraffa Papers are kept at the Wren Library, Trinity College, Cambridge (catalogue and access to documents at https://janus.lib.cam.ac.uk/db/node.xsp?id=EAD%2FGBR%2F0016%2FSRAFFA. If not otherwise stated, quoted archive numbers refer to this catalogue).
4. A folder such labelled actually exists and is classed D3/12/4 (the actual title of the folder is 'End of November 1927 (large sheets)'—Sraffa probably added the last two words to distinguish it from the set of notes now classed D3/12/11).
5. The first page of that letter was also used by Sraffa as writing paper: it is kept in another folder and marked D3/12/5/32. The letter was dated 19 November 1927 and had been sent from Britain to Sraffa's address in Milan and forwarded from Milan to Cambridge. Evidence from the correspondence between Sraffa and Tatiana Schucht suggests that a letter sent from England to Milan and readdressed to Cambridge could have completed the whole circuit in five to seven days.
6. We interpret the fact that the same calculations are strewn throughout the page in D3/12/2/32 and repeated in good order in D3/12/2/34 as revealing that solving the system came to Sraffa as an unexpected development, which he felt he had to reproduce in a more orderly fashion, not unlikely also to be able to show it to other people, as we may take he did with Keynes.
7. We borrow the word *tabulation* from Chapter I of *Production of Commodities*, where it was employed to describe this scheme (Sraffa 1960, p. 3):

$$280\,\text{qr.wheat} + 12\,\text{t.iron} \rightarrow 400\,\text{qr.wheat}$$

$$120\,\text{qr.wheat} + 8\,\text{t.iron} \rightarrow 20\,\text{t.iron}$$

8. Given that in manuscripts D3/12/2/32–35, the no surplus case is discussed by considering a three commodity system, while the positive surplus case considers only two commodities, it may be argued that the latter could have been written down first. The three-commodity no surplus scheme would have reflected an attempt to deal with a more complex case. Against this view, we would raise a twofold objection stemming from the idea that Sraffa's attention was initially focused on the reduction of inputs to an absolutely necessary commodity. In such a perspective, on the one hand, a two-commodity case could have been seen by him as trivial; on the other hand, the note appended on the margin of manuscript D3/12/3/44 would have straightforwardly directed him towards studying a no surplus case.
9. That manuscript may have been part of the notes that Sraffa, in a draft letter to the Secretary of the General Board of the University of Cambridge dated 11 January 1928, described with these words: 'now that I have prepared a certain number of lectures I am convinced that the subject I had chosen is really quite unsuitable' (B9/1/16; see also B9/1/11).
10. The two components of each commodity's output distinguish input replacement (A, B, C) and positive surplus product (A_s, B_s, C_S).
11. For similar formulations applied to no surplus cases, see D3/12/5/2–3, D3/12/11/77, 87 and D3/12/8/8.
12. As already noted by Garegnani, in systems (14.4) and (14.5) a_i, b_i, and c_i play different roles (units of commodities in the first case; quantities of commodities in the second case). Close inspection of the manuscript reveals that Sraffa's original formulation had no figures and inputs were simply described as $a_i + b_i + c_i$. Figures were inserted as an afterthought, which also gave different statuses to a_i, b_i, and c_i on one side and to A, B, C, A_s, B_s, and C_s on the other. Figures disappeared, and a_i, b_i, and c_i were returned to their original role, when Sraffa substituted 'real unknowns' for 'apparent unknowns' (see Garegnani 2004, p. 177, n. 30; 2005, pp. 469, 487, n. 26).
13. As we have argued (Naldi 2018b, pp. 16–19; 2020, pp. 15–16), almost every item in D3/12/42/32–56 may be assumed to have been written by Sraffa before the relevant documents in D3/12/3/1–77.
14. It may be appropriate to consider more closely why Sraffa felt that the subsistence community case—which certainly was a special case—deserved the attention he gave it, while he treated the existence of substitutes as an obstacle which prevented any general step forward within the physical real cost approach. Why did he not treat the hypothetical cases of an economy with no substitutes and of a subsistence community in the same way? In our view, Sraffa saw a difference between the two cases in the fact that assuming away the existence of substitutes would have meant assuming away an aspect of real life; on the contrary, a case of strict subsistence

as the one he had envisaged in his note could have been discussed as a case—however extreme—of real economic life. Such a distinction elicits an analogy with another one we find in a note most likely relating to a conversation Sraffa had with Wittgenstein in the early 1930s. In that note, Sraffa distinguished between two different 'conditional propositions' and argued: '"If I were the king" is nonsense. For either I, or the job, would have to be entirely different'. On the contrary, '"If I were a lecturer" has sense. For I was last year, and I don't think I have changed much since, nor has the job' (D3/12/7/174; see also D3/12/7/42–3). It may also be added that the choice of a three-commodity scheme may have been intended to avoid the triviality of the reduction to an absolutely necessary commodity in a two-commodity case.

15. It may be worth noting that, while the subject of physical real costs is clearly the main focus of the folder labelled 'Physical Real Costs' (where phrases like *real costs*, *real physical costs*, *physical real costs* and *physical costs* appear in most of the documents it contains), the same subject occupies less than 10% of the pages in the folder labelled 'Notes London, summer 1927 (Physical Real Costs etc.)'. This suggests that Sraffa put the latter heading on that folder (or added to its heading the phrase within brackets) after he had seen that that was the most important point in the whole manuscript, and that that approach could lead to a most interesting outcome—even though it was not envisaged in the conclusions he had reached in the sections of that very manuscript devoted to its discussion.
16. Sraffa actually simplified his equations: the commodity produced by each sector was not included among the magnitudes multiplied by *r* (see D3/12/6/18–29).
17. In Sraffa's pocket diary for the academic year 1927–1928 (E1), we find an entry indicating a meeting with Frank Ramsey on Thursday 28 June 1928.
18. This chronological approach was outlined by Kurz and Salvadori (2001, p. 264).
19. As already mentioned in Note 11 above, similar formulations can be found in D3/12/5/2–3, D3/12/11/77, 87 and D3/12/8/8.
20. This view was mentioned by Garegnani (2004, p. 175, n. 28; 2005, pp. 467, 487, n. 24), but he considered only the second of the two omissions (intentional or otherwise) discussed above.
21. We may note that system (14.9) and our reformulation of remark no. 3 ('each quantity must be expressed by <u>two</u> letters, one being the number of units *of the commodity* [e.g., *3 kg of A*], the other the *value unit* of the commodity [e.g., *2£/kg of A*]') are consistent with a proper addition between quantities of different commodities (note that, if the first of our two amendments to remark no. 3 had not been introduced, the result could not be reduced to a single magnitude).

22. The opposite view had been put forward in Kurz and Salvadori (2001, p. 264) and criticized in Garegnani (2004, p. 176; 2005, pp. 467–468).
23. The folder which contains it is the same mentioned in Note 5 above (its title being 'Winter 1927–28 Looms etc.').
24. This line of thought emerges in the lecture notes Sraffa used in his 1928–1931 teaching on the theory of value: 'Cost of production of an article is always reduced to remuneration of factors (i.e. sharers in distribution): it might be done otherwise (physical costs)' (D2/4/3/4); 'But if the materials were not measured by the labour they cost, but directly as material, there would be an homogeneity in the theory (physical cost) similar to that of Petty and Physiocrats' (D2/4/3/13); 'To day I propose to go over again the question of the relations between Marshall's theory of real costs and opportunity cost (or loss of utility) on the one hand, and the classical, or physiocratic conception of costs, regarded purely as a physical quantity of material, required for the maintenance of labour' (D2/4/3/62); 'we are left with two kinds of materials (utility, and "costs" physical) each of which can be used as the only basis of a theory of value: we can therefore have two independent theories' (D2/4/3/69).
25. Similar tabulations can also be found in Chapter II, Sect. 5, and in Chapter IV, Sect. 25.
26. See manuscripts D3/12/11/54, 89, 101; D3/12/6/4 and D3/12/5/2—already mentioned in Sect. 14.1.
27. Similar formulas can be found in Marx's *Capital* ('20 yards of linen = 1 coat'—Marx [1867] 1978, Volume I, Part I, Chapter I, Sect. 3.a—which we may presume was known to Sraffa), and in Isnard's *Traité* ('aM = bM'—Isnard 1781, Volume I, Chapter II, Section I—which Sraffa most likely never read).

References

de Vivo, G. (2000). Produzione di merci a mezzo di merci: note sul percorso intellettuale di Sraffa. In M. Pivetti (Ed.), *Piero Sraffa. Contributi per una biografia intellettuale* (pp. 265–295). Rome: Carocci.

de Vivo, G. (2003). Sraffa's Path to *Production of Commodities by Means of Commodities*: An Interpretation. *Contributions to Political Economy, 22*(1), 1–25.

de Vivo, G. (2016). Some Notes on Marx's Role in the Development of Sraffa's Thought. *Contributions to Political Economy, 35*(1), 57–70.

de Vivo, G. (2019). Marx and Sraffa: A Comment on Gehrke and Kurz. *Review of Political Economy, 31*(1), 95–99.

de Vivo, G., & Gilibert, G. (2013). On Sraffa and Marx: A Comment. *Cambridge Journal of Economics, 37*(6), 1443–1447.

Garegnani, P. (2004). Di una svolta nella posizione teorica e nella interpretazione dei classici in Sraffa nei tardi anni Venti. *Convegno internazionale Piero Sraffa, Atti dei Convegni Lincei* (pp. 159–194). Rome: Accademia Nazionale dei Lincei.

Garegnani, P. (2005). On a Turning Point in Sraffa's Theoretical and Interpretative Position in the Late 1920s. *European Journal of the History of Economic Thought, 12*(3), 453–492.

Gehrke, C., & Kurz, H. D. (2006). Sraffa on von Bortkiewicz: Reconstructing the Classical Theory of Value and Distribution. *History of Political Economy, 38*(1), 91–149.

Gehrke, C., & Kurz, H. D. (2018). Sraffa's Constructive and Interpretive Work, and Marx. *Review of Political Economy, 30*(3), 428–442.

Gehrke, C., Kurz, H. D., & Salvadori, N. (2019). On the 'Origins' of Sraffa's Production Equations: A Reply to de Vivo. *Review of Political Economy, 31*(1), 110–114.

Gilibert, G. (2001). Gramsci, Sraffa e il secondo libro del *Capitale.* In G. Petronio & M. Paladini Musitelli (Eds.), *Marx e Gramsci. Memoria e attualità* (pp. 159–172). Rome: Manifestolibri.

Gilibert, G. (2003). The Equations Unveiled: Sraffa's Price Equations in the Making. *Contributions to Political Economy, 22*(1), 27–40.

Isnard, A. (1781). *Traité des richesses.* London: Grasset.

Kurz, H. D. (2006). The Agents of Production Are the Commodities Themselves: On the Classical Theory of Production, Distribution and Value. *Structural Change and Economic Dynamics, 17*(1), 1–26.

Kurz, H. D. (2012). Don't Treat Too Ill My Piero! Interpreting Sraffa's Papers. *Cambridge Journal of Economics, 36*(6), 1535–1569.

Kurz, H. D. (2015). Sraffa's Equations 'Unveiled'? A Comment on Gilibert. In H. D. Kurz & N. Salvadori (Eds.), *Revisiting Classical Economics: Studies in Long-Period Analysis* (pp. 192–224). Abingdon: Routledge.

Kurz, H. D., & Salvadori, N. (2001). Sraffa and the Mathematicians. In T. Cozzi & R. Marchionatti (Eds.), *Piero Sraffa's Political Economy* (pp. 254–284). London: Routledge.

Kurz, H. D., & Salvadori, N. (2004). Man from the Moon: On Sraffa's Objectivism. *Économies et Sociétés, 35*, 1545–1557. Reprinted in: H. D. Kurz & N. Salvadori (Eds.). (2007). *Interpreting Classical Economics: Studies in Long-Period Analysis* (pp. 120–130). Abingdon: Routledge.

Kurz, H. D., & Salvadori, N. (2005). Representing the Production and Circulation of Commodities in Material Terms: On Sraffa's Objectivism. *Review of Political Economy, 17*(3), 69–97.

Kurz, H. D., & Salvadori, N. (2015). On the Beginnings of Sraffa's Path to *Production of Commodities by Means of Commodities*: A Comment on de Vivo. In H. D. Kurz & N. Salvadori (Eds.), *Revisiting Classical Economics: Studies in Long-Period Analysis* (pp. 226–244). Abingdon: Routledge.

Marx, K. ([1867] 1978). *Capital: A Critique of Political Economy* (Vol. 1). Harmondsworth: Penguin.

Marcuzzo, M. C. (2005). Piero Sraffa at the University of Cambridge. *European Journal of the History of Economic Thought, 12*(3), 425–452.

Naldi, N. (2018a). On the Earliest Formulations of Sraffa's Equations. In M. Corsi, C. D'Ippoliti, & J. A. Kregel (Eds.), *Classical Economics Today: Essays in Honor of Alessandro Roncaglia* (pp. 129–152). London: Anthem Press.

Naldi, N. (2018b, December). *On the Origins of Sraffa's Equations: New Evidence Following Pierangelo Garegnani's Lead* (Centro Sraffa Working Papers, no. 33). Rome: Centro di ricerche e documentazione Piero Sraffa. Available at: http://www.centrosraffa.org/public/5bb8a8ea-523e-48ca-8c91-10b455996fb0.pdf.

Naldi, N. (2020, forthcoming). The Origins of Piero Sraffa's Equations. *Contributions to Political Economy, 39.*

Sraffa, P. (1960). *Production of Commodities by Means of Commodities: Prelude to a Critique of Economic Theory.* Cambridge: Cambridge University Press.

CHAPTER 15

What Can *Still* Be Learnt from Sraffa's Study of Prices in a Surplus Economy?

Richard Arena

Sraffa's *Production of Commodities by Means of Commodities* (*PCMC*) was published nearly sixty years ago (1960). Since then drastic changes have occurred in our *real* economic system and in the meaning of what can be still called the global reproduction of this system. Today it is therefore crucial to reconsider the ability of Sraffa's intellectual legacy to grasp the working of our present economic system, taking into account the opening of his unpublished papers in 1993. Indeed, for many economists of this period, the Cambridge controversy on the theory of capital and the subsequent debates, which took place in the 1980s, greatly contributed to favouring the emergence of two opposite interpretations of Sraffa's economic theory.

The first consisted in defining what was called the 'classical theory of general economic equilibrium',[1] and crediting Sraffa with having built

R. Arena (✉)
University of Côte d'Azur, CNRS, Gredeg, France
e-mail: Richard.ARENA@unice.fr

M. C. Marcuzzo et al. (eds.), *New Perspectives on Political Economy and Its History*, Palgrave Studies in the History of Economic Thought,
https://doi.org/10.1007/978-3-030-42925-6_15

the rigorous version of a new theory of relative prices also called 'neo-Ricardian'. This version was intended to differ from the old version called 'neo-Walrasian'.

The second interpretation rejected the idea of Sraffa's contribution as a new version of the theory of general economic equilibrium (GEE) and tried to provide alternative constructions. These constructions—provided by economists like Garegnani, Kregel, Pasinetti or Roncaglia, for instance—did not always converge but shared a common refusal to reduce Sraffa's contribution to a specific version of the GEE theory of relative prices.

However, today things have changed. On the one hand, in the 1970s–1980s the 'neo-Walrasian' general economic equilibrium theory came up against insurmountable obstacles which contributed to its decline and to the predominant rise of game theory and behavioural microeconomics within what is called 'mainstream microeconomics'. On the other hand, thanks to the increasing access to Sraffa's unpublished papers, interpretation of Sraffa's contribution to economic analysis ceased to be limited to the mere construction of an alternative price theory (in spite of some exceptions like Bidard 1992 and more recently Naqvi 2011 or Nicholas 2014). To understand this new situation and take into account the substantial new material included in Sraffa's unpublished papers, we may now consider that the first interpretation clearly presents the major drawback of 'reductionism'.

If indeed we take into consideration all Sraffa's works, papers and contributions—and not only *PCMC*—it is perfectly clear that, to understand his contribution today, price theory does not offer sufficient scope. A broader view was therefore introduced which tried to promote understanding of the right approach to analysing the way the surplus of a production economy is distributed amongst economic agents and social groups, within various given historical systems of institutions and systems of social division of labour, whether including markets or not (?) (see for instance Arena 2010, 2014, 2015a, b; Arena and Lawson 2015; Blankenburg et al. 2012). This view is compatible with the second interpretation and provides the fundamental reason why Sraffa never wrote that the theory of relative prices was 'the true object of economics'; this 'object' is 'the study of the "surplus product"' (Sraffa Papers D3/12/7: 161).[2]

This crucial use of the notion of surplus implies two important consequences.

First, the notion supposes the *concrete, objective and direct measurability of the ingredients* which play a part in the various processes of production and consumption allowing for the reproduction of a real economic system. Thus these ingredients are not individual behaviours but quantities of *commodities* (basic or non-basic material goods and immaterial services) and of *labour* (hours of heterogeneous work). These processes are related through production techniques based on technology, social norms (property rights, labour and employment legislation) and forms of organization (linking intra- and inter-firm relations as well as markets and industries through the social division of labour). Therefore, they *exclude subjective magnitudes* (such as expectations or utility), which are only indirectly measurable through the individual economic agent's individual and rational choices.

Secondly, the existence of the relations between these ingredients and the stress placed by Sraffa on the laws which govern the social division and distribution amongst agents and groups imply consideration of the historical rules and institutions in which these laws are embedded and play their respective economic roles. This existence does not generally find a place in what is usually called technical input–output analysis.

The purpose of this chapter is to cast some light on the real methodological contents of these two consequences. It is based mainly on the textual indications offered by Sraffa from the 1920s to the completion of *PCMC* and it is split into four sections.

Section 15.1 considers how and why the opposition between the theory of GEE and Sraffa's approach necessarily implies an interpretation of the latter, analysing how the surplus of a production economy is distributed amongst economic agents and social groups, in the context of various given historical systems of institutions and social rules.

Section 15.2 shows how and why Sraffa's contribution cannot be reduced to the framework of general interdependence but is also founded on Sraffa's criticism of a specific part of Marshall's theory of partial equilibrium, implying the need to found analysis of prices and individual decisions on subjective magnitudes.

Sections 15.3 and 15.4 aim to reinforce the conclusions of the first and second parts of the chapter by insisting on some aspects of the work Sraffa went through from the 1920s to the 1940s, which finds scant room in the literature today. Section 15.3 stresses why Sraffa's criticism of Marshall's theory of prices does not, however, exclude some analogies between the approaches of both authors on organization and production, again underlining the importance for Sraffa of observation of the real world. This importance is also emphasized in the last part of the chapter, which comes closer to Keynes's than to Marshall's economic construction.

15.1 Sraffa and General Economic Equilibrium

As noted above, in the 1960s and the 1970s the Cambridge controversy over capital theory, the difficulties in understanding the analytical and the mathematical foundations of *PCMC* and the stress on the opposition between the 'neo-Walrasian' and 'neo-Ricardian' approaches all contributed greatly to the interpretation of Sraffa's contribution as a specific version of the theory of general economic equilibrium. In his way, Hahn (1975) contributed to reinforcing this interpretation when he argued that Sraffa only provided a construction in which 'there is not a single formal proposition ... which is not also true in a General Equilibrium model constructed on his assumptions' (Hahn 1975, p. 362). He also reinforced the assertion that Sraffa's book belongs *only* to the realm of *pure economic theory* (see Marcuzzo 2011). When we compare Arrow and Debreu's model to Sraffa's, the comparison is based on the implicit assumption that both approaches accept formal logic, if not axiomatics as the *only validity criterion* to assess a theoretical construction (in line with Debreu 1959). If we were to accept this assumption, we would also be led to accept the view which assimilates Sraffa's to a closed and self-contained system in which there is no necessity and no reason to explain the origins and the processes of determination of Sraffa's given quantities and given income distribution variables, utilizing the achievements of other social sciences.

By contrast, let us return to the second interpretation, in which the reference to the concept of GEE is replaced with a different view, where the system analysed in *PCMC* is a production economy in which the concept of surplus is central and its social rules of distribution depend on history and institutions. To better define these production economies, we may refer to two examples, namely the contributions of two economists we have already mentioned and who were quick to contribute greatly to the dissemination of Sraffa's ideas.

The first was developed by Pierangelo Garegnani. Thanks to Sraffa, we know that the system of production prices which is investigated in *PCMC* and where capitalist producers and workers share a variable part of the surplus is only an illustration, an example of '*society*' (the word Sraffa used at the beginning of *PCMC*), and not the 'true object of economics': price theory as such is not for Sraffa the main aim of economics. This is confirmed by the fact that *two* other societies are also characterized in *PCMC*. The first is the no surplus society described at the beginning of the book, in which producers and workers are equally agents and form only one social class; this society has an air of family-resemblance to the simple merchant society described by Adam Smith in the *Wealth of Nations.* The second society described in *PCMC* has a positive 'surplus product' which is entirely appropriated by capitalist producers. Wage-earners are quite distinct from these producers but their wages are fixed by social norms and therefore they cannot share in any part of the surplus; they receive a subsistence wage. Thus the rules of income distribution differ in the two different societies characterized in *PCMC*.

This is why in *Il capitale nelle teorie della distribuzione* (Garegnani 1960), without having had the possibility to read *PCMC* (his book was written *before* 1960), Garegnani opened his book noting that 'in the classical theories of distribution, *the central problem is the determination of the circumstances which rule the size of the social surplus*' (Garegnani 1960, p. 3, emphasis added) and *not* price theory. In 1985, Garegnani highlighted the notion of '"core" in the surplus theories' (Garegnani 1985, p. 8) and made a distinction between the 'net product', the 'necessary consumption' and the 'part of the social product which differs from wages' (Garegnani 1985, p. 10). He represented the general relations between these magnitudes through what he called the 'scheme of the "core" of the surplus theories' (Garegnani 1985, p. 14, Fig. 1), contrasting for example, with the same picture or 'representation', the two different cases of societies considered above (Garegnani 1985, p. 51, Fig. 4). Garegnani's 'core' was not, therefore, devoted exclusively to studying modern capitalism but also other surplus-based societies.

The second economist we look to is Luigi Pasinetti. Let us see what he had to say:

> By 'pure theory', I mean an exercise of abstraction aimed at singling out those elements of reality that have a high degree of persistence (*i.e.* of invariance) through time. Human behavior does not share this characteristic and hence should not be part of this first stage of economic investigation. Human beings are intrinsically endowed with discretion of action and enjoy many degrees of freedom of behavior in this respect. (Pasinetti 2007, p. 212)

For Pasinetti, 'full economic analysis' includes pure theory. The difference between the two approaches is the fact that, contrary to the latter, the former introduces

> a second stage of investigation, mainly concerning institutional analysis, [dealing] with various hypotheses on individual and social behavior, and consequently [introducing] different (and sometimes alternative) institutional set-ups, within which human beings organize themselves. (ibid., p. 213)
>
> ...
>
> in so doing, we are able to open up the second stage of economic investigation to the contributions of the other social sciences, which may have a lot to say about human behavior, besides and beyond what economists may consider. Finally, we are enabled to take full account of the historical and geographical specificities of various economic systems. (ibid.)

Obviously, Garegnani's and Pasinetti's developments did differ but both defended the idea that *PCMC* does not represent a closed system but, rather, the 'core' or the 'pure theory' of Sraffa's construction. Now the core or the pure theory must be completed by transforming it into an *open system*, i.e. a system which has to be articulated with other social issues and sciences and therefore to become interdisciplinary.

In two previous papers (Arena 2013, 2015a), I tried to relate this view to the reciprocal influences between Sraffa and Wittgenstein concerning the possible relation between Sraffa's 'snapshots' and Wittgenstein's 'surveyable representations'. These analogies support the idea of a partially common morphological and 'physiognomic' conception of societies which is totally different from the neo-Walrasian concept of a self-contained system.

15.2 Sraffa and Partial Economic Equilibrium

We know that the painstaking drafting of *PCMC* was not Sraffa's only contribution to *pure theory* as well as *full economic analysis*. We must also look back to the 1920s–1930s when Sraffa made a searching and exhaustive critique Marshall's theory of value. As we know, Marshall never defended axiomatics or pure logic exclusively as such. He also stressed the crucial role played by real observations and empirical causes.

What did Sraffa really think of the Marshallian and respective neo-Marshallian contributions? We need to investigate this issue in order to piece together a complete interpretation of Sraffa's construction.

A very useful starting point for this construction may be found in an excellent paper by Salvadori and Signorino (2007). This paper provides a textual analysis of Sraffa's contributions to pure economics in order to elaborate a rational reconstruction of an aspect of Sraffa's implicit methodology which had yet to be investigated. Reference here is to the threefold relationship between '*economic reality*', '*the economist/observer*' and '*economic theory*'. It elucidates the constraints which, for Sraffa, should curb the economists' arbitrariness and traces the elements of continuity and evolution from the 1925 to 1926 critique of Marshallian economics to *PCMC*.

First the interpretation it offers of the 1960 book completes the points recalled in the previous section. Sraffa does not only refer to pure theory defined as Pasinetti had it. In fact, to build a full economic analysis Sraffa stressed the need also to take into account economic reality, or, to use Sraffa's own terminology the 'actual system' (Sraffa 1960, p. 24), 'which in the Italian edition is more explicitly mentioned as "sistema reale" or "sistema economico della realtà" (p. 24)' (Salvadori and Signorino 2007, p. 196). Now, in this context 'the economist/observer's' choice 'is discretionary but cannot be arbitrary: the distribution of the surplus depends on the (political, legal, etc.) institutions and social norms which, in a given historical period, characterize the economy under investigation' (Salvadori and Signorino 2007, p. 197). These remarks on *PCMC* cannot be disregarded. They show that to define a specific production economy, the observer or the economist is not assumed to use axiomatic and general assumptions but to define a given social and historical context related to the real social rules of the distribution of a specific surplus.

Secondly, this importance attributed to the distinction between 'economic reality' and 'the economist/observer' is not only noted in *PCMC* but also in Sraffa's Marshallian episode of the 1920–1930 decade. As Salvadori and Signorino again noted,

> Careful reading of the texts of the 1925-1926 papers and of the 1932 exchange with Hayek shows that Sraffa makes continuous reference to economic reality. In 'Sulle Relazioni fra Costo e Quantità Prodotta' (1925) Sraffa speaks of 'circostanze obbiettive inerenti alle varie industrie' (1925, p. 278) – 'objective circumstances inherent in the various industries' (1998, p. 324) – and of 'condizioni obbiettive del Sistema produttivo studiato' (1925, p. 320) – 'objective conditions of the economic system studied' (1998, p. 357). Moreover, Sraffa frequently uses expressions

> like 'esperienza' (1925, p. 279) – 'experience' (1998, p. 325) – 'fatto di comune esperienza' (1925, p. 302) – 'commonly observed fact' (1998, p. 343) – 'fatto generale' (1925, p. 287) – 'general fact' (1998, p. 331) – 'realtà' and 'realtà concreta' (1925, pp. 286, 298, 303, 307, 310, 325, 326, 327 and 328) – 'reality' and 'concrete reality' (1998, pp. 330, 340, 344, 347, 350, 361, 362 and 363). Similarly, in 'The Laws of Returns under Competitive Conditions' Sraffa (1926) makes use of expressions like 'in fact' (p. 538), 'in reality' (pp. 540 and 541, fn. 1), 'the reality of things' (p. 543), 'the actual conditions of industry [in the different industries]' (pp. 540 and 542), 'the actual process of determining the price and the quantity produced' (p. 544), 'real conditions' (p. 541), 'the actual state of things' (p. 542) and 'everyday experience' (p. 543). (Salvadori and Signorino 2007, p. 191)

Moreover, our authors made ample use of Sraffa's arguments critical of the *unrealism* of Marshall's arguments in his construction of his symmetric price theory based on various arguments related to the forms of returns to scale (see Salvadori and Signorino 2007, pp. 187–190). Therefore, Sraffa's insistence on economic reality in the 1930s actually paves the way to his surplus approach of the 1960s, which is not an axiomatic construction but also insists on the need to include the features of the real and observed world.

This conclusion is confirmed by the outstanding contribution by Marcuzzo and Rosselli (2011) on Sraffa's arguments against 'marginism'. In fact, Marcuzzo and Rosselli carefully and clearly reconstruct these arguments dealing with a crucial aspect of Sraffa's contribution. Of these arguments we will only focus here on Sraffa's stress on observation and empiricism. Marcuzzo and Rosselli (2011, p. 224, emphasis added) noted that, for Sraffa, '*marginal magnitudes*, which are the differences between an observable situation and one imagined at the level of a mere thought experiment, could not satisfy the criteria that Sraffa ascribed to scientific inquiry'. They went on to quote a passage included in the Sraffa Papers, dated 5 December 1955:

> The marginal product [cost] has *no objective existence in the real world* and that is why no observation however accurate can discover it. The experiments that are suggested by theory to 'ascertain' it must be directed in the first place to 'make' [create] it (whether they can succeed in doing so is another matter). (D3/12/42, emphasis added)

> In economic theory, there are three types of magnitudes. First we have those that are directly measurable in production and consumption processes (hours of work, tons of grain, etc.). Then there are the purely subjective magnitudes (such as expectations or utility), which are only indirectly measurable through the individual economic agent's disposition to pay. The third type of magnitude is 'virtual', existing only in the economists' thought experiments. (D3/12/13/3)

And again, returning to Marcuzzo and Rosselli: 'Now economics as a science can only work on the basis of magnitudes characterised by unequivocal, objective measurability' (Marcuzzo and Rosselli 2011, p. 224).

Our references to Marcuzzo and Rosselli, Salvadori and Signorino are obviously closely (albeit not only) related to the period of the 1920s–1930s during which Sraffa elaborated his criticisms with the aim of undermining Marshall's 'symmetric theory of value' (see also Rosselli 2005).

Reconsideration of Sraffa's papers shows, however, that his opposition to Marshall's theory of prices and 'marginism' does not mean that he rejected every single piece of the Marshallian construction. This construction is theoretically ambiguous, as indeed are all attempts at compromise or synthesis in economic theory, and Sraffa knew it perfectly. Some developments of the *Principles* provided the foundations of what, after Pigou and Viner, became the neo-Marshallian predominant theory of prices, still based on marginism, while others amongst Marshall's followers moved in the direction of a completely different research programme. This latter programme is more easily retraced in *The Economics of Industry* and in *Industry and Trade*, which contrast with the modern trend of industrial organization.[3] Broadly speaking, it consists in investigation into the causes affecting the role of organization which account for the inequality in performance of different spatial systems of production. Of the three levels of organization which Marshall distinguished ('business organization'; 'industrial organization'; systemic organization which Marshall assimilated to social division of labour, seen from the viewpoint of the whole economy), Sraffa paid particular attention to the last two. He read carefully, quoted and commented on *The Economics of Industry* as well as *Industry and Trade* (D1/36) in relation to these themes, but his views on classical political economy certainly played a crucial role, too, and they do not clash with Marshall's conception of a national system of production (Arena 1998).

There is therefore no doubt that striking analogies exist between some of the points made by Marshall and Sraffa on the need to take into account institutional and organizational aspects of the economic system, in order to understand how economic agents coordinate within the process of the social division of labour. Let us now take two crucial examples. One of these analogies corresponds to what Sraffa called the theory of the 'semi-monopoly'.

15.3 Semi-Monopoly and Obstacles to Competition

We know the major role played by Sraffa in the destruction of Marshall's 'symmetric theory of value'. He not only identified the inconsistencies in its use of marginism but also in the incompatibility of the assumption of increasing returns with the framework of perfect competition; of the assumption of decreasing returns with the framework of partial equilibrium; and of the assumption of constant returns with the idea of 'symmetric forces'.

He identified the origin of the problem in the use of the two former assumptions within the common framework of price theory, while they were introduced quite separately, coming from heterogeneous intellectual constructions. Now, we know that this critique was developed in the Italian article of 1925 and in the first part of the English article of 1926 (Sraffa 1925, 1926). The second part of the latter article, however, included remarks which were later interpreted as amongst the origins of the theory of imperfect competition. Moreover, this part was often interpreted as a kind of compensation for the English reader, in order to make the article less negative as regards what was the prevailing theory of price. Actually, this interpretation cannot be seriously defended.

On the one hand, on looking into the bundle dedicated to 'semi-monopoly' within the Sraffa Papers it becomes apparent that, far from thinking of constructing a theory of imperfect competition, Sraffa wished to build a general theory of *real competition* characterized by the existence both of a tendency to competition and of a tendency to monopoly due to the eternal efforts of entrepreneurs to create what Marshall called 'private markets', through product differentiation.

This conception is perfectly compatible with the view that there were only two cases: free competition and 'monopoly', which included all the cases in which competition was restricted by natural as well as legal, technological or strategic obstacles (see Arena 1992b). Moreover, it is impossible to interpret the second part of the 1926 article as a concession or suggestion dictated by circumstances. The Sraffa Papers show that Sraffa worked on this theory over a very long period of time, trying to give it precise and rigorous form, in order to build a general theory of real competition.

The theory of semi-monopoly also points out the sharp division of labour which characterizes modern capitalism. Semi-monopolistic entrepreneurs favour this tendency by increasing the differentiation of their products. This is why semi-monopoly is a concept which provides a good representation of the real world, namely 'le industrie reali [che] si troveranno sparse sul cammino dall'uno estremo all'altro [real industries that will be found along the path from one end to the other; pure competitive and pure monopoly]' (D1/32/22/1r). This attention paid to the real world is also shown in the second part of the 1926 article when Sraffa criticizes the theory of perfect competition because of its inability to take into account two major empirical features which characterize modern concentrated capitalism, namely the fact that, in the real world, entrepreneurs are generally price-setters and not price-takers, and the existence of internal economies within the firm. Thus, Sraffa also revives Marshall's aim to illustrate through economics 'the practice of businessmen' (Marshall, *Industry and Trade*, p. 457, copied and quoted by Sraffa, D1/29).

The importance that Sraffa attributed to this concept of semi-monopoly is also attested by a letter from Sraffa in Milan to Keynes, dated 6 June 1926,[4] in which the theory of semi-monopoly plays a central role.

We know that this line of research proved *a failure*. The obstacles were tremendous. On the one hand, Sraffa had to solve a problem of aggregation of individual cost curves into a collective one, considered at the level of the industry. On the other hand, this aggregation had to be compatible with the existence of interdependences between consumers and producers, and amongst producers, too. How was it possible to take into account strategic interactions amongst agents within the industry?

Finally, there was also the problem of going beyond partial equilibrium in order to build a more general theory. Sraffa admitted to having failed to complete analysis.

However, the semi-monopoly approach characterized the contents of Sraffa's general research programme and the importance he attributed to concreteness and the observation of the real world.

On the one hand, Sraffa's approach clearly illustrated his rejection of the usual theory of competition. Not only did he criticize the 'Marshallian' symmetric theory of prices but he also rejected the methodological device which distinguished perfect from imperfect cases. For Sraffa, the real world can never be a source of 'imperfections' contrasting with the 'perfection' of the theory of pure competition. The theory of competition must, on the contrary, use semi-monopolies (or monopolies) as the prevailing case since it better reflects *what economic reality is.* Therefore, at least in the 1920s and the 1930s, free competition did not represent for Sraffa a kind of reference which he would necessarily have to take into account in order to build a satisfactory theory of the working of a market economy.

Sraffa's rejection of the usual economic theory also explains why he tried to eliminate any subjective element inherited from Marshall. On the one hand, he interpreted semi-monopoly pricing as a kind of 'full-cost' pricing (D1/29/1).

On the other hand, in line with his critique of marginism, he tried to retain a concept of demand devoid of its subjectivist foundations. Demands had to be represented by monetary demand elasticities and they were supposed to be observed rather than micro-economically founded (cf. D1/44 or D1/68/29).

Sraffa's approach also exhibited a Marshallian flavour insofar as it stressed the importance of market organization as a crucial element of the social division of labour. *But* this flavour went along with Sraffa's own stress on organization and the rules of the real world. Thus, Sraffa's view of the semi-monopoly places at the heart of its scheme entrepreneurs seen as the 'integrating force'. They take the decisions on production and pricing; they try to influence consumers through advertising and product differentiation; they try to reduce uncertainty by organizing their own 'private markets'; they might also coordinate their activities with those of their competitors within the industry. In short, they play the major role of coordinating production and exchange activities; they form the 'integrating force' of the social division of labour. However, they are not free competitive entrepreneurs but semi-monopolistic. This confirms Sraffa's view of entrepreneurs as the actors of both the division of labour and of the tendency of the economy to monopoly.

Modern tendencies to monopoly are not limited to market organization. They also concern the control of firm activities. This is the second and last theme we shall now consider; again, it brings out the fundamental attention Sraffa paid to observed reality.

15.4 Organization and the Control of Production

Many developments included in the Sraffa Papers concern the role played by organization in the working of the economic system. However, two texts must be mentioned more specifically. Here we are referring respectively to the *Lectures on Continental Banking* given by Sraffa in 1929 (D2/5) and to the *Lectures on Industry* held in 1941, 1942 and 1943 (D2/8).

Both lectures concern the theme of the organization and control of production within the modern phase of capitalism. Thus, the *Lectures on Industry* stress the growing importance of the separation of ownership and control. The replacement of individual firms by joint companies in modern market economies raises the question of understanding who, between owners and managers, now have the power of control which was traditionally in the hands of entrepreneurs. Similarly, the *Lectures on Continental Banking* emphasize the emergence of banks specialized in financing industry. Here again, one of the major themes considered is the nature of the control the banking system exerts over firms. From this perspective, Sraffa developed both a theoretical and an empirical approach. On the one hand, he commented on the respective conceptions of the major economists interested in industrial organization at the time, from Robertson, who held that in modern companies, managers serve the interests of shareholders, to Arnold, Berle and Means or J.M. Clark, who argued, rather, that managers do in fact control the firm activities, using them sometimes to defend interests which are not those of the owners. Sraffa also developed similar reflections on the relations between entrepreneurs and bankers. In both cases, the tools and forms of control of business are meticulously described since they are not equivalent when the aim is to identify whose interests are favoured by firm decisions.

This discussion on asymmetric relations amongst agents was not the only object of Sraffa's attention. In this respect, Sraffa raised the problem of the validity of the usual conception of economic activity seen as a community of free and equal individuals contracting on markets. Did drastic changes—like the rise of modern joint companies, the growing tendency to monopoly or the increasing influence of the banking system on industry—contribute to making this conception obsolete? Having in mind competition observed in the real world, Sraffa was convinced that the answer was positive and advanced several reasons to support this answer.

He first stressed the fact that in the real world changes replaced symmetric relations between agents with asymmetric ones, implying hierarchy or inequality in contrast with the neo-Marshallian views. For instance, the concept of semi-monopoly demolished the myth of free competition according to which all the entrepreneurs had the same weight, were price-takers and adjusted (but did not decide) the levels of their quantities and prices. The influence of banks also appeared to be a major and differentiated constraint for firms. Finally, the emergence of joint companies created an inequality between owners and managers which depended on the legal forms of firms: 'majority control' companies are more beneficial to shareholders than 'minority control' ones (*Lectures on Industry*, D2/8/5/1–7).

Secondly, Sraffa noted the growing importance of vertical integration. Now, integrating is equivalent to preferring firm production to market exchange: 'The difference between production and exchange is … twofold: that the first implies lapse of time and the second does not; that the latter involves dealing with other industries and the first does not' (D3/12/52).

This does not mean, in Sraffa's view, that vertical integration implies the disappearance of market economies. It merely means that it is increasingly difficult to characterize modern market economies as economies in which individualistic exchanges are growing and spreading.

Thirdly, referring to Keynes, Sraffa also described the generalization of organized financial markets as a supplementary drastic change in the working of market economies. He noted that Keynes' *End of Laissez-Faire* made his author 'first among orthodox economists in this country to show how control was passing out of hands of individuals' (D2/8: 26).

On the one hand, the relation between a shareholder and the firm he owns partially is becoming looser and looser. The existence of financial speculation implies that 'in fact, the connection of the shareholder with the business is no more intimate or permanent than that which the holder of a ticket in the Derby Sweep has with the horses; and he certainly takes less interest in its activities' (D/8: 8).

On the other hand,

> another consequence of the system is that more and more intangible properties are capitalized and the sphere of capital extended.
>
> More things become capital: monopoly power, goodwill created by advertisement, skill of workpeople and their willingness to accept low wages, ability of salesmen, etc. are now valued as capital. All these things, which form the organization of a business and which used to be bound up with the person of the owner who could not think of selling them bits, have become objective, external objects and are readily saleable on Stock Exchange.
>
> This result is as far-reaching a revolution in the nature of property as has been the transition from feudalism to capitalism and in same direction. (lecture 5 (53) D2/8: 7)

This shows that the unity of the entrepreneurial entity is seriously threatened by the growing separation of its former activities. Traditionally, entrepreneurs were defined as the agents who took risks, who combined production factors on the market and who earned a specific income in payment for their 'business abilities' (D2/8: 39(8); Sraffa uses here an expression from Marshall).

Now, modern managers take financial risks more than industrial risks.

Sraffa is thus describing a process which replaces the world of entrepreneurial individualistic coordination with a world where the 'integrating force' of the social division of labour lies in a compromise between organizations and institutions (like banks, big firms or financial institutions).

Here again, therefore, Sraffa provided developments based on observation of the new realities of organization and the emergence of financial markets in the capitalism of his time. He stressed the emergence of new financial markets, new firms and new banks. This emergence implied a new form of distribution of the surplus based on new social rules, new institutions and a restructuration of social groups. This is certainly compatible with an interpretation of Sraffa's contribution in terms of a socially and historically embedded surplus. For various reasons, Sraffa went no further on this road and decided to limit analysis in *PCMC* to a less complex construction ('a prelude') but the latter was, however, incompatible with a GEE framework based on an axiomatic approach.

15.5 Concluding Remarks

We began our contribution by stating two objectives.

On the one hand, we set out to develop an interpretation of Sraffa's intellectual construction which differs from the traditional one and presents a more stimulating and promising research programme. On the other hand, we also questioned the ability of Sraffa's contribution to grasp the foundations of the working of the real economic system. Obviously, achievement of our first objective is of great help in achieving the second.

In conclusion, we may also, however, consider the present validity of Sraffa's contribution from the perspective of helping us to understand the contemporary working of our economic and productive systems.

Today various observed and empirical phenomena are emerging, increasing and may cast doubt on the validity of the concept of economic surplus; let us take some significant examples.

The first is the increasing scope for the production of services in our modern economic system, in relation to or in the place of traditional industrial commodities. This phenomenon does not as yet represent a challenge to the concept of economic surplus. Services are measurable in the sense which we recalled at the beginning of our paper. They can be considered as basic goods if they are used in the industry or as non-basic goods if they are supplied to consumers; they can also contribute to the definition of new goods and new industries if they are combined with more traditional commodities, as is the case with the new cellular phones, for instance. Obviously, today services form a catch-all category, but this is only a problem when we make commodities distinct and define them a priori *and not* when we define and measure the surplus a posteriori.

A second phenomenon is the growth of what is called human capital and is related to factors like the quality of human relations at work, the capabilities of managers, employees or workers, the atmosphere at the workplace, etc. But these characteristics of 'human capital' can be expressed in Sraffian terms as an increase in the heterogeneity of work and therefore taken into account when the surplus is measured.

A third phenomenon lies in the emergence and growth of self-employment and/or auto-entrepreneurship. It is actually familiar to economists who accept the concept of surplus, since Sraffa himself took it into account at the beginning of *PCMC*, considering the case of producers who do not employ persons but participate in the distribution of profits.

A fourth phenomenon lies in the increasing number and variety of social uses of commodities or services, especially in relation to digitalization. Pasinetti had already shown how this emergence of new goods and the disappearance of old ones can be modelled in the framework of structural economic dynamics that is compatible with the existence of an economic surplus.

These examples are not exhaustive. They do not cover all the new contemporary economic phenomena. Some others cases are probably more complex, as indeed is the growing internationalization of industries and supply chains. They are, however, promising since they show that the concept of economic surplus is still useful and relevant for an understanding of contemporary phenomena, encouraging economists to use it in their contributions.

Acknowledgements I am grateful to Jonathan Smith, archivist of the Wren Library (Trinity College, Cambridge), and to his staff for their competent and constant help.

Notes

1. We may refer here, for instance, to the convincing and stimulating book by Walsh and Gram on 'classical and neo-classical theories of general economic equilibrium' (Walsh and Gram 1980).
2. The Piero Sraffa Papers are kept at the Wren Library, Trinity College, Cambridge (catalogue and access to documents at https://janus.lib.cam.ac.uk/db/node.xsp?id=EAD%2FGBR%2F0016%2FSRAFFA. Quoted archive numbers refer to this catalogue).
3. For a characterization of this approach in relation to the history of economic thought, see Arena (1992a, 2017).
4. A first draft of this letter is present in the Sraffa Papers but the original letter is included amongst the Keynes Papers held in the Marshall Library in Cambridge. It was discovered by Roncaglia (1978, Chapter 1).

References

Arena, R. (1992a). La dynamique industrielle, tradition et renouveau. *Revue d'Economie Industrielle, 53,* 5–17.

Arena, R. (1992b). Libre concurrence et concurrence entravée: trois exemples historiques. *Cahiers d'Economie Politique, 20*(21), 77–91.

Arena, R. (1998). The Concept of National System of Production: From the Classical School to Marshall. In M. Bellet & C. L'Harmet (Eds.), *Industry and Space in History of Economic Thought*. London: Routledge.

Arena, R. (2010). Corporate Limited Liability and Cambridge Economics in the Interwar Period: Robertson, Keynes and Sraffa. *Cambridge Journal of Economics, 34*(5), 869–883.

Arena, R. (2013). Sraffa's and Wittgenstein's Reciprocal Influences: Forms of Life and Snapshots. In E. Levrero, A. Palumbo, & A. Stirati (Eds.), *Sraffa and the Reconstruction of Economic Theory, Vol. 3, Sraffa's Legacy: Interpretations and Historical Perspectives* (pp. 84–105). Basingstoke: Palgrave Macmillan.

Arena, R. (2014). On the Importance of Institutions and Forms of Organisation in Piero Sraffa's Economics: The Case of Business Cycles, Money, and Economic Policy. *European Journal of History of Economic Thought, 21*(5), 775–800.

Arena, R. (2015a). Order, Process and Morphology: Sraffa and Wittgenstein. *Cambridge Journal of Economics, 39*(4), 1087–1108.

Arena, R. (2015b). The Role of Technical and Social Factors in the Distinction Between Necessaries and Surplus: Classical Economics After Sraffa. *Cahiers d'Economie Politique/Papers in Political Economy, 2*(69), 185–202.

Arena, R. (2017). Histoire et dynamique industrielle: faits, idées et theories. *Revue d'économie industrielle, 160*(4), 11–22.

Arena, R., & Lawson, T. (2015). Introduction [Special Issue: *Contributions to the History of Ontological Thinking in Economics, with a Specific Focus on 'Process and Order'*]. *Cambridge Journal of Economics, 39*(4), 987–992.

Bidard, C. (1992). Équilibre général et synthèse post-classique. *L'Actualité Economique, 68*(4), 632–646.

Blankenburg, S., Arena, R., & Wilkinson, F. (2012). Piero Sraffa and 'the True Object of Economics': The Role of the Unpublished Manuscripts. *Cambridge Journal of Economics, 36*(6), 1267–1290.

Debreu, G. (1959). *Theory of Value: An Axiomatic Analysis of Economic Equilibrium*. New Haven and London: Yale University Press.

Garegnani, P. (1960). *Il capitale nelle teorie della distribuzione*. Milan: Giuffrè.

Garegnani, P. (1985). Deux voies pour la demande effective. *Cahiers d'Économie Politique, 10*(11), 21–31.

Hahn, F. (1975). Revival of Political Economy: The Wrong Issues and the Wrong Argument. *Economic Record, 51*(3), 360–364.

Marcuzzo, C. (2011). The 'Elusive Figure Who Hides in the Preface of Cambridge Books': An Appraisal of Richard Kahn's Contributions. In C. Gehrke, N. Salvadori, I. Steedman, & R. Sturn (Eds.), *Classical Economics Versus Modern Theories: Essays in Honour of Heinz D. Kurz* (Vol. 2, pp. 185–206). Abingdon: Routledge.

Marcuzzo, C., & Rosselli, A. (2011). Sraffa and His Arguments Against 'Marginism'. *Cambridge Journal of Economics, 35*(1), 219–231.

Naqvi, N. (2011). *Demystifying Sraffa's Theory of Value in the Light of Arrow and Debreu* (MAGKS—Joint Discussion Paper Series in Economics, no. 50-2011). Marburg: University of Marburg.

Nicholas, H. (2014). Whither Sraffa's Theory of Price? *World Review of Political Economy, 5*(3), 315–330.

Pasinetti, L. (2007). *Keynes and the Cambridge Keynesians: A Revolution in Economics to Be Accomplished.* Cambridge: Cambridge University Press.

Roncaglia, A. (1978). *Sraffa and the Theory of Prices.* New York: Wiley.

Rosselli, A. (2005). Sraffa and the Marshallian Tradition. *European Journal of the History of Economic Thought, 12*(3), 403–423.

Salvadori, N., & Signorino, R. (2007). Piero Sraffa: Economic Reality, the Economist and Economic Theory: A Suggested Interpretation. *Journal of Economic Methodology, 14*(2), 187–209.

Sraffa, P. (1925). Sulle relazioni fra costo e quantità prodotta. *Annali Di Economia, 2,* 277–328.

Sraffa, P. (1926). The Laws of Returns Under Competitive Conditions. *Economic Journal, 36,* 535–550.

Sraffa, P. (1960). *Production of Commodities by Means of Commodities: Prelude to a Critique of Economic Theory.* Cambridge: Cambridge University Press.

Sraffa, P. (1998). On the Relations Between Cost and Quantity Produced. English Translation by A. Roncaglia & J. Eatwell of P. Sraffa (1925), *Sulle relazioni fra costo e quantità prodotta.* Available at https://www.hetwebsite.net/het/texts/sraffa/sraffa25.pdf. Accessed 22 Jan 2020.

Walsh, V., & Gram, H. (1980). *Classical and Neo-classical Theories of General Equilibrium: Historical Origins and Mathematical Structure.* Oxford: Oxford University Press.

PART V

The Legacy of Keynes: Liquidity, Method and *Laissez-faire*

CHAPTER 16

Keynes, Schumpeter, Mercantilism and Liquidity Preference: Some Reflections on How We Do History of Economic Thought

Richard van den Berg

16.1 A Doubly Curious Passage

Hidden away in a footnote in Joseph Schumpeter's *History of Economic Analysis* (1954), there is a striking comment on a curious passage in a publication of the mid-eighteenth-century commercial author Malachy Postlethwayt (1707–67). In the passage in question, the payment of interest is considered as an enticement to compensate hoarders for the risk of giving up the command over their money savings to borrowers for some time:

> In Order to bring [locked up] Money back into Trade, those who are in great Want of it will offer a Profit to its Proprietors to part with it for a Time. That Profit will be proportioned to the Borrower's Want, the

R. van den Berg (✉)
Kingston University, Kingston, UK
e-mail: r.van-den-berg@kingston.ac.uk

M. C. Marcuzzo et al. (eds.), *New Perspectives on Political Economy and Its History*, Palgrave Studies in the History of Economic Thought,
https://doi.org/10.1007/978-3-030-42925-6_16

> Advantage the Money may be of to him, and the Risk run by him that lends it. (Postlethwayt 1757, p. 337)

Schumpeter commented:

> *Great Britain's True System*... (1757), ... contains a passage that interprets interest as a payment to hoarders by those who stand in need of it, i.e. as a payment necessary in order to overcome people's reluctance to part with cash. This reads like a clumsy version of Lord Keynes's own-rate theory of interest. (Schumpeter 1954, p. 372, n. 15)

This is of course a minor passage in Schumpeter's monumental *History*, but a contemporary reader who pauses to reflect on it may have mixed feelings. On the face of it at least, Schumpeter's comment is a small example of the kind of long-range comparisons of ideas that was common in the mid-twentieth century, but of which many historians of economic thought have grown weary in recent decades. In order to draw an analogy like the one he suggested between theoretical arguments formulated by authors living nearly two centuries apart, does one not have to ignore the thoroughly different circumstances in which they wrote? If so, should one not reject a historiography that favours long-term persistence of broad similarity in economic discourses at the expense of readings that do justice to the unique content of time-bound individual contributions? Alternatively, however, a contemporary reader may still marvel at Schumpeter's vast knowledge of the history of the economic literatures and his steadfast ability to 'place' even minor contributions of long-forgotten authors within a multi-layered, but single account of the history of economic analysis.

In the following pages, I argue that a historical assessment of a passage like Schumpeter's suggestive comment requires one to address at least two dimensions. First, the comment does, of course, raise questions about the original passage identified. Regardless of the merits of the particular reading Schumpeter gave to the passage, the mere fact that it was picked out by such an eminent scholar raises one's curiosity about this early contribution and invites one to 'go back' and have a closer look at it. As Annalisa Rosselli (2013, pp. 873–874) has cautioned, in particular when it comes to pre-classical monetary thought, the historical context needs to be given careful consideration. It will be shown that there are some surprising aspects about Postlethwayt's passage that Schumpeter failed to appreciate. The second kind of question, however, focuses more on Schumpeter's interpretation of the passage. Put differently, the focus shifts from the 1750s to the 1940s, when Schumpeter wrote his *History*. What later readers 'made of' a text is of course just as valid an object of historical study as the 'original purposes' of its author. Here the appropriate historical context of the passage becomes, not the thinking about public and private credit and interest at the time of the Seven Years' War, but the aftermath of the world recession of the 1930s and the intellectual responses to Keynes's *General Theory*.

A third dimension that a discussion of the history of 'a passage about a passage' would normally address consists of the various subsequent responses to it. In a sense, this would involve a further shift in focus from the 1940s to the present day: the current author (me in this case) would assess how other commentators have responded to Schumpeter's interpretation of Postlethwayt's curious passage and thus he would place his own reading in the context of the range of opinion up to his time of writing. In the little case study attempted here, this third dimension can be dealt with pretty quickly: I have been unable to find a single mention of Schumpeter's suggested reading of Postlethwayt's theory of interest anywhere in the literature since the 1950s. This silence is somewhat surprising given the fact that for several post-war decades intense discussions raged about the merits or otherwise of reading 'Mercantilist' authors of the seventeenth and eighteenth centuries through Keynesian spectacles.

Rather than attempting to provide an explanation for this lacuna, in the following I concentrate on the two other dimensions instead. Section 16.2 provides a sketch of Schumpeter's wider considerations that help understand his particular reading of the passage that he found in Postlethwayt's work of 1757. It argues that Schumpeter's assessment fits into one of the main themes of his *History*, which consisted of a grand sequence of time periods which he conceived as the alternate dominance of 'monetary' and of 'real' theories of interest. Section 16.3, on the other hand, concentrates on the mid-eighteenth-century origins and circumstances of the production of Postlethwayt's publication. Section 16.4 offers some thoughts about the divergent conclusions that can be drawn from the previous sections.

16.2 Mercantilist Monetary Theory After Keynes

That Schumpeter would associate Keynes's monetary views with those of 'Mercantilist' authors is not surprising in the light of the fact that, in the penultimate chapter of the *General Theory*, Keynes himself had gone out of his way to point out a number of parallels. Keynes, it will be remembered, had chosen to bookend his famous work by a pair of historical discussions. Chapter 2 was devoted to a critique of 'the postulates of the classical economics', by which he meant 'the followers of Ricardo, those, that is to say, who adopted and perfected, the theory of the Ricardian economics, including (for example) J.S. Mill, Marshall, Edgeworth and Prof. Pigou' (Keynes [1936] 1973, p. 3, n. 1). In his 'Notes on Mercantilism' in Chapter 23, in turn, he sought to highlight the views of earlier authors that had been rejected by the 'Classicals' and with which Keynes, almost by implication, felt an affinity.

It should be clear that in both chapters Keynes's purposes were in the first place polemical.[1] That is to say, he lined up those dominant theories of the more immediate past, with which he had come to disagree, against any older ones that he felt could now, in the light of his own new theories, be credited with renewed relevance. His surprising championing of much earlier monetary thought and practice that had long been derided as 'pre-scientific', served primarily to highlight the revolutionary nature of his own General Theory. As such, the pages 333–351 were not an attempt at detailed, contextualized historiography. This is quite clear from the fact that Keynes freely acknowledged that he simply copied most of the historical examples of views with which he sympathized from Eli Heckscher's *Mercantilism*, a detailed two-volume study that had just been published in English translation in 1935 (Keynes [1936] 1973, p. 341).[2]

In the decades that followed the publication of the *General Theory*, economists and historians responded in variety of ways to aspects of Keynes's impressionistic re-evaluation of 'Mercantilism'. Some picked up on the similarities Keynes had sketched between his ideas and those of early 'under-consumptionists', or early discussions of involuntary unemployment, or of the stimulating effects on domestic activity of a positive balance of trade. On these and other topics controversies existed that ranged from whether Keynes had identified the most relevant early authors, to whether the Keynesian perspective was at all similar to that of 'Mercantilist' authors.[3]

Undoubtedly, Schumpeter shared some of the criticism of the details of Keynes's Notes. In his *History*, he declared that Keynes 'is not only generous but overgenerous in his recognition of the "Mercantilist" contribution' since it conveyed 'a somewhat misleading picture' that obscured 'the amount of preanalytic wisdom and error that went into those works' (Schumpeter 1954, p. 283, n. 11).[4] This did not mean, however, that Schumpeter rejected the very premise that one could find in 'Mercantilist' authors' anticipations of various aspects of Keynes's theories. On the contrary, he followed the latter's lead by proffering further examples of early authors who could be read as having presented in 'rudimentary form' ideas found in the *General Theory*. For example, he highlighted the apparent emphasis on the importance of domestic investment that could be found in J.J. Becher's *Politischer Discurs* of 1668.[5]

More importantly, Schumpeter affirmed the momentous implications of Keynes's monetary views for the history of theories of interest. 'During the seventeenth century and far into the eighteenth', he declared, 'the large majority of economists looked upon interest – *as many of us do again now* – as a monetary phenomenon' (Schumpeter 1954, p. 329; emphasis added). Indeed, the long Chapter 6 of Part II of his *History*, covering the seventeenth and eighteenth centuries, was cast in the terms of a struggle for dominance between Real Analysis and Monetary Analysis '... that has acquired additional interest for the student of modern economics owing to the fact that *Monetary Analysis has once more conquered in our own time*' (Schumpeter 1954, p. 276; emphasis added).[6] Surely, here he was referring to the impact in the 1940s of Keynes's theory of money and interest. Not unlike Keynes himself, Schumpeter suggested that the former's ideas had turned the tide on 'a victory of Real Analysis that was so complete as to [have] put Monetary Analysis practically out of court for well over a century' (Schumpeter 1954, p. 282).

Where Schumpeter differed from Keynes's sketchy periodization was that he attempted to pinpoint precisely the early writers who had been primarily responsible for the 'victory of Real Analysis'. In the first place, he laid great emphasis on a passage in Nicolas Barbon's *Discourse of Trade* (1690) that defined interest as a payment for 'Wrought or Artificial Stock', that is 'real capital', rather than a payment for the use of money. Barbon's identification of interest with the return on capital investments was, Schumpeter asserted, 'the decisive step towards the "real" analysis of the nineteenth century, according to which money was just a "veil" that it was the business of analysis to lift' (Schumpeter 1954, p. 330).[7] Since, however, Barbon's tract had been 'forgotten very soon', Real Analysis had 'remained in abeyance' until the third quarter of the eighteenth century. It was during that period that, beside the writings of Massie and more importantly Hume, it had been especially Turgot who had brought real analysis to prominence. Turgot's contribution was 'not only by far the greatest performance in the field of interest theory the eighteenth century produced but it clearly foreshadowed much of the best thought of the last decades of the nineteenth century' (Schumpeter 1954, p. 332).

In Schumpeter's view, Turgot's historic performance had been twofold. First, 'Turgot, exploiting Cantillon's or Quesnay's conception of capital, tied the phenomenon of interest to a most elementary fact about production' (Schumpeter 1954, p. 333). That is to say, Turgot thought of the interest rate as being determined by the supply of savings (instead of the supply of money) and the demand for funds, as demand for productive advances. Borrowers were able to pay interest since 'capital yields interest because it bridges the temporal gap between the productive effort and the product'.[8] In other words, Turgot had established a close relation between the monetary rate of interest and the return on real capital, or profit.

Second Turgot had been responsible for the 'first serious analysis' of the process of capital formation that 'broke away from an anti-saving tradition established in his circle' (Schumpeter 1954, pp. 324, 325). That was to say, in his *Réflexions* Turgot had transformed a conception of capital, already found in 'Cantillon and the physiocrats', as a stock of produced *avances*, by emphasizing the act of saving as an essential step in the process of the accumulation of capital. Especially seminal had been Turgot's insistence on the point that typically savings were made with the express aim of investment, i.e. the increase in real capital goods productively employed, and that therefore one should consider that 'savings are converted into capital *sur-le-champ* [immediately]'.[9] This was what Schumpeter called the 'Turgot-Smith theory of saving and investment' and its influence on subsequent economists had been momentous:

> The theory was not only swallowed by the large majority of economists: it was swallowed hook, line and sinker. As if Law- and others- had never existed, one economist after another kept on repeating that only (voluntary) saving was capital creating. And one economist after another failed to look askance at the word 'immediately' … this came to mean that every decision to save coincides with a corresponding decision to invest so that

saving is transformed into (real) capital practically without a hitch .... The reader need not strain his imagination unduly in order to realize what a difference it would have made to doctrinal history if the possibility and, in depressive situations, likelihood of the occurrence of hitches had been pointed out from the first –of hitches that may paralyze the mechanism described by Turgot and cause saving to become a disturber of the economic process, hence possibly a destroyer instead of a creator of industrial apparatus. (Schumpeter 1954, pp. 325–326)

In this forceful assessment of the 'historic performance' of Turgot's role in preparing the way for the dominant classical 'real analysis' and the associated ideas about the near identity of savings and investment, Keynes's spirit, one may say, loomed large.[10] Without in this case naming Keynes by name, he mentioned 'modern attacks upon the theory' in the wake of the Keynesian revolution.

Thus, whilst Schumpeter's changed pivotal characters in Keynes's much more impressionistic history, he did not alter the main narrative as far as theories of interest were concerned. A similar thing can be said for commentators who in the decade or so after the publication of Schumpeter's *History* discussed the interest theories of the eighteenth and nineteenth centuries. For example, the monographs by Vickers (1959) or Tucker (1960), to take two of the most scholarly contributions of this type, presented casts of early authors that had not been presented by Keynes, but they clearly endorsed a broadly Keynesian perspective of the transition that had taken place as one from 'monetary' to 'real' theories of interest. By the time Mark Blaug published the first edition of his successful *Economic Theory in Retrospect* in 1962, Keynes's perspective on 'Mercantilism' was recognized as an unavoidable take on 'pre-adamite economics'. As far as monetary theory was concerned, Blaug's account (1962, pp. 22–24) was perhaps closest to the one presented by Schumpeter, arguing similarly that 'real theories of interest came to the fore with Cantillon, Hume and Turgot' (p. 23).[11] He had very little time, however, for comparisons between earlier explanations of the rates of interest with that of Keynes. Authors like 'Locke, Petty, and Law' had held that 'the rate of interest varies inversely with the quantity of money', but this view rested on 'common-sense ideas' and 'casual empiricism', and that was 'all there is to the Mercantilist theory of interest, and it is extraordinary indeed that Keynes saw merit in it or, for that matter, in any *purely* monetary theory of interest' (Blaug 1962, p. 23). Blaug dismissal of early theories of interest in this way was very generic and did of course not mention the supposed exception that Schumpeter had hinted at.

16.3 Back to the 'Postlethwayt' Passage

This reference by Schumpeter to the passage from Postlethwayt's *Great Britain's True System* is surely only a minor one. Not only did it, as I noted, apparently fail to elicit *any* subsequent commentary, Schumpeter himself refrained from elaborating upon his view that there was here a resemblance with Keynes's theory of interest. This is perhaps a little surprising, because judging by his wording, Schumpeter appears to have felt that he had found perhaps the most precise early anticipation of a crucial part of Keynes's monetary theory of interest.[12] This is suggested by the close correspondence of his characterization of Postlethwayt's theory of interest with his description of Keynes's own position. The former, Schumpeter stated, saw interest 'as a payment necessary in order to overcome people's reluctance to part with cash' (Schumpeter 1954, p. 372, n. 15). Compare this to Schumpeter's description of Keynes's position which had gone 'in the direction of the propositions that interest is nothing but *a payment for overcoming one's reluctance to part with* the one ideally liquid asset in existence (own-rate theory of interest) and that the quantity of money, considered relatively to the amount of it that is absorbed by transactions, is the sole directly governing factor in its determination' (Schumpeter 1954, p. 1179; emphasis added).[13]

It should be noted that although Schumpeter was first to point out this apparent strong similarity with Keynes, at least two authors before him had put some emphasis on the relevant passages in Postlethwayt's publication. In 1923, Arthur E. Monroe in his *Monetary Theory before Adam Smith* had noted Postlethwayt's 'curious theory' of interest. This theory of 'Composite Circulation', Monroe remarked, held that '[i]n order to bring hoarded money back into trade, people in great need will offer to pay for the use of it, and thus arises interest as part of the expenses of every undertaking' (Monroe [1923] 1966, p. 285). This conception, he added, 'appears to be quite unique' (ibid.). In a similar vein, some years later Jacob Viner (1937) in his widely read *Studies in the Theory of International Trade* stated that

> Postlethwayt, in a curious argument, claimed that lending of money at interest involved hoarding .... In order to bring the hoarded money back into trade, those in great need of it will offer interest ('profit') for its loan.

> The result will be that other moneyed men, instead of 'circulating their money' in trade, will 'lock it up', while awaiting the opportunity to lend it, preferring to get their income by usury instead of by trade. (Viner 1937, p. 47)

Since Monroe and Viner wrote before Keynes published his *General Theory*, they could of course not have made a connection with the views expressed in that work. But the fact that they had both flagged up Postlethwayt's theory linking hoarding and the payment of interest as being 'curious' may well have alerted Schumpeter to it some years later.[14] The association he then made with Keynes was not a big leap if one recalls the view expressed in the *General Theory* that 'the concept of hoarding may be regarded as a first approximation to the concept of liquidity-preference', in the sense that interest 'is the reward of not-hoarding' (Keynes [1936] 1973, p. 174).

The works of Monroe and Viner will have been of little further use to Schumpeter, however, in providing context to the writings of Postlethwayt. They followed a then common historiographical practice of offering erudite gleanings that in the space of a few pages mined many decades, or even centuries, of commercial writing, for what were considered thematically relevant passages. Moreover, other historical literature of the period that did discuss Postlethwayt's work at greater length, ignored what originality there may have been to the monetary thought in *Great Britain's True System*. It did little to alter Schumpeter's offhand opinion that generally speaking Postlethwayt's name was 'associated with substandard performance' (Schumpeter 1954, p. 372, n. 15).[15]

What none of the commentators on Postlethwayt's (1757) work realized was that large parts of it were taken directly from a contemporary French source. Even though since the later nineteenth century it was known that Postlethwayt had in several of his publications borrowed extensively and without acknowledgement from Cantillon's *Essay*, another of his acts of plagiarism, equally audacious, went unnoticed. It was his lifting of hundreds of pages from the work *Elemens du commerce*, published in 1754, by François Véron de Forbonnais (1722–1800). Amongst these pages was an English translation of most of Chapter 9 of the *Elemens* with the title 'De la Circulation de l'Argent'.[16] It was in this chapter that the 'curious' passage occurred that much later would be puzzled over by Monroe, Viner and Schumpeter.

It would probably have come as a surprise to Schumpeter had he known the French source of the 'curious passage'. During much of the nineteenth and twentieth centuries, Forbonnais tended to get a rough deal from historians who either ignored him or dismissed him as a late Mercantilist author who had simply failed to appreciate the novel truths contained in the economic doctrines of the physiocrats.[17] In keeping with this low reputation, Schumpeter wrote damningly that

> [Forbonnais] is the prototype of the 'useful' or 'sound' economist of whom the public approves. No historian will ever sing his praises; for the historian who is interested only in what policy a man is for or against will not be satisfied and will put down Forbonnais as an eclectic without originality; and the historian who looks for contributions to our analytical apparatus will also be dissatisfied, for he will not find it, and he will notice clumsy and pedestrian behavior whenever Forbonnais did venture upon theoretical ice. (Schumpeter 1954, p. 174)

It may be doubted whether Schumpeter knew the few French works that, with the revival of interest in monetary thought in the inter-war period, had started paying more than passing attention to Forbonnais, namely the studies by Paul Harsin (1928, pp. 249–259) and René Gonnard (1936, pp. 92–105).[18] Familiarity with these works might have prompted Schumpeter to have another look at Forbonnais's monetary ideas in *Elemens du commerce*. That this did not happen is ironic in the sense that Forbonnais's case fits very well into Schumpeter's grand view that the watershed moment in the shifting dominance of 'monetary' towards 'real' theories of interest had come with Turgot's treatment of saving and investment, profit and interest in the *Réflexions* (see above Sect. 16.2). Forbonnais, it must be understood, was perhaps the most prominent French monetary theorist of the 1750s and 1760s (for a more detailed assessment, see van den Berg 2019a). Turgot's views, if not formulated in direct response to those of Forbonnais, provided at least striking alternative explanations to those of his then more famous contemporary (on the latter's Europe wide fame, see Alimento 2014).

Forbonnais was an admirer of the British system of public credit, which allowed the state to borrow at lower cost than its rival France. Following Vincent de Gournay (1712–59), who also encouraged Turgot's early economic writings, Forbonnais saw low interest rates as the deciding factor for the profitability of all kinds of economic activity. In *Elemens du commerce*, he argued that

> ... there is no branch of commerce to which the reduction of interest does not give motion. Every soil is fit for some production or other: but if the sale of its products does not yield so much as the interest of the money employed in the cultivation, that cultivation will be neglected or abandoned .... The same reasoning should be applied to the establishment of manufactures, to navigation, fisheries, the settling of colonies. The lower the interest of the advances which these undertakings require is, the more they are deemed profitable. (Forbonnais 1754, ii.146–147 and 161–162; translation from Anonymous 1767, pp. 171 and 176)[19]

This view of the level of interest as the arbiter of the required profitability of economic activity was rather similar to Turgot's later depiction in the *Réflexions* of the money rate of interest as 'a kind of level below which all work, all cultivation, all industry, all trade seizes' (Turgot 1770, p. 593). However, when it came to the question what determined the money rate of interest Forbonnais offered a very different theory. To be sure, like Hume and Cantillon, and later Turgot, he held that in commercial countries the balance between the 'supply of' and 'demand for' savings (rather than 'money') ruled interest rates. However, he conceived of the factors that determined this 'supply' and 'demand' in a decidedly different manner from Hume, Cantillon or Turgot.

With regard to the demand for loans, Forbonnais emphasized the large role played by government borrowing. Especially the British government had since the late seventeenth century been successful at financing its many wars through a developing credit market. To avoid its high demand for loans driving up interest rates, the British government, and its agent the Bank of England, had developed a new kind of management of public credit (see Forbonnais 1753, pp. cxi–cxvii). Instead of relying on 'natural' forces to reduce interest rates, Forbonnais argued that an active management of credit as practised in Britain was required in France too.

With regard to the 'supply' of money capital, in *Elemens* Forbonnais developed the novel theory that money, besides functioning as means of payment in 'simple circulation', also functioned, due to the superior suitability of precious metals, as the store of value preferred by rich citizens. The payment of interest could be understood as an enticement to compensate hoarders for the risk of giving up the command over their savings for some time. It was in this context that the 'curious' passage, noted by Schumpeter in Postlethwayt's publication, appeared. In the original French, it read:

> Pour rapeller cet argent [resserrée] dans le commerce, ceux qui en auront un besoin pressant, offriront un profit à ses propriétaires pour s'en désaisir pendant quelque temps. Ce profit sera en raison du besoin de l'emprunteur, du bénéfice que peut lui procurer cet argent, du risqué couru par le prêteur. (Forbonnais 1754, ii.145–146)[20]

Forbonnais described the return of hoarded money to trade as a circuit that existed alongside 'simple' money circulation, namely that of 'compound circulation' (*circulation composée*). The preparedness of lenders to supply savings was related to the psychological factor of 'mistrust' (*défiance*). Whenever the nation's commerce and prosperity were threatened, the owners of money would be scared into hoarding more of it and a higher premium would have to be paid to tempt them to lend it (see Forbonnais 1754, ii.147–148, consequences 1, 2, 6, 8). At the same time, the abundant availability of money reserves amongst rich citizens constituted a great potential source of power over other states (see Forbonnais 1754, ii.176). Public borrowing allowed the state to maintain its military strength and to defend its commercial and colonial interests (see Forbonnais 1754, ii.170). This would again prevent interruptions to trade and guarantee a peaceful state of affairs conducive to coaxing rich people to voluntarily lend their money at lower rates. And such reductions would be reflected in lower rates of commercial loans, which would animate all kind of economic activity by allowing producers to operate at lower rates of profit.

Thus in Forbonnais's view, the fundamental rate of interest in the economy that acted as an arbiter for other rates of return was the price at which government borrowed: 'the Merchant's Profit in Commerce is regulated by the Value of his Money placed out at Interest in the public Stocks' (Forbonnais 1753, p. cv). If this was a 'monetary theory of interest', it must be said that it was of a sophisticated type. It appealed to political and psychological factors and was quite different from the simple idea that the rate of interest was inversely related to the amount of money in circulation, which according to a commentator like Blaug (see above) was 'all there was to the Mercantilist theory of interest'. It is another matter, however, whether this also means that there is at all any close affinity between Keynes's theory of liquidity preference and Forbonnais's views that rich citizens tend to withdraw sums of money from circulation, which then are only lent if a rate of interest is offered that they judge sufficient. This, I suggest, is like beauty, entirely in the eye of the beholder.[21]

What can be said is that Turgot did have very little use for Forbonnais's theory of interest with its interrupted circuit of money hoarding. Turgot conceived of the supply of savings not as a stock of 'money/silver placed in reserve' (*l'argent mis en réserve*) but as a much wider class of 'moveable wealth' (*richesses mobiliaires*):

> It is not ... the quantity of silver existing as metal which causes the rate of interest to rise or fall, or which brings more money into the market to be lent; it is simply the sum of capitals to be found in commerce, that is to say, the current sum of moveable values of every kind, accumulated, saved gradually out of the revenues and profits, to be employed by the owner to procure himself new profits and new revenues. It is these accumulated savings which are offered to the borrowers, and the more there are of them, the lower the interest of money will be, at least if the number of borrowers is not augmented in proportion. (Turgot 1770, p. 581; translation in Groenewegen 1977, p. 84)

Since Turgot insisted that savers either accumulated capital with the predominant motive of investment in their own enterprises or of lending it to other entrepreneurs who would invest it in theirs, he left very little space for a 'purely monetary' determination of interest rates. Turgot thus strongly played down the possibility of interrupted circuit, or 'hitch', as Schumpeter put it, that the notion of saving-as-hoarding suggested. And perhaps one of the reasons why Turgot insisted on this point was precisely that Forbonnais had proposed the opposite theory.[22]

16.4 Conclusion

Historians of economic thought are fond of quoting Keynes's well-known quip that 'practical men, who believe themselves to be quite exempt from any intellectual influences, are usually the slaves of some defunct economist' ([1936] 1973, p. 383). It is a view that offers solace to 'academic scribblers' as to their unacknowledged relevance. More specifically, it provides historians of economics with a validation for their attempts to 'trace back' policies, views and theories to their 'intellectual origins'. It needs to be borne in mind, however, that historians, like practical men, are not immune either to the spells cast by powerful thinkers. To put it unkindly, historians of economic thought who believe themselves quite exempt from any retrospective intellectual frameworks are usually the 'slaves' of some economist *of their own day*.

Schumpeter's account of the theories of interest of the eighteenth century is a case in point. Surely, Schumpeter was nobody's slave and on many points his assessment of Keynes was highly critical.[23] Nevertheless, this did not prevent him from acknowledging the significance of the success of the *General Theory*, to which he devoted the final chapter of his *History*, for his reading of earlier literatures. In particular, as we saw, Schumpeter recast the history of interest theories as the alternate dominance of Monetary Analysis (up to the mid-eighteenth century, and again in Keynes's day) and Real Analysis (from the late eighteenth century until the early twentieth century). This, of course, introduced a new retrospective reading of earlier economic literatures. However, it would be short-sighted to dismiss such a reading merely *because* we know it to be retrospective. Not only would this be short-sighted since, to a significant extent, one's views of the past are very often unavoidably mediated by present-day beliefs and insights. It also would prevent us from appreciating the context in which new retrospective viewpoints arise. In other words, all we need to do, it may be suggested, is to recognize that frameworks applied to the history of economic thought, just like the contributions that they frame, have their own historical context. They provide changing perspectives, often insightful but also 'of their time', by which old texts are interpreted.

This applies to the readings of specific old passages too. Thus, for instance, Schumpeter's observation that Postlethwayt's (i.e. Forbonnais's) theory of interest 'reads like a clumsy version of Lord Keynes's own-rate theory of interest' may be taken quite literally: to a perceptive student of early economic literatures writing in the wake of the Keynesian revolution, like Schumpeter, the 'curious' old passage *read like* an anticipation of the idea that owners of money savings require an interest payment to overcome their 'liquidity preference'. Put in that way, Schumpeter's claim was not that the historical context in which, and specific purposes for which, Forbonnais originally formulated his theory of interest were at all similar to those of Keynes. All the claim involves is that the latter's writings made a novel reading of the former's writings possible. Without telling us much about the time-bound historical circumstances in which a passage was *written*, such new *readings* become part of its reception history and should be studied by the historian of economic thought in that sense and for that reason.

Notes

1. In a similar sense, Adam Smith's fateful decision to depict the extensive and varied British economic literature that had preceded him as a single 'Mercantile system' served his polemical purposes of contrasting his own theories to anything that went before.
2. As Magnusson (2019, p. 296) points out, Keynes's cherry-picking approach in Chapter 23 contrasted with, for example, his *Essays in Biography* which were 'composed with an acute eye for the historical detail, trying hard to understand the historical context in which these figures acted and thought'. The fact that Keynes largely relied on Heckscher's work also explains why he paid relatively little attention to eighteenth-century authors: Heckscher had heavily concentrated on the literatures up to the seventeenth century and early decades of the eighteenth century.
3. The literature is too large to cite here. For short overviews of the controversies, see, for example, Hutchison (1978, pp. 127–135), or Magnusson (1994, pp. 45–49; 2019). Coleman (1969) or Blaug (1991) collected articles that in many cases commented on the Keynes's take on Mercantilism.
4. The last remark was probably a comment on Keynes's statement that he wished to highlight 'the element of scientific truth in Mercantilist doctrine' (Keynes [1936] 1973, p. 335). In fact, it seems fair to say that both men clearly believed that it was perfectly feasible to separate the 'scientific' or 'analytic' reasoning in older economic texts from the accompanying 'pre-scientific' or 'pre-analytic' content. Schumpeter merely suggested that Keynes should have been more discerning in doing this.
5. See Schumpeter (1954, pp. 283–284). Subsequently Hutchison (1978, p. 136), for example, picked up on this suggestion. In an earlier contribution, Hutchison (1953) had identified a 'low road' in British economic thinking that ran from Bishop Berkeley and Mandeville and via unorthodox nineteenth-century economists to Keynes.
6. This chapter was one of a few that Schumpeter never completed. For details, see Elizabeth Boody Schumpeter's 'Editor's Appendix' (1954, pp. 1190–1192).
7. Whilst greatly emphasizing the significance of Barbon's passage, he also pointed out that it could be judged a 'service or disservice' since considering money simply as a mere veil 'is precisely the center of the analytical difficulties created by Real Analysis' (Schumpeter 1954, p. 330). In the

final chapter of the *History*, he added that 'Keynes broke away ... from what I have termed the Barbon tradition and, in intent at least, established a monetary theory of interest, according to which interest is not derived from, or expressive of, anything that has, in whatever form, to do with the net return from capital goods' (Schumpeter 1954, p. 1178).

8. Schumpeter implied that by hinting at the time element as an explanation for the payment of interest, Turgot anticipated Böhm-Bawerk, an interpretation endorsed by Groenewegen ([1971] 2002, especially p. 312, n. 55), although subsequently qualified by Groenewegen ([1982] 2002, pp. 314–330).
9. See Schumpeter (1954, p. 324, n. 2) where the insistence shared by Turgot and Smith on the 'immediate' conversion of savings into investments is called 'an essential feature of both theories and indeed their most serious shortcoming'.
10. It is worth noting that Schumpeter did not emphasize an important role for interest in Turgot's theory of saving and investment as the equilibrating variable between the latter two. This was perhaps mostly due to the fact that he discussed Turgot's theory of saving and investment in a separate section (6) from his discussion of his theory of interest (section 7).
11. An indebtedness is suggested by Blaug's comment (1962, p. 34) that 'Schumpeter deals brilliantly with the struggle between monetary and real analysis in the eighteenth century: *History*, Part II, Chapter 6)'.
12. The footnote in which the comment occurs was left unfinished and thus it is possible that Schumpeter intended to get back to it.
13. Schumpeter was keen to emphasize Keynes's as a 'purely' monetary theory of interest. He acknowledged that in Chapter 13 of the *General Theory* Keynes seemed to say that the rate of interest depended 'on the interaction of the schedule of the marginal efficiency of capital with the psychological propensity to save' and that there the notion of liquidity preference appeared as 'not more than an amendment. Later on however [Schumpeter probably had primarily Keynes (1937) in mind, but], even in the *General Theory*' he, and more explicitly 'orthodox followers' like Lerner had tended towards a more purely 'monetary' theory. For this interpretation of Keynes's theory of interest, which has had a distinct following, see Chick (2019).
14. The wording of the passage quoted above had been identical in Viner's earlier journal publication (Viner 1930, p. 295), which would form the basis of the first two chapters of Viner (1937). Schumpeter (1954, p. 336) acknowledged his general 'indebtedness to this excellent piece of work'. It seems plausible that amongst this indebtedness was Viner's flagging up of the 'curious' passage in Postlethwayt's publication.
15. Schumpeter was familiar with E.A.J. Johnson's *Predecessors of Adam Smith* of 1937, which contained a detailed and sympathetic discussion

of Postlethwayt (Schumpeter 1954, p. 157). He also appears to have known the rather tendentious article by Fay (1934) (see Schumpeter 1954, p. 372, n. 15).

16. To be precise pages 332–362 of Postlethwayt (1757) are a straightforward translation of volume 2, pages 137–188 of the second edition of Forbonnais (1754). The full chapter runs from page 117 to 226. In van den Berg (2018), I discuss the precise extent of Postlethwayt's plagiarism from Forbonnais.
17. The tone for this was set by, amongst others, McCulloch (1824, p. 33), Blanqui (1842, ii.17) and Daire and de Molinari (1847, p. 169).
18. Schumpeter only mentions other works by these French historians that did not deal with monetary theory or international trade. Instead, the French historian of monetary thought he esteemed highly was Charles Rist, whose *History of Monetary and Credit Theory* (1940; the English translation from the French original of 1938) is referenced several times. This work, however, completely ignored Forbonnais. The only other contemporaneous work in English that actually contained a positive discussion of Forbonnais's ideas of international trade and money, and which was referenced by Schumpeter (1954, p. 336, n. 4) was Angell (1926, see pp. 216–219). Even if Schumpeter would have noted this discussion, which is not clear, it would have exposed him only to a discussion of some of the ideas found in the partial reprint of Forbonnais (1767) in Daire and de Molinari (1847) which was the only work Angell had relied on. Inter alia, the same was true for Monroe's discussions of various opinions of de Forbonnais. Had Monroe studied Forbonnais (1754) as well, he would surely have recognized Postlethwayt's plagiarism.
19. Postlethwayt's translation in this case was not very literal. Especially the first sentence altered Forbonnais advocacy of 'managed' reductions in the interest rate, translating it as: 'In Fact, there is not any of its Branches to which *the natural, not the forced Reduction of Interest does not give a new Life*' (Postlethwayt 1757, p. 346; emphasis in the original).
20. Note that Postlethwayt's translation (1757, p. 337; see above Sect. 16.1) of the French *profit* as 'profit' causes a slight confusion, since what is meant is 'interest' (as Viner realized; see above Sect. 16.3). Since the French term was used in a wider sense than what was customary amongst English commercial writers, perhaps the English term 'reward' would have expressed this wider sense better.
21. As far as I have been able to establish the case that Forbonnais anticipated Keynes's theory of liquidity preference has been made in any detail only once, see Morrisson and Goffin (1967, pp. 16–20).
22. In van den Berg (2019b), I discuss the differences between the theories of capital and interest of Forbonnais and Turgot in more detail.

23. Hagemann (2019) assesses the complicated attitude of Schumpeter towards Keynes. For a comparison between Schumpeter's and Keynes's monetary economics, see Bertocco (2006).

References

Alimento, A. (2014). Translation, Reception and Enlightened Reform: The Case of Forbonnais in Eighteenth-Century Political Economy. *History of European Ideas, 40*(8), 1011–1025.

Angell, J. W. (1926). *The Theory of International Prices: History, Criticism and Restatement.* Cambridge: Harvard University Press.

Anonymous. (1767). *The General Principles of Commerce. Part 1* [n.p.].

Bertocco, G. (2006). The Characteristics of a Monetary Economy: A Keynes-Schumpeter Approach. *Cambridge Journal of Economics, 31*(1), 101–122.

Blanqui, A. (1842). *Histoire de l'économie politique en Europe depuis les anciens jusqu'à nos jours.* Paris: Guillaumin.

Blaug, M. (1962). *Economic Theory in Retrospect.* Homewood, IL: Irwin.

Blaug, M. (Ed.). (1991). *Pioneers in Economics, Vol. 4: The Early Mercantilists.* Aldershot: Edward Elgar.

Chick, V. (2019). Liquidity Preference. In R. W. Dimand & H. Hagemann (Eds.), *The Elgar Companion to John Maynard Keynes* (pp. 249–254). Cheltenham, UK and Northampton, MA: Edward Elgar.

Coleman, D. C. (1969). *Revisions in Mercantilism.* London: Methuen.

Daire, E., & de Molinari, G. (1847). *Mélanges d'économie politique. Collection des principaux économistes* (Vols. 14–15). Paris: Guillaumin.

Fay, C. R. (1934). America, and the Doctrinal Defeat of the Mercantile System. *The Quarterly Journal of Economics, 48*(2), 304–316.

Forbonnais, F. Véron Duverger de. (1753). *Le Négotiant anglois, ou traduction libre du livre intitulé 'The British Merchant'.* Dresden: Estienne.

Forbonnais, F. Véron Duverger de. (1754). *Elemens du commerce* (2nd ed.). Paris: Leyde.

Forbonnais, F. Véron Duverger de. (1767). *Principes et Observations Œconomiques.* Amsterdam: M. M. Rey.

Gonnard, R. (1936). *Histoire des Doctrines Monétaires.* Paris: Sirey.

Groenewegen, P. D. ([1971] 2002). A Re-interpretation of Turgot's Theory of Capital and Interest. As reprinted in: *Eighteenth-Century Economics: Turgot, Beccaria and Smith and Their Contemporaries* (pp. 299–313). London and New York: Routledge.

Groenewegen, P. D. (1977). *The Economics of A.R.J. Turgot.* The Hague: Nijhoff.

Groenewegen, P. D. ([1982] 2002). Turgot: Forerunner of Neo-Classical Economics? As reprinted in: *Eighteenth-Century Economics: Turgot, Beccaria and Smith and Their Contemporaries* (pp. 314–330). London and New York: Routledge.

Hagemann, H. (2019). Joseph Alois Schumpeter. In R. W. Dimand & H. Hagemann (Eds.), *The Elgar Companion to John Maynard Keynes* (pp. 324–334). Cheltenham, UK and Northampton, MA: Edward Elgar.

Harsin, P. (1928). *Les doctrines monétaires et financières en France du XVIe au XVIIIe siècle*. Paris: Félix Alcan.

Heckscher, E. ([1935] 1955). *Mercantilism* (2nd Rev. English ed.). London: Allen and Unwin.

Hutchison, T. W. (1953). Berkeley's Querist and Its Place in the Economic Thought of the Eighteenth Century. *The British Journal for the Philosophy of Science, 4*(13), 52–77.

Hutchison, T. W. (1978). *On Revolutions and Progress in Economic Knowledge*. Cambridge: Cambridge University Press.

Johnson, E. A. J. (1937). *Predecessors of Adam Smith: The Growth of British Economic Thought*. New York: Prentice-Hall.

Keynes, J. M. ([1936] 1973). *The General Theory of Employment Interest and Money*. As reprinted in: D. E. Moggridge & E. Johnson (Eds.), *The Collected Writings of John Maynard Keynes* (Vol. 7). London: Macmillan for the Royal Economic Society.

Keynes, J. M. (1937). Alternative Theories of the Rate of Interest. *Economic Journal, 47*(186), 241–252.

Magnusson, L. (1994). *Mercantilism: The Shaping of an Economic Language*. London and New York: Routledge.

Magnusson, L. (2019). Mercantilism. In R. W. Dimand & H. Hagemann (Eds.), *The Elgar Companion to John Maynard Keynes* (pp. 296–301). Cheltenham, UK and Northampton, MA: Edward Elgar.

McCulloch, J. R. (1824). *A Discourse on the Rise, Progress, Peculiar Objects and Importance of Political Economy*. Edinburgh: Constable.

Monroe, A. E. ([1923] 1966). *Monetary Theory Before Adam Smith*. Reprint. New York: A. M. Kelley.

Morrisson, C., & Goffin, R. (1967). *Questions financières aux XVIIIe et XIXe siècles*. Paris: PUF.

Postlethwayt, M. (1757). *Great-Britain's True System*. London: Millar, Whiston, White, and Sandby.

Rist, C. (1940). *History of Monetary and Credit Theory from John Law to the Present Day*. London: Allen and Unwin.

Rosselli, A. (2013). Economic History and History of Economics: In Praise of an Old Relationship. *The European Journal of the History of Economic Thought, 20*(6), 865–881.

Schumpeter, J. A. (1954). *History of Economic Analysis.* London: Allen and Unwin.

Tucker, G. S. L. (1960). *Progress and Profits in British Economic Thought, 1650–1850.* Cambridge: Cambridge University Press.

Turgot, A. R. J. ([1770] 1914). *Réflexions sur la formation et la distribution des richesses.* In G. Schelle (Ed.), *Œuvres de Turgot et documents le concernant* (Vol. 2, pp. 533–601).

van den Berg, R. (2018, August 29–31). *Forbonnais in an English Guise.* Paper presented at the THETS Conference at Balliol College, Oxford.

van den Berg, R. (2019a). Circular Reasoning: Forbonnais and the Intricate History of Circular Flow Analysis in the 1750s. *European Journal of the History of Economic Thought, 26*(5), 1107–1152.

van den Berg, R. (2019b, June 20–23). *Turgot's Theory of Capital and Interest in Its Contemporary Context.* Paper presented at the HES Conference in New York.

Vickers, D. (1959). *Studies in the Theory of Money, 1690–1776.* Philadelphia and New York: Chilton.

Viner, J. (1930). English Theories of Foreign Trade Before Adam Smith. *Journal of Political Economy, 38*(3), 249–301.

Viner, J. (1937). *Studies in the Theory of International Trade.* New York and London: Harper.

CHAPTER 17

The Original Meaning of 'Liquidity Trap' in the Early Discussions Between Robertson and Keynes

Luca Fantacci and Eleonora Sanfilippo

17.1 Introduction

The concept of 'liquidity trap' has recently seen a revival in macroeconomics.[1] It was first resumed at the end of the 1990s as a theoretical tool to interpret the stagnation of the Japanese economy (Krugman 1998). After the outbreak of the global financial crisis, it was used as an analytical device to explain the persistence of low levels of economic activity and the failure of conventional monetary policy to boost the economy (Blanchard et al. 2010; Werning 2011; Korinek and Simsek 2014).

The definition of 'liquidity trap', however, is not univocal; indeed, there are differing views on the analytical conditions that characterize it

L. Fantacci (✉)
Bocconi University, Milan, Italy
e-mail: luca.fantacci@unibocconi.it

E. Sanfilippo
University of Cassino and Southern Lazio, Cassino, Italy
e-mail: e.sanfilippo@unicas.it

M. C. Marcuzzo et al. (eds.), *New Perspectives on Political Economy and Its History*, Palgrave Studies in the History of Economic Thought,
https://doi.org/10.1007/978-3-030-42925-6_17

(e.g. Krugman 2010; Barens 2011). In most textbooks and macroeconomic models, the liquidity trap is identified with the so-called zero lower bound on interest rates (e.g. Blanchard 2017). Other well-known contributions have, by contrast, stressed that monetary policy may prove ineffective even at positive levels of the interest rate (e.g. Hicks 1937, 1939; Fellner 1992). The impression is that, despite its wide use in macroeconomics textbooks and modelling, there is some ambiguity as to what the liquidity trap really is and the theoretical reasons for its occurrence.[2]

In the article that contributed to reviving the use of the concept, Krugman (1998, p. 137) identified the liquidity trap as a condition of ineffectiveness of monetary policy occurring when money and bonds become perfect substitutes, at a zero level of the nominal interest rate. This situation is known in literature as the 'zero lower bound', since it is assumed that the nominal interest rate cannot become negative.[3] This interpretation of the liquidity trap is also endorsed by Blanchard (2017, pp. 80–81), who directly refers to Keynes: 'The concept of a liquidity trap (i.e. a situation in which increasing the amount of money ["Liquidity"] does not have an effect on the interest rate [the liquidity is "trapped"]), was developed by Keynes in the 1930s, although the expression itself came later' (Blanchard 2017, p. 80, square brackets in the original text).

However, this definition does not correspond to Keynes's description of the case of ineffectiveness of monetary policy envisaged in Chapter 15 of the *General Theory*:

> There is the possibility that,... after the rate of interest has fallen to a certain level, liquidity-preference can become virtually absolute in the sense that almost everyone prefers cash to holding a debt which yields so low a rate of interest. In this event the monetary authority would have lost effective control over the rate of interest. (Keynes [1936] 1973, p. 207)

According to Keynes, as already noted by Barens (2011), ineffectiveness of monetary policy is not associated with perfect substitutability between money and bonds (at an interest rate equal to zero) but rather with the opposite condition, i.e. that money is ***absolutely*** preferred to any other asset (at a low level of the interest rate). In Keynes's perspective, as this chapter will clarify, the possible failure of monetary policy to influence the interest rate[4] is ascribed to the inherent characteristics of money as a store of value in a context of 'radical' uncertainty, which makes liquidity behave as a 'trap', rather than to the instance of an interest rate equal or very close to zero. As we shall see, in Keynes and Robertson's early discussions on this issue, liquidity is not 'trapped', as Blanchard's reading of Keynes's thought suggests, but liquidity is itself the trap.

In the *General Theory* (*GT*), nevertheless, the loss of control over the interest rate by the central bank is described as a very rare occurrence: 'whilst this limiting case might become practically important in the future, I know of no example of it hitherto' (Keynes [1936] 1973, p. 207). The only instance that he mentions concerns 'a financial crisis or crisis of liquidation' in the US in 1932, 'when scarcely anyone could be induced to part with holdings of money *on any reasonable terms*' (Keynes [1936] 1973, pp. 207–208, emphasis added).

In a lecture entitled 'The economic prospects 1932', Keynes had described the situation precisely in terms of a 'competitive struggle for liquidity' induced by uncertainty about the future value of assets, financed with liabilities fixed in monetary terms:

> We are now in the phase where the risk of carrying assets with borrowed money is so great that there is a competitive panic to get liquid. And each individual who succeeds in getting more liquid forces down the price of assets in the process of getting liquid, with the result that the margins of other individuals are impaired and their courage undermined. And so the process continues. (Keynes [1932] 1982, pp. 39–40)

The misalignment between Keynes's analysis of the phenomenon and the way contemporary macroeconomists understand the liquidity trap calls for closer investigation into the original meaning of the expression. Only two scholars have specifically devoted attention to the way the liquidity trap concept evolved in the history of economic thought: Boianovsky (2004), who focused mainly on Hicks's interpretation of the liquidity trap and the following developments in macroeconomics, and Barens (2011, 2018), who put it in relation with the 'banana parable' used by Keynes in his *Treatise on Money* to illustrate the paradox of thrift. None of these contributions analyse the correspondence between Keynes and Robertson subsequent to publication of the *GT* on the role of liquidity as a 'trap', which is the central part of our investigation.[5]

17.2 Robertson–Keynes Exchanges in 1936

The first reference we found in Robertson's writings to the word 'trap' in relation to liquidity is contained in 'Some Notes on Mr. Keynes' General

Theory of Employment', published in the *Quarterly Journal of Economics* (*QJE*) in November 1936. Robertson had sent a copy to Keynes,[6] who carefully read and commented on it, as testified by his handwritten annotations in the margins (Keynes Papers, KP hereafter, L/R/121–133).[7] Numerous studies have been dedicated to the correspondence between Keynes and Robertson (Presley 1992a; Mizen et al. 1997; Moggridge 2006; Sanfilippo 2005, 2008), as well as their intellectual and personal relationship (Samuelson 1963; Hicks 1964; Dennison 1968; Robinson 1975; Moggridge 1992; Skidelsky 1992; Fletcher 2000), not to speak of the liquidity preference vs. loanable funds controversy, which saw them sharply opposed on the question of interest rate determination (e.g. Hicks 1939; Presley 1992b; Fletcher 2000). Nevertheless, to the best of our knowledge, no study has hitherto focused on Keynes's manuscript comments on Robertson's 1936 article, and particularly those regarding the possible ineffectiveness of monetary policy. Analysis of this unpublished material is one of the contributions offered in this chapter, together with closer analysis of the correspondence that has been published but has received only scant reference in the literature, and in particular Keynes's letter containing his notes on Robertson's review, and Robertson's reply with his counternotes.[8]

When, on 28 August 1936, Robertson wrote to Keynes to inform him that he had spent 'a lot of time' on the *GT* that Summer and that he intended to publish 'in the *QJE* or elsewhere' some notes on the book without any further confrontation with him, Keynes (then Editor of the *Economic Journal*) replied:

> I agree that it is much better that you should print your criticisms without any further prior debate with me. But I would be grateful if you could let me have them for the E.J. The number of contributions sent me, which deal with different aspects of my book, is embarrassing me as editor and it is difficult to decide how many it is right and reasonable to print. But it would help the position a good deal if I could have a critique from you; at any rate it might do a little to protect me from the charge of making the E.J. a propagandist organ! (letter from JMK to DHR, 20 September 1936, Robertson Papers, C2/5/13–17)[9]

Robertson evidently did not accept Keynes's offer, since he eventually published his paper in the *QJE*. It is impossible to say if this decision was due merely to the fact that he had already sent the manuscript to the *QJE* or also to the need he felt to mark a distance from Keynes and the Keynesian creed. Having received Robertson's *QJE* article, Keynes replied to him both privately and publicly. As far as the public debate is concerned, Keynes published in the *QJE* the famous article (1937a), in which he provided not only a clarification of the notion of 'fundamental' uncertainty in the *GT*, but also a collective reply to the reviews that appeared in the November 1936 issue of the *QJE*, including the one by Robertson.[10] But Keynes also replied to Robertson in private, in a letter dated 13 December 1936,[11] where he refers to the annotations he had written in the margins of his paper, clarifying that he had summarized 'the substance' of them in the letter. Nevertheless, comparing Keynes's original manuscript comments on his copy of Robertson's article and what Keynes wrote in the above letter—as we may have expected, given the different nature of the two documents—we have found several significant differences, and this is why we consider Keynes's manuscript annotations worth investigating in their own right, as we shall see in the next section.

Indeed, the annotations in the margins represent Keynes's first and unfiltered reaction on reading Robertson's published comments—which Keynes had not seen before, as we have reconstructed above. These annotations were jotted down by Keynes for his own use, while we may presume that the letter sent to Robertson was a mediated text, which had been 'adjusted' by Keynes in relation to the intended reader (Robertson himself); a reader who was not simply a colleague, a long-life friend, a fundamental collaborator of Keynes in the 1920s and a staunch opponent in the 1930s, but also one of the most renowned Cambridge monetary economists at the time.[12]

Robertson, in turn, made his own manuscript 'counternotes' on specific points in Keynes's letter and sent them back to Keynes at the end of December, together with an accompanying letter, some general comments on Keynes's remarks and an additional note written '[a]fter reading Harrod's *Econometrica* article and discussing it with Pigou' (in Keynes 1973, p. 99).[13]

The two letters, together with their respective notes and counternotes, represent relevant sources of information for our study on the origin of the notion of 'liquidity trap'.

17.3 Robertson's Analysis of Liquidity as a Trap in the 1936 Article and the Ensuing Debate with Keynes

While the first two sections of Robertson's review are devoted to a discussion of effective demand and the multiplier, the third section focuses on Keynes's treatment of the interest rate. Robertson answers to the liquidity preference theory with his own loanable funds theory. We shall not enter into the arguments that Robertson uses to refute Keynes's theory of interest, since they belong to a much broader controversy that continued over several years and has been extensively discussed in the literature.[14] Suffice it to recall here that in Keynes's liquidity preference theory the interest rate 'serves to equate demand and supply of hoards' (Keynes 1973, p. 213), whereas Robertson explains the interest rate as the price equating the demand and supply of loanable funds (Robertson 1936, p. 183). It is only towards the end of Robertson's article, in §8, that Robertson discusses the potential threat that the liquidity preference represents for real investments. He also acknowledges that a monetary expansion may not be an effective countermeasure against this threat. This is where Robertson describes liquidity itself as a potential 'trap for savings'.

Robertson is concerned with the consequences of an act of saving that takes the form of a purchase of securities on the stock market. If there is a negatively inclined liquidity preference, and if the producers of consumption goods do not issue new securities to cover the losses following from the reduced sales, then an increase in savings will cause the prices of securities to rise, and hence the interest rate to decline; this, in turn, will induce part of the public to hold an increased quantity of money, and hence to sell part of their securities, partially counterbalancing the purchase of securities on the part of those who have increased their savings, and so will dampen the reduction of the interest rate caused by the enhanced savings.

If, on the contrary, the demand for money is not affected by changes in the interest rate (i.e. if the liquidity preference schedule is a vertical line), then the increase in savings will lead to a more substantial increase in the price of securities, and hence to a more substantial reduction in the interest rate, since the increased demand for securities will not be counterbalanced by an increased supply. Therefore, the existence of a negatively sloping liquidity preference will reduce the expansionary effects of an increase in savings on investments and income.

Here Robertson makes some concessions to Keynes's perspective admitting that the interest rate is at least partially a monetary phenomenon, depending on the demand for money for the purpose of holding it and not only of spending it on real investments. Hence, Robertson concludes that: 'Liquidity appears on the demand side of the market for savings as an equal partner (tho no more) with Productivity, and as a potential source of damage' (Robertson 1936, p. 189).

In other words, savings may take the form of investments (with a view to enhancing productivity) or of hoarding (liquidity); in the latter case, they will have a harmful effect in terms of lower income. Robertson insists that the options of hoarding and investing are 'equal partners', thereby suggesting, as he has claimed from the beginning of his *Notes*, that the demand for money does not depend only on 'the desire of holding more money in lieu of income-yielding assets' but also on the 'prospect of using more money profitably in business' (Robertson 1936, p. 176).

In the last part of the article, Robertson suggests that such a situation would call for an expansionary monetary policy, or in other words for a reduction of the bank rate to match the (now lower) 'natural rate' in order to ensure that money be 'neutral' (and that savings be equal to investments) (Robertson 1936, p. 189, fn. 7). Keynes reacts to this passage noting in the margin: 'Impossible to say until "neutral" is defined' (L/R/132). In his letter of reply to Robertson, Keynes makes his perplexity even more explicit, by adding: 'I believe it [neutral money] to be a nonsense notion' (Keynes 1973, p. 93). This passage is of crucial importance, because it bears evidence of a radical difference between the positions of Robertson and Keynes. Robertson remained of the idea, throughout his life, that 'the trouble about [Keynes's] theory is that while it tells us something about what determines the divergence between the actual and the normal rates, it tells us nothing whatever about what determines the normal rate and therefore, given the degree of divergence, the actual rate' (Robertson 1963a, p. 65; see also Robertson 1940a, p. 25 and a letter to R.F. Harrod [Harrod 2003, vol. 2, p. 589], quoted by Bridel 2019, p. 6).

This is the true theoretical ridge that marks the divergence and misunderstanding between the two Cambridge economists (and the strands of thought that they have inspired). Robertson believes that Keynes, with the liquidity preference, captured only a factor of temporary disturbance, failing to explain the structural determinants of the natural interest rate, namely 'thrift' and 'productivity', i.e. savings and investments. Keynes, instead, does not even believe in the existence of a natural interest rate and is not afraid 'to leave the rate of interest hanging in the air' (Keynes 1973, p. 212), and to make it depend entirely on the speculative demand for money in relation to the supply of money to accommodate it. Indeed, in the logic of the *GT*, there is nothing natural about the interest rate: on the contrary, it is 'highly conventional' (Keynes [1936] 1973, p. 203). Significantly, Robertson does not reply on this point in his counternotes: it remains his blind spot, which causes him to miss the essence of the liquidity preference theory as a full and consistent theory of the interest rate.

In fact, Robertson concedes that it is theoretically possible that, under certain circumstances, liquidity preference can create a difficulty for monetary policy to reduce the interest rate with a view to boosting the economy. However, Robertson immediately advances several counterarguments to downplay the role of liquidity preference in preventing the interest rate from falling (to the level required to restore what he calls equilibrium), particularly in the long run.

(1) Robertson's first objection to the relevance of monetary policy ineffectiveness revolves around the speculative demand for money as a decisive component of the liquidity preference in the determination of the interest rate: 'According to Mr. Keynes, the liquidity schedule proper is a phenomenon of "speculation," turning on the expectation of *reversals* in the downward movement of interest rates. It is not evident that it is right to attach much importance to it in connection with the long period problem now under discussion' (Robertson 1936, p. 189).

Robertson seems to suggest that, since the speculative demand for money depends on the expectation of future increases in the interest rate, it should be relevant only in the short run (where indeed fluctuations of the interest rate can be expected).

It is worth noting that this notion of the speculative demand for money advanced by Robertson is consistent with the notion implied by Keynes in *GT*, where he describes the speculative demand as dependent on 'the desire on the part of certain individuals to hold cash (because at that level they feel "bearish" of the future of bonds)' (Keynes [1936] 1973, p. 171).

It is all the more surprising, then, that on reading the passage quoted above, Keynes should suggest a significant correction in the description of the factor underlying the liquidity preference: in fact, he put brackets around the expression 'the expectation of *reversals* in the downward movement of interest rates' and proposed to substitute it with 'the uncertainty of the future'.

This correction seems to signal a significant shift in what Keynes himself regarded as the determinants of the liquidity preference (and hence, through the latter, of the interest rate): this is, indeed, the first instance in which Keynes lays emphasis on the fact that the demand for money may be determined not so much by the expectation of a change in the interest rate as, rather, by the fear of unexpected changes. In other words (adhering more closely to Keynes's *Theory of Probability*), what counts for the decision to retain cash is not merely the probability associated with future interest rates, but the 'weight of the arguments' upon which those probabilities are calculated.[15] Hence, the demand for money may be altered by a change not only in expectations but also in the degree of confidence with which expectations are held.

Given the dramatic implications of this new perspective, it is even more surprising that this comment is the only major note that Keynes did not include in the letter he sent to Robertson. It is hard to believe that Keynes deliberately decided to exclude this point because he thought that it was not relevant. It is perhaps safer to assume, instead, that Keynes believed the issue to be too important to leave to a short note at the bottom of a letter. In fact, it seems to capture a crucial aspect of the liquidity preference, to which Keynes eventually gave prominence in his 1937 article for the *QJE* where he intended to better clarify the aspects of his theory to which he attached most importance. It is here that Keynes—as is well known[16]—defines the interest rate as 'the measure of the degree of our disquietude', reflecting lack of confidence in the ability to produce reliable forecasts in the face of radical uncertainty (Keynes 1937a, p. 216).

(2) Robertson's second argument against the danger of hoarding revolves around the other component of the demand for money. In fact, Robertson argues that also the demand for money for transaction and precautionary purposes may respond to variations in the interest rate. Moreover, he suggests that those who hold money for these purposes will weigh the advantage of holding money (in terms of convenience and security) against the disadvantage of not earning the 'rate of return actually obtainable from investment'. Therefore, Robertson concludes that, in the long run, the interest rate will depend predominantly on Productivity rather than on Liquidity [preference]: 'Liquidity in the long run appears perhaps rather as a kind of ghost or poor relation of Productivity than as its equal partner, and as likely to furnish *a progressively less dangerous*

trap for savings as, with a successful process of saving, the normal rate of interest declines' (Robertson 1936, p. 190; emphasis added).

This observation reiterates Robertson's argument that, in the long run, the interest rate is mainly determined by real factors (the productivity of capital), rather than by monetary factors (liquidity preference).

Keynes objects, both in the pencil notes and in his letter of reply to Robertson, that the causal relationship is necessarily reversed, since productivity depends on investments, which in turn depend on the interest rate: 'But productivity depends on quantum of capital which depends on what liquidity preference has been. This sentence looks like a relapse into a confusion between the marginal efficiency of capital and the rate of interest' (Keynes 1973, p. 94).

Once again, Keynes's remarks seem to be guided by the intention, not to dispute the relevance of productivity in affecting the interest rate, but to show that it only enters the picture 'through the back door', i.e. under the conditions for the supply of loans that are determined by the liquidity preference.

To this Robertson replies in his counternotes insisting on the fact that, even when we consider the demand for money as determined by the 'convenience and security' of holding it (instead of spending it), it is only possible to translate such convenience into a quantity by referring to the return that the money would yield if it were invested:

> I do not think you have apprehended my point (2), which is that the translation of a schedule of psychic doses of convenience and security into a schedule of rates per cent will be influenced by the rate of return obtainable from investment, – people who, when capital is scarce, would regard the nth dose of convenience and security as worth (say) 8 per cent will, when capital is abundant, come to regard it as only worth (say) 5 per cent. I'm afraid this sentence shows our minds are still pretty far from meeting! (Keynes 1973, p. 94)

Robertson's argument builds on the implicit application of a concept of the marginal utility and opportunity cost of holding money, as opposed to investing it. Following this line of reasoning, however, Robertson fails to acknowledge that the 'convenience and security' of holding cash depend on the uncertainty of the future, and not on the level of the interest rate.

In fact, concluding his review Robertson accuses Keynes of having unduly complicated the whole matter: 'I could wish that Mr. Keynes had found it possible to say his say about it without, as I think, encumbering our judgments with an apparatus which accords to Liquidity a unique position in the theory of interest to which, even in the short run, it is not, I have attempted to argue, entitled' (Robertson 1936, p. 191).

To which Keynes replies epigrammatically, both in the manuscript notes and in the letter, in a final attempt to distil in one sentence the gist of his entire theory of the interest rate: 'What I say is that other factors work *through* liquidity' (KP L/R/132; emphasis in the original).

But Robertson, even on this occasion, remains faithful to his loanable funds theory, as the counternotes testify: 'And I say that liquidity preference proper, defined usefully like the Marshallian K and not so as to be a portmanteau of everything, works through affecting the supply of loanable funds!' (Keynes 1973, p. 94).

It is this line of reasoning that Robertson would continue to develop even in his subsequent writings, as we shall see in the next section.

17.4 The Development of the Concept of 'Liquidity Trap' in Robertson's Writings After 1936

After the intense theoretical confrontation with Keynes in the autumn of 1936, Robertson returned to the subject in two subsequent writings to discuss the risk that liquidity might behave as 'a trap'. The first occasion was his rejoinder to Keynes's article 'Alternative theories of the rate of interest', published in September 1937 in the *EJ*, where he discussed the theme again, although he did not use the wording 'liquidity trap'; the other is his essay on 'Mr. Keynes and the rate of interest', which opens his book *Essays in Monetary Theory*, where the expression first appeared (Robertson 1940b, p. 35).

In the rejoinder, Robertson clarifies some points which are relevant to our reconstruction. In his opinion, the liquidity function 'is ultimately a reflection of less ghostly forces', i.e. a less dangerous source of damage for the economic system as a whole, than argued by Keynes (a view that, with very similar wording, he had already expressed in Robertson 1936, p. 190). Notwithstanding this position, he is ready to admit that the variability of the liquidity function plays a significant role in causing short-term fluctuations; and also that—following Hawtrey (1937) and Hicks (1937)—'"liquidity" considerations might in certain conditions set a limit to the practicable fall in the long-term rate of interest' (Robertson 1937, pp. 433–434). What he considers inacceptable is Keynes's denial of the connection between idle money and the process of savings (Keynes 1937a, b). According to Robertson, in fact, even if it is true 'that a shift may occur in the liquidity function without any change occurring in the desire to save' (Robertson 1937, p. 434), it is also true that the role of the liquidity function as a '*chronic* obstacle to the growth of wealth' (emphasis in the original) can be justified not so much on the basis of its variability, but on the ground of its supposed (infinite) elasticity, which in Robertson's understanding of the matter makes liquidity 'a death-trap (from the social point of view) for acts of thrift' (Robertson 1937, p. 434). Robertson's claim (Robertson 1937, p. 435) is grounded on the line of thought advanced by Keynes himself in the 'banana parable' in the *Treatise on Money*, where the 'devil of excessive thriftiness' had been first underlined. This explains why it is particularly difficult for Robertson to follow Keynes in his 'new' theoretical position, accusing him of an 'astonishing change of front' on this point. It is paradoxical for Robertson to see that once he had made the effort (Robertson 1936, p. 188, fn. 6) to concede the validity of Keynes's reasoning on the potential risk of additional acts of thrift in the *Treatise on Money*, Keynes had changed his mind again, formulating in the *GT* a new theory of the interest rate in which savings have no role at all. The final conclusion of Robertson's discussion is a reaffirmation of the same view:

> Whether the sting of the liquidity function lies in its variability or elasticity, the degree of its malignity *will* find reflection in the behaviour of idle money. And our knowledge ... seems to support the view ... that the antics of the liquidity function (broadly interpreted) are a significant ingredient in the story of industrial fluctuation, but that its importance as a secular obstacle to the growth of wealth is unproven. (Robertson 1937, p. 435, emphasis in the original)

What Robertson means by 'our knowledge' is simply the traditional theory of the interest rate based on the more or less explicit view that, in the long run, where the forces of thrift are balanced with those of productivity, a 'natural' interest rate will necessarily tend to prevail.

The 1940 essay offers the most systematic account given by Robertson of past discussions with Keynes, and, to some extent, the conclusive one.[17] Returning to the question of what happens in the economic system if a person decides to divert an amount of his income from consumption to buying an equivalent amount of securities, Robertson defines as a 'siding or a trap' the circumstance that, when the interest rate starts to decrease, some people will be induced to sell securities and hold increased money balances, which will counteract the initial fall of the interest rate (Robertson 1940b, pp. 18–19). At the end of the essay, Robertson then comes to the other aspect of the liquidity trap, linked to the expansionary monetary policy in the long run, and it is exactly here that the famous expression appears: 'How far is the existence of the liquidity trap for thrift likely to hamper the banking system in its long run task of executing the chosen policy, and so bringing the fruits of thrift to birth?' (Robertson 1940b, p. 34).

Here Robertson is substantially repeating the same arguments as in his review of the *GT*, while at the same time he seems here to understand, better than in 1936, that the desire for liquidity due to the speculative motive (Keynes's liquidity preference) is affected by 'uncertainty in a broader sense' (Robertson 1940b, p. 35). On this specific point, nevertheless, Robertson does not change his optimistic position as far as the long run is concerned[18]:

> To an enormous extent the contemporary troubles of the world are due to the prolonged prevalence of a state of affairs that is neither peace nor war; real peace would do more than anything – more even than real war – not only to raise the curve of marginal productivity of investable funds, but to rotate and stiffen the roof of the liquidity trap into a straight line as vertical and rigid as Mr. Chamberlain's umbrella. (Robertson 1940b, p. 35)

Here Robertson appears to be following Keynes's argument, not only in accepting the idea that the liquidity preference may affect the interest rate, but also in ascribing the liquidity preference to uncertainty, particularly with regard to the incipient state of war (and indeed to a chronic blurring of the distinction between war and peace). But he also reiterates his belief that, ultimately, a steady state will prevail, in which the interest rate will no longer depend on the demand for money as a protection against uncertainty (and hence the liquidity preference curve will become vertical), but solely on the need to finance real investments.

17.5 Conclusions

In this chapter, we have provided a reconstruction of the original meaning of 'liquidity trap' through a detailed analysis of the early theoretical exchanges between Keynes and Robertson between 1936 and 1940, where the expression was coined. From our investigation, we may draw the following provisional conclusions.

The concept of a 'liquidity trap' is a discovery made by Robertson: meditating on the *GT*, he captures with the metaphor of the trap the possibility that money hoarding may represent an obstacle to a fall in the interest rate. Robertson's attention is caught by the possibility that the beneficial effects of saving, or of monetary expansion, can be offset by the accumulation of idle balances.

However, having admitted this possibility, Robertson tends to attribute minor importance to it. He remains ultimately convinced, on the basis of his own theory, that counterforces will be activated so as to overcome this block and restore the natural interest rate. He therefore tends to downplay the practical relevance of the liquidity trap as an explanation of persistent economic depression.

Keynes, on the contrary, even though he had barely touched upon the inefficacy of monetary policy in the *GT*, is stimulated by Robertson's remarks on the possibility that liquidity could play the role of a *chronic* obstacle to full employment and eventually appears to have recognized the relevance of this case, emphasizing the importance of the propensity to hoard in holding the interest rate at a level that is not compatible with full employment. In particular, it is only upon reading Robertson's review that Keynes becomes aware of the fact that not only is uncertainty about the future interest rate the necessary condition for the existence of the liquidity preference (as he had written in Keynes [1936] 1973, p. 168), but that the degree of uncertainty about the future, i.e. the lack of confidence in formulating expectations, is a major determinant of the level of the interest rate (as he would state explicitly only in Keynes 1937a, p. 216).

However, even when Keynes eventually acknowledged the importance of the point raised by Robertson for his theory of the interest rate as 'barometer of the degree of our distrust of our own calculations and conventions concerning the future' (Keynes 1937a, p. 216), he did not pick up the expression 'liquidity trap', which eventually entered and gained prominence in economic analysis with a rather different meaning.

In fact, the expression 'liquidity trap' would have remained buried in economic literature, leaving no trace in policy debate, if John Hicks had not picked it out in his review of Robertson's 1940 book and had not associated it with Keynes's idea of the existence of a floor to the interest rate (Hicks 1942, p. 56), visualizing it, in the framework of the IS–LM model, as the left horizontal segment of the LL curve (Hicks 1957, pp. 279 and 286), thereby influencing all the subsequent debate.[19]

However—as we have seen—the notion was employed by Robertson with a wider analytical meaning, and in a different context than the IS–LM model, to refer to the power of liquidity, considered as an alternative form of wealth, to divert savings from becoming investment. This may explain why Robertson himself, in his 1940 essay, did not make the association of his 'liquidity trap' with the left horizontal segment of the LL curve, despite his intense exchanges with Hicks and his general sympathy with the latter's approach. In Robertson's reasoning, this 'chronic obstacle to the growth of wealth' or 'this potential source of damage' does not have to do merely with the ineffectiveness of monetary expansion at low (or zero) levels of the interest rate, but in principle can occur at whatever level of the interest rate, and in any case at a level exceeding that which is necessary to reach full employment.

Unlike the prevailing use of the concept in contemporary literature, for Robertson 'liquidity trap' does not mean a trap *for liquidity*, which prevents monetary expansion from feeding through to interest rates, but the trap *of liquidity*, or in other words the trap for savings represented by the accumulation of idle balances. It is the demand for money as a store of wealth and as a hedge against uncertainty that prevents the transformation of savings into investments.

Having discovered this concept, however, Robertson hastily dismisses its possible relevance in explaining persistent economic slumps. In Robertson's view, the role that liquidity preference could in principle exercise in accounting for short-run fluctuations cannot be admitted as acting in a long run, where the forces of productivity will sooner or later regain their influence in determining the interest rate. Robertson was ready to follow Keynes, but only up to the point where this did not lead him to question his faith in the neoclassical traditional apparatus.

For Keynes, instead, the impossibility of reducing the interest rate further is not due to speculation, in the sense of expectation of reversal in the downturn trend of the interest rate and thus a condition that will sooner or later be overcome (as believed by Robertson), but is due rather to the 'radical' uncertainty of the future, against which liquidity can provide only illusory protection. This central message by Keynes, which gives uncertainty a definite analytical role in accounting for long-term stagnation, may prove particularly relevant, and perhaps more useful for an understanding of the conditions of most economies throughout the world today, than the more restricted notion of liquidity trap that has prevailed hitherto in economic analysis.

Notes

1. For an overview of the changing fortunes of the concept of liquidity trap in macroeconomic thought, see Boianovsky (2004, pp. 92–93).
2. Quite recently, even the possibility of the liquidity trap occurring has been questioned from a neoclassical perspective (Ahiakpor 2018).
3. Over the past few years, in fact, interest rates have dropped below zero: nominal yields on excess bank reserves, as well as on numerous government and corporate bonds, are negative. However, to the extent that investors have the alternative possibility of holding wealth in the form of cash, interest rates cannot fall below zero by more than the carrying costs of cash. This means that, if the lower bound is not zero, it is only slightly lower.
4. Following the assumption made by Keynes in the *General Theory*, we shall make abstraction from the existence of various rates of interest for debts of different maturities (Keynes [1936] 1973, p. 167, fn. 2). For a discussion of Keynes's analysis of the term structure of interest rates, see Fantacci et al. (2014).
5. Dow and Dow (1988) and Tily (2007) considered the correspondence between Robertson and Keynes in 1936 to clarify some theoretical aspects of their systems of thought but made only scant reference to the concept of liquidity trap, without discussing its first use and meaning.
6. The document is undated, but it was certainly sent between November (the date of publication of the article) and 13 December 1936 (the date of Keynes's reply).
7. Keynes Papers are kept at King's College, Modern Archives, Cambridge, UK (catalogue at https://janus.lib.cam.ac.uk/db/node.xsp?id=EAD/GBR/0272/PP/JMK; quoted archive numbers refer to this catalogue).
8. We believe that the correspondence greatly helps to contextualize and better understand the theoretical controversies among Cambridge economists, as Marcuzzo and Rosselli (2005) have excellently shown.
9. Robertson Papers are kept at the Wren Library, Trinity College, Cambridge, UK (catalogue at https://janus.lib.cam.ac.uk/db/node.xsp?id=

EAD%2FGBR%2F0016%2FROBERTSON; quoted archive numbers refer to this catalogue).

10. The debate between Keynes and Robertson on the liquidity preference theory continued for a couple of years in the pages of several journals (Keynes 1937b, c, 1938; Robertson 1937, 1938a, b).
11. KP GTE/2/4/78–86 (published in Keynes 1973, pp. 89–95).
12. Robertson was the author of the famous Cambridge Handbook on *Money* (Robertson [1922], rev. ed. 1928) and *Banking Policy and the Price Level* (Robertson 1926).
13. The letter, together with the additional note, is published in Keynes (1973, pp. 95–100). Robertson's counternotes to Keynes's letter are reproduced in the footnotes to the latter (Keynes 1973, pp. 89–95).
14. See Bibow (2000) and Bridel (2019) for two recent reappraisals of the debate from different viewpoints.
15. On this point, see Cristiano (2019).
16. See, e.g., Kregel (1976), Davidson (1978), Chick (1983).
17. Even though it was not the last time Robertson dealt with the matter (see, e.g., Robertson 1947).
18. See also Robertson (1940c, 1963b, c), where he refutes Keynes's stagnation thesis once again.
19. Even in relation to the notion of liquidity trap, one can argue what Bridel (2019, p. 4) has shown to be true more generally, namely that Robertson had a major influence on Hicks in establishing the neoclassical synthesis.

References

Ahiakpor, J. C. W. (2018). On the Impossibility of Keynes's Liquidity Trap: Classical Monetary Analysis Helps to Explain. *History of Economic Ideas, 26*(1), 31–58.

Barens, I. (2011). *'To Use the Words of Keynes…': Olivier J. Blanchard on Keynes and the 'Liquidity Trap'* (Darmstadt Discussion Papers in Economics, no. 208). Darmstadt: Department of Law and Economics, Darmstadt University of Technology.

Barens, I. (2018). *Robertson's 'Liquidity Trap' as an Answer to Keynes's 'Banana Parable', or: Did the* General Theory *Really Have to Be Written?* Paper presented at the ESHET Conference, Madrid, 7–9 June 2018.

Bibow, J. (2000). The Loanable Funds Fallacy in Retrospect. *History of Political Economy, 32*(4), 789–831.

Blanchard, O. (2017). *Macroeconomics* (7th ed.). London: Pearson.

Blanchard, O., Dell'Ariccia, G., & Mauro, P. (2010, February 12). *Rethinking Macroeconomic Policy* (IMF Staff Position Note, no. SPN/10/03). Washington, DC: International Monetary Fund.

Boianovsky, M. (2004). The IS–LM Model and the Liquidity Trap Concept: From Hicks to Krugman. *History of Political Economy, 36*(Annual Suppl.), 92–126.

Bridel, P. (2019). *The Twilight of 'Marshallian Macroeconomics': The Liquidity Preference vs. Loanable Funds Episode (1936–1956)*. Mimeo.

Chick, V. (1983). *Macroeconomics After Keynes: A Reconsideration of the General Theory*. Cambridge, MA: MIT Press.

Cristiano, C. (2019). Keynes's Theory of Rationality, the 'Weight of Arguments' and Keynes as an Investor in the Financial Markets. In A. Rosselli, N. Naldi, & E. Sanfilippo (Eds.), *Money Finance and Crises in Economic History: The Long-Term Impact of Economic Ideas* (pp. 117–128). London and New York: Routledge.

Davidson, P. (1978). *Money and the Real World* (2nd ed.). London and Basingstoke: Palgrave Macmillan.

Dennison, S. R. (1968). Robertson Dennis Holme. In D. L. Sills (Ed.), *International Encyclopaedia of the Social Sciences* (Vol. 13, pp. 529–533). New York: Macmillan and Free Press.

Dow, A., & Dow, S. (1988). Idle Balances and Keynesian Theory. *Scottish Journal of Political Economy, 35*(3), 193–207.

Fantacci, L., Marcuzzo, M. C., & Sanfilippo, E. (2014). A Note on the Notions of Risk-Premium and Liquidity-Premium in Hicks's and Keynes's Analyses of the Term Structure of Interest Rates. *European Journal of the History of Economic Thought, 21*(6), 1102–1108.

Fellner, W. (1992). The Robertsonian Evolution. In J. R. Presley (Ed.), *Essays on Robertsonian Economics* (pp. 127–147). London: Palgrave Macmillan.

Fletcher, G. A. (2000). *Understanding Dennis Robertson*. Cheltenham, UK and Northampton, MA: Edward Elgar.

Harrod, R. F. (2003). *The Collected Interwar Papers and Correspondence* (D. Besomi, Eds., 3 Vols.). Cheltenham, UK and Northampton, MA: Edward Elgar.

Hawtrey, R. G. (1937). *Capital and Employment*. London: Longmans, Green and Co.

Hicks, J. R. (1937). Mr. Keynes and the Classics: A Suggested Interpretation. *Econometrica, 5*(2), 147–159.

Hicks, J. R. (1939). *Value and Capital* (2nd ed.). Oxford: Clarendon Press.

Hicks, J. R. (1942). The Monetary Theory of D.H. Robertson. *Economica*, New Series, *9*(33), 53–57.

Hicks, J. R. (1957). A Rehabilitation of 'Classical' Economics? *Economic Journal, 67*(266), 278–289.

Hicks, J. R. (1964). Dennis Holme Robertson, 1890–1963. *Proceedings of the British Academy, 50*, 305–316.

Keynes, J. M. ([1932] 1982). The Economic Prospects 1932. Lecture to the International Economic Society of Hamburg, 8 January 1932. In D. E. Moggridge & E. Johnson (Eds.), *The Collected Writings of John Maynard Keynes*, vol. 21: *Activities 1931–1939: World Crisis and Policies in Britain and America* (pp. 39–48). London: Macmillan for the Royal Economic Society.

Keynes, J. M. ([1936] 1973). *The General Theory of Employment, Interest and Money*. As reprinted in: D. E. Moggridge & E. Johnson (Eds.), *The Collected Writings of John Maynard Keynes* (Vol. 7). London: Macmillan for the Royal Economic Society.

Keynes, J. M. (1937a). The General Theory of Employment. *The Quarterly Journal of Economics, 51*(2), 209–223.

Keynes, J. M. (1937b). Alternative Theories of the Rate of Interest. *Economic Journal, 47*(186), 241–252.

Keynes, J. M. (1937c). The Ex-Ante Theory of the Rate of Interest. *Economic Journal, 47*(188), 663–669.

Keynes, J. M. (1938). Mr. Keynes and 'Finance' Comment. *Economic Journal, 48*(190), 318–322.

Keynes, J. M. (1973). *The General Theory and After: Part II: Defence and Development*. In D. E. Moggridge & E. Johnson (Eds.), *The Collected Writings of John Maynard Keynes* (Vol. 14). London: Macmillan for the Royal Economic Society.

Korinek, A., & Simsek, A. (2014). *Liquidity Trap and Excessive Leverage* (IMF Working Paper, no. 14/129). Washington, DC: International Monetary Fund.

Kregel, J. A. (1976). Economic Methodology in the Face of Uncertainty: The Modelling Methods of Keynes and the Post-Keynesians. *Economic Journal, 86*(342), 209–225.

Krugman, P. (1998). It's Baaack: Japan's Slump and the Return of the Liquidity Trap. *Brookings Papers on Economic Activity, 1998*(2), 137–187.

Krugman, P. (2010, July 14). Nobody Understands the Liquidity Trap (Wonkish). *New York Times*. Online at https://krugman.blogs.nytimes.com/2010/07/14/nobody-understands-the-liquidity-trap-wonkish/. Accessed 23.01.2020.

Marcuzzo, M. C., & Rosselli, A. (Eds.). (2005). *Economist in Cambridge: A Study Through Their Correspondence, 1907–1946*. London and New York: Routledge.

Mizen, P., Moggridge, D., & Presley, J. (1997). The Papers of Dennis Robertson: The Discovery of Unexpected Riches. *History of Political Economy, 29*(4), 573–592.

Moggridge, D. E. (1992). *Maynard Keynes: An Economist Biography*. London and New York: Routledge.

Moggridge, D. E. (2006). Keynes and His Correspondence. In R. E. Backhouse & B. W. Bateman (Eds.), *The Cambridge Companion to Keynes* (pp. 136–159). Cambridge: Cambridge University Press.

Presley, J. R. (1992a). J.M. Keynes and D.H. Robertson: Three Phases of Collaboration. In J. R. Presley (Ed.), *Essays on Robertsonian Economics* (pp. 80–96). London and Basingstoke: Palgrave Macmillan.

Presley, J. R. (Ed.). (1992b). *Essays on Robertsonian Economics.* London and Basingstoke: Palgrave Macmillan.

Robertson, D. H. ([1922] 1928). *Money* (Rev. ed.). Cambridge: University Press.

Robertson, D. H. (1926). *Banking Policy and the Price Level.* London: P.S. King & Son.

Robertson, D. H. (1936). Some Notes on Mr. Keynes General Theory of Employment. *The Quarterly Journal of Economics, 51*(1), 168–191.

Robertson, D. H. (1937). A Rejoinder to Mr. Keynes's 'Alternative Theories of the Rate of Interest'. *Economic Journal, 47*(187), 428–436.

Robertson, D. H. (1938a). Mr. Keynes and 'Finance'. *Economic Journal, 48*(190), 314–318.

Robertson, D.H. (1938b). A Reply to Keynes's Comment on 'Mr. Keynes and "Finance"'. *Economic Journal, 48*(191), 555–556.

Robertson, D. H. (1940a). *Essays in Monetary Theory.* London: Staples Press.

Robertson, D. H. (1940b). Mr. Keynes and the Rate of Interest. In D. H. Robertson (Ed.), *Essays in Monetary Theory* (pp. 1–38). London: Staples Press.

Robertson, D. H. (1940c). The Snake and the Worm. In D. H. Robertson (Ed.), *Essays in Monetary Theory* (pp. 104–113). London: Staples Press.

Robertson, D. H. (1947). The Economic Outlook. *Economic Journal, 57*(228), 421–437.

Robertson, D. H. (1963a). *Lectures on Economic Principles* (3 Vols.). London: Collins, The Fontana Library.

Robertson, D. H. (1963b). Banking and the Monetary Equilibrium. In D. H. Robertson (Ed.), *Lectures on Economic Principles* (Vol. 3, pp. 362–374). London: Collins, The Fontana Library.

Robertson, D. H. (1963c). The Stagnation Thesis. In D. H. Robertson (Ed.), *Lectures on Economic Principles* (Vol. 3, pp. 375–392). London: Collins, The Fontana Library.

Robinson, E. A. G. (1975). A Personal View. In M. Keynes (Ed.), *Essays on John Maynard Keynes* (pp. 9–23). Cambridge: Cambridge University Press.

Samuelson, P. A. (1963). D.H. Robertson (1890–1963). *The Quarterly Journal of Economics, 77*(4), 517–536.

Sanfilippo, E. (2005). Keynes's Valuable Opponent and Collaborator: The Correspondence Between Keynes and Robertson. In M. C. Marcuzzo & A.

Rosselli (Eds.), *Economists in Cambridge: A Study Through Their Correspondence, 1907–1946* (pp. 58–91). London: Routledge.

Sanfilippo, E. (2008). The Collaboration Between Keynes and Robertson During the Second World War: A Perspective from the National Archives. In R. Leeson (Ed.), *Archival Insights into the Evolution of Economics: The Keynesian Tradition* (pp. 42–64), Basingstoke: Palgrave Macmillan.

Skidelsky, R. (1992). *John Maynard Keynes: The Economist as Saviour 1920–1937*. London: Macmillan.

Tily, G. (2007). *Keynes Betrayed: The General Theory, the Rate of Interest and 'Keynesian' Economics*. London: Palgrave Macmillan.

Werning, I. (2011). *Managing a Liquidity Trap: Monetary and Fiscal Policy* (NBER Working Paper, no. 17344). Cambridge, MA: National Bureau of Economic Research.

CHAPTER 18

An Outline of a Keynesian-Sraffian Macroeconomics

Jan Kregel and Alessandro Roncaglia

18.1 Introduction

This chapter explores some similarities in the approach employed by Keynes and Sraffa to challenge the dominant economic theory of their time. Both challenged an existing neoclassical explanation of price determination: Keynes the explanation of the price level via the quantity of money and Sraffa the Marshallian microeconomic theory of supply and demand. Keynes formulated a 'monetary theory of production'[1] that eventually led him to propose a liquidity preference theory of financial asset prices, while Sraffa produced a theory of prices based on the production of commodities by means of commodities as a prelude to a critique of economic theory.

J. Kregel
Levy Economics Institute of Bard College, Annandale-on-Hudson, NY, USA
e-mail: kregel@levy.org

A. Roncaglia (✉)
University of Rome La Sapienza, Rome, Italy
e-mail: alessandro.roncaglia@uniroma1.it

M. C. Marcuzzo et al. (eds.), *New Perspectives on Political Economy and Its History*, Palgrave Studies in the History of Economic Thought,
https://doi.org/10.1007/978-3-030-42925-6_18

Both approaches thus differ from traditional neoclassical approaches in that they consider the role of prices in establishing equilibrium in production rather than exchange. And in this sense both may be considered as a reversion to the concerns of the Classical economists. In addition, both give a central role to the rate of interest in determining equilibrium in the system, Keynes rejecting the idea of a natural or real rate of interest determined by conditions of production, instead arguing that it is endogenously determined by asset preferences subject to policy decisions of the central bank, while Sraffa rejects the productivity determination of the rate of profits, also hinting to monetary influences on income distribution through a monetary determination of the rate of interest.

These similarities suggest that rather than being diametrically opposed, a fruitful symbiosis of the two approaches would lead to a better understanding of the operation of the economy in which we live. This contribution will focus on the similarity in the analytical methods employed in both approaches. We may simplify by noting that this method consists in isolating for analysis a specific objective and identifying the most important specific elements relevant for the problem under consideration, leaving aside complicating factors that have little impact on the final result. This approach allows for compatibility between the analysis of different issues, whenever the underlying conceptual framework (the general vision of the working of the economy) is, or can be considered to be, unique.[2] The existence of a common method at the basis of the theoretical work of the two economists provides an additional element in favour of the joint consideration of the approach of the two authors.

It is important to note that a number of economists of diverse formation have engaged in identifying and amplifying these similarities as the basis for a more general approach to economic analysis. In particular, contributions to the history of economic thought such as Annalisa Rosselli's are most useful, indeed necessary, for the reconstruction and specification of the set of concepts that constitute a common methodological approach or 'vision', which Schumpeter considered a vitally important stage of theorizing in economics.

The chapter is structured as follows. In Sect. 18.2, we illustrate our methodological standpoint. It combines two elements. First, there is the need for conceptual consistency of how a 'monetary production economy' works, requiring much greater attention than that implicit in the simple list of assumptions usually prefixed to theoretical models. Second, the requirement for strict internal analytical consistency in theoretical contributions implies the need of well-specified separate theories dealing with different issues.

In Sect. 18.3, we sketch the main elements of the general vision, namely, the Classical 'circular-flow' approach, and we recall the 'photograph' interpretation of Sraffa's analysis of prices and their relationship with income distribution between wages and profits. Then the structure of Keynes's theory is discussed in Sect. 18.4. Our (provisional) conclusions are sketched in Sect. 18.5.

18.2 Method: The House and the Bricks

The two basic methodological requirements for a theory to be useful in interpreting reality are what Paolo Sylos Labini used to call the two 'R's: Rigour, namely internal logical consistency, and Relevance (or Realism), namely the reference to the actual conditions of the world in which we live, not to some imaginary mental construction which meets the theoretician's dreams for clear analytical results.

There is no need to dwell on internal logical consistency. Some additional considerations are instead necessary for the second 'R'. As Friedman (1953) intimated, barring a one-to-one replication of reality (which by the way, following the Sraffa-Wittgenstein debate recalled below, we consider to be impossible), no theory can be fully realistic: some simplification is unavoidable. We also agree with Friedman that the simpler a model is, the better, the ideal being a model that explains while focusing attention on very few elements.

Nonetheless, we must depart from Friedman's idea that the model should be accepted or rejected on the basis of its ability to forecast the future; ceteris paribus never rules in practice so it is impossible to differentiate changes in initial conditions from failures in the theory underlying the predictions. Friedman and his allies have always referred to the variations in actual economic events (what Marx, defending his own 'laws', christened 'counter-tendencies') to explain forecasting failures. If we have to rely on prediction failure to refute a theory, as in Lakatos's (1978) delineation of research programmes, the decision will depend on the subjective assessment of how large the failure must be (how much is enough?), so that we are led to Feyerabend's (1975) method of rhetorical debate (of which Adam Smith [1795], was a forerunner).[3]

In fact, Friedman's test more than anything else served a (misleading) rhetorical purpose in resolving first, in the early 1950s, a conundrum raised by what appeared to be non-rational behaviour contradicting the rationality assumption of the new von Neumann-Morgenstern-Savage microeconomics; then, in the early 1970s, a supposedly similar conundrum raised by stagflation to neo-Keynesian fine-tuning policy: inflation was to be confronted with restrictive demand policy while unemployment required expansion of demand.[4] The Phillips curve appeared to provide policy-makers with a menu of policy choices between inflation and unemployment, but it proved to be impossible to evaluate policy results based on the Phillips curve since the NAIRU, the unemployment rate which was presumed to be compatible with stable prices, was continually revised (upwards) and error attributed to the statistical identification of the slope and position of the curve. Eventually, the expectations augmented curve led to the specification of a vertical curve in which there was no longer any trade off and policy to reduce unemployment would only produce inflation.

In simplifying reality, theory can adopt two complementary strategies (or, perhaps, two faces of the same strategy): the Weberian method of ideal types (Weber [1920–21], in many ways equivalent to the Kaldorian method of stylized facts, cf. Kaldor [1957]), and preservation—if not directly, at least as potential compatibility—of the main characteristics of the real-world object of our enquiries. In economics, this means simplifications that do not contradict the fact that we refer to a world: (i) where the division of labour prevails, (ii) where there are many commodities (more precisely: various basic commodities, namely commodities directly or indirectly utilized in all processes of production) so that perfect substitution in production and consumption does not exist, (iii) in which continuous change leads to uncertainty over future outcomes, (iv) a market institutional set-up prevails open to private ownership of means of production, and (v) a variety of agents holds a variety of opinions. As we shall see, these are the five basic characteristics of the real world that are present in both the Keynesian and Sraffian viewpoints.

This approach to simplification implies that each theoretical issue under investigation may involve the choice of a different set of the most relevant simplifying assumptions. Each separate specification will then provide 'building blocks' or 'analytical bricks' that, when considered together, may provide a theoretical structure for analysing the functioning of the economy.

In this regard, a model of aggregate income (such as Harrod's dynamic theory) does not necessarily contradict this general 'vision', when it aims at results (the instability of the warranted growth path) and provides results that will carry, though in a more complex form, in a multi-sectoral economy. In contrast, the trade-off between real wage rate and unemployment in a one sector model does not produce results that apply to a multi-commodity world. Analogously, the Sraffian analysis of the relationship between prices and income distribution does not contradict the presence of uncertainty in the real world, because it refers to a 'photograph' of the economy at a point in time and does not try to explain those phenomena—such as the rate of interest, or investments—where uncertainty is directly relevant, nor how uncertainty may influence the evolution of these variables over time. So a theory such as Fama's (1970) on efficient financial markets cannot be considered of general application since its results depend on exclusion of (Keynesian-type) uncertainty. Division of labour in a capitalist society implies the presence of conflicts (and alliances) of interests, requiring abandonment of the abstract notion of the 'representative agent' (that, in modern macroeconomics, is analytically equivalent to the one-commodity assumption).

Construction of a general theory/model representing economic reality in all its aspects is impossible. The very outcome of the research programme of general economic equilibrium testifies to this: multiple equilibria and instability void the model of useful results and call into question the relevance of its conceptual foundations (equilibrium prices determined by demand and supply, convex preference and production sets, absence of uncertainty).

The idea of a full axiomatization of the economy (along the lines of the Bourbaki ideal of axiomatization in mathematics) relies on something similar to Wittgenstein's original ideas in the *Tractatus* ([1921] 1922): a system of propositions, simple and complex, representing the world—with the exception of the 'unspeakable': religious convictions, aesthetic judgements et similia. This idea was abandoned by Wittgenstein, in the wake of Sraffa's criticisms to it.

An alternative way is suggested by Wittgenstein himself in his posthumous book on *Philosophical Investigations* (1953) pointing to the possibility of constructing 'word games', where the same word may acquire different meanings in different contexts. Each 'word game' can usefully represent an aspect of reality; producing a unique theory of different 'word games' is nonsensical, since as just recalled the terms acquire somewhat different meanings within different games. In our view, while no general theory is possible, it is possible to add up different word games in a loosely identified commonly understood language: in our context, a 'view', or approach, unified by the reference to a common conceptual representation of reality.[5]

In other terms, we may conceive of individual components or 'analytical bricks' each dealing with a well-specified issue and thus relying on a set of specific assumptions, with such assumptions chosen in such a way as to be conceptually compatible with an underlying vision of the working of the economy, so that the different bricks can contribute to a theoretical building, though not adding up to a unique general analytical structure.

Keynes points in a similar direction in his *Treatise on Probability*, with his 'theory of groups'.[6] Confronted with the substantial differences in the confidence we may have in our evaluation of the situation when confronted with different kinds of decisions, Keynes proposes the application of the mathematics of probability (or, we may suggest by extension, theoretical reasoning) separately to issues of the same kind, namely to which a similar level of confidence may be applied.

More specifically, Keynes provides a logical specification of a 'group' as a set of propositions, a sub-set of which constitutes the 'premises' (independent of each other), while all other propositions are logically derivable from the premises. When applied to economics, this method implies specification of the premises on the basis of the requirements set out above. Thus, in a way, 'groups' may be considered as a forerunner of the proposed individual components or 'bricks'.

More generally, Keynes suggests such a versatile method when he says

> The division of the determinants of the economic system into the two groups of given factors and independent variables is, of course, quite arbitrary from any absolute standpoint. The division must be made entirely on the basis of experience, so as to correspond on the one hand to the factors in which the changes seem to be so slow or so little relevant as to have only a small and comparatively negligible short-term influence on our quaesitum; and on the other hand to those factors in which the changes are found in practice to exercise a dominant influence on our quaesitum. ([1936] 1973, p. 247; cf. 1973a, pp. 481–483)

This division will thus be different for every specific aspect of the system that is under investigation. Thus, economics is a science—the need for logical consistency is essential, and in the realm of the analysis of concepts the philological method of analysis of text and context also provides a scientific foundation for distinguishing what is scientifically acceptable from what is not—but it is also an art, requiring historical, social and human sensibility. (Again, we should add that in choosing the relevant theories the economist should look at their internal consistency and their compatibility with the main characteristics of the economic world in which we live—those indicated above.)

In other terms, we have a conceptual representation of the working of a monetary production economy—and a set analytical results, or bricks which provide its foundation. Two of such bricks are recalled below: Sraffa's analysis of the relationship between prices of production and income distribution, and Keynes's analysis of output and employment.

18.3 Sraffa's Photograph

The 'vision' of the monetary production economy, as we conceive it, has been built gradually over centuries. It relies on the Classical ('surplus', 'circular flow') approach, adding to it the Keynesian notion of uncertainty, the corresponding notion of liquidity and the corresponding interpretation of the way financial factors affect the economy.

Traditionally, the Classical approach is presented by contrasting it to the marginalist (or 'neoclassical') one. Sraffa (1960, p. 93) speaks of 'circular flow of production and consumption' in contrast to the 'one-way avenue' leading from scarce resources to the satisfaction of economic agents' needs and desires. Within the Classical approach, economics (or, as the Classical authors used to call it, political economy) studies the conditions of society's economic reproduction and development; the marginalist approach instead focuses on the conditions of optimal utilization of the scarce resource available. This difference in approach has multiple implications.

First, the 'circular flow' (or 'spiral', as Sylos Labini [1985] prefers to call it, since the point of arrival of the cycle is different from the point of departure) is intrinsically dynamic, representing processes that take place in time. Essentially, in an economy based on the division of labour, each productive unit at the end of the production period obtains a certain quantity of products, that is usually of greater value than the means of production employed, but consists in a different bundle of commodities; thus, it needs to enter into relations of exchange with other productive units for obtaining the means of production (and the means of subsistence for its workers) so as to start a new production process. Thus the market is a web of exchange (and distributive) relations connecting the different sectors and productive units (while within the marginalist approach it is conceived as a point in time and space to which offers and demands converge, as in Medieval fairs or in today's stock exchange). Exchange ratios must be such as to ensure that each sector obtains what is necessary to repeat the production process, plus a profit incentive to renew it.

This view of the problem of value—namely, the determination of exchange ratios and distributive variables—is thus different from the marginalist (one-way avenue) approach. In the latter, each agent has an original endowment of resources, and has the problem of allocating it among different uses in such a way as to maximise utility, keeping into account the preferences (utility maps) for the different uses. The imperative of equilibrium between supply and demand implies full utilization of the available resources.

Also, within the Classical approach the decision to produce a certain amount of product precedes the production process, and this in turn precedes the 'realization' problem, namely that of selling the product on the market; this implies that the theoretical variable 'natural prices' has nothing to do with equality between supply and demand.

The presence of differing groups with conflicting interests on the distribution of the surplus product (social classes and social strata) implies that the distributive variables are 'socially embedded' magnitudes, where economic and political processes interact. Within the marginalist approach instead the distributive variables are simply the demand and supply determined prices of the 'factors of production'; thus, by implication, the equilibrium prices of the distributive variables thus conceived automatically ensure equality between quantity demanded and supplied of such factors of production, namely full employment of labour, land and capital. Such a full employment implication is absent from the Classical notion of a distributive variable.

Sraffa's (1960) contribution focuses on the analysis of the relationship connecting prices to income distribution between wages and profits. Its conceptual context is the Classical one just recalled above. Sraffa's aim is to solve the Classical problem of value, by rigorously delimiting it.[7] Sraffa's solution involves abandoning the labour theory of value, so as to keep into account the influence of distributive variables over prices:

an influence already recognized by Classical authors such as Ricardo or Marx, but without providing a satisfactory solution.

Following the Classical tradition, Sraffa distinguishes prices of production—the theoretical variable that is the object of analysis—from market prices, not considered theoretical variables. Also, Sraffa explicitly assumes production levels as given, so that no assumption about returns is necessary. This point is quite important, as shown by the fact that Sraffa repeats it three times in the Preface to his book. This means that his analysis refers to a given moment in time: a 'photograph', not a theory of long-run prices connected to a theory of short run prices identified with market prices, as in the Marshallian tradition, nor a theory of 'long period positions' acting as 'centres of gravitation' for market prices, as Garegnani and others have interpreted it.[8] In this way, the issue of value as tackled by Sraffa is kept separate from other issues, such as accumulation, technical change and development of the economy over time. The analysis focuses solely on the relationship between prices (interpreted as theoretical variables, hence 'natural' or 'production' prices, to be kept distinct from 'market prices', not considered as a theoretical variable) and distributive variables for a given set of output levels and a given state of technology.

Let us summarize Sraffa's analysis. When commodities are at one and the same time products and means of production, the price of one commodity cannot be determined independently of the others, nor the set of relative prices independently of income distribution between profits and wages. We must consider income distribution and the determination of relative prices simultaneously. The solution is thus provided by a set of equations, each one describing what happens in one of the sectors of production in which the economy is subdivided. Quantities of means of production and of labour employed in each sector, multiplied by their respective prices and by the wage rate, plus a rate of profits which is uniform in all sectors of the economy multiplied by the value of means of production employed in the sector, is equal to the value of the product, namely the quantity of the products multiplied by their respective prices. Once one of the distributive variables is exogenously given, and once a unit of measure has been chosen, the set of equations—as many as there are sectors in the economy—determines relative prices and the second distributive variable.

As far as distributive variables are concerned, at each point in time (hence, given the levels of production and the technology in use) there is a given surplus (a multi-dimensional magnitude, represented by a vector of quantities indicating the surplus produce of the different commodities) to be distributed between the two social classes of capitalists and workers. Thus, one of the two variables is determined within Sraffa's system of equations, while the second one is determined as a consequence. This means that the distribution of the surplus between the two classes is not determined within the model: it is determined outside of it, in a historical-social-political context.[9]

Thus Sraffa's analysis, by focusing on given activity levels and a given technology in use, 'cuts out' all other issues different from the one under consideration. It is a perfect 'brick' to build our edifice: internally consistent, and conceptually compatible with the Classical approach (circular flow, market as a web of exchanges allowing reproduction of the economy, a uniform rate of profits corresponding to the Classical hypothesis of free competition meant as freedom of capitals to move from one sector to another), while open to a Keynesian solution for the determination of levels of output and employment and to the overarching influence of the financial sector over the real economy, income distribution included.

Sraffa himself points in the direction of the influence of finance on income distribution, referring to the influence of the interest rate on the profit rate: a not-well understood point in common with Keynes's approach which requires an interest rate to be set independently of the other rates of return on assets, and considers the action of the central bank in setting interest rates as an independent variable.

Other complications may also be quite easily introduced in the analysis. For instance, in the case of oligopolistic sectors, we might introduce multiplicative coefficients for the sectoral profit rates determined by the size of the barriers to competition. Equally, different qualifications can be easily recognized for labour. These are but other bricks, superimposed on the one that represents a founding pillar in our Classical-Keynesian approach.

18.4 Keynes's Restatement of the 'General' Theory of Employment

Though Keynes entitles his main work *The General Theory of Employment, Interest and Money*, it was certainly not intended to be a general theory in the sense that it encompasses all aspects of economic reality, as proposed in general equilibrium theory. In the Preface to the *General Theory*,

Keynes ([1936] 1973, p. xxii) defines his objective as 'primarily a study of the forces which determine changes in the scale of output and employment as a whole; .... We are thus led to a more general theory, which includes the Classical theory with which we are familiar, as a special case'.

As noted above, the choice of this particular problem to be analysed required the selection of variables to be classed as independent, given and dependent. 'Our present object is to discover what determines at any time the national income of a given economic system and (which is almost the same thing) the amount of its employment; which means in a study so complex as economics, in which we cannot hope to make completely accurate generalisations, the factors whose changes mainly determine our quaesitum'. And perhaps most importantly for the economist, 'Our final task might be to select those variables which can be deliberately controlled or managed by central authority in the kind of system in which we actually live' (Keynes [1936] 1973, p. 247; 1973a, p. 483). That is, to be able to formulate policy implications of the analysis.

In the case of the determination of the volume of employment and output he selected the following factors as having insufficient impact on the objective that they could be considered as given:

1. The existing skill and quantity of labour.
2. The existing quality and quantity of productive equipment.
3. The existing techniques of production.
4. The degree of competition.
5. The tastes and habits of consumers.
6. The disutility of different intensities of labour and activities of supervision and organization.

However, note that, while these factors are considered as given, this did not imply that they could be considered as constant or unchanging, but that the effect and consequences of changes in them were not sufficiently important to be taken into consideration. These given factors then 'influence our independent variables, but do not completely determine them' (Keynes [1936] 1973, pp. 245–246).

The independent variables that Keynes proposes are the three 'psychological' or behavioural relations: the propensity to consume, the marginal efficiency of capital and liquidity preference. In addition, Keynes considers behavioural factors which are determined by other actors in the economy and thus also independent: the wage unit and the quantity of money as determined by the central bank.

But, Keynes notes in the Preface quoted above ([1936] 1973, p. xxii) that 'A monetary economy, we shall find, is essentially one in which changing views about the future are capable of influencing the quantity of employment and not merely its direction'. Since the three 'psychological' variables are classified as 'independent', it is clear that they will be mostly influenced by individual expectations. Yet, what Keynes calls the 'state of expectations' is not present in the independent variables listed above. In this regard, Keynes employs a variation in the degree of 'independence' assigned to expectations.

He first notes that the impact of changing expectations might better be differentiated for decisions concerning investment, consumption and portfolio choice. In general, he considers the impact of expectations on the consumption function to be of minimal significance and thus best considered amongst the givens, while they are of much greater significance for production decisions, capital investment decisions and portfolio choice. For production decisions, Keynes notes following Marshall that short-period expectations will dominate, while for capital investment decisions long-term expectations will be crucial. Finally, as Richard Kahn (1972) and Joan Robinson (1952) were to subsequently explicate, for widows and orphans subject to income risk, long-term expectations would be more important while for money market traders, subject to price risk, short-term expectations would be more important.

> Having, however, made clear the part played by expectations in the economic nexus and the reaction of realised results on future expectations, it will then be safe for us in what follows often to discard express reference to expectations. It is important to make the logical point clear and to define the terminology precisely so that it will apply without ambiguity in all cases. (Keynes 1973b, p. 397)

The assumption thus meant keeping at the back of our minds that 'we shall not in any way be precluded from regarding the propensity itself as subject to change' (Keynes 1973a, p. 440) due to a change in general expectations when analysing the real world.

The relative importance of long- and short-period expectations is thus given varying weight in discussion of various elements of the independent variables in the *General Theory*. It is possible to provide a general summary of three classes of analysis of the influence of expectations on the independent variables of the *General Theory* via three informal models (cf. Kregel 1976). In comments written after the publication of the book Keynes alludes in 1937 to what may be called a model of static equilibrium in which the state of general expectations is given and constant, supported by individual short-period expectations that are confirmed. The theory of effective demand could thus be set out without reference to comparison of ex-ante or ex-post expectations nor the assumption of perfect certainty.

In a stationary equilibrium the state of general expectations remains constant, but the now admitted possibility of present disappointment would have no effect on long-period expectations. This is the model that Keynes implicitly assumes in the first 18 chapters of the *General Theory* where he notes that it is possible to 'disregard express reference' to the impact of expectations since they function as givens for the analysis of the principle of effective demand.

Finally, it is possible to discern a model of 'shifting equilibrium', where current disappointment affects the state of general expectations and thus the independent individual expectational functions are free to shift over time and will normally be disappointed. This is the model that corresponds to his reference to 'changing ideas' about the future becoming crucially important, noting that 'it is not the economy under observation which is moving in the one case and stationary in the other, but our expectations of the future environment which are shifting in one case and stationary in the other' (Keynes 1973b, p. 511). In the *General Theory* (Keynes [1936] 1973, p. 293) Keynes also refers to this 'line of division between the theory of stationary equilibrium and the theory of shifting equilibrium—meaning by the latter the theory of a system in which changing views about the future are capable of influencing the present situation'.

The extreme complexity of such a situation shows the advantage of the approach of specifying the objective of analysis by choice of independent and given variables.

Note that there is correspondence between Keynes's stationary model and the assumption of 'tranquil conditions' made by Joan Robinson (1952) in her analysis of growth and distribution. It seems obvious that the study of growth and capital accumulation, for example, requires productive capacity to become a dependent variable instead of being given:

liquidity preference may become a datum as well as the propensity to consume. Population must be assumed to be constant or growing in a specified manner. The independent variable is then the marginal efficiency of capital or 'animal spirits'. One can then analyse the system with a stationary equilibrium approach, by looking at the effect of two different given constant levels of expectations on the rate of change of the quantity of productive equipment. Likewise the direct analyses of distribution, technical progress, the determination of prices and mark-ups would require their own particular divisions of the determinants of the economic system.

18.5 Provisional Conclusions

In this chapter, we have illustrated a method of theory construction—'analytical bricks' connected in a common conceptual framework—indirectly suggested, though in different ways, by both Keynes and Sraffa. We have then shown that this method is employed by these two authors. These analyses can thus be interpreted as two foundational bricks for an evolving reconstruction of economics along Classical-Keynesian-Sraffian lines.

We might recall here a number of examples of bricks, quite different in nature, but conceptually compatible with a Keynes-Sraffa approach. First, Harrod's (1939) model defining the warranted rate of growth, interpreted as extending to dynamics the instability problem of non-convergence to a full employment equilibrium path, or indeed to any stable share of employment on population. Second, Minsky's (1975, 1982, 1986) analysis of financial fragility, as well as his notion of money manager capitalism. Third, Sylos Labini's (1956) analysis of oligopoly (interpreted as the general case of market forms, with free competition and monopoly as the limit boundaries characterized by a zero and an infinite barrier to entry). But the list may be quite long.

The field is wide, and we can only hope that young scholars will take on the task.

Acknowledgements Thanks for useful comments are due to Mario Tonveronachi and to an anonymous referee.

Notes

1. As Keynes himself labels it, in the title of his autumn 1932 lecture course: cf. Keynes (1973a, p. 420).
2. The interpretations of Keynes's and Sraffa's analyses and of their connections presented here find their genesis in Kregel (1973, 1976, 1980), Roncaglia (1975, 2009a, b), Tonveronachi (1983, 1992), Roncaglia and Tonveronachi (2014).
3. On the history and nature of the method of rhetorical debate, cf. Roncaglia (2005, pp. 8–12, 118–120).
4. On Friedman's method, cf. Roncaglia (2019, § 8.5). On the history of the debate on the strict rationality assumption, cf. Heukelom (2014).
5. On Wittgenstein's change of views, and on Sraffa's influence on it, cf. Roncaglia (2009b, pp. 25–28), summarizing an interpretation already set out in Roncaglia (1975), for which he is greatly indebted to discussions with Piero Sraffa.
6. Cf. Keynes ([1921] 1973, Chapter 11, in particular, p. 134). The point is illustrated in Roncaglia (2009a).
7. Here, we do not consider Sraffa's second objective: providing the foundations for an internal criticism to the traditional marginalist theory of value and distribution. Nor do we consider a long-debated issue concerning the relevance, and compatibility with Sraffa, of an absolute notion of value connected to labour and hence to Marx's exploitation.
8. On this point and more generally for this interpretation of Sraffa's analysis, as well as for references to the 'long period'/'centres of gravity' interpretations, see Roncaglia (2009b).
9. See, for instance, Sylos Labini's analysis of income distribution (e.g. in Sylos Labini 1984).

References

Fama, E. F. (1970). Efficient Capital Markets: A Review of Theory and Empirical Work. *The Journal of Finance, 25*(2), 383–417.

Feyerabend, P. (1975). *Against Method: Outline of an Anarchist Theory of Knowledge*. London: New Left Books.

Friedman, M. (1953). *Essays in Positive Economics*. Chicago: University of Chicago Press.

Harrod, R. (1939). An Essay in Dynamic Theory. *Economic Journal, 49*(193), 14–33.

Heukelom, F. (2014). *Behavioral Economics: A History*. Cambridge: Cambridge University Press.

Kahn, R. F. ([1954] 1972). Some Notes on Liquidity Preference. As reprinted in: *Essays on Employment and Growth* (pp. 72–96). Cambridge: Cambridge University Press.

Kaldor, N. (1957). A Model of Economic Growth. *Economic Journal, 67*(268), 591–624.

Keynes, J. M. ([1921] 1973). *Treatise on Probability*. As reprinted in: D. E. Moggridge & E. Johnson (Eds.), *The Collected Writings of John Maynard Keynes* (Vol. 8). London: Macmillan for the Royal Economic Society.

Keynes, J. M. ([1936] 1973). *The General Theory of Employment, Interest and Money*. As reprinted in: D. E. Moggridge & E. Johnson (Eds.), *The Collected Writings of John Maynard Keynes* (Vol. 7). London: Macmillan for the Royal Economic Society.

Keynes, J. M. (1973a). *The General Theory and After: Part 1. Preparation*. In D. E. Moggridge & E. Johnson (Eds.), *The Collected Writings of John Maynard Keynes* (Vol. 13). London: Macmillan for the Royal Economic Society.

Keynes, J. M. (1973b). *The General Theory and After: Part 2. Defence and Development*. In: D. E. Moggridge & E. Johnson (Eds.), *The Collected Writings of John Maynard Keynes* (Vol. 14). London: Macmillan for the Royal Economic Society.

Kregel, J. A. (1973). *The Reconstruction of Political Economy*. London: Macmillan.

Kregel, J. A. (1976). Economic Methodology in the Face of Uncertainty: The Modelling Methods of Keynes and the Post-Keynesians. *Economic Journal, 86*(342), 209–225.

Kregel, J. A. (1980). Markets and Institutions as Features of a Capitalistic Production System. *Journal of Post Keynesian Economics, 3*(1), 32–48.

Lakatos, I. (1978). *The Methodology of Scientific Research Programmes: Philosophical Papers*. Cambridge: Cambridge University Press.

Minsky, H. P. (1975). *John Maynard Keynes*. New York: Columbia University Press.

Minsky, H. P. (1982). *Can 'It' Happen Again? Essays on Instability and Finance*. Armonk, NY: Sharpe.

Minsky, H. P. (1986). *Stabilizing an Unstable Economy*. New Haven: Yale University Press; new ed., New York: McGraw Hill, 2008.

Robinson, J. (1952). The Rate of Interest. In *The Rate of Interest and Other Essays*. London: Macmillan.

Roncaglia, A. (1975). *Sraffa e la teoria dei prezzi*. Roma–Bari: Laterza. English transl. *Sraffa and the Theory of Prices*. Chichester: Wiley, 1977.

Roncaglia, A. (2005). *The Wealth of Ideas*. Cambridge: Cambridge University Press.

Roncaglia, A. (2009a). Keynes and Probability: An Assessment. *European Journal of the History of Economic Thought, 16*(3), 489–510.

Roncaglia, A. (2009b). *Piero Sraffa*. Basingstoke: Palgrave Macmillan.
Roncaglia, A. (2019). *L'età della disgregazione. Storia del pensiero economico contemporaneo*. Bari–Roma: Laterza. English transl. *The Age of Fragmentation*. Cambridge: Cambridge University Press.
Roncaglia, A., & Tonveronachi, M. (2014). Post-Keynesian, Post-Sraffian Economics: An Outline. In D. Papadimitriou (Ed.), *Contributions to Economic Theory, Policy, Development and Finance: Essays in Honor of Jan A. Kregel* (pp. 40–64). Basingstoke: Palgrave Macmillan.
Smith, A. ([1795] 1980). *Essays on Philosophical Subjects*. In W. P. D. Wightman & J. C. Bryce (Eds.), *The Glasgow Edition of The Works and Correspondence of Adam Smith* (Vol. 3). Oxford: Oxford University Press.
Sraffa, P. (1960). *Production of Commodities by Means of Commodities*. Cambridge: Cambridge University Press.
Sylos Labini, P. (1956). *Oligopolio e progresso tecnico*. Milano: Giuffrè. English transl. *Oligopoly and Technical Progress*. Cambridge, MA: Harvard University Press, 1962.
Sylos Labini, P. (1984). *The Forces of Economic Growth and Decline*. Cambridge, MA: MIT Press.
Sylos Labini, P. (1985). La spirale e l'arco. *Economia Politica, 2*(1), 3–11.
Tonveronachi, M. (1983). *J.M. Keynes. Dall'instabilità ciclica all'equilibrio di sottoccupazione*. Roma: NIS.
Tonveronachi, M. (1992). Keynes and Equilibrium: A Note. In M. Sebastiani (Ed.), *The Notion of Equilibrium in the Keynesian Theory* (pp. 18–31). London: Palgrave Macmillan.
Weber, M. (1920–21). *Gesammelte Aufsätze zur Religionssoziologie*. Tübingen: Mohr.
Wittgenstein, L. ([1921] 1922). Logisch-philosophische Abhandlung. *Annalen der Naturphilosophie, 14*, 185–262. Revised English edn., *Tractatus Logico-Philosophicus*. London: Kegan Paul.
Wittgenstein, L. (1953). *Philosophical Investigations*. Oxford: Basil Blackwell.

CHAPTER 19

The State and the Market in John Maynard Keynes and His Relevance Today

Mario Sebastiani

Whether market is hero, or villain, or tragic hero, remains to be seen.
John Hicks (1969, p. 25)

19.1 Background

The central issue that, paraphrasing the great question about Macbeth, Hicks (1969, p. 25) raises over the nature of the market runs through the entire history of economics and beyond. Since no one has ever really seen the market as a hero without any blemish, the questions all economists (?) have sought to address, rather, are: Who should take on the task of 'accompanying' (or redeeming) it—supposing it might be worthwhile—and, in the affirmative case, how?

Basically, the issue lies in the relationship between private and social calculation, and in the comparative failures of the market and the State to bring about a satisfactory synthesis. This being an area subject not so

M. Sebastiani (✉)
University of Rome Tor Vergata, Rome, Italy
e-mail: sebastiani@economia.uniroma2.it

M. C. Marcuzzo et al. (eds.), *New Perspectives on Political Economy and Its History*, Palgrave Studies in the History of Economic Thought,
https://doi.org/10.1007/978-3-030-42925-6_19

much to technical toolkits as to political views, the borderlines between State and market have wavered, due both to the 'accidents' of history, changes in ideologies and forms of government, and as a result of physiological political cycles.

However, the oscillations of the pendulum have not always been synchronized with the alternation of predominant economic theories. Indeed, public ownership, particularly of enterprises supplying utilities (electricity, gas, railways and, later on telephone networks, etc.), has been the main area for economic regulation in Europe as from the nineteenth century. After all, Bismarck, Mussolini, Franco and De Gaulle, for example, were amongst the keenest nationalizers, although hardly figures that might be associated with left-wing ideologies.

Leaping over a considerable stretch of history of economic theory and policy, and coming straight to Keynes, his best-known and most revolutionary work, focused on the macroeconomics of employment and money, was the end result of a radical critique of the doctrine of *laissez-faire* as a whole—a critique encompassing all the shortcomings of the free, unregulated market and levels of public action, which Keynes continued to develop throughout his entire production. It was a long progression he embarked upon as early as the beginning of the 1920s, contesting the parallelism between economic *laissez-faire* and Darwinism, according to which 'free competition had built man' (Keynes [1926] 1972, p. 276), as well as the assumptions on which it was based.

Keynes's attack went far deeper than criticism of the mere assumptions underlying *laissez-faire*, to address the very nature of human relations and the market:

> Let us clear from the ground the metaphysical or general principles upon which, from time to time, *laissez-faire* has been founded. It is not true that individuals possess a prescriptive 'natural liberty' in their economic activities. There is no 'compact' conferring perpetual rights on those who Have or on those who Acquire. The world is not so governed from above that private and social interest always coincide. It is not so managed here below that in practice they coincide. It is not a correct deduction from the principles of economics that enlightened self-interest always operates in the public interest. Nor is it true that self-interest generally is enlightened; more often individuals acting separately to promote their own ends are too ignorant or too weak to attain even these. Experience does not show that individuals, when they make up a social unit, are always less clear-sighted than when they act separately. (ibid., pp. 287–288)

The clash between individual and social calculation is not a passing illness, negligible as a transitory deviation from a steady state of good health, but a structural condition affecting every aspect of economic and social life, economic life being viewed as a sort of 'parody of an accountant's nightmare', and calculation of social expediency performed solely on a, even self-defeating, basis of financial profitability.[1] Individual rational calculations are in fact basically affected by fallacy of composition and uncertainty, which forces decisions to be led by conventions, a sort of 'beauty contest' where people devote their intelligence to anticipate what the average opinion expects the average opinion to be ('and there are some who practice the fourth, fifth and higher degree', Keynes [1936] 1973, p. 156). For these reasons, basically, there are no natural tendencies towards stable equilibria, and even less to full employment, just as there are no natural tendencies towards a just society. Fallacy also affects *laissez-faire* policies, as is proved by the 'Treasury Opinion' neglecting the paradox of saving. Hence the need for active public policies able to look through, internalize and govern the effects of non-coordinated individual choices.

All of Hicks's questions about the market ('hero, or villain, or tragic hero') are shared by Keynes, probably with a preference for a 'villain' to be redeemed through public action, or, perhaps better, a demon requiring the constant attendance of the exorcist.

Thus Keynes's broad design was to identify a 'third way', being well aware that (to paraphrase an aphorism attributed to Winston Churchill) 'capitalism is the worst form of economic and social organization, except for all the others'. Hence liberal socialism remains the only practicable means of avoiding the destruction of existing economic forms in their entirety and as the condition of the successful functioning of individual initiative (Keynes [1936] 1973, p. 380).

Keynes's recipes for a 'wisely managed' capitalism (a liberal socialism) relies on the principle of horizontal subsidiarity, according to which the chief task of economists should be to distinguish the *agenda* of government from the *non-agenda*, and the companion task of politics to devise forms of government capable of accomplishing the agenda—where the most important portion of States' agenda is to be related not to things which individuals are already doing or doing them a little better or a little worse, but to do those that at present are not being done at all (ibid., pp. 288, 291).

Keynes also anticipated reforms on vertical subsidiarity by proposing to decentralize the governments' tasks to autonomous bodies, like the independent authorities today established in modern States:

> I believe that in many cases the ideal size for the unit of control and organisation lies somewhere between the individual and the modern State. I suggest, therefore, that progress lies in the growth and the recognition of semi-autonomous bodies within the State – bodies whose criterion of action within their own field is solely the public good as they understand it, and from whose deliberations motives of private advantage are excluded, though some place it may still be necessary to leave, until the ambit of men's altruism grows wider, to the separate advantage of particular groups, classes, or faculties – bodies which in the ordinary course of affairs are mainly autonomous within their prescribed limitations, but are subject in the last resort to the sovereignty of the democracy expressed through Parliament. … . It is easy to give examples, from what already exists, of separate autonomies which have attained or are approaching the mode I designate – the universities, the Bank of England, the Port of London Authority, even perhaps the railway. (Keynes [1936] 1973, pp. 288–289)

Another trend which Keynes detected and hoped for implementation was the progressive transformation of largest enterprises into public companies[2]—a kind of socialization evidently far from nationalization—where the separation between ownership and management would promote the entrepreneurship of the latter and allay the mania for immediate gains. A view, however, that seems to clash with the argument against speculation in the *General Theory*, for it is hard to see why diffuse shareholding might not also be tempted to take such a line and the management in turn tempted to fuel it at the cost of sound long-run targets.

19.2 Keynes's Agenda Today

Coming to the present day, the 'final death' of Keynes's relevance has repeatedly been proclaimed by many economist and politicians. Keynes's fiercest enemies have labelled his proposals as illiberal, mainly due to his propensity to '*somewhat comprehensive*' socialization of investments, as well as a somehow elitist conception of the political powers, almost as if he had inspired the large-scale nationalizations carried out in Great Britain in the immediate aftermath of the war[3] and followed in many other countries. Keynes has often been seen as the inspirer of the welfare policies urged by William Beveridge (1942, 1944) in Great Britain and to a great extent implemented in that country and indeed in others in the post-war period. Though sympathizing with Beveridge's aims in principle (the elimination of the 'five great evils' of humanity—'want, disease, ignorance, squalor, idleness'), Keynes did not agree with the extensive scope of the agenda Beveridge advocated to achieve them.[4]

However, Keynes's legacy is at least traceable in the modern economic constitutions as pillars on which the social market economies of many industrialized countries rest, notably in Europe. It is hard to say whether some developments in the construction of the European Union were inspired by Keynes's ideas, but in principle they certainly do not clash with them. A few points about the affinities and differences between Keynes's proposals and Europe's policies can be outlined.

In 1926, Keynes stated that the public agenda must relate to activities falling outside the sphere of the individual, meaning by these activities incompatible with the free play of individual motivations. Specifically, 'We must aim at separating those services which are technically social from those which are technically individual' (Keynes [1926] 1972, p. 291), where reference to services was due to the impact they have on welfare and employment. However, Keynes's distinction between agenda and non-agenda is not clear-cut, being based on the principle of horizontal subsidiarity, so that the borderline between the two 'kinds' of services may shift over time according to economic and social conditions and the policies for the implementation of the agenda are flexible.

Leaving aside the restrictive, short-terministic interpretation of the *General Theory* and taking it within the framework of Keynes's comprehensive vision, investments do not only serve to sustain demand but must also prove to be useful in the long run. Public investment should aim at generating social capital first, and in general to promote sectors with high social returns but with private returns too low or too long deferred to attract private capital:

> Whether we like or not, *it is a fact* that the rate of capital development in the transport system, the public utilities and the housing of this country largely depends on the policy of the Treasury and the government of the day. If they ... facilitate and inspire, the equipment of the country moves forward. ... Roads, afforestation, reclamation and drainage, electrification, slum clearance and town planning, the development of canals, docks and harbours; these are the things we need to absorb large sums of capital

today, and in any case the initiative necessarily lies with a public authority. (Keynes [1929] 1972, p. 113)

Commenting the *General Theory*, Joan Robinson grasps the junction between Keynes's macro- and micro-policies:

It is impossible for the State to divest itself of responsibility for the direction of employment once it has accepted responsibility for the total amount of employment. ... The task of deciding between these needs [housing, education, health, public utilities, etc.] and reducing them to a scheme of priorities, must be the duty of the Government. Once we have accepted that it is the business of the Government to see that labour is always employed, we must go on to admit it is the business of the Government to see that labour is employed in the most useful possible way .... (Robinson [1946] 1966, p. 108)

Without dwelling on the modernity of these 'green economy' hints, it is fairly evident that the preferential destination of investment is the 'technically social' services, those the European law defines as services of general economic interest (SGEIs)—economic activities that would not be supplied by the market without public intervention, or would be supplied without complying with adequate conditions of quality, safety, affordability, equal treatment and universal access. Inadequate endowment of social capital and SGEIs is now largely acknowledged as one of the most important causes of the low propensity to private investment and the inequality of incomes. For that reason, Article 14 of the Treaty on the Functioning of the European Union (TFUE) grants public administrations ample discretionary powers for the national, regional and local authorities to identify the services that come within the category of SGEIs, and indeed to supply, commission and finance them although potentially representing market services. The freedom granted to the States is only limited by 'manifest errors' in identifying them and by exercising control over the proportionality of any restrictions on competition and the fundamental freedoms. Taking into consideration their social impact, the provision of SGEIs can be exempted from competition rules, *insofar as* the application of such rules obstructs the performance, in law or in fact, of the particular tasks assigned to them (TFUE, article 106, par. 2). Today, the services referred to are public local services (water, waste, transportation) and network infrastructures sharing the characteristic of essential facilities.

Indeed, Keynes emphasizes the need to boost the supply of them as the most effective means for the redistribution of welfare, as compared with growth in nominal wages (Keynes [1930] 1981).

Another point to be made is that the socialization of investments Keynes proposes should not necessarily lead to a role for the State as nationalizer or direct investor, but that the State should take on a role as director of them. Keynes would certainly have endorsed the principle that public intervention should be tempered by criteria of proportionality, i.e. should be the least intrusive compatibly with the pursuit of objectives of public interest. The State as regulator rather than as producer finds a perfectly natural place in his vision of liberal socialism. What counts is that the State maintains its role as promoter of investments—and more in general as a guide of industrial and social policy—which can be achieved in the field of utilities and SGEIs through public-private partnership or concession systems, planning and investment decisions being entrusted to public authorities and concretely carried out by concessionaires at the expense of the consumers, on the basis of tariffs established by public regulators (Keynes [1937] 1982, p. 394). In most European countries, public utilities services are now provided by enterprises under public concession regimes, subject to public service obligations to guarantee the fulfilment of their mission of general interest. Similarly Keynes:

> Building and transport and public utilities, which can use large amounts of capital, lie half way between private and public control. They need therefore the combined stimulus of public policy and a low rate of interest. But a wise public policy to promote investments needs long preparation. … . The railways companies, the port and river authorities, the water, gas, and electricity undertakings, the building contractors, the local authorities and the other great Corporations should be asked to investigate what projects could be useful undertaken …. (Keynes [1937] 1982, p. 394)

Socializing investments does not mean that the State necessarily looks to the taxpayers to pay the costs; alternatively, it may be up to the users themselves, on the decision of the public authorities. This is certainly one of the options for the socialization of investments that Keynes would have advocated, together with that—which, however, has had rather less success—of creating public companies.

Hence the need for ex ante regulation of access to the essential facilities and SGEIs, as well as, if necessary, of the dominant players in the downstream markets. After a long-lasting phase of direct governmental regulation entailing considerable limitations—such as a rigid command-and-control type of approach and the risk of capture of the 'prince' by vested interests—authorities independent of the governments began to be established in modern countries, albeit somewhat belatedly and following non-linear paths in Europe.[5] These new independent bodies strikingly resemble the semiautonomous bodies proposed by Keynes in 1926 and, as he deemed appropriate, are subject to the parliaments only.

On the macroeconomic level, the constitutionalization of the balanced budget rules, introduced by the Maastricht Treaty and implemented with the Fiscal Compact[6]—in Italy Article 81 of the Constitution—cannot be ascribed to Keynes, being the long wave of the legacy of the Freiburg Ordoliberal School. For some European countries, this is the '*bête noire*' standing in the way of growth of the European economy and in particular of countries with higher public debts in proportion to their gross domestic product (GDP). For many, this is seen as the de profundis of Keynesian policies. This opinion, however, relies on a 'selective' and misleading interpretation of Keynes's views. On the contrary, Keynes would probably not have been opposed in principle to some structural constraints on deficit spending, provided that they do not turn into numbers carved in stone.

Indeed, the European stability pact provides elements of flexibility, binding member States' fiscal policies not to current but to *structural* balance budgets driven by the 'output gap', i.e. the gap between the actual and the potential GDPs.

However, though broadly sharing that principle, Keynes would have objected to the way it is applied.

First of all, according to many observers and in contrast to its alleged aim, the rule gives rise to pro-cyclical effects which amplify economic downturns. The most critical point lies in the concrete finality of the approach as well as on the European commission's way of calculating the potential output, which fundamentally rests, as far as the labour factor is concerned, on a combination of the Phillips curve and the structural (*read* natural) 'rate of unemployment doctrine', a threshold beneath which the rate of inflation could rise. Similar considerations hold for the degree of utilization of other productive factors too. Moreover, the methodology is based on analyses of the time series of unemployment, consumption and investments, so that severe downturns turn into lower potential GDPs, then into lower output gap and, ultimately, into lower 'compatible' deficit spending. In short, while fuelling the virtuous circle of growth during economic expansions, this approach gives rise to opposite effects during crises. Meaningful in this regard is the criticism raised by the IMF, an organization that would hardly be suspected of being open to free public spending, according to which 'the standard advice of letting automatic stabilizers operate fully in response to a positive/negative growth shocks likely implies a strengthening/weakening of the structural position', so that the cyclically adjusted primary balances were revised downwards during crisis years for most European countries (Tereanu et al. 2014, pp. 4, 8).

By this way, Italy's 'natural' rate of unemployment was set at 10.4% in 2013, 11% in 2015 and 9.8% in 2019–20 by the European Commission projections.[7] While welcoming structural reforms, Keynes would certainly have rejected both the underlying and today unwarranted obsession with inflation and the notion of unemployment as a 'natural' condition, aware as he was that high levels of employment are prerequisites for social reforms and policies of income redistribution.

Moreover, Keynes would have disagreed with considering the ceiling to expenditure without distinguishing between current and investment spending. In fact, subject to the conditions above, he was in favour of the current balance budget rule, while funding investment in deficit, when necessary.

Turning to the dynamics of public (and private) European investments in 2007–17 (see Table 19.1), we see an appreciable drop in proportion to the (also declining) GDPs in almost all the Eurozone countries, which bears out the conclusion that the impact of the European policies has not been anticyclical.

Taking into consideration that properly selected public investments, besides being prerequisite for increasing private investments, also boost economic growth in the long run, it follows that a fall in them gives rise to a perverse vicious circle.

Little effect seems to have been achieved with the expansive monetary policies launched by the European Central Bank as from 2011 and successively implemented through quantitative easing, which led to interest rates close to zero.

The present slowdown of investments, despite the negligible level of interest rates, demonstrates what Keynes had foreseen about the ineffectiveness of monetary policy when the propensity to hoarding prevails, also in the form of semiliquid investments, such as government bonds

Table 19.1 Investment at current market prices, 2007, 2012 and 2017 (% of GDP)

	Total investment			*Public investment*			*Business investment*			*Household investment*		
	2007	*2012*	*2017*[a]	*2007*	*2012*	*2017*[a]	*2007*	*2012*	*2017*[b]	*2007*	*2012*	*2017*[b]
EU-28	22.9	20.1	20.6	3.2	3.1	2.8	13.1	11.9	12.7	6.6	5.1	5.1
Euro area (EA-19)	23.6	20.5	20.8	3.2	2.9	2.6	13.0	11.9	12.8	7.3	5.7	5.4
Belgium	23.2	22.6	23.4	2.0	2.5	2.2	14.5	14.3	15.4	6.7	5.9	5.8
Bulgaria	28.3	21.3	18.6	5.2	3.4	2.6	21.7	16.3	12.8	14	1.6	3.2
Czech Republic	29.5	25.9	24.7	4.8	4.2	3.3	19.1	17.2	16.6	5.6	4.5	4.7
Denmark	23.5	18.8	20.5	3.0	3.8	3.5	12.9	10.9	12.5	7.6	4.1	4.5
Germany	20.1	20.1	20.0	1.9	2.2	2.1	12.2	11.6	11.9	6.0	6.3	6.0
Estonia	36.6	28.6	22.3	6.0	6.3	4.8	22.4	18.6	12.2	8.2	3.7	5.3
Ireland	28.7	19.7	31.8	4.6	2.0	1.8	12.3	15.0	27.2	11.8	2.7	2.9
Greece	26.0	12.6	11.7	4.9	2.5	3.2	7.8	4.9	.7	13.3	5.2	2.8
Spain	31.1	19.8	20.0	4.6	2.5	1.9	17.2	13.3	15.1	9.2	4.0	3.0
France	23.1	22.5	22.0	3.9	4.1	3.4	12.3	12.4	12.9	6.9	6.0	5.7
Croatia	26.8	19.6	–	6.1	3.5	–	16.2	12.7	–	4.5	3.4	–
Italy	21.6	18.4	17.5	2.9	2.6	2.0	10.9	9.4	9.9	7.7	6.4	5.6
Cyprus	25.6	15.1	17.4	3.1	2.9	2.6	8.6	6.2	9.3	13.8	6.0	5.5
Latvia	36.4	25.4	18.2	5.9	4.9	3.5	22.8	16.9	11.9	7.7	3.6	2.8
Lithuania	28.6	17.4	18.9	5.4	4.0	3.0	19.4	10.4	11.4	3.7	3.0	4.5
Luxembourg	18.4	20.2	17.2	3.6	4.0	3.9	9.8	12.2	9.2	5.0	4.0	4.1
Hungary	23.7	19.4	21.7	4.3	3.7	6.6	14.4	12.7	12.3	5.0	2.9	2.8
Malta	22.4	18.2	23.8	3.7	3.3	2.6	–	–	–	–	–	–
Netherlands	21.8	18.9	20.3	3.9	3.7	3.5	10.2	10.6	10.9	7.8	4.6	5.9
Austria	22.9	22.7	23.1	3.0	2.9	3.0	14.7	14.4	15.1	5.3	5.3	5.0
Poland	22.5	19.8	18.1	4.5	4.8	3.3	12.4	10.1	10.4	5.6	5.0	4.4
Portugal	22.5	15.8	16.2	3.2	2.5	1.8	13.4	9.6	11.1	5.9	3.7	3.3

	Total investment			*Public investment*			*Business investment*			*Household investment*		
	2007	*2012*	*2017*[a]	*2007*	*2012*	*2017*[a]	*2007*	*2012*	*2017*[b]	*2007*	*2012*	*2017*[b]
Romania[c]	30.2	27.3	22.8	6.4	4.7	3.6	21.8	16.8	13.9	2.1	5.9	5.3
Slovenia	28.8	19.2	17.6	4.5	4.1	3.2	18.0	11.5	11.0	6.2	3.7	3.4
Slovakia	26.8	21.3	21.2	3.2	3.4	3.2	18.3	13.3	13.5	5.4	4.6	4.5
Finland	24.2	22.3	22.2	3.5	4.0	4.1	13.6	11.8	11.5	7.1	6.5	6.5
Sweden	23.9	22.6	24.9	4.1	4.6	4.6	16.5	15.7	17.2	3.3	2.4	3.1
UK	18.1	15.9	16.7	2.5	2.8	2.6	9.7	9.0	9.1	5.9	4.1	4.9
Iceland	29.4	16.0	19.0	4.8	2.6	2.9	18.0	10.9	–	6.6	2.5	–
Norway	23.5	22.4	23.9	3.8	3.9	5.5	14.4	13.2	11.8	5.4	5.3	6.7
Switzerland	24.4	23.8	24.1	2.7	3.0	3.1	17.1	16.8	17.0	4.6	4.0	3.9
Serbia	25.3	21.2	–	–	–	–	–	–	–	–	–	–
Turkey[d]	22.0	26.9	29.5	3.9	3.1	3.3	12.5	16.5	17.7	5.6	7.4	8.4

Source Eurostat, September 2019

[a]Belgium, Bulgaria, Germany, Estonia, Ireland. Greece, Spain, Cyprus, Latvia, Lithuania, Luxembourg, Malta, Austria, Poland, Romania, Slovenia, Slovakia, UK and Switzerland: 2016. Hungary, Iceland and Turkey: 2015

[b]Belgium, Bulgaria, Germany, Estonia, Ireland. Greece, Spain, Cyprus, Latvia, Lithuania, Luxembourg, Austria, Poland, Romania, Slovenia, Slovakia, UK and Switzerland: 2016. Hungary and Turkey: 2015

[c]Business investment and household investment 2013, break in series

[d]2009 instead of 2007

or graded corporate bonds to increase a provision of liquidity which turn into real investments poorly. In fact, according to Keynes monetary and fiscal policy are complementary tools to boost investment and employment, to be used in coordination by focusing on one or the other according to circumstances. This is exactly what is not happening in Europe, as is constantly being observed.

This situation has revived discussion on possible modification of the Fiscal Compact by introducing the 'golden rule' originally proposed by Richard Musgrave (1939, 1959),[8] which Keynes would certainly have endorsed, particularly in concomitance with an expansive monetary policy. The main (declared) reasons why this proposal meets with opposition in Europe are to avoid burdening future generations with further debt and the 'tyranny' of global financial investors. To the first reason, it should be opposed that deficit spending for investment does not violate the principle of intergenerational equity, provided that it is directed to creating *social capital* in the long run, so that future generations will benefit from it in return for the burden of the debt by means of which it was generated.[9] It must also be recalled that in Keynes's view, socialization of investment does not necessarily imply public expenditure, as pointed out above.

As for the second reasons, the sustainability of public debts depends mainly on the state of confidence of investors, which is in turn based on the speculative beauty contest mentioned above. The basic reason for this rests on the sovereign (national) nature of these debts. It is a current refrain that the Europe Union would need fiscal union to be fully accomplished, while the fiscal compact philosophy is exactly the opposite, what is indicative of the fact that the today rampant and widely criticized national sovereignism is much more widespread than acknowledged. As the former President of the European Central Bank, Mario Draghi, recently noted, countries lose their sovereignty 'when debt become so high that each policy action has to be … scrutinised by the markets, i.e. by people … who are outside the democratic accountability process'.[10] That statement is obviously correct *within* the present condition of national fiscal policies.

In this regard, too, Keynes[11] would have shown staunch opposition. Suffice it to consider his contribution to the creation of post-war international organizations like the International Monetary Fund (IMF) and the World Trade Organization (WTO). The Clearing Union he conceived to finance temporary disequilibria in the balance of trade between countries, with the creation of a fund amounting to half the global value of world imports, went far beyond the IMF itself.[12]

Surveying today's political and social scenarios, we see the rise of national and individualistic fundamentalisms on both sides of the Atlantic. It is a political tendency that is now making the contrast between the growing need for economic regulation and the decreasing capability of the political systems to cope with it increasingly dramatic.

Needless to say, national self-interest was widespread in Keynes's times, too,[13] but post-World War I experience led him to combine pragmatism with a considerable dose of optimism of the will, stating that 'the power of vested interests is vastly exaggerated compared with the gradual encroachment of ideas' (Keynes [1936] 1973, p. 383). The author of the present chapter could hardly fail to share Keynes's view. However, another major question remains, concerning who, in Keynes's view, should run the State, who should govern economic and social policies inspired by this enlightened ideas. Keynes believed that the British political and economic system would be governed by the intellectual elites of the upper middle class—an intellectual aristocracy made up of politicians, economists[14] and civil servants sharing his enlightened views on the conduct of public affairs. An elite which by virtue of its moral integrity would be free from political bias and weaknesses of any kind[15]—not, immediately, he argued, but, 'apart from this contemporary mood', after a certain interval. On the other hand, Keynes does not go into the issue of selection of the political class, whose wisdom and sightedness would call for a symmetric conversion of people in democratic regimes.

What remains of the Keynesian legacy—which, as Luigi Pasinetti (2017, p. 11) wrote, should represent the starting point 'to be back to the future of the Keynesian revolution'—is his vision of a just society, the need for a new world economic and social constitution and his basket of economic proposals. The entire scientific output of Keynes is dominated by the rebuttal of economics as a natural science, seasoned by social justice: 'I also want to emphasize strongly the point about economics being a moral science. … It deals with introspection and with values, with motives, expectations psychological uncertainties … ' (Keynes [1938] 1973, p. 300). Consistently with the profile of the economist, as he traced it out (see above), for Keynes economics is not a mere toolbox separable from policy. Hence his life-project to reform capitalism.

However, the radical changes he predicted entail genuine elites in power selected by equally enlightened and conscious public opinions, at both the national and supranational level. Without embracing the public choice school' views,[16] this definitely seems like a visionary hope vis-à-vis (quoting Keynes) our contemporary (passing?) mood.

Notes

1. 'To suggest social action for the public good to the City of London is like discussing the Origin of Species with a bishop sixty years ago. The first reaction is not intellectual, but moral' (Keynes [1926] 1972, p. 287).
2. 'One of the most interesting and unnoticed developments of recent decades has been the tendency of big enterprise to socialize itself, particularly a big railway or big public utility enterprise, but also a big bank or a big insurance company' (Keynes [1936] 1973, p. 289).
3. See British Nationalization Acts, 1945–51: Bank of England (1946), Civil Aviation (1946), Coal Industry (1947), Cable and Wireless (1947), Transport (1948), Electricity (1948), Gas (1949), Iron and Steel (1951) (House of Commons 2018, p. 27).
4. Basically, Keynes and Beveridge came from different political and cultural backgrounds: 'Beveridge, the Fabians' heir, relied on neoclassical economic theory while Keynes, the revolutionary economist, relied on reformed liberalism for his social policy' (Marcuzzo 2010, p. 198).
5. Significantly, national competition laws, with simultaneous institution of the Competition Authorities, were introduced in most European countries some 30 years after the Treaty of Rome and a hundred years after the Sherman Antitrust Act in the United States.
6. 'Treaty on Stability, Coordination and Governance in the Economic and Monetary union', 2012, in turn derived from the Maastricht Treaty of 1993 and the Stability Pact of 1997.
7. European Commission, *European Economic Forecast*, various annual issues at https://data.europa.eu/euodp/it/data/dataset/european-economic-forecast.
8. Unlike the Juncker-Plan or other more ambitious plans to boost public or (publically supported) investment through investment funds, the golden rule provides a direct boost to public investment on the national level and does not have to rely on highly insecure shifting and leveraging of public funds at the European level in the hope of finding private investors at times when business confidence is extremely low (see Truger 2015).
9. As argued by Keynes, this is all the more so if the rate of interest is kept low; in fact, (i) on the one hand, the trend in the debt/GDP ratio depends on the differential between real interest rates and the rate of GDP growth; (ii) on the other hand, if the interest rates are low, the cost of financing private investments does not rise due to the competition of public investments and there is no crowding out of private investments—so feared by

the orthodox economists of the last century. Now, the present-day situation in Europe is of real rates standing at practically zero.

10. Hearing of the Committee on Economic and Monetary Affairs of the European Parliament, Brussels, 28 January 2019 (available at https://www.ecb.europa.eu/press/key/date/2019/html/ecb.sp190128_transcript.en.pdf, p. 12).
11. The position taken by Keynes in 1933 against economic internationalism (in 'National Self-Sufficiency' [1933] 1982) must be viewed in the context of the *laissez-faire* and gold standard regimes, where the struggle to conquer foreign markets was the only way for governments to combat economic downturns.
12. Unlike the IMF, member countries would not be required to commit any amount of money in any form to the Clearing Union, but they would be simply assigned a current account denominated in a new, international unit of account called 'bancor'.
13. See, for instance, Keynes ([1925] 1972).
14. Keynes's depiction of the economist is significant: '... the master-economist must possess a rare combination of gifts. He must be mathematician, historian, statesman, philosopher—in some degree. He must contemplate the particular in terms of the general, and touch abstract and concrete in the same flight of thought. He must study the present in the light of the past for the purposes of the future. He must be purposeful and disinterested in a simultaneous mood; as aloof and incorruptible as an artist, yet sometimes as near the earth as a politician' (Keynes [1924] 1972, pp. 173–174).
15. However, on the one hand this auspice contradicts Keynes's own personal experience and opinion on politicians, which he had the opportunity to acquire as a civil servant, in the time between World War I and World War II (see Ferencak et al. 2014, p. 119).
16. As we know, Keynes's vision was overturned by the public choice theoreticians, holding that the political actors and bureaucracies, just like the consumers, pursue selfish aims (maximization of their own utilities), while voters cast their votes on the basis of their most immediate individual interests. Thus, it is better to refrain from interfering in market mechanisms. A different approach, although converging on the conclusion that the public decision-makers are far from being inspired by the general interest, was embarked upon by George Stigler (1971) with the 'theory' of the capture of the regulator by the economic powers that should actually be subordinate to him. This is a current of thought that left an indelible mark in the neoliberal policies of the 1970s and 1980s, especially in the United States and Great Britain.

References

Beveridge, W. H. (1942). *Social Insurance and Allied Services.* Report presented to Parliament by Command of His Majesty. London: His Majesty Stationery Office.

Beveridge, W. H. (1944). *Full Employment in a Free Society.* London: Allen & Unwin.

Ferencak, I., Crnković, B., & Rudan, S. (2014). State and Market. *Ekonomski Vjesnik/Econviews, 27*(1), 113–126.

Hicks, J. (1969). *A Theory of Economic History.* London: Oxford University Press.

House of Commons. (2018, May 31). *Public Ownership of Industries and Services* (Briefing Paper No. CBP8325). London: House of Commons Library.

Keynes, J. M. ([1924] 1972). Alfred Marshall, 1842–1924. *The Economic Journal, 34*(135), 311–372. As reprinted in: D. E. Moggridge & E. Johnson (Eds.), *The Collected Writings of John Maynard Keynes,* Vol. 10, *Essays in Biography* (pp. 161–231). London: Macmillan for the Royal Economic Society.

Keynes, J. M. ([1925] 1972, July 22–24). The Economic Consequences of Mr. Churchill. *The Evening Standard.* As reprinted in: D. E. Moggridge & E. Johnson (Eds.), *The Collected Writings of John Maynard Keynes,* Vol. 9, *Essays in Persuasion* (pp. 207–230). London: Macmillan for the Royal Economic Society.

Keynes, J. M. ([1926] 1972). *The End of Laissez-faire.* London: Hogarth Press. As reprinted in: D. E. Moggridge & E. Johnson (Eds.), *The Collected Writings of John Maynard Keynes,* Vol. 9, *Essays in Persuasion* (pp. 272–294). London: Macmillan for the Royal Economic Society.

Keynes, J. M. ([1929] 1972). Can Lloyd George Do It?—The Pledge Examined. As reprinted in: D. E. Moggridge & E. Johnson (Eds.), *The Collected Writings of John Maynard Keynes,* Vol. 9, *Essays in Persuasion* (pp. 86–125). London: Macmillan for the Royal Economic Society.

Keynes, J. M. ([1930] 1981). The Question of High Wages. *The Political Quarterly, 1*(1), 110–124. As reprinted in: D. E. Moggridge & E. Johnson (Eds.), *The Collected Writings of John Maynard Keynes,* Vol. 20, *Activities 1929–1931: Rethinking Employment and Unemployment Policies* (pp. 3–16). London: Macmillan for the Royal Economic Society.

Keynes, J. M. ([1933] 1982). National Self-Sufficiency. *The New Statesman and Nation*, 6, 8 and 15 July, pp. 36–37, 65–67. As reprinted in: D. E. Moggridge & E. Johnson (Eds.), *The Collected Writings of John Maynard Keynes,* Vol. 21, *Activities 1931–1939: World Crises and Policies in Britain and America* (pp. 233–246). London: Macmillan for the Royal Economic Society.

Keynes, J. M. ([1936] 1973). *The General Theory of Employment, Interest and Money*. London: Macmillan. As reprinted in: D. E. Moggridge & E. Johnson (Eds.), *The Collected Writings of John Maynard Keynes*, Vol. 7. London: Macmillan for the Royal Economic Society.

Keynes, J. M. ([1937] 1982, January 12). How to Avoid a Slump. *The Times*. As reprinted in D. E. Moggridge & E. Johnson (Eds.), *The Collected Writings of John Maynard Keynes*, Vol. 21, *Activities 1931–1939: World Crises and Policies in Britain and America* (pp. 384–395). London: Macmillan for the Royal Economic Society.

Keynes, J. M. ([1938] 1973, July 16). Letter to R. F. Harrod. In: D. E. Moggridge & E. Johnson (Eds.), *The Collected Writings of John Maynard Keynes*, Vol. 14, *The General Theory and After: Part 2. Defence and Development* (pp. 299–301). London: Macmillan for the Royal Economic Society.

Marcuzzo, M. C. (2010). Whose Welfare State? Beveridge vs. Keynes. In R. Backhouse & T. Nishizawa (Eds.), *No Wealth but Life: Welfare Economics and Welfare State in Britain, 1880–1945* (pp. 189–206). Cambridge, UK: Cambridge University Press.

Musgrave, R. A. (1939). The Nature of Budgetary Balance and the Case for a Capital-Budget. *American Economic Review, 29*, 260–271.

Musgrave, R. A. (1959). *The Theory of Public Finance: A Study in Public Economy*. New York: McGraw-Hill.

Pasinetti, L. (2017). Keynes and the Cambridge Keynesians. Preface to the Japanese Translation of L. Pasinetti, *Keynes and the Cambridge Keynesians. A Revolution in Economics to be Accomplished*. Also reprinted (2018) *Annali della Fondazione Luigi Einaudi, 52*(2), 99–112.

Robinson, J. ([1946] 1966). Obstacles to Full Employment. *Nationalokonomisk Tidsskrift*. As reprinted in: J. Robinson, *Collected Economic Papers* (Vol. 1, pp. 105–114). Oxford: Blackwell.

Stigler, G. J. (1971). The Theory of Economic Regulation. *Bell Journal of Economics and Management Science, 2*(1), 3–21.

Tereanu, E., Tuladhar, A., & Simone, A. (2014). *Structural Balance Targeting and Output Gap Uncertainty* (IMF Working Paper No. WP/14/107). Washington, DC: International Monetary Fund.

Truger, A. (2015). Implementing the Golden Rule for Public Investment in Europe (Working Paper Reihe der AK Wien – Materialien zu Wirtschaft und Gesellschaft, No. 138). Vienna: Abteilung Wirtschaftswissenschaft und Statistik der Kammer für Arbeiter und Angestellte.

Index

M. C. Marcuzzo et al. (eds.), *New Perspectives on Political Economy and Its History*, Palgrave Studies in the History of Economic Thought, https://doi.org/10.1007/978-3-030-42925-6

The manufacturer's authorised representative in the EU is Springer Nature Customer Service Centre GmbH, Europaplatz 3, 69115 Heidelberg, Germany. If you have any concerns regarding our products, please contact ProductSafety@springernature.com

Printed and bound by CPI Group (UK) Ltd, Croydon, CR0 4YY

30/09/2026

02225459-0020